海外优秀教材编译文丛 ①

张健鹏 胡足青/主编

马浩岚/编译

American Literature

上

美国语文

美国著名中学课文精选

中国妇女出版社

图书在版编目(CIP)数据

美国语文/张健鹏,胡足青主编;马浩岚编译. —北京:中国妇女出版社,2008.7

ISBN 978-7-80203-582-9

Ⅰ.美… Ⅱ.①张…②胡…③马… Ⅲ.英语课—中学—教学参考资料 Ⅳ.G634.411

中国版本图书馆 CIP 数据核字(2008)第 083902 号

美国语文

主　　编:张健鹏　胡足青
编　　译:马浩岚
责任编辑:陈　元
封面设计:形式书籍设计
责任印刷:王卫东
出　　版:中国妇女出版社出版发行
地　　址:北京东城区史家胡同甲 24 号　　**邮政编码**:100010
电　　话:(010)65133160(发行部)　　65133161(邮购)
网　　址:www.womenbooks.com.cn
经　　销:各地新华书店
印　　刷:北京正合鼎业印刷技术有限公司
开　　本:170×240　1/16
印　　张:58
字　　数:980 千字
版　　次:2008 年 7 月第 1 版
印　　次:2009 年 8 月第 2 次
书　　号:ISBN 978-7-80203-582-9
定　　价:98.00 元(全二册)

序言

另一种学习

据编者所知，本书应该是中国第一套系统引进的西方中学语文教材。

长期以来，我们对于西方教育的了解，仅仅限于一些短文的零星介绍，少有系统的研究和分析，这不能不说是一个遗憾。但作为一个民间的研究机构，要想完成这样一个庞大的系统工程，我们显然力有未逮，只能是知其难而勉力为之，以达抛砖引玉之效。

近年来，随着对国内教育制度的反思和与国际社会交流的日益增多，很多有条件的家长选择在中学时期即将孩子送出国门留学。从教育效果来说，此举引起诸多争议。当然，基于不同的文化传统和社会土壤，东西方的教育模式各有自己的特点，不可简单地就其一点进行优劣评价。而且，对于大多数普通百姓而言，一则在国内上学已然负担不轻，就更别说去国外了；二来也没有时间和精力介入关于教育制度改革的争论研讨之中。我们能做的，也许只是力所能及地结合自己孩子的具体情况，做些适当的弥补和引导。那么，在国内的日常教与学中，我们可以有选择地借鉴一些国外教育中的具体做法，让孩子了解国外的同龄人在学什么、怎样学，培养良好的思维方式，以便将来能更轻松地与国际同龄人接轨。

我们希望这套《美国语文》能给大家提供这方面切实的帮助。

一般来说，美国多数中学在语文教育方面会选择三部教程：一部《英语》，主要讲解语法知识；一部是《拼写》，注重单词的拼写训练；还有一部《文学》，介绍各种题材的美国文学读本，本书就是较权威的一个《文学》版本的中文节选译本。该书原版内容繁多，考虑到阅读习惯及篇幅，我们删去了原文中的诗歌与剧本部分，本书课文编排顺序沿袭了原版教材，并且在中文译文后附有英文原文，以便有兴趣的读者阅读参考。

本书的内容庞大，几乎涵盖了文学的所有形式，包括日记、神话、小说、散文、诗歌、游记、戏剧等，而且其课文的设置与编排顺序非常有特色，它以美国历史的发展为线索，将美国二百余年的历程分为六个不同的主题时代，而相对应的课文则取材于同时代的具有广泛社会影响及文学代表意义的文章。每个主题时代都配以时代故事来讲解此时代中发生的大事件以及本时代文学的变迁与发展特征。每篇课文都有作者的生平介绍，课文的写作背景、分析、要点聚焦，整个内容布局一目了然，简洁明快。学生通过文学的学习，即可了解到美国历史的演进、文明的传承以及社会方方面面的发展过程。

而全书最精彩的莫过于每篇课文后的问题设置。美国的中学教育注重于学生的智力启发与创新，这些课后问题与练习很好地证明了这一点。其课后问题的提出并不限于让学生理解作者所要表达的思想主旨，而是更侧重置学生于时代事件、背景以及作者身处之环境中，充分调动学生的想象力、创造力，全方位启发学生的多元化思维与独特体验，注重在提高文学素养的同时，增强学生收集、整理素材以及解决社会生活问题的实践能力。充满趣味性、现实性的习题无疑是触动学生学习乐趣的有效方法，这让学生体会到的是学习的快乐，而不是沉重的负担。这样的教材完全体现了语文教育的人文性、开放性、综合性，不仅仅是语文教程，更是历史人文教程、思想实践教程。

很显然，“听说读写”仅仅是对一种语言的基本性的工具要求，语文则应是在此基础上对语言和文化、文明的系统学习。通过长达十多年的语文学习，我们应该体验到文学的美感，了解到历史文明的演进，领略到思想的力量和智者的智慧，具备坚实的人文基本素质，培养在不同环境中解决实际问题的能力。

所以，我们诚挚建议家长和教师不要把本书仅仅作为学习英语的工具，那样无异于买椟还珠。我们要认真注意的是：

他们的课文为什么这样编选？他们的习题为什么会这样设计？他们想达到什么样的目的？这样的方式训练出来的孩子与我们有什么不同？

本书的策划、翻译、编辑和出版是一个浩大的工程。在历时两年的过程中，我们得到了众多专家和朋友的大力帮助，在此一并表示感谢！

需要说明的是，书中部分文章的观点及表述有不少值得商榷之处，因为编译本书的主要目的是出于对其教材编排的了解，所以我们基本忠实于原文，未作编辑处理，请读者理解。

另外，由于本书涉及美国二百余年历史的方方面面，译者和编者的局限和疏忽在所难免，敬请读者批评指正。

编 者

目 录

第1部分 文明的交会

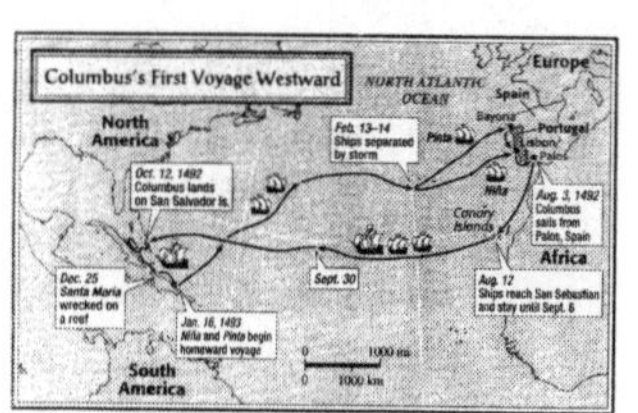

第三课 “有趣的故事”

第四课 弗吉尼亚通史

第五课 罪人在愤怒的上帝手中

第2部分 国家的诞生

第四课　穷理查德的年鉴

第五课　从新白宫里写给女儿的信

第 3 部分　国家的发展

第一课 《日晷》的通告

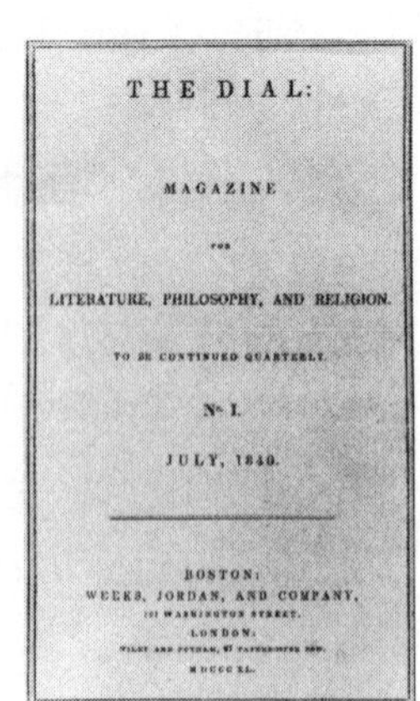
THE DIAL:

MAGAZINE

FOR

LITERATURE, PHILOSOPHY, AND RELIGION.

TO BE CONTINUED QUARTERLY.

No. I.

JULY, 1840.

BOSTON:
WEEKS, JORDAN, AND COMPANY,
121 WASHINGTON STREET.
LONDON:
WILEY AND PUTNAM, 67 PATERNOSTER ROW.
MDCCCXL.

第二课 魔鬼和汤姆·沃克

第三课 穿越大裂谷

第四课 厄舍府的倒塌

第五课 自然

第三课 内战中的声音

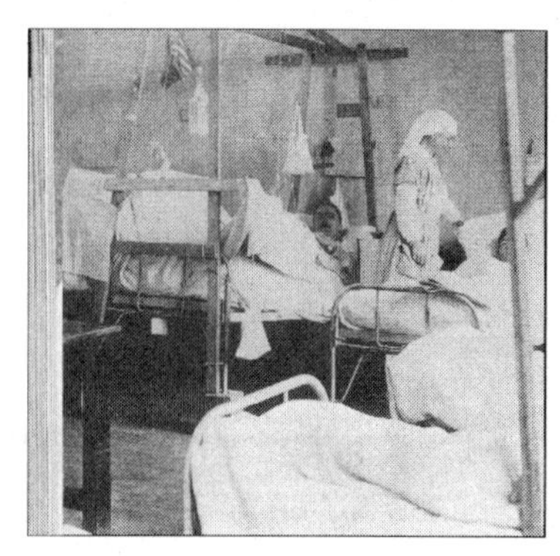

第四课 密西西比河上的生活

第五课 生火

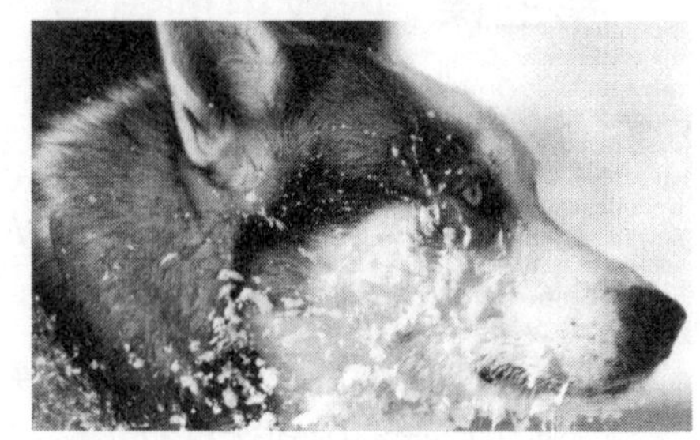

第六课 一小时的故事

第七课 一场瓦格纳音乐会

第5部分 不满、觉醒与反抗

第一课 龟

第二课 在另一个国家

第三课 四月沐浴

第四课 被遗弃的韦瑟罗尔奶奶

第五课 幽灵进来的那一夜

第 6 部分　繁荣与保护

第一课　前七年

第二课　棕色的大箱子

第三课　女勇士

第四课　做了抵押的心

第五课　稻草变黄金:日常生活中的蜕变

第六课　家里的作家

第1部分 Unit One

文明的交会

Meeting of Culture

时代故事

开始—1750

欧洲探险家登陆北美洲之后一个世纪，在圣奥古斯丁北部的西半球上仍然没有固定的定居点。然而，到了1607年，一小群英国移民在詹姆士河中的一个湿地小岛上生存下来，这个小岛就在现在的弗吉尼亚州。1611年，这个殖民地的总督托马斯•戴尔给国王写了一份报告，表达了殖民地的居民们继续生活下去的决心。尽管受到疾病和饥荒的困扰，但詹姆士镇还是生存了下来。

最初的移民们被当地的土著居民迷住了，但他们起初并没意识到这些更早的美洲人像欧洲人一样拥有自己的文化价值和文学传统。因为北美洲的部族还没有发展自己的文字，所以他们的文学全都是口头文学。多样的口头文学和殖民者的早期作品就形成了美国文学传统的开端。

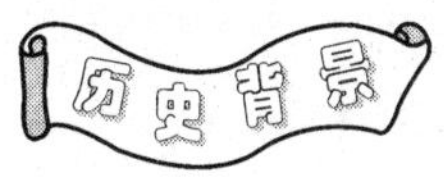

1492年，当克里斯托弗·哥伦布到达北美洲的时候，这片大陆上已经居住着几百个美洲土著部落了，但是他们稀稀落落地分散在各处。欧洲人并没有在同一时间遇见所有这些部落，各国探险家在不同的时期与他们建立了联系。据我们所知，这些分布广泛的美洲土著部落在语言、管理形式、社会组织、风俗习惯、房屋建筑和生存方法上有很大的不同。

美洲土著 没人能准确地说出最早的美洲人是什么时候或怎样到达现在的美国的，他们到达这里的时间可能晚到1.2万年以前，也可能早到7万年以前。即使那比较近的估计是正确的，土著美洲人在这片大陆上的时间也比欧洲殖民者在这里的时间长了30倍，欧洲人是16世纪晚期才开始到达北美洲的东海岸的。

在那么多个世纪里，最早的美洲土著人一直在做什么呢？这个问题的答案在很大程度上是神秘而不可解的。美洲土著人并没有留下文字记载，然而，考古学家们根据他们的手工制品做出了很多推测，民俗学家们也记录了丰富的歌曲、传说和神话。

我们可以肯定的是：美洲土著人经常将最早来自欧洲的移民作为朋友来欢迎。他们对这些新来的人在农业耕作和森林环境知识方面加以指导，教他们认识玉蜀黍、豆子、西葫芦、槭糖、雪地鞋、长雪橇和桦树皮独木舟。事实上，如果没有这些美洲土著人的帮助，会有更多的欧洲移民在东北部严酷的冬季中饥寒而死。

朝圣者与清教徒 1620年，一小群欧洲人乘“五月花”号从英国航行到美洲。他们是一群宗教改革者——对英国教会不满的清教徒。他们放弃了从内部“净化”教会的希望，转而选择退出教会，这一行动使他们被称为“独立派”，而我们将他们称为“朝圣者”。他们在北美洲登陆，在现在的马萨诸塞州的普利茅斯建立了一个定居点。在友好的美洲土著部落的帮助下，普利茅斯定居点在北美洲严酷的条件下生存了下来。然而，这个殖民群体并没有发展壮大，最后，它被北方的一个大得多的定居点——马萨诸塞海湾殖民区吞并了。

清教徒在建造房屋

像普利茅斯定居点一样，马萨诸塞海湾殖民区也是由宗教改革者建立的。然而，这些改革者并没有从英国教会中退出。与“独立派”不同的是，他们是试图从内部改革教会的清教徒。在美洲，这些清教徒希望能建立一个像殖民地总督约翰·文斯洛普所说的那样一个“山上之城”，一个在所有的方面都受《圣经》

指导的模范社会。他们的管理形式将是一个神权政治，即一个直接受上帝指引的政府。

清教徒的中心信念包括：人类是为了信仰上帝而存在的，而《圣经》则是上帝意旨的唯一表达。他们还相信得救宿命论——这是约翰·卡尔文的信条，他们认为上帝已经决定了哪些人将得到拯救，哪些人不能。然而，那些被选中得救的人——或者叫圣徒，却不能认为他们自己被选中是理所当然的。因此，所有虔诚的清教徒都要通过艰难困苦以及时时发现的上帝恩宠来寻求自己的灵魂。清教徒们认为他们获得善终的唯一途径就是辛勤的工作和自律。这就是今天当人们谈到"清教徒伦理"时所指的思想。

到18世纪早期，由于比较宽容的新教团体吸引了大批追随者，清教主义在新英格兰全境呈现衰败趋势。然而，对于这种新自由的反响在18世纪20年代左右开始兴起。大觉醒运动是一系列席卷了殖民地区的宗教复兴运动，其领导者是雄辩的牧师们，包括著名的乔那森·爱德华兹和乔治·怀特费尔德，大觉醒运动吸引了成千上万的皈依者参加众多的新教组织，但却并没使旧式的清教主义重获生机。然而清教徒关于勤劳、节俭、自我改善和自立的信念却至今仍是美国的基本美德。

南部的种植者　南部的殖民地区与新英格兰在气候、作物、社会组织和宗教等各方面都有所不同。虽然和北部一样，在南部也同样产生了繁荣的沿海城市，但在这些城市的远方，却是大片的种植园，而不是小农场。种植园虽然有着浪漫的形象，但实际上就是大面积的农场和商业中心。在一个种植园中可能有多至1000人在生活和工作，而其中的很多人都在受着奴役。

第一批黑奴是在1619年被运到弗吉尼亚来的，这是朝圣者们在普利茅斯登陆的前一年。虽然奴隶制度存在于包括马萨诸塞在内的每一个殖民地区，但是种植园制度和奴隶制仍然是从一开始就紧密相关的。

大多数种植园主都是英国教会的成员，他们认为自己属于贵族阶级。第一代种植园主，也就是建立了那些大种植园的人，同清教徒一样，雄心勃勃、精力充沛、严格自律并且足智多谋。然而，他们的生活方式却

非洲奴隶的生活环境

比清教徒要舒适优雅得多。1750年，清教在各地开始衰退，而南方的种植园制度则正在走向它的高峰。

建立美国文学基础的是一个奇特的包含各类人群的整体：有着口头文学传统的美洲土著人、相信罪恶和拯救的清教徒和过着繁忙社会生活的南部种植者。实际上，生活在殖民地的人们当时所读的很多文学作品并不是产生在殖民地区的——而是从英国传来的。然而，到了1750年，美国本土文学有了清晰的开端，而这种文学终有一天在英语世界中受到高度评价。

美国土著文学传统　在很长一段时期里，美国土著文学主要被看做是民间传统。其结果是人们更多地研究歌词、英雄故事、迁移传说和起源故事的内容，而不是它们的文学价值。根据口头文学的传统，故事的讲述会随着每个讲述者变化，而词句也几乎一定会随着时间改变。因此，这种形式的文学作品没有固定的版本留存下来。然而，当美国土著歌词或故事中的词句用书面形式记录下来的时候，其语言经常是富有诗意而感人的。在这种口头文学的氛围里，我们可以料想到美洲土著人是具备高度评价雄辩的才能的。某些雄辩家的名字，例如罗根和红夹克，在美国广为人知。

这一单元中选录的美国土著文学体现了最初的美洲声音所具有的深度和力量。

"在亚当的堕落中/我们都犯了罪"　正如宗教占据了清教徒的生活一样，它也占据了他们的写作——根据现代的标准，这些写作中的大部分都不应被看做文学作品。清教徒的典型作品是神学研究、赞美诗、历史记录、人物传记和自传。他们写作的目的是为了提供精神上的洞察力和指导。当清教徒们为自己写作日志和日记时，他们的目的也是为了对生活的方方面面进行严格的自我监督。清教徒既不创作小说也不创作戏

1670年的清教徒儿童

剧，因为他们将其视为罪恶。

然而，清教徒却写作诗歌，并将诗歌作为一种精神的启迪，虽然他们更多关心的是诗歌的内容而不是文学形式。在17世纪，出现了几个杰出的清教徒诗人，其中包括安·布莱德斯特里特和爱德华·泰勒。安·布莱德斯特里特亲切感人的声音和爱德华·泰勒强烈的虔诚透过传统的清教主义主题闪耀着光芒。

清教徒对于男性和女性的教育有着强烈的信念。1636年，他们建立了哈佛大学，以保证神职人员的教育。两年以后，他们建立了殖民地区的第一家印刷厂。1647年，在马萨诸塞建立了免费的公共学校。而在1690年左右开始发行的《新英格兰初级读本》则结合了拼写、阅读指导和类似"在亚当的堕落中/我们都犯了罪"这样的道德说教。

《海湾圣诗集》是最早在殖民地区印刷的图书之一，它是当时的标准赞美诗集。英克里斯·马特是这本书的三个作者之一，他在波士顿的北方教会做了很多年的牧师，他还写了大约130本书，其中《关于罪恶灵魂的良知案例》发表于1693年，内容是关于前一年撒勒姆巫术审判的对话。当时的审判是在一种歇斯底里的氛围中进行的，最终结果是有20个人作为女巫被吊死。

英克里斯的大儿子考顿·马特的文学作品的产量远远超过了他父亲，他一生中发表了至少400部作品。考顿·马特和他的父亲一样，人们记住他的部分原因是他和撒勒姆巫术审判之间的联系。虽然实际上他并没有参加审判，但是他关于巫术的作品却激起了部分人的歇斯底里的情绪。然而，考顿·马特仍然是那个时代最有学识的人之一，是这个国家的一种精神和著名的作家。他的写作理论很简单（虽然他的写作并不简单）：一部作品包含的信息越多，它的风格就越好。

事实上，清教徒有一个关于文学风格的普遍理论。他们相信一种朴素的写作风格——在这种风格中，清楚的论述就是最高目标。华丽或故弄玄虚的风格则被认为是一种虚荣的表现，是与上帝的意旨不相符的。虽然清教徒在自己的生活和文学作品中设立

1636 年清教徒建立了哈佛大学

了很多限制，但他们仍然成功地创作出了一小部分优秀的文学作品。

南部的声音 考虑到后来在南部，尤其是在弗吉尼亚出现的精通文学的优秀政治家的数量，那么1750年以前南部只出现了几个作家，就让人感到很惊讶了。和居住在新英格兰的清教徒一样，南方的那些受过教育的人也创作了大量的作品，但是这些作品大部分都具有实用的性质。例如，弗吉尼亚的詹姆士镇定居点的领导人约翰•史密斯写作了《弗吉尼亚通史》，其目的是向欧洲人描述他的经历。除了像史密斯所写的这样的报告以外，南部种植者写的信件也表现了对这个时代的洞察。与清教徒不同的是，南方人并不反对小说或戏剧，美国第一家剧院就是1716年在弗吉尼亚的威廉姆斯堡开始使用的。

维斯特奥弗的种植者 革命前南部的重要的文学成就可以归结为一个名字——威廉姆•比尔德。比尔德生活在维斯特奥弗，詹姆士河边的一个宏伟的种植园里，这是他富有的父亲遗留给他的。1728年，他受到委任，视察弗吉尼亚和北卡罗来纳之间的边界线，他将自己的经历都记录在一本日志里。那本日志就成为他的《分界线的历史》的基础，这本书的手稿在他英国的朋友之间广泛传阅。在比尔德逝世后几乎过了一个世纪，这本书才得以出版并马上被看做是一部精致的幽默杰作。之后比尔德的更多文章得到了出版，使他赢得了革命前南部最优秀作家的声誉。

这个单元中出现的作家并不是美国文学史上的伟大的作家，但他们是后来有巨大成就的美国文学的启蒙者。在这个单元里我们将看到，现代美国文学意识在初期的朦胧觉醒。

The Story of the Times

Beginnings to 1750

More than a century after European explorers first landed in North America, there were still no permanent settlements in the Western Hemisphere north of St. Augustine, Florida. By 1607, however, a small group of English settlers was struggling to survive on a marshy island in the James River in the present state of Virginia. In 1611, Thomas Dale, governor of the colony, wrote a report to the king expressing the colonists' determination to succeed. Despite disease and starvation, Jamestown did survive.

The first settlers were entranced by the native inhabitants they met. They did not at first realize that these earlier Americans, like Europeans, had cultural values and literary traditions of their own. Their literature was entirely oral, for the tribes of North America had not yet developed writing systems. This extensive oral literature, along with the first written works of the colonists, forms the beginning of the American literary heritage.

Historical Background

When Christopher Columbus reached North America in 1492, the continent was already populated, though sparsely, by several hundred Native American tribes. Europeans did not encounter these tribes all at one time. Explorers from different nations came into contact with them at different times. As we now

know, these widely dispersed tribes of Native Americans differed greatly from one to another in language, government, social organization, customs, housing, and methods of survival.

<u>The Native Americans</u> No one knows for certain when or how the first Americans arrived in what is now the United States. It may have been as recently as 12,000 years ago or as long ago as 70,000 years. Even if the shorter estimate is correct, Native Americans have been on the continent thirty times longer than the Europeans. Colonists from Europe did not begin arriving on the east coast of North America until the late 1500's.

What were the earliest Americans doing for those many centuries? To a great extent, the answer is shrouded in mystery. No written story of the Native Americans exists. Archaeologists have deduced a great deal from artifacts, however, and folklorists have recorded a rich variety of songs, legends, and myths.

What we do know is that the Native Americans usually, but by no means always, greeted the earliest European settlers as friends. They instructed the newcomers in their agriculture and woodcraft, introduced them to maize, beans, squash, maple sugar, snowshoes, toboggans, and birch bark canoes. Indeed, many more of the European settlers would have succumbed to the bitter northeastern winters had it not been for the help of these first Americans.

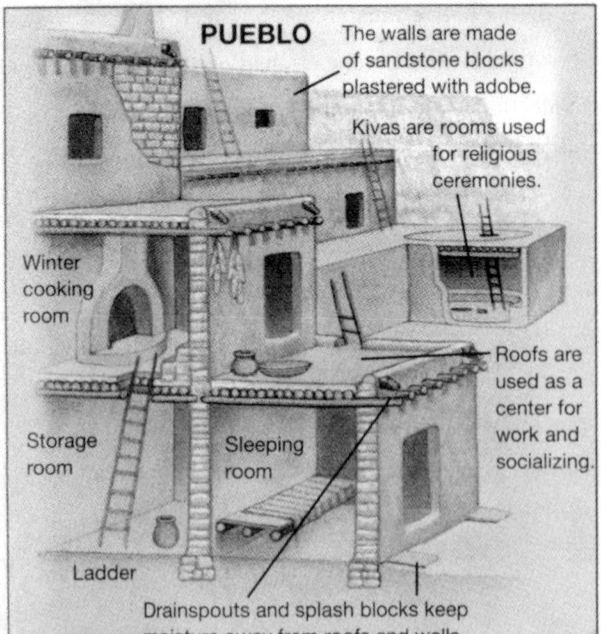

PUEBLO
The walls are made of sandstone blocks plastered with adobe.
Kivas are rooms used for religious ceremonies.
Winter cooking room
Roofs are used as a center for work and socializing.
Storage room
Sleeping room
Ladder
Drainspouts and splash blocks keep moisture away from roofs and walls.

<u>Pilgrims and Puritans</u> A small group of Europeans sailed from England on the Mayflower in 1620. The passengers were religious reformers—Puritans who were critical of the Church of England. Having given up hope of "purifying" the Church from within, they chose instead to withdraw from the Church. This

action earned them the name Separatists. We know them as the Pilgrims. They landed in North America and established a settlement at what is now Plymouth, Massachusetts. With help from friendly tribes of Native Americans, the Plymouth settlement managed to survive the rigors of North America. The colony never grew very large, however. Eventually, it was engulfed by the Massachusetts Bay Colony, the much larger settlement to the north.

Like the Plymouth Colony, the Massachusetts Bay Colony was also founded by religious reformers. These reformers, however, did not withdraw from the Church of England. Unlike the Separatists, they were Puritans who intended instead to reform the Church from within. In America, the Puritans hoped to establish what John Winthrop, governor of the Colony, called a "city upon a hill," a model community guided in all aspects by the Bible. Their form of government would be a theocracy, a state under the immediate guidance of God.

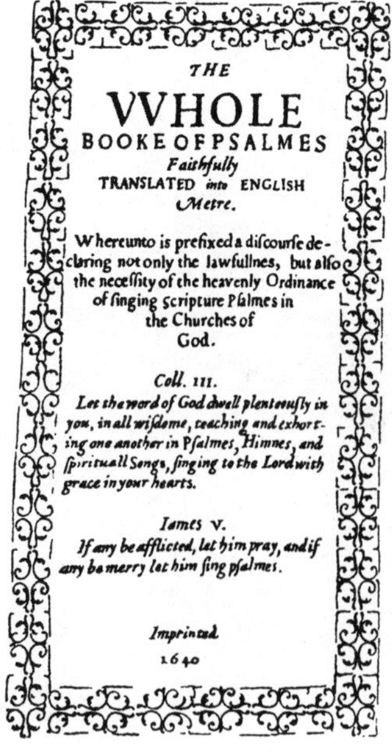

THE
VVHOLE
BOOKE OF PSALMES
Faithfully
TRANSLATED into ENGLISH
Metre.

Whereunto is prefixed a discourse declaring not only the lawfullnes, but also the necessity of the heavenly Ordinance of singing Scripture Psalmes in the Churches of God.

Coll. III.
Let the word of God dwell plenteously in you, in all wisdome, teaching and exhorting one another in Psalmes, Himnes, and spirituall Songs, singing to the Lord with grace in your hearts.

Iames V.
If any be afflicted, let him pray, and if any be merry let him sing psalmes.

Imprinted
1640

Among the Puritans' central beliefs were the ideas that human beings exist for the glory of God and that the Bible is the sole expression of God's will. They also believed in predestination—John Calvin's doctrine that God has already decided who will achieve salvation and who will not. The elect, or saints, who are to be saved cannot take election for granted, however. Because of that, all devout Puritans searched their souls with great rigor and frequency for signs of grace. The Puritans felt that they could accomplish good only through continual hard work and self-discipline. When people today speak of the "Puritan ethic", that is what they mean.

Puritanism was in decline throughout New England by the early 1700's, as more liberal Protestant congregations attracted followers. A reaction against this new freedom, however, set in around 1720. The Great Awakening, a series of reli-

gious revivals led by such eloquent ministers as the famous Jonathan Edwards and George Whitefield, swept through the colonies. The Great Awakening attracted thousands of converts to many Protestant groups, but it did little to revive old-fashioned Puritanism. Nevertheless, Puritan ideals of hard work, frugality, self-improvement, and self-reliance are still regarded as basic American virtues.

The Southern Planters The Southern Colonies differed from New England in climate, crops, social organization, and religion. Prosperous coastal cities grew up in the South, just as in the North, but beyond the southern cities lay large plantations, not small farms. Despite its romantic image, the plantation was in fact a large-scale agricultural enterprise and a center of commerce. Up to a thousand people, many of them enslaved, might live and work on a single plantation.

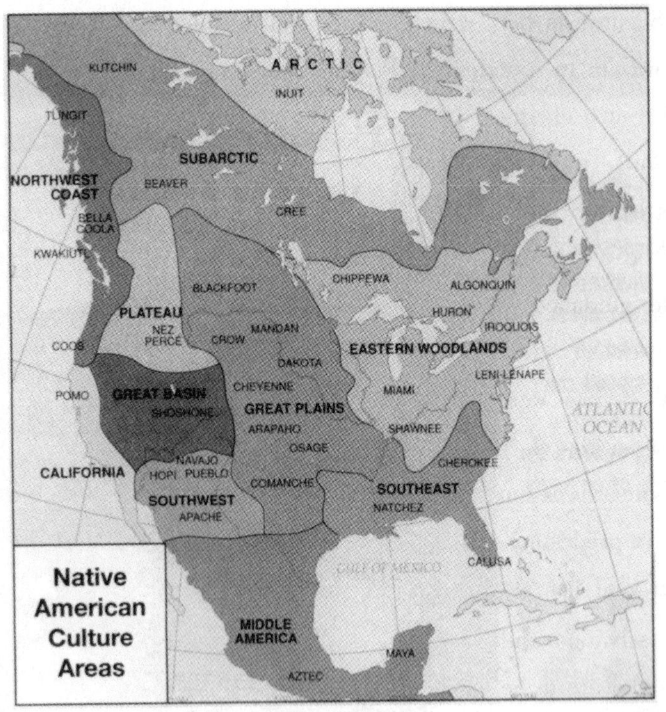

Native American Culture Areas

The first black slaves were brought to Virginia in 1619, a year before the Pilgrims landed at Plymouth. The plantation system and the institution of slavery were closely connected from the very beginning, although slavery existed in every colony, including Massachusetts.

Most of the plantation owners were Church of England members who regarded themselves as aristocrats. The first generation of owners, the men who established the great plantations, were ambitious, energetic, self-disciplined, and resourceful, just as the Puritans were. The way of life on most plantations, however, was more sociable and elegant than that of any Puritan. By 1750, Puritanism was in decline everywhere, and the plantation system in the South was just reaching its peak.

Literature of the Period

It was an oddly assorted group that established the foundations of American literature: the Native Americans with their oral traditions, the Puritans with their preoccupation with sin and salvation, and the southern planters with their busy social lives. Indeed, much of the literature that the colonists read was not produced in the colonies—it came from England. Yet, by 1750, there were the clear beginnings of a native literature that would one day be honored throughout the English-speaking world.

Native American Tradition For a long time, Native American literature was viewed mainly as folklore. The consequence was that song lyrics, hero tales, migration legends, and accounts of the creation were studied more for their content than for their literary qualities. In an oral tradition, the telling of the tale may change with each speaker, and the words are almost sure to change over time. Thus, no fixed versions of such literary works exist. Still, in cases where the words of Native American lyrics or narratives have been captured in writing, the language is often poetic and moving. As might be expected in an oral setting, oratory was much prized among Native Americans. The names of certain orators, such as Logan and Red Jacket, were widely known.

The samples of Native American literature in this unit reveal the depth and power of those original American voices.

"In Adam's Fall/We Sinned All" Just as religion dominated the lives of the Puritans, it also dominated their writings—most of which would not be considered literary works by modern standards. Typically, the Puritans wrote theological studies, hymns, histories, biographies, and autobiographies. The purpose of such writing was to provide spiritual insight and instruction. When Puritans wrote for themselves in journals or diaries, their aim was the serious kind of self-examination they practiced in other aspects of their lives. The Puritans produced neither fiction nor drama because they regarded both as sinful.

The Puritans did write poetry, however, as a vehicle of spiritual enlightenment. Although they were less concerned with a poem's literary form than with its message, some writers were naturally more gifted than others. A few excellent Puritan poets emerged in the 1600's, among them Anne Bradstreet and Edward Taylor. Anne Bradstreet's moving, personal voice and Edward Taylor's devotional intensity shine through the conventional Puritanism of their themes.The Puritans had a strong belief in education for both men and women. In 1636, they founded Harvard College to ensure a well educated ministry. Two years later, they set up the first printing press in the colonies. In 1647, free public schools were established in Massachusetts. The New England Primer, first published around 1690, combined instruction in spelling and reading with moralistic teachings, such as "In Adam's fall/We sinned all."

One of the first books printed in the colonies was the Bay Psalm Book, the standard hymnal of the time. Increase Mather, one of the book's three authors, served for many years as pastor of the North Church in Boston. He was also the author of some 130 books. Cases of Conscience Concerning Evil Spirits, published in 1693, was a discourse on the Salem witchcraft trials of the previous year. The trials, conducted in an atmosphere of hysteria, resulted in the hanging of twenty people as witches.

Increase's eldest son, Cotton Mather, far exceeded his father's literary output, publishing at least 400 works in his lifetime. Cotton Mather, like his father, is remembered in part because of his connection with the Salem witchcraft trials. Although he did not actually take part in the trials, his works on witchcraft had helped to stir up some of the hysteria. Still, Cotton Mather was one of the most learned men of his time, a power in the state and a notable author. His theory of writing was simple (although his writing was not): The more information a work contains, the better its style.

In fact, the Puritans in general had a theory of literary style. They believed in a plain style of writing—one in which clear statement is the highest goal. An ornate or clever style would be a sign of vanity and, as such, would not be in accordance with God's will. Despite the restrictions built into their life and literature, the Puritans succeeded in producing a small body of excellent writing.

Southern Voices Considering the number of brilliantly literate statesmen who would later emerge in the South, especially in Virginia, it seems surprising that only a few notable southern writers appeared prior to 1750. As in Puritan New England, those who were educated produced a substantial amount of writing, but it was mostly of a practical nature. For example, John Smith, the leader of the settlement at Jamestown, Virginia, wrote The General History of Virginia to describe his experiences for Europeans. In addition to accounts like Smith's, letters written by southern planters also provide insight into this time period. Unlike the Puritans, southerners did not oppose fiction or drama, and the first theater in America opened in Williamsburg, Virginia, in 1716.

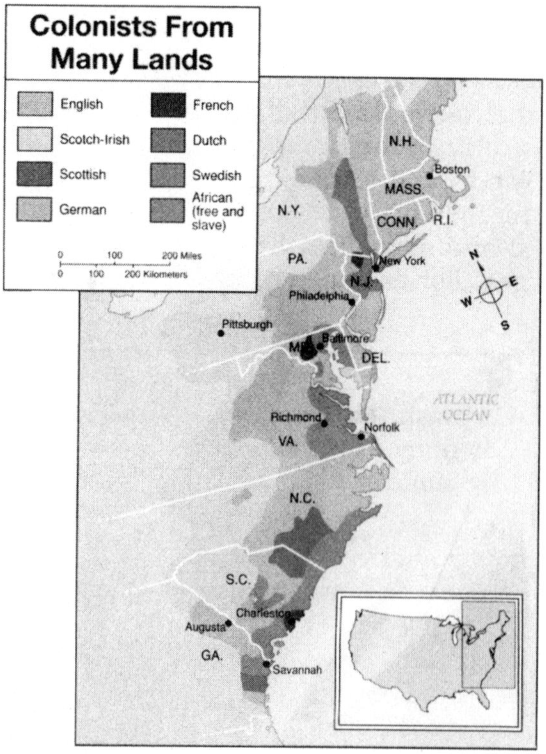

Colonists From Many Lands

The Planter From Westover The important literature of the pre-Revolutionary South can be summed up in one name—William Byrd. Byrd lived at Westover, a magnificent plantation on the James River bequeathed to him by his wealthy father. Commissioned in 1728 to survey the boundary line between Virginia and North Carolina, Byrd kept a journal of his experiences. That journal served as the basis for his book, The History of the Dividing Line, which was circulated in manuscript form among Byrd's friends in England. Published nearly a century after Byrd's death, the book was immediately recognized as a minor humorous masterpiece. More of Byrd's papers were published later, establishing his reputation as the finest writ-

er in the pre–Revolutionary South.

The writers whose work appears in this unit are not the great names in American literature. They are the founders, the men and women who laid the groundwork for the towering achievements that followed. The modest awakening of American literature seen in this unit had repercussions that echoed down the years.

第一课

第一次美洲航海日志

克里斯托弗·哥伦布 (1451—1506)

克里斯托弗·哥伦布是历史上最著名的探险家之一。关于他的早期生活人们知之甚少，可以确定的是，他很早就离开了他在意大利各诺亚的家庭，开始航海。哥伦布25岁时，在葡萄牙海岸外遭遇了沉船。他回到陆上以后，马上开始学习绘制地图和导航技术。他还学习了拉丁文，并阅读了马可·波罗关于富饶的亚洲的描述。

克里斯托弗·哥伦布

1480年至1482年之间，哥伦布远航到了阿佐里斯和非洲附近的加纳利群岛。此后他就开始梦想进行更有挑战性的航海。

哥伦布一生执著于一个目标：向西环游世界，一直到达传说中亚洲神奇的城市。

起初，哥伦布试图说服葡萄牙的约翰二世国王资助他向西航行，当这一请求被约翰二世拒绝之后，他又转向欧洲其他的统治者寻求资助。经受了一系列挫折之后，哥伦布终于得到了西班牙伊丽莎白王后的支持。

有利的条件　1492年，伊丽莎白王后和她的丈夫费尔南德国王，同意资助哥伦布的第一次远航。在他们的协议中，这位探险家为自己争取到了有利的条件。在他的请求之下，除了资助之外，国王夫妇还授权他统治他征服的所有陆地，并且拥有这些陆地上财富的十分之一。

大航海　哥伦布于8月3日出发航行，10月12日，他到达了巴哈马群岛中的一个岛，并把这个岛误认为是印度附近的岛屿，然后他继续向加勒比海进发。在此后的12年中，他又进行了三次穿越大西洋的航行，而且一直坚信自己到达了亚洲，希望能找到马可·波罗传说中的城市。

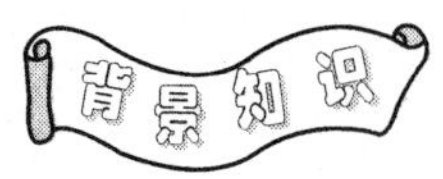

历史：探险时代

15世纪50年代，人们所知道的唯一从欧洲到达印度的路线就是穿过土耳其。1453年，土耳其人宣布对欧洲与印度之间的利润丰厚的贸易征收一项新税后，葡萄牙人和西班牙人就开始寻找一条可以代替陆路的海上路线。他们的探索使欧洲和南、北美洲取得了联系，在那之后的一个世纪里，这两个大洲的大部分土地都落入了欧洲人的控制之中。直到1498年，巴思科·达·伽玛才发现了绕过非洲海角通往印度的全程海路。

如这张地图所示，哥伦布在航行中先经过葡萄牙里斯本，到达西班牙帕罗斯和加纳利群岛，然后穿越大西洋。他首先在圣萨尔瓦多岛登陆，这篇游记就从这里开始。

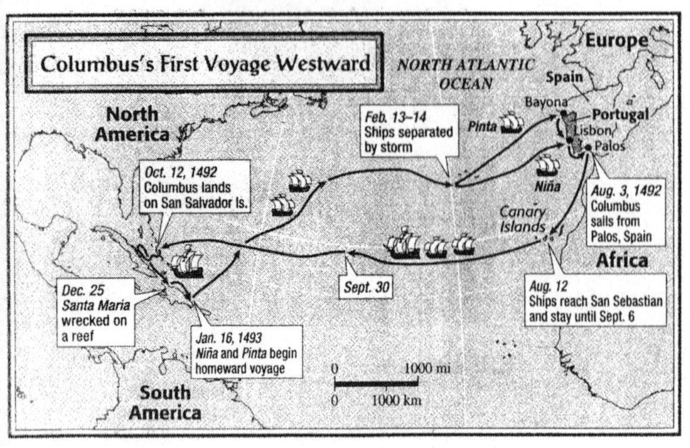

哥伦布航海路线图

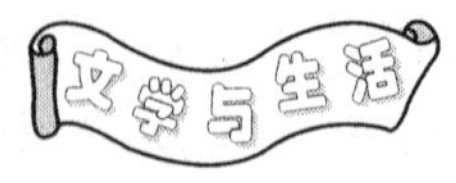

联系你的经历　有一句励志格言："只要你有梦想，你就能够做到。"然而，有一些梦想，例如乘小船环游世界或是发明治

疗绝症的方法，不是只有愿望就能做到的。一个人要完成梦想就需要经济上的支援。即使是克里斯托弗•哥伦布也需要为他的航海事业寻求一个强有力的后盾作保证。他的很多篇航海日志都强调了新大陆有丰富的资源，这样才能保证伊丽莎白王后在读了他的航海日志后，决定继续对他进行资助。

日志写作 有些人认为环游世界的航行不值得资助，得不到足够的回报，你怎样才能让他们接受这个想法，进行资助呢？就这个题目，在你的日志里写一篇有说服力的文章。

专题聚焦：文化的交会 在最初欧洲人对北美洲进行的探索中，北美的土著居民遇见了奇怪的外来者。当这两种文化第一次相遇时将会发生什么事情呢？

日志 欧洲人对于美洲的探索和征服过程都被记录在探险家的日志中。“日志”就是一个人对每天发生的事情的记录，其中记录的细节只有亲自参加或亲眼目睹事件的人才能知道。日志中记录了作者个人对事件的反应和想法，使人们能了解作者的各个方面。

日志虽然能使人们深入地了解它的作者，但并不一定是事实的可靠记录。作者本人的印象，特别当他或她置身于事件之中的时候，会对事件的描述产生影响。如果作者写日志的目的是出版发行，而不是私人保存的话，这种日志就可能更不客观了。你在阅读哥伦布日志的过程中，试着寻找他在为某些读者写作的证据。

第一次美洲航海日志(节选)

克里斯托弗•哥伦布

这篇日志开始于哥伦布在圣萨尔瓦多岛登陆后的第九天。

1492年，10月21日，星期日。10点钟，我们到达了这个岛的一个海角，船队的其他船只也抛锚停下了。匆匆吃了一顿饭之后，我上了岸，发现除了一栋空

无一人的房子之外，这里没有人烟的迹象。我们相信房子的主人由于我们的到来深感恐惧，弃家而逃，因为房子里面生活用具样样俱全。我下令不许动房子里的东西，然后带着我的船长们和一些船员去视察岛屿全境。这座岛屿比其他的岛屿更加美丽富饶。到处是高大茂盛的小树林，还有四周绿树环绕，浓荫覆盖的大湖，景色优美迷人。整个世界就像四月的安塔露西亚一样青翠欲滴。鸟儿歌声动听，让人不忍离去，成群的鹦鹉连天空都能遮没。这里的鸟类和我们国家的鸟类看起来极其不同，还有上千种不同的树木，树上长满果实，香味使人垂涎欲滴。让我感到非常遗憾的是我不知道这些树的名字，但我确认它们都很有价值，所以我保存了这些树和植物的标本。在湖周围视察时，我们发现了一条蛇，它逃到了水里，我们一直跟着它，因为水不深，最后用长矛把它捉住了。这条蛇有七指长，我估计这一带还有很多这样的蛇。我还发现了芦荟树，并决定明天带十昆多（当时的一种计量单位——译者注）上船，因为有人告诉我这种树很值钱。在寻找饮用水的过程中，我们在距离停船处半里格（旧时长度单位，1里格约4.8公里——译者注）的地方见到了一座当地人的村庄，那里的居民一发现我们就弃家逃走，还把值钱的东西都带到了山里。我命令我们的人不许拿走任何他们留下的东西，连一根针也不行。不久我们就看到几个当地人向我们走过来，其中有一个接近了我们，我们给了他一些鹰铃和玻璃珠，他很高兴。作为交换，我们向他要一些水。当我回到船上时，那些

哥伦布在西半球登陆

当地人已经带着装满水的葫芦来到了岸边，而且表现得很高兴。我下令再给他们一些玻璃珠，他们答应第二天再来。我希望能在这个地方将船上的水桶装满水，如果天气许可，就马上离开，绕岛航行，直到我找到这里的国王。因为我听说他拥有很多黄金，所以想试试看能否得到一些。之后我打算向另外一个很大的岛屿进发，根据船上的印第安人提供的信息，我相信这个岛就是西潘哥岛。那些印第安人称这个岛为寇芭岛，说那里有很多大船和海员。还有一个岛屿他们称为波西亚岛，据说这个岛也很大。对于在我们航线上的其他岛屿，我也会在经过的时候进行探查，并且根据是否发现了大量的黄金或香料来决定我的行动。无论发生什么事情，我决心向大陆航行，访问那个城市，把陛下的信呈给大汗，并且带着他的答复回来。

文学和生活

读者反应 如果你是哥伦布航行的资助者，读到他的这段经历记录，你会有什么样的感受？

领导能力测试 和同学们组成小组，列出优秀的领导者所需具备的素质，和同学们讨论你的结论。

主题焦点 哥伦布的日志记录了欧洲人和北美洲当地人最早的相遇。这两类人有什么样不同的反应？你从文中能找到什么证据？

阅读理解

1. 哥伦布看到景色之后的反应是什么？

2. 根据哥伦布的叙述，为什么当他和船员们到达那些房屋的时候，里面空无一人？

3. 哥伦布打算在这个岛上停留多长时间？

思考

解释

1. 你怎么判断岛上的美景给哥伦布留下了深刻印象？（证据支持）

2. 哥伦布选择送回西班牙的“样本”，最大的初衷是什么？（分析）

3. 根据哥伦布的叙述,第一次与当地人的相遇是怎样进行的?(概括)

评价

4. 如果哥伦布写作的目的是请求进一步的支持,那么他在证明自己探险活动的价值方面做得如何?(做出你的判断)

应用

5. 如果这篇描述是由一名船员写的,将会有怎样的不同?(假设)

6. 如果这篇描述是由一名观察到船员们活动的美洲当地人写的,将会有怎样的不同?(假设)

文学聚焦

日志

日志是一个人对每天发生的事件和其个人感受的记录。大部分的日志都是作为个人记录保存的,但是哥伦布却把他的美洲航海日志记入编年史,以便他的资助者西班牙国王和王后查阅。

1. 根据你的理解,哥伦布为什么经常在见到事物时想到它们的金钱价值?

2. 在你看来,哥伦布试图表达的对美洲的印象是什么?

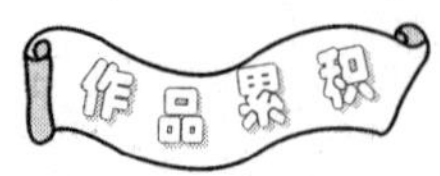

点子库

写作

1. 船员日志　想象你是哥伦布的一名船员,从你的角度重写本文。

2. 续写　从哥伦布停止的地方续写,写一篇日志来描述你探索加勒比海时的想法。

3. 比较日志　哥伦布进行了多次的航行,但是一直没有抵达亚洲,利用图书馆资源,找一篇哥伦布后来的航海日志,在你的文章中比较哥伦布后期的日志与早期的日志中表达出来的情感有什么不同,并解释为什么有这些不同?(社会研究连线)

项目

1. 地图　画一张岛上的地图，表现哥伦布登陆和探查的地点。

2. 哥伦布纪念收集　说明哥伦布对当今世界的贡献。找到以他的名字命名的重点公共场所（例如：城市和公园），了解在全国各地是怎样庆祝“哥伦布日”的。将你的发现制成一本剪贴簿。

微型写作课

口头航海报告

哥伦布能筹集到资金是因为他有能力使没见过他探险的大陆的人接受他的想法。假设你是哥伦布，口头作出一篇报告，在回到欧洲时报告给西班牙国王和王后。

写作技巧重点：生动细致的说明

为使你的听众分享你的经历，你需要通过深入细致的描述来说明纳入感官的细节，叙述可以看到、听到、感觉到、触摸到或闻到的东西。在以下范例中，哥伦布使他的读者感受到他们没有亲身经历的事件。

日志中的范例

到处是高大茂盛的小树林，还有四周绿树环绕，浓荫覆盖的大湖，景色优美迷人。整个世界就像四月的安塔露西亚一样青翠欲滴。鸟儿歌声动听，让人不忍离去，成群的鹦鹉连天空都能遮没。

哥伦布通过感官细节来描述这个岛屿，他认为这个富饶的岛屿非常美丽。

构思

想象哥伦布见到的自然风光，列出他可能碰到的热带风光、声音、触觉、气味和味道。

写稿

在描述这个岛的时候，尽可能纳入你最多的感官细节。通过细节来表现这一地区的富饶繁茂，而不是告诉你的听众它有多美丽。

修改

对你描述的每一个形象都加入细节来强化，在只有视觉和听觉的描述中加入嗅觉，考虑在适当的地方加入触觉或味觉的描写。

Guide for Interpreting

Christopher Columbus(1451—1506)

Not much is known about the early life of Christopher Columbus, one of history's most famous explorers. Evidently, he left his home in Genoa, Italy, and went to sea at a young age. At age 25, he was shipwrecked off the coast of Portugal. Once back on land, Columbus studied mapmaking and navigation. He also learned Latin and read Marco Polo's account of tile riches of Asia.

Between 1480 and 1482, Columbus sailed to the Azores and to the Canary Islands off Africa. He then began to dream of more challenging voyages.

One goal became the focus of Columbus's life: reaching the fabled cities of Asia by sailing westward around the world.

First, Columbus tried to convince King John II of Portugal to fund a westward voyage. When his requests were rejected there, Columbus sought funding from other European rulers. After a series of unsuccessful attempts, Columbus won the support of Queen Isabella of Spain.

A Hard Bargain Queen Isabella and her husband, King Ferdinand, agreed to finance Columbus's first voyage in 1492. In forging the agreements, the explorer had negotiated favorable terms. In addition to funding, he asked for and received the right to rule any lands he conquered. He would also be entitled to 10 percent of all wealth from those lands.

The Famous Voyage Columbus set sail on August 3. On October 12, he reached one of the Bahama islands, which he mistook for an island off India. Columbus named the island San Salvador. Then he continued to explore the Caribbean. Over the next twelve years, he made three more transatlantic voyages, ever convinced that he had reached Asia and always hopeful of finding Marco

Polo's fabled cities.

Background for Understanding

HISTORY: THE ERA OF EXPLORATION

In the 1450's, the only known way to India from Europe involved traveling through Turkey. When the Turks announced a new tax on Europe's profitable overland trade with India in 1453, Portugal and Spain began to look for an alternate sea route to India. Their search brought Europe into contact with North and South America. Within a century, much of these two vast continents would come under European control. It was not until 1498 that Vasco da Gama found the all-sea route to India—around the horn of Africa.

As this map shows, Columbus's voyages took him from Lisbon, Portugal, to Palos, Spain, and the Canary Islands before crossing the Atlantic. He landed first on the island of San Salvador, where this account begins.

Literature and your Life

CONNECT YOUR EXPERIENCE

"If you can dream it, you can do it", one motivational motto asserts. However, to fulfill the desire to circle the globe in a boat or discover the cure for a deadly disease takes much more than sheer will. A dreamer needs financial resources. Even Christopher Columbus had to secure and retain backers for his voyages. Many of his journal entries stressed the rich potential of the new lands, so that, upon reading them, Queen Isabella would decide to continue her sponsorship.

Journal Writing How would you have sold the idea of traveling around the globe to people who believed it would not be worth the expense? Write a convincing argument in your journal.

THEMATIC FOCUS: MEETING OF CULTURES

The earliest days of European exploration of North America brought native

peoples into contact with curious newcomers. What kind of things can happen when cultures first meet?

Literary Focus

JOURNALS

The European encounters with and conquest of the Americas are recorded in the journals of the explorers. A journal is an individual's day-by-day account of events. It provides valuable details that can be supplied only by a participant or an eyewitness. As a record of personal reactions, a journal reveals much about the writer.

While offering insight into the life of the writer, a journal is not necessarily a reliable record of facts. The writer's impressions may color the telling of events, particularly when he or she is a participant. Journals written for publication rather than private use are even less likely to be objective. As you read Columbus's journal, look for evidence that the explorer was writing for an audience.

Journal of the First Voyage to America

Christopher Columbus

This account begins nine days after Columbus landed on San Salvador.

SUNDAY, OCT. 21ST [1492]. At 10 o'clock, we arrived at a cape of the island, and anchored, the other vessels in company. After having dispatched a meal, I went ashore, and found no habitation save a single house, and that without an occupant; we had no doubt that the people had fled in terror at our approach, as the house was completely furnished. I suffered nothing to be touched, and went with my captains and some of the crew to view the country. This island even exceeds the others in beauty and fertility. Groves of lofty and flourishing trees are abundant, as also large lakes, surrounded and overhung by the foliage, in a most enchanting manner. Everything looked as green as in April in Andalusia. The melody of the birds was so exquisite that one was never willing to part from the spot, and the flocks of parrots obscured the heavens. The diversity in the appearance of the feathered tribe from those of our country is extremely curious. A thousand different sorts of trees, with their fruit were to be met with, and of a wonderfully delicious odor. It was a great affliction to me to be ignorant of their natures, for I am very certain they are all valuable; specimens of them and of the plants I have preserved. Going round one of these lakes, I saw a snake, which we killed, and I have kept the skin for your Highnesses; upon being discovered he took to the water, whither we followed him, as it was not deep, and dispatched him with our lances; he was seven spans in length; I think there are many more such about here. I discovered also the aloe tree, and am determined to take on board the ship tomorrow, ten quintals of it, as I am told it is valuable. While we were in search of some good water we came upon a village of the natives about half a league from the place where the ships lay; the inhabitants on discovering us abandoned their houses, and took to flight, carrying off their goods to the mountain. I ordered that nothing which they had left should be taken, not even the value of a pin. Presently we saw several of the natives advancing towards our party, and one of them came up to us, to whom we gave some hawk's bells and glass beads, with which he was delighted. We asked him in return, for water, and after I had gone on board the ship, the natives came down to the shore with their calabashes full, and showed great pleasure in presenting us with it. I ordered more glass beads to be given them, and they promised to return the next day. It is my wish to fill all the water casks of

the ships at this place, which being executed, I shall depart immediately, if the weather serve, auld sail round the island, till I succeed in meeting with the king, in order to see if I can acquire any of the gold, which I hear he possesses. After–wards I shall set sail for another very large island which I believe to be Cipango, according to the indications I receive from the Indians on board. They call the island Colba, and say there are many large ships, and sailors there. This other is–land they name Bosio and inform me that it is very large; the others which lie in our course, I shall examine on the passage, and according as I find gold or spices in abundance, I shall determine what to do; at all events I am determined to proceed on to the continent, and visit the city of Guisay where I shall deliver the letters of your Highnesses to the Great Can, and demand an answer, with which I shall return.

第二课

龟背上的土地

昂昂达嘎族

作为最初的五个民族之一，昂昂达嘎族是伊罗奎伊斯联盟，一支说伊罗奎伊斯语的美洲土著联盟中有影响的部族。昂昂达嘎族生活在现纽约州中部，他们住在由木头和树皮建成的长状房子中，以血缘关系聚集而居。美国革命之后，伊罗奎伊斯联盟解体了，随后昂昂达嘎族中的小分支就分散到国家的不同地区，但是其中的大多数都回到了纽约他们的祖先曾经居住过的山谷，那里就是现存的昂昂达嘎族居留地。

莫多克族

莫多克族人从前住在奥雷根和加利福尼亚的北部地区，并在那里耕种、捕鱼和打猎。每个村庄都是独立的，有各自的头领，但在战争发生的时候，他们就会团结起来一致对外。19世纪中期，莫多克族人被迫居住在奥雷根的一个印第安人居留地。后来，在一个名叫“杰克队长”的小头领的带领下，有一小群莫多克人逃离了这个居留地。这些追随者最终定居在俄克拉何马，并在随后的几年中一直与美国军队处于敌对状态。后来他们被允许回到奥雷根的居留地，但这个居留地在20世纪50年代中期也被取消了。

纳瓦霍族

今天，纳瓦霍族是美国最大的美洲土著民族，拥有超过10万族众。其中有很多人住在纳瓦霍居留地，这个居留地覆盖了亚利桑那州、犹他州和新墨西哥州的2.4万平方英里土地。古纳瓦霍人是勇猛的战士和猎手，他们在大约1000年以前定居在西南部，最终与爱好和平的普埃布罗人通婚，并从他们那里学会了织布和种植谷物。在打退美国移民长达几十年的侵犯之后，纳瓦霍人在1864年被美国军队从他们的领地里驱赶了出来。但最后他们还是得到允许回到了他们在纳瓦霍土地上的居留地。很多纳瓦霍人仍然延续着传统的风俗，他们住在泥土和圆木结构的房屋里，信奉部落的宗教。

伊罗奎伊斯族

强大的伊罗奎伊斯族住在现美国东北部地区。在14世纪，一个名叫德卡纳维达的神秘主义者和预言家在村庄之间穿行，竭力主张说伊罗奎伊斯语的人们停止争斗，和平共处。德卡纳维达努力的最终结果形成了五族伊罗奎伊斯联盟，这个联盟由五个说伊罗奎伊斯语的部落组成：莫霍克、欧内达、赛内卡、卡由加和昂昂达嘎。

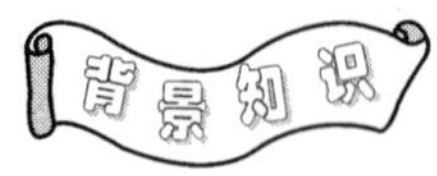

文化：人类与自然界

美洲土著人对自然界极为崇敬，他们相信每种生物都拥有一种赖以生存并影响其他生物的力量。每种美洲土著文化都给这种力量起了不同的名字，但是最早定居在那里的白人学到的是一个阿尔刚奎恩语的名字：玛尼托。玛尼托以不同的形状和大小出现，但很多美洲土著文化都认为有一种主要的玛尼托，或者叫“大神”——一种作为人类生命和美好事物的来源的无形力量。很多为早期的美洲土著人提供食物和衣服的动物都被他们认为是玛尼托，有很多美洲土著的民间故事和艺术中都刻画了动物，反映出对动物的崇敬。

联系你的经历 “我出生的时候是什么样子的？”“你知道关于我祖父母的什么事吗？”出于一个共同的原因，我们都会提出像这样的问题。我们都有一种共同的渴望，就是了解我们的起源——我们从哪里来，我们在这个世界上的位置。就像你收集关于你家族历史的故事一样，各种文化也会创造出故事来解释他们所知道的世界。

美洲土著人陶器

日志写作 仔细观察一下这片美洲土著人陶器上的老鼠和熊的形象，讲叙一下你现在了解到的美洲土著人的信仰，解释一下箭头可能代表着什么。

专题聚焦：文化的交会 这些神话故事是美洲土著人对于人类起源问题做出的回答。在你阅读的时候，注意这四篇作品中都充满了来自自然界的形象。自然界在改变和维持美洲土著人的生活中发挥了什么作用？

起源神话 神话产生于人类解释生命开端的需要，是人们代代相传的传统故事，大多是关于神灵精怪的。我们把这些重述早期生命起源的故事称为起源神话。神话经常也会解释很多其他的现象，包括风俗习惯、宗教仪式、自然景观(例如一座大山)或人们无法控制的事情。在你读到每个神话的时候，注意是谁或什么造成了地球上最早的生命起源，并找出关于自然现象的解释。

龟背上的土地

昂昂达嘎族

迈克尔·J.·卡杜托 和 约瑟夫·布鲁卡克 复述

在土地存在之前，世上只有水。一个人能看到多远，那水就伸展到多远，

鸟儿和动物都在水里游来游去。在水的上方很远的地方，有一片“天陆”。在那片“天陆”上，长着一棵巨大美丽的树。它有四条白色的根，每条伸向一个神圣的方向[①]，而它的枝条上长着各种果实和花朵。

在那片“天陆”上住着一个老首领。他年轻的妻子怀了孕，一天夜里，她梦见那棵大树被连根拔起。第二天，她把这个梦讲给了她的丈夫。

在她讲完了她的梦以后，他点点头，说：“我的妻，你做的这个梦让我感到很悲伤。这很显然是个具有巨大力量的梦。按照我们的传统，当有人做了这样一个有力的梦时，我们就要尽全力让它实现。大树必须被连根拔起。”

然后老首领就把所有的年轻人叫到一起，告诉他们必须要把那棵树拔起来。可是那棵树的根扎得那么深，他们根本就推不动它。最后老首领自己走到树前。他双臂抱着树干，弯下膝盖，身体紧绷着。终于，他猛地用了一下力，把那棵树连根拔了起来，平放在了地上。这棵树原本深深扎根的那块“天陆”现在就变成了一个大洞。首领的妻子走近前来，抓住大树的一根树枝稳住身子，探身向下看。她好像在下面很远的地方看见有什么东西像水一样熠熠生辉，于是又向前探了探身子，想看清楚。就在她向前探身的时候，她失去了平衡，掉进了那个洞里。她的手从那树枝上滑下来的时候抓了一把种子，然后她就一直向下掉，向下，向下，向下……

在远远的下方，有些鸟和动物在水中向上望去。

“有人从天上朝我们这儿掉下来了。”有一只鸟说。

美洲龟

“我们应该帮帮她。”另一只鸟说。然后就有两只天鹅向上飞去，它们把那从天上掉下来的女人架在宽阔的翅膀之间。慢慢地，它们带着她向水面飞来，而鸟儿和动物们都在水中看着它们。

“她不像我们，”一只动物说，“看，她的脚上没有蹼。我想她不能生活在水里。”

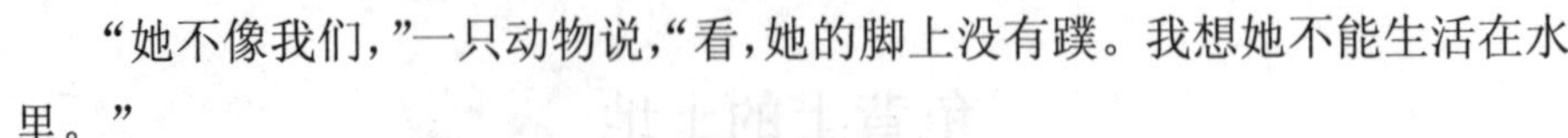

“那我们应该怎么办呢？”另一只水里的动物问。

“我知道。”有只水鸟说，“我听说过在水下很远的地方有泥土。如果我们

① 神圣的方向：东、南、西、北。

潜水下去，把泥土拿上来的话，她就可以有个地方站了。”

于是鸟儿和动物们就决定要有谁去把泥土拿上来。它们一个接一个地尝试。

有的说，是鸭子第一个潜了下去。它向下游啊游，到了水面下很远的地方，但是没碰到底就又浮了上来。然后轮到海狸，它潜得更深，深得周围一片黑暗，但是它也碰不到底。不久，好像所有的动物都试过了，但是都失败了。然后有一个小小的声音说话了：

“我要不把泥土拿上来，就死在水下。”

它们都想看看那是谁，原来那是小麝鼠。它潜入水下，游啊游。它不像其他动物那样强壮，也不像它们那样敏捷，可是它有坚定的决心。它潜到周围一片黑暗的深处，仍然向更深处游去。它游得那么深，它的肺都要爆炸了，可它还是向更深处游去。最后，就在它快要失去知觉的时候，它伸出了一只小爪子，抓到了水底，它刚刚碰到底，就向上浮去，那时它几乎已经死了。

当其他动物看见它浮出水面的时候，它们以为它失败了。然后它们看见它的右爪紧紧攥在一起。

“它拿到泥土了。”他们说，“现在我们能把土放在哪儿呢？”

“放在我的背上吧。”一个深沉的声音说。那是大龟，它是从水下的深处上来的。

于是它们把麝鼠放在大龟身上，把它的爪子放在它的背上。直到今天，龟壳上还有麝鼠爪子留下的痕迹。那一点儿泥土刚一落到龟的背上，马上就开始变得越来越大，越来越大，直到变成了整个世界。

然后那两只天鹅就带着天上的女人落到了地上。她踏上了新的土地，张开手，让手里的种子掉到光秃秃的地面上。从那些种子里长出了树和草。地上的生命开始了。

文学和生活

读者反应 如果你是老首领的话，你会把那棵大树拔起来吗？为你的回答做出解释。

主题焦点 这个神话故事中刻画的动物们怎样体现了人类本性中最好的方面？

非正式辩论 和一组同学进行一次非正式辩论，讨论麝鼠和龟是否应该因为创造了陆地而获得更多称赞。

阅读理解

1. 根据这个神话，在这片土地之前存在的是什么？
2. 是什么引发了一系列事件，最终导致陆地的产生？
3. 天上的女人从“天陆”上带来了什么，这对陆地产生了什么影响？

思考

解释

1. 说出至少两种在“天陆”上失去了或牺牲了的东西，因此陆地上才有生命。（分析）

2. 这个神话里的动物怎样表现了人类的美德？（解释）

3. 你认为昂昂达嘎族把创造陆地的功劳主要归于谁？（推断）

4. 你能从这个神话中得出关于昂昂达嘎族人与他们周围的自然环境之间的关系的什么结论？为你的回答做出解释。（得出结论）

扩展

5. 为了拯救天上的女人，麝鼠宁愿牺牲自己的生命。描述你在文学或真实生活中看到的同样无私的人。（综合）

在灰熊直立行走的时候

莫多克族

里察德·埃尔多斯 和 阿尔方索·沃第兹 复述

在地上有人类存在之前，天神的首领对他在上界的家感到厌倦了，因为那里的空气总是冷得像冰一样，所以他用一块石头在天空上挖了一个洞，把所有的冰雪都从那儿推了下去，直到形成了一个从地面通到天上的大雪堆。今天人们把它称做莎斯塔山。

然后天神拿着他的手杖，从一朵云迈到山峰上，向山下走去。在离下面的山谷还有大约一半路程的时候，他开始用手指到处碰触地面，他的手指碰到哪里，哪里就长出一棵树来。冰雪在他的脚下融化，水向下流成了河海。

天神把他那根巨大手杖的较小的一端弄碎，把碎片扔到河里。长一些的碎片就变成了海狸和水獭，小一些的碎片变成了鱼。当树叶从树上掉下来的时候，他把它们捡起来，向它们吹气，就这样创造了鸟。然后他拿起那根巨大手杖的较大的一端，创造出了所有在地上行走的动物，这些动物中最大的就是灰熊。

当灰熊最初被创造出来的时候，它们和今天的熊一样全身是毛，有尖利的爪子，但是它们用两只脚行走，还能像人一样说话。它们看起来非常凶猛，所以天神把它们送到远离他的山脚下的森林里居住。

天神的首领对他自己所做的一切感到非常满意，决定把他的家人带下来，和他一起住在地上。冰雪堆成的大山变成了他们的房子。他在大山的中心点起一堆大火，并在山顶上挖了一个孔，以便烟和火星能从那里飘出去。当他把一大块木头扔到火里的时候，火星就会飞起来，整个大地都会颤抖。

春末的一天，天神和他的家人正围火而坐，风神送来一阵大风，摇动了山顶。这阵风一直吹啊吹，吼啊吼。烟被吹回到他们的家里，弄疼了他们的眼睛。终于天神对他最小的女儿说："你爬到烟孔上去，请风神吹得轻一点儿。告诉他我恐怕他会把整座山吹翻。"

正当小女儿要向上爬的时候，她的父亲又说："小心别把头伸到山顶外去。如果你伸出去的话，风会抓住你的头发，把你吹走的。"

那女孩很快爬到山顶上，一直待在烟孔里面和风神说话。就在她想要向下爬回来的时候，她记起她的父亲曾经说过，在他们家的顶上能看到大海。这个小女儿完全被自己的好奇心控制住了，很想知道大海是什么样子。她把头伸到了孔外面，转向西方，可是她还什么都没看见，风神就抓住了她的长头发，把她拉到山外面，吹到了冰雪下面。她落到了树木和冰雪交界处的低矮的杉树中间，她长长的红头发在雪地上飘曳。

有一只灰熊在外出为全家觅食的时候发现了这个小女孩。它把她带回了家，小女孩就和家庭里的小熊一起被它的妻子养大。这个红头发的小女孩和小熊一起吃饭，一起玩耍，一起长大。

当她长成一个年轻女人的时候，她嫁给了灰熊的大儿子。在后来的那些

年里，他们生了很多孩子，这些孩子不像灰熊那样多毛，但也长得不完全像他们的天神妈妈。

森林里所有的灰熊都为这些新生命感到骄傲，所以它们为红头发的妈妈和她的孩子们造了一栋房子。它们把这房子造在莎斯塔山的旁边——今天人们叫它小莎斯塔山。

很多年过去了，灰熊妈妈知道自己快要死了。因为藏起了天神首领的女儿，它知道应该请求天神首领的原谅，所以它把所有的灰熊都聚集到它们建起的房子旁边。然后它把它的大儿子送到一朵云里，一直到莎斯塔山的顶上，让它去告诉天神首领在哪里能找到他丢失已久的女儿。

天神首领得到这个消息的时候，非常高兴，所以大步地从山的一侧走下来，在他的脚下冰雪融化，大地崩裂。直到今天在莎斯塔山南侧的岩石路上还能看到他留下的足迹。

当他走近那所房子的时候，他大声叫道："这里是我小女儿住的地方吗？"

天神首领本以为他的孩子会像他最后一次见到她的时候一样，然而他见到的是一个成年的女人，又发现她正在照顾的那些奇怪的动物是他的外孙，他非常生气。一种新的动物居然不经他的创造就产生了！他非常严厉地对那灰熊老祖母皱着眉头，它马上就倒下死去了。然后他对所有的灰熊发出了诅咒：

"你们欺骗了我，从现在开始你们都要用四只脚走路，而且永远不能再说话。"

他把他的外孙们都从那所房子里赶了出去，把他的女儿扛在肩膀上，爬回山上去。他再也没回到过森林。有人说他熄灭了他房子中心的火，带着他的女儿回到天上去住了。

那些奇怪的动物，他的外孙们，在地上四处散布游荡。他们就是最早的印第安人，所有印第安部落的祖先。

这就是为什么住在莎斯塔山附近的印第安人决不会杀死一只灰熊的原因。当一个印第安人被灰熊杀死，他的尸体就被当

美洲灰熊

场火化。之后的很多年里，每个经过那里的人都会往那个地方扔一块石头，最后就形成了一个大石堆，标志着那个印第安人被灰熊杀死的地方。

纳瓦霍起源传说（节选）

纳瓦霍族

华盛顿·马修斯 复述

在第十二天的早晨，人们认真地清洗了自己的身体。女人们用黄色的玉米粉把自己擦干；而男人们用白色的玉米粉把自己擦干。这个洗礼刚一结束，他们就听到从远处传来慢慢靠近他们的神[①]的呼唤。像以前一样，这呼唤重复了四次——每次重复都更近一些，声音更大一些——然后，在这四次呼唤之后，神们出现了。蓝身神和黑身神每人拿着一张神圣的鹿皮。白身神拿着两个玉米穗，一个是黄色的，一个是白色的，每个玉米穗的底端都长满了谷粒。

神们把一张鹿皮头朝西方铺在地上，然后把那两个玉米穗头朝东放在上面，他们又把另一张鹿皮头朝东方铺在玉米穗上。在白色的玉米穗下，他们放了一只白鹰的羽毛，而在那黄色的玉米穗下，他们放了一只黄鹰的羽毛。然后他们让人们站远一些，让风能吹进来。白色的风从东方吹来，黄色的风从西方吹来，吹进了两张鹿皮之间。在风吹的时候，来了八个幻影人，他们绕着地上的那些东西走了四圈。鹰的羽毛从鹿皮之间伸了出来，当他们踏到羽毛上的时候，人们看见羽毛在动。幻影人走完之后，上面的那张鹿皮被掀了起来；玉米穗不见了，取而代之的是一个男人和一个女人躺在那里。

那个白色的玉米穗变成了一个男人，而那个黄色的变成了一个女人，是风给了他们生命。现在，我们嘴里吹出的风给了我们生命，当这风不吹了，我们就死了。在我们手指尖的皮肤上，能看见风的痕迹，这告诉我们当我们的祖先被创造出来的时候，风是从什么地方吹来的。

这样创造出来的那一对人就是“第一个男人”和“第一个女人”。神们指导人们为这对人用柴枝建起了一圈围墙。当围墙建好以后，“第一个男人”和“第

---

① 靠近他们的神：纳瓦霍族的四神：白身神、蓝身神、黄身神和黑身神。

一个女人"就走了进去，神们对他们说："现在，作为丈夫和妻子生活在一起吧。"

文学和生活

读者反应 如果要你描述这些故事里的形象和他们留给你的印象，你将使用什么样的词句？

主题焦点 当神灵和自然界相遇的时候发生了什么事情？

小组活动 《纳瓦霍起源传说》描述了一个由神和幻影人共同完成的仪式。有哪些正式和不正式的仪式是我们今天生活的组成部分？考虑社会、宗教、教育、甚至与体育有关的仪式，例如用扔硬币来作为一场比赛的开始。在黑板上列出大家提出的建议。

阅读理解

1. 根据这个故事，地上的自然风景和生物是怎样产生的？
2. 总结纳瓦霍创造人的仪式。

思考

解释

1. (a)在莫多克族的天神看来，灰熊真正犯了什么罪？(b)他的反应揭示了他的什么方面？(分析)

2. 莫多克族人标志印第安人被灰熊杀死的地点的风俗有什么意义？(解释)

3. 为什么纳瓦霍人把手指尖和风留下的痕迹联系起来？(解释)

4. 从这个故事中找出证据证明对于纳瓦霍族人来说"四"是个神圣的数字。(分析)

应用

5. 这两个故事在哪些方面有所不同？(对比)

伊罗奎伊斯宪章(节选)

伊罗奎伊斯族

亚瑟·C·帕克 译

我是德卡纳维达，我和五族[①]同盟的首领们一起种下这棵“大和平树”。我把这棵树命名为“大长叶树”。在这棵大和平树的树荫下，我们用球蓟像羽毛一样的白色绒毛铺成座位，给您，阿多达霍，和您的兄弟首领们。

我们把你们安置在那些座位上，在和平树伸展的枝叶下的树荫中，像羽毛一样的球蓟绒毛铺得很柔软。你们将坐在那里，看着五族联盟的集会火焰，五族中所有的事情都应该在这个地方，在你们面前处理。

大和平树的根伸展出去，一条伸向北方，一条伸向东方，一条伸向南方，一条伸向西方。这些根的名字叫做“大白根”，他们的本质是和平与力量。

如果五族之外的任何人或任何族愿意遵守大和平的法令，并且把他们的意向告诉联盟的首领们，他们就可以顺着这些根找到这棵树。如果他们的思想纯净，而且愿意顺从，保证服从联盟会议的意愿，我们就欢迎他们在长叶树下受到庇护。

我们把一只可以看得很远的鹰放在长叶树顶上。如果它在远方看见任何邪恶在靠近我们或任何危险在威胁我们，它就会立刻向联盟里的人发出警告。

联盟的集会火焰的烟雾应该一直向上升入天空，以便其他可能成为我们的同盟的部族能够看见大和平的集会火焰……

无论何时，只要联盟首领为了召集会议而聚集在一起，昂昂达嘎的首领就应该在会议开始之前表达对兄弟首领的感谢并且问候他们，然后他们应该做出一个演说，感谢人们居住的土地、水流、水塘、泉水和湖泊；感谢玉蜀黍和果实；感谢药草和树；感谢森林里的树，因为它们非常有用；感谢动物，它们是我们的食物，还贡献毛皮让我们做衣服；感谢大风和微风；感谢雷电；感谢太

① 五族：莫霍克、欧内达、赛内卡、卡由加和昂昂达嘎部落，这些部落一起组成了伊罗奎伊斯联盟。

阳，那强大的战士；感谢月亮；感谢传达造物者意旨的信使们；感谢住在天上的造物者，他给了人们所有需要的东西，他是健康和生命的源泉和统治者。

然后昂昂达嘎的首领应该宣布会议开始……

五族联盟的首领应该在所有的事情上都保持诚实……任何人如果使一个首领卷入繁琐的事情，他就是犯了严重的错误，因为出于对首领们崇高职务的尊敬，人们必须对他们抱有最高的评价。

当一个首领候选人即将就职的时候，他应该提供四串长长的贝壳（或贝壳做的小珠子），一端系在一起。这些珠串就代表了他对联盟首领们的誓言，他发誓要遵守大和平宪章，在所有的事情中都做到公正判断。

伊罗奎伊斯族老人

当他交出了这信物以后，会议的发言人必须手中拿着珠串，对集会火焰对面的人们发言，他应该这样开始他的发言："现在看着他。他已经成为了一名联盟首领。看他是多么雄壮。"然后他可以继续作出一个演讲。在演讲结束时，他应该把珠串送到对面去，这束珠串将被作为誓言的信物收下。然后对面的首领应该说：

"现在我们授予你神圣的鹿角冠，这是你成为首领的象征。你现在应该成为五族人民的良师益友。你的皮肤应该有七指厚——也就是说你应该抵御愤怒、侮辱的行为和批评。你的心里应该充满和平和良好的愿望，你的思想里应该充满对联盟人民幸福的渴望。你应该用无尽的耐心来履行你的职责，你的强硬应该和你对你的人民的温和相融合。你的思想中不应该有愤怒或暴怒的容身之处，你的言行都应该经过理智地谨慎考虑。你在联盟会议中的所有考虑，在制定法律的过程中，在所有的正式行为中，个人利益都应被抛诸脑后。如果你的下一代指责你犯了错误或做错了事，不要对他们的警告置之不理，而是应该回到公正正确的大法中去判断。为整个民族的人们的幸福去听去看，总是要不仅看到现在这一代人，而且还要看到后面的几代人，甚至那些脸还在地面下的人——还没出生的未来的民族。"

文学和生活

读者反应 如果你是一个美洲土著部族的首领，这篇演讲会说服你加入联盟吗？解释原因。

主题焦点 德卡纳维达怎样在伊罗奎伊斯宪章中使用了自然界中的形象？这些参照告诉了你关于伊罗奎伊斯族的什么信息？

阅读理解

1. 德卡纳维达使用了哪三个与大和平相联系的自然形象？
2. 根据伊罗奎伊斯宪章，总结要求大会首领具有的品质和行为。

思考

解释

1. 宪章要求首领们“感谢人们居住的土地”。这条法令表现了伊罗奎伊斯人的什么思想？（推断）

2. 从德卡纳维达制定的宪章中，你了解到关于他的什么方面？（推断）

评价

3. 你认为一棵树能充分代表和平吗？解释理由。（评价）

应用

4. 宪章列出了伊罗奎伊斯首领的品质。你认为现代领袖应该具有其中的哪些品质？解释原因。（综合）

文学聚焦

起源神话

人是由麦穗变来的。类似这样的精灵神怪和神秘的事件就是典型的起源神话——代代相传地解释世界和世上一切由来的故事。

1. 请描述在《在灰熊直立行走的时候》中解释的自然现象、风俗习惯和生物（除人类以外）。

2. 列出《在灰熊直立行走的时候》《龟背上的土地》和《纳瓦霍起源传说》

中将人类生命带到地球上的过程中的共同之处。

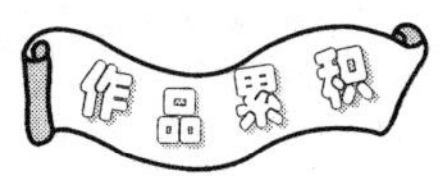

点子库

写作

1. 新结尾　根据《龟背上的土地》，麝鼠在创造“新土地”中作出了关键贡献。为这个神话写一个新结尾，包括对天神怎样奖励她的解释。

2. 起源神话　写出一个神话来解释一个地方自然风景的起源，例如附近的一个湖、一个山谷或一块岩石。

3. 散文《伊罗奎伊斯宪章》需要吸引听众的注意力　写一篇散文，分析这篇文章是怎样利用形象化的描述和短语来创造一个令人难忘的印象的。

项目

1. 图腾柱　研究美洲土著人在直立的木头上雕刻各种形象的风俗。在一根你研究或制造的图腾柱上用标记或说明来解释每个图像的意义。

2. 徽标　利用《伊罗奎伊斯宪章》中包含的形象激发你的灵感，设计一个代表伊罗奎伊斯联盟的徽标。（艺术连线）

微型写作课

复述一个神话

神话是一种口头的流传形式，年复一年地被讲故事的人不断重复，每个人都会在自己的复述中加入一点儿个人的东西。选择一个你熟悉的神话故事并把它复述给一个朋友听。保持故事的结构和事件的顺序，但是可以对故事进行改编以便能适应你的听众的需要。例如，你可以更新故事的发生背景。

写作技巧重点：有效的重复

有效的重复——重复动作、词组或单词来产生一种期待的效果——可以使一个口头讲述的故事更加好记、产生戏剧性并加强悬念。

故事里的范例

它潜入水下，游啊游。它不像其他动物那样强壮，也不像它们那样敏捷，可是它有坚定的决心。它潜到周围一片黑暗的深处，仍然向更深处游去。

在你进行复述的时候,利用重复的方法来吸引你的听众。

构思

根据你所记得的神话写出一个粗略的情节提纲。然后列出这个神话中你要保留的元素和你要改变的元素。

写稿

根据你的情节提纲,写出一个草稿。找出你可以利用重复来制造戏剧效果并产生节奏感的地方。

修改

大声朗读你的故事,听一听它是不是既有戏剧性又便于记忆。你的重复是不是成功地产生了你所希望的声音效果呢?对你的写作进行润色,以达到期望的效果。

Guide for Interpreting

Onondaga

As one of the original five member nations, the Onondaga were an influential force in the Iroquois Confederation, a league of Iroquoian-speaking Native Americans. The Onondaga live in what is now central New York State, in village of wood and bark longhouse occupied by related families. Following the breakup of the Iroquois Confederation after the American Revolution, factions of Onondaga scattered to various parts of the country, but the majority returned to their ancestral valley in New York, where the Onondaga reservation now exists.

Modoc

The Modoc once lived in villages in the area of Oregon and northern California, where they farmed, fished, and hunted. Though each village was independent and had its own leaders, in times of war they would band together. In the mid-nineteenth century, the Modoc were forced onto a reservation in Oregon. A band of Modoc,under the leader ship of a subchief known as Captain Jaek, later fled the reservation. The result was several years of hostilities with United States troops and the eventual relocation of Captain Jack's followers to Oklahoma. They were later allowed to return to the Oregon reservation, which was dissolved in the mid-1950's.

Navajo

Today, the Navajo nation is the largest Native American nation in the United States, with more than 100,000 members. Many live on the Navajo reservation, which covers 24,000 square miles of Arizona, Utah, and New Mexico. Fierce warriors and hunters, the ancient Navajo settled in the Southwest about 1,000 years ago and eventually intermarried with the peaceful Pueblo people, who taught them to weave and raise crops. In 1864, after decades of fighting off encroaching

American settlers, the Navajo were driven from their territory by the United States Army. They were eventually allowed to return to a reservation on Navajo land. Many Navajo still carry on traditional customs, living in earth-and-log structures and practicing the tribal religion.

Iroquois

The powerful Iroquois nation lived in what is now the northeastern United States. During the fourteenth century, an Iroquoian mystic and prophet named Dekanawidah traveled from village to village urging the Iroquois-speaking people to stop fighting and band together in peace and brotherhood. Dekanawidah's efforts led to the formation of the Iroquois Confederation of the Five Nations, a league of five Iroquois tribes: Mohawk, Oneida, Seneca, Cayuga and Onondaga.

Background for Understanding

CULTURE:HUMANS AND THE NATURAL WORLD

Native Americans have great respect for the natural world. They believe that each creature has its own power by which it maintains itself and affects others. Each Native American culture has its own name for this power, but early white settlers learned the Algonquian term manito. Manitos come in all shapes and sizes, but many Native American cultures recognize a chief manito, or Great Spirit—an invisible power that is the source of life and good for humans.

Many of the animals that helped feed and clothe the early Native Americans are revered as powerful manitos. Native American folklore and art, much of which portrays animals, reflect this great respect.

Literature and Your Life

CONNECT YOUR EXPERIENCE

"What was I like when I was born?" "What do you remember about my great-grandparents?" You ask questions like these for the same reason we all ask them. We share a fundamental desire to understand our origins — where we come from, our place in the world. Just as you collect stories of your family history, cultures create stories to explain the world as they know it.

<u>Journal Writing</u> Look closely at the images of the moose and bear on this piece of Native American pottery. Given what you now know about Native American beliefs, explain what the arrows might symbolize.

THEMATIC FOCUS: MEETING OF CULTURES

Think of these origin stories as Native American responses to the universal questions of how and why we came to be.Notice as you read them that all four works are filled with images from nature.

What role does nature play in explaining—and maintaining—Native American life?

Literary Focus

ORIGIN MYTHS

The need to explain how life began gave birth to myths, traditional stories, often about Immortal beings, that are passed down from generation to generation. When these stories recount the origins of earthly life, we call them origin myths, Myths often explain many other phenomena, including customs, institutions, or religious rites; natural landmarks, such as a great mountain; or events beyond people's control. As you read each myth, note who or what is responsible for the start of life on Earth, and look for explanations of natural phenomena.

The Earth on Turtle's Back

Onondaga

Retold by Michael J. Caduto and Joseph Bruchac

Before this Earth existed,there was only water.It stretched as far as one could see, and in that water there were birds and animals swimming around. Far above, in the clouds, there was a Skyland. In that Skyland there was a great and beautiful tree. It had four white roots which stretched to each of the sacred directions, and from its branches all kinds of fruits and flowers grew.

There was an ancient chief in the Skyland. His young wife was expecting a child, and one night she dreamed that she saw the Great Tree uprooted. The next day she told her husband the story.

He nodded as she finished telling her dream. "My wife," he said, "I am sad that you had this dream. It is clearly a dream of great power and, as is our way, when one has such a powerful dream we must do all we can to make it true. The Great Tree must be uprooted."

Then the Ancient Chief called the young men together and told them that they must pull up the tree. But the roots of the tree were so deep, so strong, that they could not budge it. At last the Ancient Chief himself came to the tree. He wrapped his arms around it, bent his knees and strained. At last, with one great effort, he uprooted the tree and placed it on its side. Where the tree's roots had gone deep into the Skyland there was now a big hole. The wife of the chief came close and leaned over to look down, grasping the tip of one of the Great Tree's branches to steady her. It seemed as if she saw something down there, far below, glittering like water. She leaned out further to look and, as she leaned, she lost her balance and fell into the hole. Her grasp slipped off the tip of the branch, leaving her with only a handful of seeds as she fell, down, down, down, down.

Far below, in the waters, some of the birds and animals looked up.

"Someone is falling toward us from the sky," said one of the birds.

"We must do something to help her," said another. Then two Swans flew up. They caught the Woman From The Sky between their wide wings. Slowly, they began to bring her down toward the water, where the birds and animals were watching.

"She is not like us," said one of the animals. "Look, she doesn't have webbed feet. I don't think she can live in the water."

"What shall we do then?" said another of the water animals.

"I know," said one of the water birds. "I have heard that there is Earth far below the waters. If we dive down and bring up Earth, then she will have a place

to stand."

So the birds and animal decided that someone would have to bring up Earth. One by one they tried.

The Duck dove first, some say. He swam down and down, far beneath the surface, but could not reach the bottom and floated back up. Then the Beaver tried. He went even deeper, so deep that all was dark, but he could not reach the bottom either. The Loon tried, swimming with his strong wings. He was gone a long, long time, but he, too, failed to bring up Earth. Soon it seemed that all had tried and all had failed. Then a small voice spoke.

"I will bring up Earth or die trying."

They looked to see who it was. It was the Tiny Muskrat. She dove down and swam and swam. She was not as strong or as swift as the others, but she was de-termined. She went so deep that it was all dark, and still she swam deeper. She swam so deep that her lungs felt ready to burst, but she swam deeper still. At last, just as she was becoming unconscious, she reached out one small paw and grasped at the bottom, barely touching it before she floated up, almost dead.

When the other animals saw her break the surface they thought she had failed. Then they saw her right paw was held tightly shut.

"She has the Earth," they said. "Now where can we put it?"

"Place it on my back," said a deep voice. It was the Great Turtle, who had come up from the depths.

They brought the Muskrat over to the Great Turtle and placed her paw against his back. To this day there are marks at the back of the Turtle's shell which were made by the Muskrat's paw. The tiny bit of Earth fell on the back of the Turtle. Almost immediately, it began to grow larger and larger and larger until it became the whole world.

Then the two Swans brought the Sky Woman down. She stepped onto the new Earth and opened her hand, letting the seeds fall onto the bare soil. From those seeds the trees and the grass sprang up. Life on Earth had begun.

When Grizzlies Walked Upright

Modoc

Retold by Richard Erdoes and Alfonso Ortiz

Before there were people on earth, the Chief of the Sky Spirits grew tired of his home in the Above World, because the air was always brittle with an icy cold. So he carved a hole in the sky with a stone and pushed all the snow and ice down below until he made a great mound that reached from the earth almost to the sky. Today it is known as Mount Shasta.

Then the Sky Spirit took his walking stick, stepped from a cloud to the peak, and walked down to the mountain. When he was about halfway to the valley below, he began to put his finger to the ground here and there, here and there. Wherever his finger touched, a tree grew. The snow melted in his footsteps, and the water ran down in rivers.

The Sky Spirit broke off the small end of his giant stick and threw the pieces into the rivers. The longer pieces turned into beaver and otter; the smaller pieces became fish. When the leaves dropped from the trees, he picked them up, blew upon them, and so made the birds. Then he took the big end of his giant stick and made all the animals that walked on the earth, the biggest of which were the grizzly bears.

Now when they were first made, the bears were covered with hair and had sharp claws, just as they do today, but they walked on two feet and could talk like people. They looked so fierce that the Sky Spirit sent them away from him to live in the forest at the base of the mountain.

Pleased with what he'd done, the Chief of the Sky Spirits decided to bring his family down and live on earth himself. The mountains of snow and ice

became their lodge. He made a big fire in the center of the mountain and a hole in the top so that the smoke and sparks could fly out. When he put a big log on the fire, sparks would fly up and the earth would tremble.

Late one spring while the Sky Spirit and his family were sitting round the fire, the Wind Spirit sent a great storm that shook the top of the mountain. It blew and blew and roared and roared. Smoke blown back into the lodge hurt their eyes, and finally the Sky Spirit said to his youngest daughter, "Climb up to tile smoke hole and ask the Wind Spirit to blow more gently. Tell him I'm afraid he will blow the mountain over."

As his daughter started up, her father said, "But be careful not to stick your head out at the top. If you do, the wind may catch you by the hair and blow you away."

The girl hurried to the top of the mountain and stayed well inside the smoke hole as she spoke to the Wind Spirit. As she was about to climb back down, she remembered that her father had once said you could see the ocean from the top of their lodge. His daughter wondered what the ocean looked like, and her curiosity got the better of her. She poked her head out of the hole and turned toward the west, but before she could see anything, the Wind Spirit caught her long hair, pulled her out of the mountain, and blew her down over the snow and ice. She landed among the scrubby fir trees at the edge of the timber and snow line, her long red hair trailing over the snow.

There a grizzly bear found the little girl when he was out hunting food for his family. He carried her home with him, and his wife brought her up with their family of cubs. The little red-haired girl and the cubs ate together, played together, and grew up together.

When she became a young woman, she and the eldest son of the grizzly bears were married. In the years that followed they had many children, who were not as hairy as the grizzlies, yet did not look exactly like their spirit mother, either.

All the grizzly bears throughout the forests were so proud of these new creatures that they made a lodge for the red-haired mother and her children. They placed the lodge near Mount Shasta—it is called Little Mount Shasta today.

After many years had passed, the mother grizzly bear knew that she would soon die. Fearing that she should ask of the Chief of the Sky Spirits to forgive her for keeping his daughter, she gathered all the grizzlies at the lodge they had built. Then she sent her eldest grandson in a cloud to the top of Mount Shasta, to tell the Spirit Chief where he could find his long-lost daughter.

When the father got this news he was so glad that he came down the mountainside in giant strides, melting the snow and tearing up the land under his feet. Even today his tracks can be seen in the rocky path on the south side of Mount Shasta.

As he neared the lodge, he called out, "Is this where my little daughter lives?"

He expected his child to look exactly as she had when he saw her last. When he found a grown woman instead, and learned that the strange creatures she was taking care of were his grandchildren, he became very angry. A new race had been created that was not of his making! He frowned on the old grandmother so sternly that she promptly fell dead. Then he cursed all the grizzlies:

"Get down on your hands and knees. You have wronged me, and from this moment all of you will walk on four feet and never talk again."

He drove his grandchildren out of the lodge, put his daughter over his shoulder, and climbed back up the mountain. Never again did he come to the forest. Some say that he put out the fire in the center of his lodge and took his daughter back up to the sky to live.

Those strange creatures, his grandchildren, scattered and wandered over the earth. They were the first Indians, the ancestors of all the Indian tribes.

That's why the Indians living around Mount Shasta would never kill a grizzly bear. Whenever a grizzly killed an Indian, his body was burned on the spot. And for many years all who passed that way cast a stone there until a great pile of stones marked the place of his death.

The Navajo Origin Legend

Navajo

Retold by Washington Matthews

On the morning of the twelfth day the people washed themselves well. The women dried themselves with yellow cornmeal; the men with white cornmeal. Soon after the ablutions were completed they heard the distant call of the approaching gods. It was shouted, as before, four times—nearer and louder at each repetition—and, after the fourth call, the gods appeared. Blue Body and Black Body each carried a sacred buckskin. White Body carried two ears of corn, one yellow, one white, each covered at the end completely with grains.

The gods laid one buckskin on the ground with the head to the west: on this they placed the two ears of corn, with their tips to the east, and over the corn they spread the other buckskin with its head to the east; under the white ear they put the feather of a white eagle, under the yellow ear the feather of a yellow eagle. Then they told the people to stand at a distance and allow the wind to enter. The white wind blew from the east, and the yellow wind blew from the west, between the skins. While the wind was blowing, eight of the Mirage People came and walked around the objects on the ground four times, and as they walked the eagle feathers, whose tips protruded from between the buckskins, were seen to move. When the Mirage People had finished their walk the upper buckskin was lifted; the ears of corn had disappeared, a man and a woman lay there in their stead.

The white ear of corn had been changed into a man, the yellow ear into a woman. It was the wind that gave them life. It is the wind that comes out of our mouths now that gives us life. When this ceases to blow we die. In the skin at the tips of our fingers we see the trail of the wind; it shows us where the wind blew when our ancestors were created.

The pair thus created were First Man and First Woman (Atsé Hastin and Atsé Estsán). The gods directed the people to build an enclosure of brushwood for the pair. When the enclosure was finished, First Man and First Woman entered it, and the gods said to them:"Live together now as husband and wife."

The Iroquois Constitution

Iroquois

Translated by Arthur C.Parker

I am Dekanawidah and with the Five Nations confederate lords I plant the Tree of the Great Peace.I name the tree the Tree of the Great Long Leaves. Under the shade of this Tree of the Great Peace we spread the soft white feathery down of the globe thistle as seats for you, Adodarhoh, and your cousin lords.

We place you upon those seats, spread soft with the feathery down of the globe thistle, there beneath the shade of the spreading branches of the Tree of Peace. There shall you sit and watch the council fire of the confederacy of the Five Nations, and all the affairs of the Five Nations shall be transacted at this place before you.

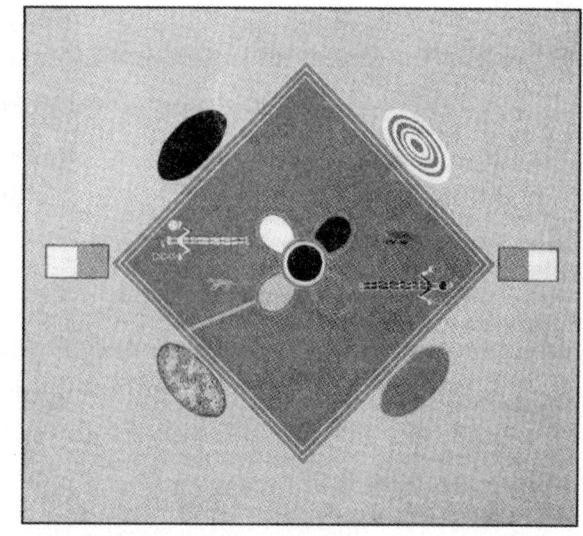

Roots have spread out from the Tree of the Great Peace, one to the north, one to the east, one to the south and one to the west. The name of these roots is the Great White Roots and their nature is peace and strength.

If any man or any nation

outside the Five Nations shall obey the laws of the Great Peace and make known their disposition to the lords of the confederacy, they may trace the roots to the tree and if their minds are clean and they are obedient and promise to obey the wishes of the confederate council, they shall be welcomed to take shelter beneath the Tree of the Long Leaves.

We place at the top of the Tree of the Long Leaves an eagle who is able to see afar. If he sees in the distance any evil approaching or any danger threatening he will at once warn the people of the confederacy.

The smoke of the confederate council fire shall ever ascend and pierce the sky so that other nations who may be allies may see the council fire of the Great Peace...

Whenever the confederate lords shall assemble for the purpose of holding a council, the Onondaga lords shall open it by expressing their gratitude to their cousin lords and greeting them, and they shall make an address and offer thanks to the earth where men dwell, to the streams of water, the pools, the springs and the lakes, to the maize and the fruits, to the medicinal herbs and trees, to the forest trees for their usefulness, to the animals that serve as food and give their pelts for clothing, to the great winds and the lesser winds, to the thunderers, to the sun, the mighty warrior, to the moon, to the messengers of the Creator who reveal his wishes and to the Great Creator who dwells in the heavens above, who gives all the things useful to men, and who is the source and the ruler of health and life.

Then shall the Onondaga lords declare the council open...

All lords of the Five Nations' Confederacy must be honest in all things... It shall be a serious wrong for anyone to lead a lord into trivial affairs, for the people must ever hold their lords high in estimation out of respect to their honorable positions.

When a candidate lord is to be installed he shall furnish four strings of shells (or wampum) one span in length bound together at one end. Such will constitute the evidence of his pledge to the confederate lords that he will live according to the constitution of the Great Peace and exercise justice in all affairs.

When the pledge is furnished the speaker of the council must hold the shell strings in his hand and address the opposite side of the council fire and he shall commence his address saying: "Now behold him. He has now become a confederate lord. See how splendid he looks." An address may then follow. At the end of it he shall send the bunch of shell strings to the opposite side and they shall be received as evidence of the pledge. Then shall the opposite side say:

"We now do crown you with the sacred emblem of the deer's antlers, the emblem of your lordship. You shall now become a mentor of the people of the Five Nations. The thickness of your skin shall be seven spans—which is to say that you shall be proof against anger, offensive actions and criticism. Your heart shall be filled with peace and good will and your mind filled with a yearning for the welfare of the people of the confederacy. With endless patience you shall carry out your duty and your firmness shall be tempered with tenderness for your people. Neither anger nor fury shall find lodgement in your mind and all your words and actions shall be marked with calm deliberation. In all of your deliberations in the confederate council, in your efforts at law making, in all your official acts, self-interest shall be cast into oblivion. Cast not over your shoulder behind you the warnings of the nephews and nieces should they chide you for any error or wrong you may do, but return to the way of the Great Law which is just and right. Look and listen for the welfare of the whole people and have always in view not only the present but also the coming generations, even those whose faces are yet beneath the surface of the ground—the unborn of the future nation."

第三课

“有趣的故事”

欧拉乌达·艾库维阿诺(1745—1797)

1798年出版的《欧拉乌达·艾库维阿诺自传》引起巨大反响。

《有趣的故事》使全社会开始正视奴隶制度的残忍，为奴隶贸易在美国和英格兰的废除作出了贡献。

欧拉乌达·艾库维阿诺

艾库维阿诺出生于强大的贝宁王国，是部落长老的儿子。若不是被卖做农奴，他可能沿袭父亲的足迹。11岁的艾库维阿诺和他的姐姐在西非的家乡被抢掠，并被卖给英国的奴隶贩子。和姐姐分开后，他先被运送到了西印度群岛，然后又到了弗吉尼亚，在那里一个英格兰船长买下了他，让他在海上劳动。

攒钱买自由 艾库维阿诺被人改名为古斯塔夫斯·瓦萨，做了近10年的奴隶。他在费城替主人掌管经济，从中赚到足够的钱为自己赎身。后来他定居英国，致力于废除奴隶制度。为了将奴隶们的境况公布于众，他写下了两卷自传——《有趣的故事》。尽管艾库维阿诺的著作引起了人们对缺乏人性的奴隶制的关注，但是直到1808年美国才宣布从法律上废除奴隶制，此时该书已出版近20年。

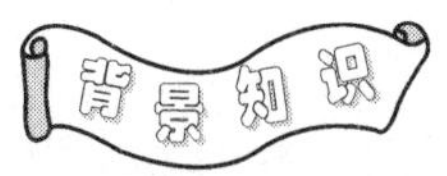

历史:奴隶贸易

艾库维阿诺描述的奴隶贸易,当时在西半球殖民地正处于全盛时期。当很多人为了寻求财富来到新大陆的同时,另外有很多人却是被卖到这里来的。

16世纪到19世纪之间,大约有1500万非洲人被捕捉并通过船只运送到西半球。如艾库维阿诺所述,穿过大西洋的航行,或被称为“中间通道”,其条件是极其可怕的。在连续6到10个月的时间里,黑奴们挤在甲板下面,那里的空间高度有时候都不到5英尺。家庭被拆散,男人和女人被分开关押。在航行中,男人们经常被成对地锈在一起。过度拥挤、疾病和绝望夺去了许多人的生命。有的非洲人发动了叛乱,有的试图绝食或者跳海。历史学家估计大约有200万奴隶在抵达目的地之前丧命。

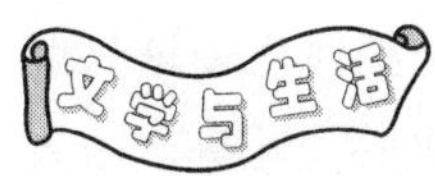

联系你的经历 想象如下情景:你所属的群体是有价值的商品,你的家庭则可能被运送到遥远的岛上被迫从事体力劳动!如果你生活在一个存在奴隶制的世界,你对自由的甜蜜和生命的价值将产生一种新的看法。

日志写作 如果你被强行送到另一个国度,你的感受将会怎样?简单记下你的所想。

专题焦点:文明的交会 欧洲的传统和思想经常与美洲本土习俗发生冲突。然而,这并不是新大陆唯一存在的文化碰撞。艾库维阿诺,一名被强行卖到这里的非洲人,代表了融入美国背景的另一种文化。

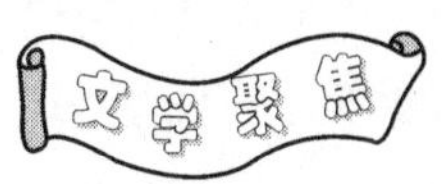

奴隶故事 艾库维阿诺对“中间通道”的描述是奴隶故事的一个早期范例。奴隶故事作为美国文学里一种独特的文体,是对奴隶生活的自传性描述。

通过从奴隶的视角记录他们的亲身经历，这种文体表现了那种人类奴役的可怕之处。

南北战争之前，在废奴主义者的鼓励下，很多获得自由和逃脱的奴隶都发表了奴隶故事。

欧拉乌达·艾库维阿诺一生的“有趣的故事”（节选）

欧拉乌达·艾库维阿诺

在前几章里，艾库维阿诺描述了他和姐姐是如何在西非的家中被奴隶贩子绑架并运往非洲海岸的。在这六七个月的旅程中，艾库维阿诺和姐姐分开了，他被辗转监禁在随后一系列的驿站中。抵达海岸后，艾库维阿诺和其他黑奴一起被运往新大陆。下面的故事就描述了这次可怕的旅行。

最后，我们的船载满了人，他们在做最后的准备工作，弄出可怕的巨大声响。我们全部都被关在甲板下，这样我们就不能看见他们是如何驾驶这只船的。不过这一遗憾只是我所有痛苦中最微不足道的。船舱里的气味臭得令人难以忍受，在那里，片刻的停留都是对生命的威胁。我们当中一部分人获准待在甲板上面，能够呼吸到新鲜空气。但是，现在船上所有的人都挤在一起，很容易引发疾病的流行。船舱非常拥挤，几乎没有办法翻身。狭窄的空间、炎热的空气，再加上船上的人数，人们几乎连转个身的地方都没有，这差点儿使我们窒息。大量的排汗，使得空气很快就没有办法呼吸，成为一种难闻的味道，导致奴隶中很多人得病并死亡——我把这样的牺牲归咎为他们买主的“短见的贪婪”。锁链的摩擦更加重了这种悲惨，令人难以支撑下去。小孩子经常摔倒在那装秽物的必备的桶里头，几乎要被憋死。女人们的尖叫、垂死的人在呻吟，制造出一种难以想象的恐怖气氛。然而让我高兴的是因为我的身体很快就变得

奴隶主家餐厅一角

虚弱，他们认为我有待在甲板上的必要。而且，因为我年龄太小，可以不用戴脚镣。在这种情况下，我希望能将我命运的每一小时与我的同伴们分享，他们当中有的人每天被带上甲板，因为他们正处于死亡边缘。我开始希望能尽快结束我的苦难。不管我遇到哪种情况，都只能使我更加痛苦，加强我的恐惧以及对白人残暴的认识。

有一天，奴隶主抓了很多鱼。他们吃得心满意足后，出乎我们这些在甲板上的人的意料，他们没有给我们一丁点儿，而是把剩下的鱼扔回海里，尽管我们拼命乞求、恳请他们赐给我们一点点，但这都是徒劳。我的同胞在饥饿的驱使下，以为没有人看见，伺机偷了一点儿，却被发现了。这一图谋带给他们的是一顿严厉的鞭打。又一天，海面风平浪静，两个锁在一起的疲惫的同胞(我当时离他们很近)，试图以死结束痛苦的命运。不知通过何种方法，他们挣脱了束缚跳进海里。紧接着，又一个绝望的伙伴，由于生病没有戴镣铐，也效仿了他们。我相信，要不是立即警觉起来的船员们加以阻止，更多人将做出同样的事情。我们之中那些最活跃的人被立即赶下甲板。船上的人为了停船引发了巨大的嘈杂和混乱，是我前所未闻的。他们放出一条小艇去寻找奴隶。然而，两个不幸的人淹死了，一个被救了上来，接着他就受到了毫不怜悯的鞭刑，这是他试图寻死的结果。就这样，我们经历了更多的苦难，远非我在这里所能叙述的。苦难是与这一邪恶的交易不能分割的一部分。我们经常整天整天地缺乏新鲜空气，好多次我们都濒临窒息。船舱里粪桶的恶臭和新鲜空气的缺乏，夺去了很多人的生命。

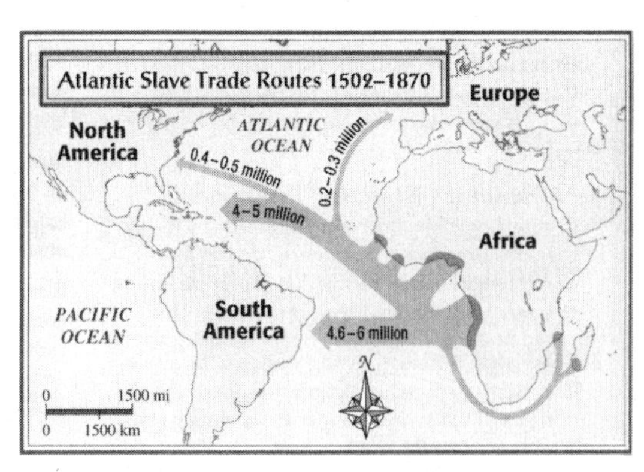

奴隶贸易的“中间通道”

在旅行中，我第一次看到飞鱼，非常惊讶。它们频繁地掠船而过，很多掉在甲板上。我也第一次看到了四分仪的使用，我经常惊讶地看到水手们用它来观测。我弄不明白它的意思。他们最终注意到我的惊讶，有一个水手想让我更加惊讶，同时又满足我的好奇心，把一个四分仪给我看了一天。在我看来，

云就像是大陆，随着船的前行消失在视野中。这更增加了我的好奇，使我更相信我身处另一个世界，每一样事物都那么的奇妙。最后，我们看到了巴巴多斯岛，船上的白人们大声叫喊，表现出很快乐的样子。我们并不知道这是什么意思，但是随着船逐渐靠岸，我们清楚地看到了港口，还有大大小小各种各样的其他船只。我们很快就停泊在这些船之间，这里是布里奇顿。虽然已经是黄昏时分，还是有很多商人和种植园主走上船来。他们把我们分成小组，仔细地检查我们。他们还让我们蹦跳。他们又指向大陆，示意我们将要前往那里。我们根据这手势猜想，这些丑男人可能要把我们吃掉。当我们很快又被放到甲板下面时，我们恐惧万分、颤抖不已。整夜没有别的声音，只有悲苦的哭泣。最后白人从岸上找来几个老黑奴安慰平息我们。他们告诉我们不是要被送去吃掉，而是去劳动，我们很快就要上岸，那里我们将遇到很多我们的同胞。这些话使我们放松了很多。果然，我们很快上了岸，以后遇到不少非洲人，说着各种不同的语言。

我们被带到贸易市场，在那里，我们被关在一起，就像羊栏里的羊，不分性别和年龄……我们在商人的看管下没几天，就按照他们的规则被卖掉了。这个规则是这样的：信号一起（比如一通鼓声），买家就马上冲进关押奴隶的场地，选出他们最喜欢的货物……

文学和生活

读者反应 根据艾库维阿诺的叙述，你对他有什么印象？

日志写作 记下看完艾库维阿诺的叙述后的反应。它激起你哪一种情感？

主题焦点 当一种文明统治另一种文明的时候，一个社会将会面临什么样的困难？

阅读理解

1. 艾库维阿诺的年龄对他在此次航行中的经历有什么影响？
2. (a)奴隶们因为什么罪行而受惩罚？(b)惩罚的内容是什么？
3. 总结船上奴隶们的生活条件。

思考

解释

1. 为什么艾库维阿诺把船上的疾病归咎于商人“短见的贪婪”？（证据支持）

2. 虽然艾库维阿诺声称自己想要死亡，但你怎样能够判断出他拥有对生命的热望？从文中举例说明。（证据支持）

应用

3. 艾库维阿诺的叙述对美国废除奴隶贸易的斗争起着帮助性的作用。在他对“中间通道”的描述中提供了哪些具有说服力的证据？（辩护）

扩展

4. 艾库维阿诺的航行与那些探险者和殖民者有什么相同点和不同点？（社会研究连线）

文学聚焦

奴隶故事

奴隶故事是对奴隶生活自传性的描述。在对作者一生重大事件的描绘中，作者通常记录了奴隶制的可怕。本篇艾库维阿诺的故事节选，提供了一幅刻画“中间通道”和奴隶贸易的凄惨画面。

1. 艾库维阿诺在这篇记录中强调了船上情况的哪个方面？

2. 奴隶们对自己处境的普遍感觉是什么？

3. 举出两个说明奴隶贩子对奴隶们的残酷行为的例子。

4. 举出两个说明奴隶贩子关心奴隶健康的例子。

5. 是什么促使奴隶贩子对他们的人类货物采取那样的行为？解释原因。

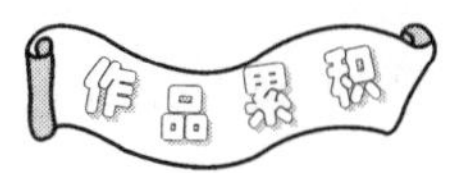

点子库

写作

1. 活动者的列表　艾库维阿诺的自传对奴隶贸易的终结作出了贡献。制作一个当今社会所面临问题的列表，并给出人们应当如何教育，来解决这些

问题的建议。

2. 社论　想象你是一名1789年的美国报社记者，当时艾库维阿诺的《有趣的故事》刚刚上市。作为一名主张废除奴隶制的废奴主义者，请写一篇社论作为对该书的反响。

3. 角色脚本　作为重现《有趣的故事》的导演，描述艾库维阿诺这一角色。包括他的优点和弱点，以便演员能够再现这一形象。

项目

1. 因特网调研　类似Amnesty International的组织致力于唤醒人们对世界范围内的不平等的意识。利用因特网或图书馆了解Amnesty International及其发表的宗旨。将你的调查结果在班里作一个报告。（技术链接）

2. 电影海报　设计一个好莱坞版《有趣的故事》的海报。为了适合银幕观众，你需要重新命名这一作品。

微型文写作

博物馆布告

为了教育今天的观众，类似底特律非洲美国历史博物馆这样的机构正在举行展现19世纪奴隶贸易文献记录的展览。设想你被邀请写一篇序言，并且这篇序言将出现在展览开始处一幅大的布告上。要求阐明奴隶贸易中事件的顺序，从非洲人在他们家乡被俘获开始，到非洲人在美洲被拍卖成为奴隶为止。

写作技巧：时间的顺序

时间顺序可以使读者一步一步地把握事件的发展。简略列出你要讲述的顺序。遵循以下建议：

1. 从最先发生的事情开始，然后按时间顺序继续。

2. 使用next、then和finally这样的单词使顺序尽可能地清晰。

3. 避免时间顺序上的变换。

构思

利用图书馆资源收集奴隶贸易的事实。组织你的信息，最好画一张地图表明奴隶贸易的路线、日期和其他关键细节。

写稿

参照你的笔记，将事件按时间顺序叙述，使用过渡词——at first、next、

while、then、finally和after——使你的叙述顺序清晰。

修改

重读你的作文，确保你的布告能够突出奴隶贸易的重要阶段。剔除不重要的细节，增加过渡语句使事件的顺序清晰。

Guide for Interpreting

Olaudah Equiano (1745—1797)

When published in 1789, the autobiography of Olaudah Equiano created a sensation.

The Interesting Narrative made society face the cruelties of slavery and contributed to the banning of the slave trade in both the United States and England.

The son of a tribal elder in the powerful kingdom of Benin, Equiano might have followed in his father's footsteps had he not been sold into slavery. When Equiano was eleven years old, he and his sister were kidnapped from their home in West Africa and sold to British slave traders. Separated from his sister, Equiano was taken first to the West Indies, then to Virginia, where he was purchased by a British captain and employed at sea.

Saving to Buy Liberty Renamed Gustavus Vassa, Equiano was enslaved for nearly ten years. After managing his Philadelphia master's finances and making his own money in the process, Equiano amassed enough to buy his freedom. In later years, he settled in England and devoted himself to the abolition of slavery. To publicize the plight of slaves, he wrote his two-volume autobiography, The Interesting Narrative. Although Equiano's writing raised concern about the less than humane conditions inherent ill slavery, the slave trade in the United States was not abolished by law until 1808, nearly twenty years after its publication.

Background for Understanding

HISTORY: THE SLAVE TRADE

The slave trade Equiano describes was in full operation during the colonization of the Western Hemisphere. While many people came to the new world in search of wealth or riches, many others were brought against their will.

Between 1500 and 1800, about 15 million Africans were captured and shipped to the Western Hemisphere. As Equiano attests, the conditions of the Atlantic crossing, known as "the middle passage;" were atrocious. For six to ten weeks, Africans were crammed below deck in spaces sometimes less than five feet high. Families were torn apart; men and women placed in separate holds. During the voyage, men were often shackled together in pairs. Overcrowding, disease, and despair claimed many lives. Some Africans mutinied, and others tried to starve themselves or jump overboard. Historians estimate that nearly 2 million slaves died before reaching their destination. This map shows the most common routes of the middle passage.

Literature and your Life

CONNECT YOUR EXPERIENCE

Imagine knowing that members of your community were valuable merchandise and that your family could be shipped away to a distant land to perform forced labor! Living in a world where slavery existed, you might develop a new attitude about the sweetness of freedom and the value of life.

<u>Journal Writing</u> How would you feel if you were sent to another country against your will? Jot down your thoughts.

THEMATIC FOCUS: MEETING OF CULTURES

European traditions and ideas often came into conflict with Native American customs. However, these were not the only cultures clashing on this continent. Equiano, an African brought against his will, represents another culture to be absorbed into the American scene.

Literary Focus

SLAVE NARRATIVES

Equiano's account of the middle passage is an early example of a slave

narrative. A uniquely American literary genre, a slave narrative is an autobio-graphical account of life as a slave. Often written to expose the horrors of human bondage, it documents a slave's experiences from his or her own point of view.

Encouraged by abolitionists, many freed or escaped slaves published narra-tives in the years before the Civil War.

The Interesting Narrative of the Life of Olaudah Equiano

Olaudah Equiano

In the first several chapters, Equiano describes how he and his sister were kidnapped from their home in West Africa by slave traders and transported to the African coast. During this six- or seven month journey, Equiano was separated from his sister and held at a series of way stations. After reaching the coast, Equiano was shipped with other slaves to this continent. The following account describes this horrifying journey.

At last when the ship we were in, had got in all her cargo, they made ready with many fearful noises, and we were all put under deck, so that we could not see how they managed the vessel. But this disappointment was the least of my sorrow. The stench of the hold while we were on the coast was so intolerably

loathsome, that it was dangerous to remain there for any time, and some of us had been permitted to stay on the deck for the fresh air; but now that the whole ship's cargo were confined together, it became absolutely pestilential. The closeness of the place, and the heat of the climate, added to the number in the ship, which was so crowded that each had scarcely room to turn himself, almost suffocated us. This produced copious perspirations, so that the air soon became unfit for respiration, from a variety of loathsome smells, and brought on a sickness among the slaves, of which many died—thus falling victims to the improvident avarice, as I may call it, of their purchasers. This wretched situation was again aggravated by the galling of the chains, now become insupportable, and the filth of the necessary tubs, into which the children often fell, and were almost suffocated. The shrieks of the women, and the groans of the dying, rendered the whole a scene of horror almost inconceivable. Happily perhaps, for myself, I was soon reduced so low here that it was thought necessary to keep me almost always on deck; and from my extreme youth I was not put in fetters. In this situation I expected every hour to share the fate of my companions, some of whom were almost daily brought upon deck at the point of death, which I began to hope would soon put an end to my miseries. Often did I think many of the inhabitants of the deep much more happy than myself. I envied them the freedom they

enjoyed, and as often wished I could change my condition for theirs. Every circumstance I met with, served only to render my state more painful, and heightened my apprehensions, and my opinion of the cruelty of the whites.

One day they had taken a number of fishes; and when they had killed and satisfied themselves with as many as they thought fit, to our astonishment who were on deck, rather than give any of them to us to eat, as we expected, they tossed the remaining fish into the sea again, although we begged and prayed for some as well as we could, but in vain; and some of my countrymen, being pressed by hunger, took an opportunity, when they thought no one saw them, of trying to get a little privately; but they were discovered, and the attempt procured them some very severe floggings. One day, when we had a smooth sea and moderate wind, two of my wearied countrymen who were chained together (I was near them at the time), preferring death to such a life of misery, somehow made through the nettings and jumped into the sea; immediately, another quite dejected fellow, who, on account of his illness, was suffered to be out of irons, also followed their example; and I believe many more would very soon have done the same, if they had not been prevented by the ship's crew, who were instantly alarmed. Those of us that were the most active, were in a moment put down under the deck; and there was such a noise and confusion amongst the people of the ship as I never heard before, to stop her, and get the boat out to go after the slaves. However, two of the wretches were drowned, but they got the other, and afterwards flogged him unmercifully, for thus attempting to prefer death to slavery. In this manner we continued to undergo more hardships than I can now relate, hardships which are inseparable from this accursed trade. Many a time we were near suffocation from the want of fresh air, which we were often without for whole days together. This, and the stench of the necessary tubs, carried off many.

During our passage, I first saw flying fishes, which surprised me very much; they used frequently to fly across the ship, and many of them fell on the deck. I also now first saw the use of the quadrant; I had often with astonishment seen the mariners make observations with it, and I could not think what it meant. They at last took notice of my surprise; and one of them, willing to increase it, as well as to gratify my curiosity, made me one day look through it. The clouds appeared to me to be land, which disappeared as they passed along. This heightened my wonder; and I was now more persuaded than ever, that I was in another world, and that every thing about me was magic. At last, we came in sight of the island of Barbados, at which the whites on board gave a great shout, and made many signs of joy to us. We did not know what to think of this; but as the vessel drew nearer, we plainly saw the harbor, and other ships of different kinds and sizes, and we soon anchored amongst them, off Bridgetown. Many merchants and planters now came on board, though it was in the evening. They put us in separate parcels, parcels and examined us attentively. They also made us jump, and pointed to the land, signifying we were to go there. We thought by this, we should be eaten by these ugly men, as they appeared to us; and, when soon after we were all put down under the deck again, there was much dread and trembling among us, and nothing but bitter cries to be heard all the night from these apprehensions, insomuch, that at last the white people got some old slaves from the land to pacify us. They told us we were not to be eaten, but to work, and were soon to go on land, where we should see many of our country people. This report eased as much. And sure enough, soon after we were landed, there came, to us Africans of all languages.

We were conducted immediately to the merchant's yard, where we were all pent up together, like so many sheep in a fold, without regard to sex or age .... We were not many days in the merchant's custody, before we were sold after their usual manner, which is this: On a signal given (as the beat of a drum), the buyers rush at once into the yard where the slaves are confined, and make choice of that parcel they like best ....

第四课

弗吉尼亚通史

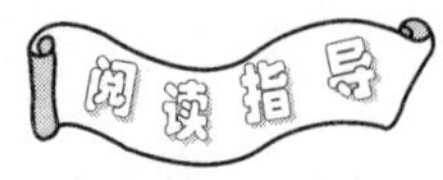

约翰·史密斯（1580—1631）

如果约翰·史密斯生活在今天的话，他会在流行冒险电影中出演阿诺德·施瓦辛格的对手戏——这至少很可能是他对自己的看法。冒险家、诗人、地图绘制者和自我中心主义者，这些只是适合史密斯的几个头衔，他对领导英国在美洲建立第一个殖民地作出了很大的贡献，因此，作为英国最著名的探险家之一而享有盛名。他的探险故事经常由他自己润色，不仅吸引了他那个时代的读者，而且一直为人们提供早期美洲探险的细节记录。

约翰·史密斯

在当了10年士兵之后，史密斯领导一队殖民者来到了这个大陆，1607年他们在弗吉尼亚登陆，并建立了詹姆士镇。史密斯在1608年至1609年期间担任殖民地总督，帮助人们获取食物、执行纪律并和当地的美洲土著人相处。

虽然史密斯在1609年回到了英国，但他后来又两次到美洲航行，去探查新英格兰海岸。在一生中他发表了几部作品，包括《弗吉尼亚通史》《新英格兰》和《夏日群岛》（1624）。

威廉姆·布拉德福特（1590—1657）

威廉姆·布拉德福特

在北美洲的生存取决于耐力、智慧和勇气，而威廉姆·布拉德福特就兼具这三者。詹姆士镇建立13年后，布拉德福特带领着朝圣者们来到了现在马萨诸塞州的这片土地。

布拉德福特出生在英国的约克郡，他加入了一群极端的清教徒，他们认为英国教会已经腐蚀，希望能脱离教会。面对着严厉的迫害，他们最终逃到了荷兰，并从那里乘船来到了北美洲。

在殖民地的第一位领导逝世后，朝圣者们将威廉姆·布拉德福特选为总督，他随后又连续当选30次之多。在他的任期内，他组织了对他们的经济援助者的债务偿还，鼓励新的移民，并且与美洲土著人建立了良好的关系，如果没有土著人的帮助，殖民地根本就不会生存下来。

1630年，布拉德福特开始写作《普利茅斯农场》，这是对于朝圣者们生存斗争的第一手记录，他们仅仅是凭着勇气和坚定不屈的信仰才坚持了下来。这部作品是用被称为“清教徒简朴风格”的简单语言写成的，直到1865年才得以发表。

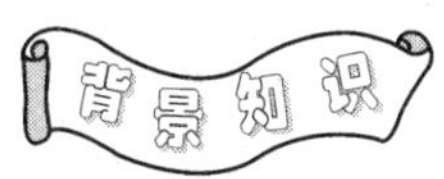

历史：在殖民地的经历

资助史密斯远征的贸易公司错误地以为在北美洲能挣到很多钱。因为没能满足赞助者经济上的期望，约翰·史密斯差点被送进了监狱。因此，有时候史密斯夸大了定居者们在新大陆上为生存而斗争的功绩，也就不足为奇了。

为生存而斗争的人不只是詹姆士镇的定居者们。1620年，经历了一艘小小的“五月花”号上的艰苦航行，朝圣者们没能按计划在弗吉尼亚登陆，而是向北走了很远到达靠近考德海角的马萨诸塞。在他们建造住处搬到岸上之前，就已经是12月中旬了。在船上几个星期沉闷的等待中，威廉姆·布拉德福特的妻子多罗茜，掉下船淹死了。

朝圣者们一搬到岸上，就发现严寒的冬天使得在陌生土地上的定居更加艰难，并且开始就原本为去弗吉尼亚而准备的特许状是否有效而进行争论。这些斗争的结果是定居者们签署了《五月花协议》，这是由殖民者制定的第一个自治协议，成为后来定居的范本。

联系你的经历 你很可能记得在生活中的某个时候，所有的事情都不顺利。考虑早期美洲殖民者所面对的一切：饥饿、疲劳、疾病和对未知世界的恐惧。正如这篇叙述文中所表现的，是决心使他们不断前进。

日志写作 写下你对早期定居者的生活的想象和看法。

专题聚焦：文化的交会 定居者们为争取一个新生活的机会，要面对很多可怕的风险。如果没有美洲土著人的帮助，他们能生存下来吗？

叙述文 叙述文讲述了真实生活中的故事。下面所选文章属于历史叙述文，记录重大历史事件的叙述文。有些历史叙述文，包括这里所选的文章，是亲身经历事件的人们的第一手记录。其他的则是二手的或次要的叙述，是由研究者而不是在生活中经历这些事件的人们记录的。在你阅读文章时，切记由于作者本人参与了事件，所以这些第一手的记录可能是主观的。

弗吉尼亚通史（节选）

约翰·史密斯

第一批供给物资到达之前发生的事情

我们就这样落入了命运的掌心，在10天之内，我们之中能继续正常活动或好好地站立的人几乎只有不到10个了，我们都被极度的虚弱和疾病困扰着。如果考虑到一个原因，这种情况就不会令人惊讶了，这个原因就是：当船只停泊在这里的时候，我们的限量供应因为每天多了一些饼干而得到一定的改善，这些饼干是船员们偷偷地送给我们，或者用来与我们交换钱、萨萨弗拉斯树或毛皮的。但是当他们离开以后，这里除了一些公有的食物储备以外，既没留下饭馆、啤酒馆，也没留下任何供人们放松的场所。如果我们像远离贪食和醉酒这两种罪孽一样远离所有的罪孽的话，我们就可以被封为圣人了。但是我们的总督就永远不可能有这个资格，因为他把除了那些公有食物储备之外的所有东西都据为己有了，包括燕麦片、干白葡萄酒、油、白兰地、牛肉、蛋，等等。他允许我们平均分配那些食物，每人每天能分到煮熟的半品脱小麦和半品脱大麦，这些粮食因为晾干后在船上存放了26个星期，所以里面的虫子都和粮食一样多了，实际上我们应该把这些粮食称做谷糠而不是谷物。我们喝的是白水，住的是空中楼阁。

在这种居住和饮食条件下，搬运和安插栅栏的极度劳累的工作使我们饱受摧残、满身伤痛，在极度炎热的天气下不间断地工作使我们变得非常虚弱，这使我们的生活和在本国或世界上任何其他地方一样悲惨。

从5月到9月，逃走的人以鲟鱼和海蟹为生。在这段时间里我们埋葬了50个人，余下的人在看到总督的行为之后乘我们的小船逃走了（他们在这段时间里并没受到食物短缺和疾病的折磨）。这大大地震动了我们麻木的精神，所以我们罢黜了总督，并选举瑞特克里弗接任他的位置……

现在我们所有的供给都耗尽了，鲟鱼离开了，所有的帮助都无望了，我们每个小时都在担心土著人的狂暴进攻。但是上帝，所有美好努力的保护神，在这种极端绝望的时候改变了土著人的感情，他们居然给我们送来了超出我们需要的水果和粮食。

现在有些人断言说委员会派出这样供给不足的人员是不明智的举动，下面这个无可辩驳的理由就能明白地说明他们抱有这样一个不理智的想法是非常欠考虑的：首先，我们航行的错误是我们自己造成的。我们装备了自己能想到的一切合适和必要的东西，但是关于我们会找到什么，需要什么，

美洲土著居民在照顾受伤的英国人

或我们将要去到哪里,我们全都一片茫然。由于送我们来的人根本不明白他们承担的是什么工作,错误地预计了情况,我们本以为可以在两个月内完成航行,有足够的食物,还能利用春季工作。但实际上我们在海上航行了5个月,耗尽了食物,还失去了耕种的时机和季节。

从古至今,这样的行为就必定导致这样的事故,所有人们认为有价值的事情都充满了艰难,但是远没有在这样荒无人烟和缺乏工具的地方建立一个独立的集体困难,在这个地方人们的思想是如此顽固,既不能独善其身,又不能容忍别人。但是我们还是要继续前进。

新总督马丁,不受人爱戴,在危险的时候没有决断力,在和平的时候又不够勤奋。他把栅栏围出的边境之外的所有事情都交给史密斯船长去管理,而史密斯船长通过自身的示范、友好的言语和公平的许诺,分配一些人去割草,另一些人绑茅草,一些人建房子,另一些人盖房顶,他自己也总是承担一份很繁重的工作。这样,不久他就使我们中的大多数人都有了住处,却没有顾及他自己的需要……

在一次对其卡荷米尼河流域的远征中,史密斯船长和他的部下受到印第安人的袭击,史密斯被抓住了。

当这个消息传到詹姆士镇的时候,人们因为失去他而感到非常悲伤,但没有人预料到接下来发生的事情。

那些土著人把史密斯船长拘禁了6个或7个星期,他们对他采用了许多奇怪的方法,但是他降低身份与他们友好相处,不仅使得他们没有突袭要塞,使自己重获自由,而且还为他和他的队伍赢得了很高的评价,以至于那些野蛮人对他非常崇敬。

土著人对待他的方式和释放他的过程是这样的:

土著人首先从乔治•卡森那里打听到了史密斯船长的去向,一支由300名弓箭手组成的队伍利用这个机会跟踪着他。这支队伍是由帕门基河的大王领导的,他们在分散搜索河流的转弯处时,在火堆边发现了罗宾逊和爱穆利,他们乱箭齐发,把这两个人杀死了。然后他们发现了船长,就像我们说过的那样,他利用做他向导的土著人保护自己(他们中的三个被杀死了,其他的几个受了伤)奋力反击,余下的土著人都不愿再靠近他。他以为这样就能回到他的船上去,但顾虑到这些土著人,他在回去的途中绕了很远的路,和他的土著人向导一起滑到了一条小溪的中间。然而直到他快要被冻死并放弃了他的武器之后，那些土著人才敢靠近他。然后根据他们的习俗，他们把他拉起来，领到火边，他手下的人正是在这里被杀害的。土著人非常卖力地摩擦他冻得麻木的四肢。

他要求见他们的首领，他们就把他带到欧佩坎卡诺——帕门基河的大王——面前。他送给大王一个圆形的象牙双面指南仪。他们对指南仪部件的运动大为惊叹，他们能够清清楚楚地看到这些部件，却因为玻璃表盘的覆盖而摸不到。但是当他利用这球形珠宝来说明地球和天空是圆形的，太阳、月亮和星星的运行范围，太阳不停地绕着地球旋转，大陆和海洋的壮观，各个种族的不同，人们肤色的变化，我们和他们就像地球的两极一样，还有其他许多这样的事情的时候，他们都站在那里，崇拜震惊得呆若木鸡。

然而，不到一个小时以后，他们就把他绑在一棵树上，他的周围站满了人，准备把他射死。但是大王举起了手里的指南仪，他们放下了弓箭，得意洋洋地把他带到了奥拉帕克斯，按照他们的习惯款待他……

最后他们把他带到了维罗乌科摩克，他们的皇帝普哈坦就在那里。200多个表情严肃的朝臣站在那里研究他，就好像他是一只怪物一样，直到最后普哈坦和他的随从们才聚集起他们最大的勇气来。普哈坦坐在火前面好像床架一样的一个座位上，身上披着一件用浣熊皮制成的大袍子，浣熊的尾巴垂在他四周。他的两边各坐着一个16或18岁的年轻姑娘，有两列男人站在房子的两边，他们身后有同样多的女人，这些人的头和肩膀都涂成了红色，很多人的头上装饰着白色的鸟毛，但是所有人的脖子上都带着一大串诸如白色的珠子之类的东西。

当史密斯走到皇帝面前的时候，所有的人一起发出了一声巨吼。皇帝命令阿波玛托克的皇后拿水来让他洗手，另外一个皇后拿来一束羽毛代替毛巾让他把手擦干。他们按照自己最好的野蛮风俗款待了他之后，就进行了一次长长的讨论，但讨论的结论却是：他们拿来两块大石头放在普哈坦的面前，然后无数的人抓住了史密斯，把他拖过去，把他的头按在石头上面，准备用他们的大棒子把他的脑浆打出来。普卡洪塔斯，大王最爱的女儿，看到任何恳求都不可能有作用了，双臂抱住他的头，把自己的头挡在他的头上，使他免于一死。在这种情况下，皇帝表示让史密斯活下来为他制造短柄小斧，为女儿制造铃铛、珠子和铜。他们认为史密斯应该和他们自己一样擅长于制造这些东西，因为大王也要像其他人一样为自己制造长袍、鞋、弓箭、器皿，还要耕种、打猎

或做其他事情。

两天以后，普哈坦尽可能地把自己装扮成最可怕的样子，叫人把史密斯船长带到森林里的一所大房子里，并把他一个人放在火旁的垫子上。不久，从房子中间的一道帘子后面传出了他听到过的最悲伤的声音。普哈坦打扮得不像人而像一个鬼，带着200多个和他自己一样穿着黑衣服的人，走到史密斯面前，告诉他现在他们是朋友了，他要马上回到詹姆士镇，然后给普哈坦送来两支大枪和一个砂轮，作为交换，普哈坦会给他卡帕好瓦西科的土地，并且永远像看待自己的儿子南塔昆德一样看待他。

就这样普哈坦让12个向导送他回到詹姆士镇。那天夜里他们在森林里宿营，他还是每个小时都在担心他可能被这样或那样地杀死（就像他在拘禁期间一直担心的一样），因为他们的宴会看起来是那样野蛮。但是全能的上帝（通过他的天意）用同情软化了这些野蛮人顽固的心灵。第二天清晨他们早早地到达了要塞，在那里史密斯尽可能友好地款待了那些土著人，他让罗汉特——普哈坦信任的仆人，看了带给普哈坦的两门大炮和一个磨盘。他们觉得这些东西有点儿太沉了，但是当他们看到他把石头装在大炮上，然后打到一棵挂满冰柱的大树的主枝之间的时候，冰和大树枝轰隆落下，那些可怜的土著人吓得半死，纷纷逃开了。最终双方协商的结果是，送给他们能让大家都满意的礼物，包括送给普哈坦、他的妻子和孩子们的玩具。

弗吉尼亚州某镇长官

现在整个詹姆士镇又陷入了混乱之中，最强壮的人又一次准备乘小船逃走。史密斯船长冒着自己的生命危险，用小加农炮和滑膛枪第三次命令他们停下，否则就打沉他们的船。

有些人昧着自己的良心，曾经和总督阴谋计划第二天利用“勒维特考法”来处死他，因为他们栽赃说是因为他才使罗宾逊和爱穆利丧了命。但是他很快就和一些律师彻底战胜了他们，并把其中一些囚犯送回了英国。

现在每隔四五天普卡洪塔斯和她的随从们就会给他带来很多供给物资，救了很多人的命，要不是这样的话他们本来会在这种情况下饿死的。

他见到的富饶土地，尤其是维罗乌科摩克，和普哈坦的慷慨大方（在那以前没有人了解)，改变了他们麻木的心灵(尤其是普卡洪塔斯的爱)，因此所有的人都不再恐惧了。

就这样你可以看出在所有美好努力中仍然充满了艰辛，事业的功绩经常要经受破坏的阶段，但是你看到了上帝用怎样奇怪的方法解决了这一切。

文学和生活

读者反应 如果你是史密斯的话，当你一有机会的时候，你是会回到英国还是留在詹姆士镇？为什么？

主题焦点 促使殖民者们离开英国，到美洲去开始新生活的原因可能是什么？

阅读理解

1. 殖民者们在这个大陆上的前几个月里经历了什么困难？
2. 殖民者们得到了什么帮助？
3. 史密斯对新总督、殖民者马丁做出了什么评价？
4. 史密斯在这篇文章里赞扬了谁或什么东西？

思考

解释

1. 你从这篇文章中得到了对史密斯的什么印象？(推断)
2. 描述史密斯对美洲土著人的态度。(分析)
3. 你认为史密斯为什么要用第三人称写作，把自己称为“他”而不是“我”？(得出结论)

评价

4. 你认为史密斯记录的每个细节都是准确的吗？为什么？(评价)

扩展

5. 如果史密斯生活在今天，他可能会有什么样的事业？解释原因。(职业联系)

普利茅斯农场(节选)

威廉姆·布拉德福特

他们的航行和他们怎样穿越了大海;以及他们安全到达考德海角。

在他们享受了一季柔和的海风和美好的天气后,他们多次遇到了侧风和猛烈的暴风雨,船在风暴中剧烈地晃动,船体上部开始漏水,而船体中部的一根主桅杆被风吹得弯曲裂开了,这使他们开始害怕这艘船是否能完成这次航行。这群人的一些领导从水手们的低语中察觉到了他们对这艘船的可靠性的担忧,于是他们与船主和船上的其他主管进行了严肃的讨论,考虑在这种危险的时刻,是否应该向回转,以免把自己置于令人绝望而又不可避免的险境之中。确实,在水手们自己心中也有巨大的分歧和不同意见:为了自己的工钱,他们愿意竭尽所能完成航行(因为现在已经走过一半海路了),而在另一方面,他们又太不愿意不顾一切地用自己的生命去冒险。然而考虑了所有的意见之后,船主和其他人确定这艘船在大浪下也足够结实坚固。至于那根弯曲的主桅杆,因为船上的乘客们从荷兰带了一个巨大的铁螺钉,所以可以用它把那根桅杆复位,然后身兼木匠的船主保证他可以用一根固定在下层甲板上的柱子撑在它的下面,其他方向也绑好,这根桅杆就可以安全使用了。至于甲板和船体上部,他们将尽可能地把漏洞堵住,虽然随着船的行进这些漏洞无法保持长时间不漏水,但是只要他们不用帆给船过大的压力,就不会有大的危险。就这样,他们决定听天由命,继续前进。

在多次的暴风雨中,狂风是那么猛烈,海浪又是那么高涨,他们根本连1小时1海里的航行速度都达不到,有好几天都只能随风漂流。一天,他们正在一次狂暴的暴风雨中漂流, 一个名叫约翰·豪兰德的健壮的年轻人在栅栏上绊了一下,随着船身的一次晃动,他被抛到了海里。然而上帝保佑,幸运的是他抓住了从船上伸出很长的上桅帆的升降索。他紧紧地抓着(虽然他已经沉入水下几英尺深了)直到又被那条绳索拉到水面上来,然后他抓住了一个船上的钩子和其他的东西,又爬上了船,就这样得救了。虽然他因此病了一场,但他后来活了很多年,并且对教会和共和国都作出了贡献。在这次航行的全程中只有一名乘客死去,那就是塞缪尔·福勒的仆人,一个年轻人,威廉姆·巴顿,他在他们靠近海岸的时候死去了。

让我省去其他的事情，这样我的叙述就可以简短一些。经过在海上的漫长搏斗后，他们到达了那片叫做考德海角的大陆，他们知道这个地方，并不感到高兴。经过他们自己之间以及和船主进行的仔细讨论，他们作Z字形航行，并且决定向南航行（风和天气都很合宜）去寻找哈德森河附近可以居住的地方。然而，他们航行了半天以后，却陷入了危险的暗礁群和咆哮的大浪之中，而他们发现自己身处险境时，已经深陷其中了。风也离开了他们，他们决定再次驶向考德海角，他们希望能在夜晚来临之前脱离险境，而在上帝善良的安排下他们做到了。第二天，他们驶入了海角港口，安全地脱险了。

就这样他们到达了一个环境良好的港湾，安全地到了陆地上，他们双膝跪下感谢上帝令他们安然渡过那广阔狂暴的大海，将他们从海上所有的危险和悲惨中解救出来，再次站在这坚实稳定的土地上，这才是他们真正的归属。

饥荒时期

然而最可悲最凄惨的却是，在2–3个月的时间里，尤其是在1月和2月，这群人中就有一半死去了，由于严冬的寒冷和缺乏房屋以及其他生活设施，也由于这次漫长的航行和他们所不适应的条件带来的坏血病和其他疾病的传播。就这样，在刚才所说的那段时间里，有时候每天有2–3个人死去，一共死去了100多个人，只剩下不到50人。而在最悲惨的时期里，这些人中只有六七个是健康人，应该说，他们应该获得高度赞扬。他们不分昼夜忍受痛苦，艰辛地劳动，冒着自己的健康也受到损害的危险。他们为人们搬木柴，生火，准备做饭用的肉，铺床，洗脏衣服，还为人们穿衣脱衣。总而言之，他们为人们做了所有必需的家务事，而这些事情是那些肠胃敏感容易呕吐的人根本连听都不能听的。他们却是非常情愿地兴高采烈地做了所有这些事，没有丝毫的勉强，从中表现了对自己朋友和教友们的真诚的爱。这是一个值得人们纪念的少见的

"五月花"号探险船

范例。这七个人中的两个是：资深教士威廉姆·布鲁斯特先生和他们的上尉兼军队指挥官迈勒斯·斯坦蒂士。我本人和其他很多人在消沉患病的情况下都受到了他们的恩惠。而这些人受到了主的鼓励，因而在这次普遍的灾难中他们根本就没有受到疾病或虚弱的困扰。我赞扬这些人的话也同样适用于其他很多在这次大灾难中丧生的人和那些仍然活着的人，在他们仍然健康时，是啊，在他们还有一点儿力气的时候，他们一直没有停止帮助需要他们的人。而我只想知道主会给他们什么样的奖励。

但我不能忽略另一个不能遗忘的重要事件。当这次灾难降临到这些将要留在这里进行耕种的乘客中时，他们被匆忙地送上了岸，只有水喝，因为这样船员们就能留下更多的啤酒。而当一个病中的人渴望能喝到仅仅一小听啤酒时，他得到的回答却是：就算他是他们的亲生父亲，他们也不会给他一点儿啤酒。疾病也开始降临到船员们身上，在他们离开之前已经有几乎一半人病死了，其中有很多是他们的长官和最健壮的人，包括水手长、炮手、三个军需官、厨师和其他人。船主几乎被这件事击倒了，于是把得病的人送到岸上，并且告诉总督即使他在回家的路上只有水喝，他也会为需要的人送来啤酒。

然而在这个悲惨的时刻，船员们的表现却与船上的乘客截然不同。在那以前，当他们健康快乐一起欢宴取乐的时候，他们曾经是亲密的伙伴，而现在在这灾难中却开始彼此遗弃。他们说他们不愿意为别人冒生命危险，如果他们到病人住的小屋中去照顾病人的话，他们会被传染的；因此，当病人来到岸上躺在小屋中以后，他们就做得很少或什么也不做了，而只是说："如果他们要死的话，就让他们死吧。"然而那些仍然在船上的乘客们却表现了最大限度的慈悲，这使他们中的一些人的心变得温和宽厚了。例如水手长(还有其他一些人)，他是个骄傲的年轻人，过去经常咒骂嘲笑那些乘客。但是当他变得虚弱的时候，他们却同情他，帮助他，然后他忏悔道他不配得到他们的照顾，他曾经用言语和行为虐待过他们。"噢！"他说，"我现在看到了，你们真像基督徒一样彼此表现出仁爱，但是我们却像狗一样任由彼此躺在那儿死去。"另一个人躺在那里咒骂他的妻子，他说如果不是她的话，他就不会来参加这次倒霉的航行，然后他很快就开始咒骂他的同伴，他说他曾经为其中一些人做过这事那事，他为他们花了那么那么多钱，可他们现在却厌烦了他，在他需要他们的时候不帮助他。还有一个人答应如果他死了，就把所有的东西都给他的同伴，以此做交换让那同伴在他虚弱的时候帮助他；那同伴拿来了一点儿香料，并为他做了一两次肉。然后,因为那个人没有像他预期的那样死得那么快,他就回到了他的同伴中,发誓说那个恶棍在欺骗他,要是再给他做肉的话,希望看见他被噎死。然而,那个可怜的家伙在早晨之前就死去了。

与印第安人的关系

在这段时间里,印第安人一直偷偷地隐藏在他们周围,有时候在远处现身,但当有任何人接近他们的时候,他们就会马上逃走。有一次他们工作以后去吃饭的时候,印第安人偷走了他们的工具。但是在3月16日左右,一个印第安人大胆地走到他们中间,并且用断断续续的英语和他们交谈,他们能清楚地明白他的意思,但是对此感到极其惊讶。最后他们通过和他的交谈知道了他不属于这些部落,而是属于东部的部落,有些英国船只到那里去打鱼,他就认识了那些英国人,并且还能说出其中几个人的名字来,他就是向那些人学会英语的。他对他们很有帮助,向他们介绍了很多关于他居住的东部部落的情况,后来他们发现这非常有用。他也向他们介绍了这里的印第安人的情况,他们的姓名、人数和力量,还有他们的生活情况、与这个地方相隔的距离,以及谁是那些印第安人的首领。这个印第安人的名字叫萨莫赛特。他也告诉他们还有一个住在这个地方的印第安人叫做斯库安多,曾经去过英国,英语说得比他要好。

普利茅斯农场一角

他们和他在一起高兴地聊了一段时间,又送了他一些礼物。过了一会儿他又来了,带来了五个人,他们带来了以前偷走的所有工具,并且为他们的大首领玛萨索伊特的到来做好了准备。玛萨索伊特四五天之后带着他的友邦的首领和其他随从,和前面说过的斯库安多一起来了。经过友好的交谈和赠送礼物,他们与他达成了一个和平协议(到现在已经持续了24年),协议约定如下:

1. 他和他部落中的印第安人都不能伤害任何一个英国人。

2. 如果他部落中的某个印第安人确实伤害了任何一个英国人，他应该把那个印第安人送来接受英国人的惩罚。

3. 如果有任何东西被从英国人那里拿走，他应该保证物归原主；英国人也应该同样对他。

4. 如果任何人不公正地与他作战，英国人应该帮助他；如果有人与英国人作战，他也应该帮助他们。

5. 他应该向与他相邻的印第安部落发出同盟协定，使他们保证不会不公正地对待英国人，而且同样地在和平协议的基础上达成一致。

6. 当印第安人来到英国人的地方时，他们应该把弓和箭留在别处。

这些事情都处理好以后，玛萨索伊特回到了他居住的叫做索瓦姆斯的地方，那里离这个地方大约40英里远，但是斯库安多却继续留下来和英国人在一起，做了他们的翻译，他是上帝为了眷顾他们而送来的一个特别的馈赠，他的到来令他们喜出望外。他教会他们怎样播种谷物，到哪里去捕鱼和获得其他商品，也是帮助他们到未知的地区去谋求福利的领航员。他一直到死都没有离开他们。

文学和生活

读者反应　如果你也参加了“五月花”号的航行，你会做些什么不同的事情来为在美洲的生活更好地做准备？

主题焦点　这篇记叙使你对朝圣者们的印象发生了什么改变？

阅读理解

1. 朝圣者们在穿越大西洋的旅行中经受了哪些磨难？

2. 他们在普利茅斯的第一个冬天里遇到了哪些困难？

3. (a)萨莫赛特用哪些方法帮助了朝圣者们？(b)斯库安多为他们做了哪些事情？

思考

解释

1. 你认为朝圣者们对在普利茅斯的第一个冬天里遇到的困难的反应有哪些特点？（归类）

2. 找出两处叙述，其中表现了朝圣者们相信他们一直受到上帝的指引和保护。（分析）

应用

3. 你认为定居者们和美洲土著人态度的改变反映了典型的与外来者相遇时的经验吗？为什么？（综合）

文学聚焦

叙述文

这里所选文章是叙述文，讲述真实生活中经历的故事。它们也都是第一手的历史叙述文，是亲身经历事件的人们记录下来的重大事件。第一手的记录能抓住时代的特色，描述亲身参与事件的感觉。然而，其中的信息并不总是准确的，因为作者经常试图说服或取悦自己的读者。

1. 在文中找到两个例子表现史密斯在复述事件时的夸张或主观。

2. (a)你认为史密斯写这篇叙述文的目的是什么？(b)布拉德福特的目的和他有什么不同？

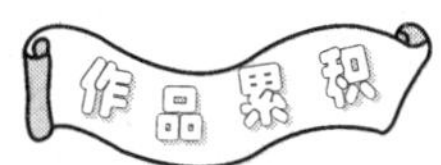

点子库

写作

1. 纪念演讲　作为一名詹姆士镇的定居者，你被邀请在纪念约翰•史密斯的典礼上讲话。写一篇演说辞，描述史密斯的探险经历和他取得的成就。

2. 戏剧场面　写一个戏剧场面，表现萨莫赛特与普利茅斯的定居者们第一次相见时的情景，其中包含对话和舞台说明。（表演艺术连线）

3. 新闻写作　普卡洪塔斯嫁给了一名詹姆士镇的定居者并到英国旅行。你作为一名《伦敦时报》的记者，对她的生平进行调查。写一篇新闻报道她在

英国的旅行。

项目

1. 广告　制作一份宣传在普利茅斯农场生活的招贴广告。鼓励其他人来到美洲加入朝圣者们的行列。

2. 菜单　由于食物中缺乏维生素C,很多朝圣者得了坏血病。了解殖民者们吃的食物和他们种植的谷物,然后根据历史条件为一个早期殖民者的一天制定菜单。(健康连线)

微型写作课

记叙文之间的比较

这两篇叙述文会使读者产生一个印象:史密斯和布拉德福特是两个对生活有着截然不同看法的人。写一篇文章将这两篇第一手的记叙文做一比较。

写作技巧重点:清楚的组织结构

当你进行比较和对比时,使用清楚的组织结构——这能帮助你确定你的比较对象之间的相似点和不同点。两种比较和对比的基本组织结构是采用逐点比较和逐个比较:

在逐点比较的组织结构中,按顺序讨论你的对象的每个方面。例如,讨论史密斯语气中的一个方面,然后马上将其与布拉德福特语气中的一个方面相对比。

在逐个比较的组织结构中,讨论一个对象的所有特征——例如,史密斯的记叙文的语气和内容——然后再讨论另一个对象的所有特征。

构思

重读这两篇记叙文,注意每位作者的风格、目的和客观性。为收集和组织细节,你可以使用如下的结构图:

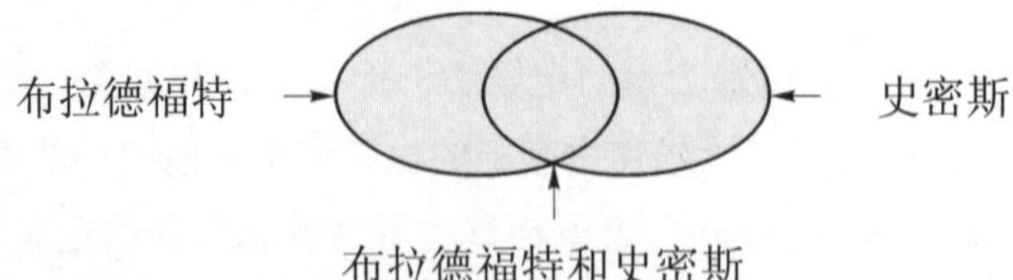

写稿

将每一段集中于一个作家或一个比较点。为了连接各段并使各点之间的关系保持清楚, 使用诸如:similarly, also, equally, in contrast, but, although, however, instead, on the other hand等过渡词语。

修改

修改你的文章，重组信息，使组织结构更清晰，同时在适宜的地方加入细节以加强你的论证。

Guide for Interpreting

John Smith(1580—1631)

If John Smith were alive today,he'd be starring opposite Arnold Schwarzenegger in blockbuster adventure films — at least, that's probably where he'd see himself. Adventurer, poet, mapmaker, and egotist are just a few of the labels that apply to Smith, who earned a reputation as one of England's most famous explorers by helping to lead the first successful English colony in America. Stories of his adventures, often embellished by his own pen, fascinated readers of his day and continue to provide details about early exploration of the Americas.

Following a ten-year career as a soldier, Smith led a group of colonists to this continent, where they landed in Virginia in 1607 and founded Jamestown. As president of the colony from 1608 to 1609, Smith helped to obtain food, enforce discipline, and deal with the local Native Americans. Though Smith returned to England in 1609, he made two more voyages to America to explore the New England coast. He published several works in the course of his life, including The General History of Virginia, New England, and the Summer Isles (1624).

William Bradford(1590—1657)

Survival in North America was a matter of endurance, intelligence, and courage. William Bradford had all three. Thirteen years after the founding of Jamestown, Bradford helped lead the Pilgrims to what is now Massachusetts.

Bradford, who was born in Yorkshire, England, joined a group of Puritan extremists who believed the Church of England was corrupt and wished to separate from it. In the face of stiff persecution, they eventually fled to Holland and from there sailed to North America.

After the death of the colony's first leader, the Pilgrims elected William

Bradford governor. He was reelected thirty times. During his tenure, he organized the repayment of debts to financial backers, encouraged new immigration, and established good relations with the Native Americans, without whose help the colony never would have survived.

In 1630, Bradford began writing Of Plymouth Plantation, a firsthand account of the Pilgrims' struggle to endure, sustained only by courage and unbending faith. The work, written in the simple language known as Puritan Plain Style, was not published until 1856.

Background for Understanding

HISTORY: THE COLONIAL EXPERIENCE

The trading company that financed the Jamestown expedition mistakenly believed that there was much money to be made in North America. John Smith was nearly sent to prison for not meeting his backers' financial expectations. It is not surprising, then, that Smith sometimes exaggerated the exploits of the settlers as they struggled to survive in the new land.

The Jamestown settlers weren't the only ones struggling. In 1620, after a difficult voyage aboard the tiny Mayflower, the Pilgrims landed not in Virginia, as intended, but much farther north near Cape Cod, Massachusetts. It was mid-December before they could build shelters and move ashore. During those dreary weeks of waiting on the ship, William Bradford's wife, Dorothy, fell overboard and was drowned. Once ashore, the Pilgrims found the hardships of settling in a strange land worsened by a harsh winter and disputes over the validity of their charter, which had been for Virginia. The conflict led the settlers to create the "Mayflower Compact", the first agreement for self-government made by the colonists and a model for later settlements.

Literature and your Life

CONNECT YOUR EXPERIENCE

You can probably remember a point in your life when everything seemed to

be going against you. Consider what the early American colonists faced: starvation, exhaustion, illness, and the terror of the unknown. As the narratives show, determination pushed them on.

Journal Writing Write down your thoughts about what you imagine it was like to be an early settler.

THEMATIC FOCUS: MEETING OF CULTURES

The settlers faced many terrible risks for a chance at a new life. Would they have survived without the help of the Native Americans?

Literary Focus

NARRATIVE ACCOUNTS

Narrative accounts tell the story of real-life events. The selections that follow are historical narratives, narrative accounts that record significant historical events. Some historical narratives, including these, are firsthand accounts by people who lived through the events. Others are secondhand, or secondary, accounts by people who researched, but did not live through, the events. As you read, keep in mind that firsthand accounts are sometimes subjective because of the writer's personal involvement in the events.

The General History of Virginia

John Smith

What Happened Till the First Supply

Being thus left to our fortunes, it fortuned that within ten days, scarce ten amongst us could either go or well stand, such extreme weakness and sickness oppressed us. And thereat none need marvel if they consider the cause and reason, which was this: While the ships stayed, our allowance was somewhat bettered by a daily proportion of biscuit which the sailors would pilfer to sell. give. or exchange with us for money, sassafras, or furs. But when they departed, there remained neither tavern, beer house, nor place of relief but the common kettle. Had we been as free from all sins as gluttony and drunkenness we might have been canonized for saints, but our President would never have been admitted for engrossing to his private. oatmeal, sack, oil, aqua vitae, beef, eggs, or what not but the kettle; that indeed he allowed equally to be distributed, and that was half a pint of wheat and as much barley boiled with water for a man a day, and this, having fried some twenty-six weeks in the ship's hold, contained as many worms as grains so that we might truly call it rather so much bran than corn; our drink was water, our lodgings castles in the air.

With this lodging and diet, our extreme toil in bearing and planting palisades so strained and bruised us and our continual labor in the extremity of the heat had so weakened us. as were cause sufficient to have made us as miserable in our native country or any other place in the world.

From May to September, those that escaped lived upon sturgeon and sea crabs. Fifty in this time we buried; the rest seeing the President's projects to escape these miseries in our pinnace by flight (who all this time had neither felt want nor sickness) so moved our dead spirits as we deposed him and established Ratcliffe in his place...

But now was all our provision spent, the sturgeon gone, all helps abandoned, each hour expecting the fury of the savages; when God, the patron of all good endeavors, in that desperate extremity so changed the hearts of the savages that they brought such plenty of their fruits and provision as no man wanted.

And now where some affirmed it was ill done of the Council to send forth men so badly provided, this incontradictable reason will show them plainly they are too ill advised to nourish such ill conceits: First, the fault of our going was our own; what could be thought fitting or necessary we had, but what we should find, or want, or where we should be, we were all ignorant and supposing to make our passage in two months, with victual to live and the advantage of the spring to work; we were at sea five months where we both spent our victual and lost the opportunity of the time and season to plant, by the unskillful presumption of our ignorant transporters that understood not at all what they undertook.

Such actions have ever since the world's beginning been subject to such accidents, and everything of worth is found full of difficulties, but nothing so difficult as to establish a commonwealth so far remote from men and means and where men's minds are so untoward as neither do well themselves nor suffer others. But to proceed.

The new President and Martin, being little beloved, of weak judgment in dangers, and less industry in peace, committed the managing of all things abroad to Captain Smith, who, by his own example, good words, and fair promises, set some to mow, others to bind thatch, some to build houses, others to thatch them, himself always bearing the greatest task for his own share, so that in short time he provided most of them lodgings, neglecting any for himself...

Leading an expedition on tile Chickahominy River, Captain Smith and his men are attacked by Indians, and Smith is taken prisoner.

When this news came to Jamestown, much was their sorrow for his loss, few expecting what ensued.

Six or seven weeks those barbarians kept him prisoner, many strange triumphs and conjurations they made of him, yet he so demeaned himself amongst them, as he not only diverted them from surprising the fort, but procured his own liberty, and got himself and his company such estimation amongst them, that those savages admired him.

The manner how they used and delivered him is as followeth:

The savages having drawn from George Cassen whither Captain Smith was gone, prosecuting that opportunity they followed him with three hundred bowmen, conducted by the King of Pamunkee, who in divisions searching the turnings of the river found Robinson and Emry by the fireside; those they shot full of arrows and slew. Then finding the Captain, as is said, that used the savage that was his guide as his shield (three of them being slain and divers others so galled), all the rest would not come near him. Thinking thus to have returned to his boat, regarding them, as he marched, more than his way, slipped up to the middle in an oozy creek and his savage with him; yet dared they not come to him till being near dead with cold he threw away his arms. Then according to their compositions they drew him forth and led him to the fire where his men were slain. Diligently they chafed his benumbed limbs.

He demanding for their captain, they showed him Opechancanough, King of Pamunkee, to whom he gave a round ivory double compass dial. Much they marveled at the playing of the fly and needle, which they could see so plainly and yet not touch it because of the glass that covered them. But when he demonstrated by that globelike jewel the roundness of the earth and skies, the sphere of the sun, moon, and stars, and how the sun did chase the night round about the world continually, the greatness of the land and sea, the diversity of nations, variety of complexions, and how we were to them antipodes and many other such like matters, they all stood as amazed with admiration.

Nothwithstanding, within an hour after, they tied him to a tree, and as many as could stand about him prepared to shoot him, but the King holding up the compass in his hand, they all laid down their bows and arrows and in a triumphant manner led him to Orapaks where he was after their manner kindly feasted and well used ....

At last they brought him to Werowocomoco, where was Powhatan, their Emperor. Here more than two hundred of those grim courtiers stood wondering at him, as he had been a monster, till Powhatan and his train had put themselves in their greatest braveries. Before a fire upon a seat like a bedstead, he sat covered with a great robe made of raccoon skins and all the tails hanging by. On either

hand did sit a young wench of sixteen or eighteen years and along on each side the house, two rows of men and behind them as many women, with all their heads and shoulders painted red, many of their heads bedecked with the white down of birds, but every one with something, and a great chain of white beads about their necks.

At his entrance before the King, all the people gave a great shout. The queen of Appomattoc was appointed to bring him water to wash his hands, and another brought him a bunch of feathers, instead of a towel, to dry them; having feasted him after their best barbarous manner they could, a long consultation was held, but the conclusion was, two great stones were brought before Powhatan: then as many as could, laid hands on him, dragged him to them, and thereon laid his head and being ready with their clubs to beat out his brains, Pocahontas, the King's dearest daughter, when no entreaty could prevail, got his head in her arms and laid her own upon his to save him from death; whereat the Emperor was contented he should live to make him hatchets, and her bells, beads, and copper, for they thought him as well of all occupations as themselves. For the King himself will make his own robes, shoes, bows, arrows, pots; plant, hunt, or do anything so well as the rest.

Two days after, Powhatan, having disguised himself in the most fearfulest

manner he could, caused Captain Smith to be brought forth to a great house in the woods and there upon a mat by the fire to be left alone. Not long after, from behind a mat that divided the house, was made the most dolefulest noise he ever heard; then Powhatan more like a devil than a man, with some two hundred more as black as himself, came unto him and told him now they were friends, and presently he should go to Jamestown to send him two great guns and a grindstone for which he would give him the country of Capahowasic and forever esteem him as his son Nantaquond.

So to Jamestown with twelve guides Powhatan sent him. That night they quartered in the woods, he still expecting (as he had done all this long time of his imprisonment) every hour to be put to one death or other, for all their feasting. But almighty God (by His divine providence) had mollified the hearts of those stern barbarians with compassion. The next morning betimes they came to the fort, where Smith having used the savages with what kindness he could, he showed Rawhunt, Powhatan's trusty servant, two demiculverins and a millstone to carry Powhatan; they found them somewhat too heavy, but when they did see him discharge them, being loaded with stones, among the boughs of a great tree loaded with icicles, the ice and branches came so tumbling down that the poor savages ran away half dead with fear. But at last we regained some conference with them and gave them such toys and sent to Powhatan, his women, and children such presents as gave them in general full content.

Now in Jamestown they were all in combustion, the strongest preparing once more to run away with the pinnace; which, with the hazard of his life, with saker falcon and musket shot, Smith forced now the third time to stay or sink.

Some, no better than they should be, had plotted with the President the next day to have him put to death by the Levitical law, for the lives of Robinson and Emry; pretending the fault was his that had led them to their ends: but he quickly took such order with such lawyers that he laid them by their heels till he sent some of them prisoners for England.

Now every once in four or five days, Pocahontas with her attendants brought him so much provision that saved many of their lives, that else for all this had

starved with hunger.

His relation of the plenty he had seen, especially at Werowocomoco, and of the state and bounty of Powhatan (which till that time was unknown), so revived their dead spirits (especially the love of Pocahontas) as all men's fear was abandoned.

Thus you may see what difficulties still crossed any good endeavor; and the good success of the business being thus oft brought to the very period of destruction; yet you see by what strange means God hath still delivered it.

Of Plymouth Plantation

William Bradford

Of Their Voyage and How They Passed the Sea; and of Their Safe Arrival at Cape Cod.

After they had enjoyed fair winds and weather for a season, they were encountered many times with cross winds and met with many fierce storms with which the ship was shroudly shaken, and her upper works made very leaky; and one of the main beams in the midships was bowed and cracked, which put them in some fear that the ship could not be able to perform the voyage. So some of the chief of the company, perceiving the mariners to fear the sufficiency of the ship as appeared by their mutterings, they entered into serious consultation with the master and other officers of the ship, to consider in time of the danger, and rather to return than to cast themselves into a desperate and in evitable peril. And truly there was great distraction and difference of opinion amongst the mariners themselves: fain would they do what could be done for their wages' sake (being now near half the seas over) and on the other hand they were loath to hazard their lives too desperately. But in examining of all opinions, the master and others affirmed they knew the ship to be strong and firm under water; and for the buckling of the main beam, there was a great iron screw the passengers brought out of Holland, which would raise the beam into his place; the which being done, the carpenter and master affirmed that with a post put under it, set firm in the lower deck and otherways bound, he would make it sufficient. And as for the decks and upper works, they would caulk them as well as they could, and though with the working of the ship they would not long keep staunch, yet there would otherwise be no great danger, if they did not overpress her with sails. So they committed themselves to the will of God and resolved to proceed.

In sundry of these storms the winds were so fierce and the seas so high, as they could not bear a knot of sail, but were forced to hull for divers days together. And in one of them, as they thus lay at hull in a mighty storm, a lusty young man called John Howland, coming upon some occasion above the gratings was, with a seel of the ship, thrown into sea; but it pleased God that he caught hold of the topsail halyards which hung overboard and ran out at length. Yet he held his hold (though he was sundry fathoms under water) till he was hauled up by the same rope to the brim of the water, and then with a boat hook and other means got into the ship again and his life saved. And though he was something ill with it, yet he lived many years after and became a profitable member both in church and commonwealth. In all this voyage there died but one of the passengers, which was William Butten, a youth, servant to Samuel Fuller, when they drew near the coast.

But to omit other things (that I may be brief) after long beating at sea they fell with that land which is called Cape Cod; the which being made and certainly known to be it, they were not a little joyful. After some deliberation had amongst themselves and with the master of the ship, they tacked about and resolved to stand for the southward (the wind and weather being fair) to find some place about Hudson's River for their habitation. But after they had sailed that course about half the day, they fell amongst dangerous shoals and roaring breakers, and they were so far entangled therewith as they conceived themselves in great danger; and the wind shrinking upon them withal, they resolved to bear up again for the Cape and thought themselves happy to get out of those dangers before night overtook them, as by God's good providence they did. And the next day they got into the Cape Harbor where they rid in safety.

Being thus arrived in a good harbor, and brought safe to land, they fell upon their knees and blessed the God of Heaven who had brought them over the vast and furious ocean, and delivered them from all the perils and miseries thereof, again to set their feet on the firm and stable earth, their proper element.

The Starving Time

But that which was most sad and lamentable was, that in two or three months' time half of their company died, especially in January: and February, being the depth of winter, and wanting houses and other comforts: being infected with the scurvy and other diseases which this long voyage and their inaccommodate condition had brought upon them. So as there died sometimes two or three of a day in the foresaid time, that of one hundred and odd persons, scarce fifty remained. And of these, in the time of most distress, there was but six or seven sound persons who to their great commendations, be it spoken, spared no pains night or day, but with abundance of toil and hazard of their own health, fetched them wood, made them fires, dressed them meat, made their beds, washed their loathsome clothes, clothed and unclothed them. In a word, did all the homely and necessary offices for them which dainty and queasy stomachs cannot endure to hear named; and all this willingly and cheerfully, without any grudging in the least, showing herein their true love unto their friends and brethren; a rare example and worthy to be remembered. Two of these seven were Mr. William Brewster, their reverend Elder, and Myles Standish, their Captain and military commander, unto whom myself and many others were much beholden in our low and sick condition. And yet the Lord so upheld these persons as in this general calamity they were not at all infected either with sickness or lameness. And what I have said of these I may say of many others who died in this general visitation, and others yet living: that whilst they had health, yea, or any strength continuing, they were not wanting to any that had need of them. And I doubt not but their recompense is with the Lord.

But I may not here pass by another remarkable passage not to be forgotten. As this calamity fell among the passengers that were to be left here to plant, and were hasted ashore and made to drink water that the seamen might have the more beer, and one in his sickness desiring but a small can of beer, it was answered that if he were their own father he should have none. The disease began to fall amongst them also, so as almost half of their company died before they went away, and many of their officers and lustiest men, as the boatswain, gunner, three quartermasters, the cook and others. At which the Master was something strucken and sent to the sick ashore and told the Governor he should send for beer for them that had need of it, though he drunk water homeward bound.

But now amongst his company there was far another kind of carriage in this misery than amongst the passengers. For they that before had been boon companions in drinking and jollity in the time of their health and welfare, began now to desert one another in this calamity, saying they would not hazard their lives for them, they should be infected by coming to help them in their cabins; and so, after they came to lie by it, would do little or nothing for them but, "if they died, let them die." But such of the passengers as were yet aboard showed them what mercy they could which made some of their hearts relent, as the boatswain (and

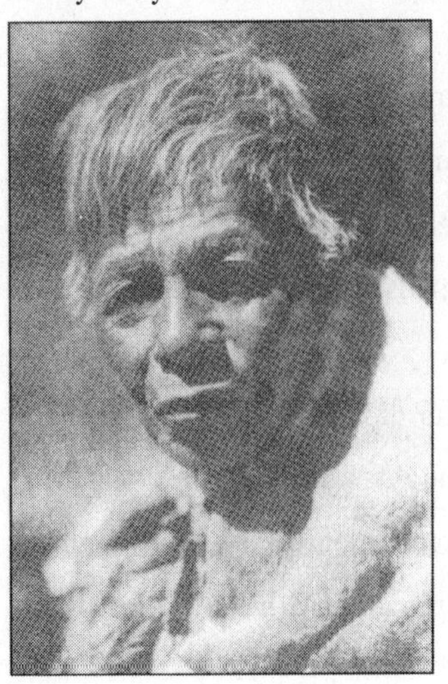

some others) who was a proud young man and would often curse and scoff at the passengers. But when he grew weak, they had compassion on him and helped him; then he confessed he did not deserve it at their hands, he had abused them in word and deed. "Oh!" (saith he) "you, I now see, show your love like Christians indeed one to another, but we let one another lie and die like dogs." Another lay cursing his wife, saying if it had not been for her he had never come this unlucky voyage, and anon cursing his fellows, saying he had done this and that for some of them; he had spent so much and so much amongst them, and they were now weary of him and did not help him, having need. Another gave his companion all he had, if he died, to help him in his weakness; he went and got a little spice and made him a mess of meat once or twice. And because he died not so soon as he expected, he went amongst his fellows and swore the rogue would cozen him, he would see him choked before he made him any more meat; and yet the poor fellow died before morning.

Indian Relations

All this while the Indians came skulking about them, and would sometimes show themselves aloof off, but when any approached near them, they would run away; and once they stole away their tools where they had been at work and were gone to dinner. But about the sixteenth of March, a certain Indian came boldly amongst them and spoke to them in broken English, which they could well understand but marveled at it. At length they understood by discourse with him, that he was not of these parts, but belonged to the eastern parts where some English ships came to fish, with whom he was acquainted and could name sundry of them by their names, amongst whom he had got his language. He became profitable to them in acquainting them with many things concerning the state of the country in the east parts where he lived, which was afterwards profitable unto them; as also of the people here, of their names, number and strength, of their situation and distance from this place, and who was chief amongst them. His name was Samoset. He told them also of another Indian whose name was Squanto, a native of this place, who had been in England and could speak better English than himself.

Being, after some time of entertainment and gifts dismissed, a while after he came again, and five more with him, and they brought again all the tools that were stolen away before, and made way for the coming of their great Sachem, called Massasoit. Who, about four or five days after, came with the chief of his friends and other attendance, with the aforesaid Squanto. With whom, after friendly entertainment and some gifts given him, they made a peace with him (which hath now continued this twenty–four years) in these terms:

1. That neither he nor any of his should injure or do hurt to any of their people.

2. That if any of his did hurt to any of theirs, he should send the offender, that they might punish him.

3. That if anything were taken away from any of theirs, he should cause it to be restored; and they should do the like to his.

4. If any did unjustly war against him, they would aid him; if any did war against them, he should aid them.

5. He should send to his neighbors confederates to certify them of this, that they might not wrong them, but might be likewise comprised in the conditions of peace.

6. That when their men came to them, they should leave their bows and arrows behind them.

After these things he returned to his place called Sowams, some 40 miles from this place, but Squanto continued with them and was their interpreter and was a special instrument sent of God for their good beyond their expectation. He directed them how to set their corn, where to take fish, and to procure other commodities, and was also their pilot to bring them to unknown places for their profit, and never left them till he died.

第五课

罪人在愤怒的上帝手中

乔纳森•爱德华兹 (1703—1758)

乔纳森•爱德华兹

乔纳森•爱德华兹这个名字和“火与硫黄”(这个词组象征罪人们在地狱里遭受的折磨)几乎代表了同样的意义，以至于许多18世纪的清教徒们仅仅听到他的名字就怕得要死了。

这位伟大的美国神学家和强有力的清教主义传道人出生于克奈克提卡特的东文德瑟，在一种虔诚修行的氛围中长大。

据说爱德华兹在童年时就在他家屋后建起简易的布道坛，对他的玩伴们布道。

他的学术成绩优异，在12岁的时候就学会了拉丁文、希腊文和希伯来文，13岁时进入耶鲁大学学习，并在4年之后作为班里致告别词的代表毕业。然后他继续进行神学专业的硕士学位学习。

布道天才　爱德华兹的祖父，索罗门•斯托达德，是马萨诸塞的北安普敦教堂的牧师，这个教堂是清教会众最多以及最富有的教堂之一。爱德华兹在1727年作为他祖父的助手，开始了他的布道生涯，他还作为一名访问牧师在新英格兰各处布道。由于回归正统的强烈渴望和对清教主义过去的热烈信仰，他成为“大觉醒”运动的一名领导者，这是在18世纪30和40年代席卷殖民地的一次宗教改革运动。

改变态度 然而，“大觉醒”运动并没持续下来。1750年，很多会众由于爱德华兹的极端保守主义而远离了教堂，他因此被免了职。此后他一生都一直坚持布道和写作，在成为新泽西大学（今天的普林斯顿大学）的校长后不久，于1758年逝世。

爱德华兹情绪热烈的布道辞《罪人在愤怒的上帝手中》是最著名的作品。这篇布道辞发布于1741年，听众是克奈克提卡特的恩菲尔德的清教会众。据说他的听众在听到这篇布道时，在一种歇斯底里的状态中纷纷从座位上站了起来。

历史：布道坛上的爱德华兹

如果看到这本现代重印版布道辞令人恐怖的封面，你可能绝对猜不到爱德华兹是用一种安静克制的语气来发布这篇“火与硫黄”的布道的。根据一篇记录，他在6个小时的布道过程中一直语调平平地朗读，同时越过听众的头顶盯着挂在后面墙上的钟绳，“就好像要把它盯成两截一样”。虽然他的举止很镇定，但据说他的听众还是因为恐惧而发出了呻吟和尖叫声。根据记录，爱德华兹不得不好几次停下布道，要求他的听众保持安静。虽然他没有采取任何戏剧性的技巧，但通过有效地运用形象的比喻和对主要观点的重复，他还是能把听众的宗教情绪推向高潮。

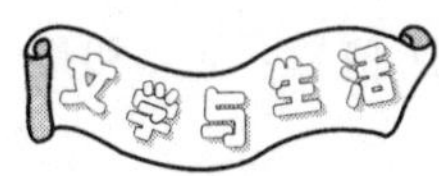

联系你的经历 假设你弟弟走上了“邪路”，你能使他回到正路的方法可能就是告诉他如果他不悔改的话，等待他的是怎样一个可怕的未来。乔纳森·爱德华兹就对他的追随崇拜者们有同样的担忧。他相信很多人正走在通向毁灭

的路上，并且不顾一切地想让他们回头走上通往天堂的道路。爱德华兹在他的布道中充分描述了不悔改的人将会经受怎样的恐怖折磨，从而达到了他的目的。

日志写作 考虑为什么爱德华兹选择采取一种安静平淡的语气，而没有用更加戏剧化或情绪化的方法来布道。解释为什么听众会认为一种安静的方式比极度戏剧化的方式更令人害怕。

专题聚焦：清教徒的影响 “把他们吓得战战兢兢”是使人们改恶向善的有效方法吗？

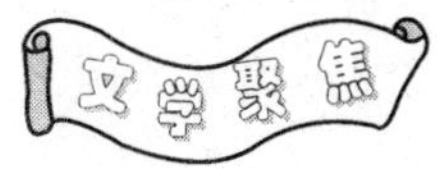

布道 虽然人们经常把“布道”与严厉的演说或是“火与硫黄”的演讲联系起来，布道其实也可以有指导意义或使人受到启发。根据宽泛的定义，布道就是在敬神的布道坛上所作的演讲，通常作为一个宗教仪式的一部分。布道与它的书面形式散文一样，表达了它的作者想传达给听众的信息或观点，我们称这些听众为“会众”。在殖民时期的美洲，布道作为一种流行的文学形式得到了蓬勃的发展。

罪人在愤怒的上帝手中（节选）

乔纳森·爱德华兹

你们中的每一个人得不到上帝庇护的时候都会身处这种境况：在你身下是一望无际的悲惨世界，硫黄在湖里熊熊燃烧。在那里，上帝愤怒的火焰在可怕的深渊里燃烧，地狱张开它的大嘴；而你无处立足，也无所依靠；在你和地狱之间是空气，只有上帝的力量和意愿才能使你免于下坠。

你很可能意识不到这一点。你知道你在地狱之外，你看不到上帝的手扶持着你，却只看着其他的事情，诸如你强健的体格，你对自己生活的关心，你为了生存而采用的方法。但实际上这些事情都毫无意义，如果上帝收回他的手，这些事情对你的下坠就都无能为力了，就好像稀薄的空气根本不能留住一个悬在空中的人一样。

你的罪恶使你的身体像铅块一样沉重，在巨大的重量压力下直落向地狱。如果上帝置你于不顾，你会马上沉下去，快速冲入无底的深渊。你健康的体魄，你自己的谨慎和智慧，最好的能力，所有这些都丝毫不能阻止你堕入地狱，就好像一张蜘蛛网无法拦住下落的石块一样。如果不是上帝至高无上的意愿，你脚下的土地一刻也不会承担你的重量……如果不是上帝至高无上的手使世界充满希望的话，你早就被扬弃在外了。现在上帝的怒火形成的黑云就笼罩在你头顶上方，里面充满着可怕的暴风和暴烈的雷电。如果不是上帝压抑着他的怒火，这黑云马上就会在你头上爆发。现在，上帝以无上的意愿控制住了他的暴风，否则这暴风就会伴随着怒火降临，你的毁灭会像旋风一样来临，你就像夏天的谷壳一样被摔打在地面上。

现在，上帝的愤怒就像被堤坝控制住的洪水一样，水越来越多，越涨越高，直到找到一个出口为止。水流被阻住的时间越长，当它一旦泄出时，就会越快、越强。没错，到目前为止对你罪恶的审判还没完成，上帝复仇的头巾还没揭开，但同时你的罪过也在不停地增长，每天你身上都积累了更多上帝的怒火。洪水不停地上涨，积累了越来越多的力量，只有上帝的意愿才能挡住这不愿停止、奋力前冲的水流。只要上帝收回他放在水闸上的手，洪水立刻就会一泻而出，上帝凶猛的怒气形成的暴烈洪水就会在无法想象的狂怒中冲刷而过，带着无所不能的力量向你扑来。即使你有比现在大一万倍的力量，是啊，即使你的力量比地狱里最强壮最有力的魔鬼的力量还大一万倍，你也根本无法抵挡或经受住上帝的怒气。

上帝愤怒的弓已经拉开，箭在弦上，正义的审判把箭瞄准了你的心窝，绷紧了弓弦。上帝，一个愤怒的上帝，对你根本没有做出任何承诺也没有任何义务的上帝，只有他的意愿才能使那箭头迟一刻喝到你的鲜血。因此，你们中间所有不曾因为灵魂受到上帝全能的精神力量影响而在心灵上产生巨大变化的人，所有

布道者画像

不曾重生而成为新人，不曾从罪恶的死亡中重新站起，达到新的境界，面对前所未有的光明和生活的人，你们都在愤怒的上帝手中。然而，你本来可以在很多方面重塑你的生活，可以拥有对宗教的爱，可以在你的家庭里和你的小屋里保持一种形式的宗教信仰，因为在上帝的房子里，只有他的意愿才能使你远离被永恒的毁灭吞噬的那一刻。无论现在你怎样不相信你所听到的真理，慢慢地你会对它坚信不疑的。

那些曾经和你处在同样的情况下但已经离去的人，在他们自己身上验证了这真理。因为毁灭突然降临到他们中的大多数人身上，而他们根本没有任何预感，还在说着：和平和安全。现在他们明白了，他们赖以获得和平和安全的那些事情只不过是稀薄的空气和空洞的影子而已。

上帝使你悬在地狱的大坑上方，就像一个人拿着一只蜘蛛或惹人讨厌的虫子放在火焰上方一样，他厌弃你，并且被你激怒了。他对你的怒气像火焰一样燃烧，在他眼里，你一文不值，他的眼睛纯净得不容你留在他视野之内，在他看来你比我们眼中最可恨的毒蛇还要讨厌一万倍……

哦，罪人！想想你正身处其中的可怕的危险吧：你在那上帝的手中，身下是充满怒火的大火炉，一个宽阔而又深不见底的深渊，而上帝正满含着对你的怒气，就好像他对地狱里受诅咒的人满含怒气一样。你被吊在一根纤细的丝线上，愤怒的火苗在它周围蹿腾，随时准备把它烤焦，烧成灰烬。而你不认识任何可以居中调停的人，抓不住任何可以拯救你自己的东西，没有什么能为你挡开那愤怒的火焰，你什么也没有，什么也不曾做过，也不能再做什么，能使上帝多宽恕你一刻……

当上帝看到你的罪恶发展到不可言喻的极端，看到你所受的折磨远远超过你的承受力，看到你可怜的灵魂被碾碎并向下沉到无边的黑暗之中时，他不会对你有丝毫的怜悯，他不会克制自己怒气的发作，也绝不会放松他手掌的重压。你不会得到任何缓和或仁慈，到那时上帝也不会再延缓他的狂风。他不会考虑你的感受，也不会因为怕你在任何其他感觉方面受太多折磨而变得小心谨慎，他只会注意不超出严格的审判所要求的对你的折磨……

上帝愿意怜悯你，这是仁慈的一天，有了能得到宽恕的鼓励，现在你可以痛哭了。但是一旦这仁慈的一天过去了，你最可怜最悲痛的哭泣和哀叫也将变得无济于事。你会完全迷失，得不到上帝的庇护，他也不再挂念你的幸福。除了让你遭受痛苦，上帝对你无法做出其他的安排，你将永远没有其他的结局。因为你会成为一个盛满怒火即将毁灭的容器，这个容器除了容纳怒火外没有别的用途……

因此，如果你执迷不悟的话，那么你自己就决定了一直停留在这种毫不转变的状态里。全能的上帝的无限的力量、权威和暴烈都会在你身上放大，并体现在你遭受的无法形容的巨大折磨中。你将在天使和基督的面前遭受折磨，每次你经受痛苦的时候，天堂里的居民都要来到你面前注视这可怕的情景，这样他们就能看到全能的上帝的怒气和威力，在他们亲眼目睹了这一切之后，他们就会俯下身躯，对那伟大的力量和权威顶礼膜拜……

全能的上帝的这种狂暴和怒火即使只经受一刻也很可怕，而你却要永远遭受它的折磨。这种强烈的可怕的痛苦将永无止境。当你向前望去的时候，你会看到在你面前的是漫长的永无止境的忍耐，它们将吞噬你的思想、麻木你的灵魂，你会完全绝望，不再期待任何释放、结束、缓和、甚至休息……

清教会众前往教堂

那些每天每小时都有危险遭受这种巨大怒气和无限痛苦的人的情况是多么可怕啊！然而这的确是这里没有经过重生的每一个会众面对的凄凉景象，无论他们在其他方面是多么道德和严格，多么审慎和认真，都无法改善这一情况。哦，还有你会想到的，无论你是年轻还是年老，情况也没什么不同！……你们当中有些人一直保持自然状态到最终，虽然这种状态能使你们最长时间地离开地狱，但没多久你们也就会到那里去了！你们被诅咒下地狱的时间不会停滞不前，它会飞快地到来，以各种可能性突然地降临到你们中很多人的身上。你有理由奇怪你为什么现在还没在地狱里。毫无疑问，这就是你见过的和认识的一

些人的情况，他们不比你更应该下地狱，在那之前看起来也像你一样本可以活到现在。他们的情况就是失去了所有的希望，他们在极度的痛苦和完全的绝望中哭泣。但是在这里，你正在活人的世界里，在上帝的房子里，有一个得到拯救的机会。那些可怜的受诅咒而毫无希望的灵魂会怎样不惜一切代价来换取像你现在拥有的这样一天的机会啊！

现在你就有了一个非同寻常的机会。在这一天，基督把仁慈之门大开，站在门口对可怜的罪人们大声召唤和呼喊；在这一天，许多人聚集到他身边，涌入了上帝的国度。每天都有很多人从东方、西方、南方和北方到这里来，很多人都处在和你们一样的悲惨情况的晚期，而现在他们生活幸福，心里充满了对一个人的热爱，那个人爱过他们，用他自己的鲜血洗去了他们身上的罪孽，现在他们因为有希望得到上帝的庇护而欢欣鼓舞。在这样一天里落在别人的后面是多可怕的事啊！看着那么多其他的人纵情欢宴，而你却在不断憔悴死去！看着那么多人为心中的欢乐而雀跃欢歌，而你却在为心中的痛苦而哀悼，为精神的烦恼而悲号！……

因此，让每个不受上帝庇护的人都觉醒过来，远离那怒火来加入我们。毫无疑问，现在全能的上帝的怒火正笼罩在这些会众中的一大部分人头上：让每个人都逃离萨德姆城吧。“赶快逃命，不要回头看，一直逃到山上，以免你被毁灭。”

文学和生活

读者反应 如果你听到爱德华兹的这次布道，你会有什么样的反应？

日志写作 你认为像爱德华兹那样的惊吓方法是改变人们行为的有效办法吗？当你在日志中回答这个问题的时候，想一想爱德华兹在他的会众身上产生的影响。

主题焦点 在“大觉醒”运动的15年中，在他的会众反对他的保守信仰并免去他的职务之前，爱德华兹成功地使成千上万的人皈依了清教。你认为爱德华兹的观点和方法在今天能成功吗？

阅读理解

1. 根据文章的第一段，是什么能使罪人们不堕入地狱？

2. 描述出至少两个爱德华兹用来比喻上帝的怒火的形象。

3. (a)在布道快要结束时，爱德华兹说罪人们能得到什么？(b)为了得到这个，他们必须做什么事情？

思考

解释

1. 你认为爱德华兹为什么从对地狱的描述来开始这部分布道？(推断)

2. (a)对“怒火”这个词的重复运用产生了什么影响力？(b)上帝怒火的象征和形象怎样加强了这种影响力？(分析)

评价

3. 爱德华兹的布道和他布道的方式对现代的听众会同样有效吗？为什么？(评价；论据支持)

应用

4. 在什么情况下(如果有这种情况的话)利用恐惧来使一个人改善自己的行为是合理的方法？为你的回答做出解释。(假设)

文学聚焦

布道

乔纳森•爱德华兹经常用布道的形式拯救人们。布道是在一次宗教仪式的过程中从布道坛上发出，有确定观点的演讲。

1. 爱德华兹在这次布道里传达的是什么观点或信息？

2. (a)在努力激励他的听众时，他试图激起他们心中的哪种情感？(b)考虑到爱德华兹的目的，这是一种合适的选择吗？为你的回答做出解释。

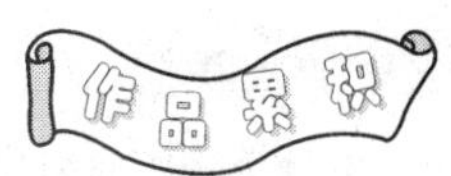

点子库

写作

1. 写日记　假设你是克奈克提卡特，恩菲尔德的一名虔诚的会众。在一

篇日记中描述你在听完爱德华兹整整六个小时的布道后的感受。

2. 新闻报道　在爱德华兹公开指出他认为在宗教信仰上达不到标准的会众之后，他作为北安普顿的牧师被解职。写一篇新闻来报道他的解职及其原因。（媒体连线）

3. 公开信　作为爱德华兹，写一封公开信，为导致你解职的行为做出辩解。解释你公开指责会众的原因。

项目

1. 电视广告　做一个广告来说服人们采取一种更健康的生活方式。在你把广告演示给你的同学时，加入音乐或声音效果。（媒体连线）

2. 清教徒手册　收集关于清教徒信仰的资料，制成一本手册，收录作为一名合格的清教徒的生活和信仰的指南和规范。

微型写作课

说服力评价

一名演讲者应该根据听众和场合的不同来选择不同的说服手段。在恩菲尔德，爱德华兹决定激发听众的情感。这是最好的选择吗？写下你对爱德华兹的说服技巧的评价。讨论他在他的听众中引起的回应和他用以获得这些回应的方法。他的方法是说服听众的合适有效的方法吗？为什么？如果在你的评价中，各部分能相辅相成，达到统一的效果，那么你的评价就会更加清楚有力。

写作技巧重点：统一

统一指的是达成同一个效果。当一篇写作的各元素和各部分表达同一个主旨观点的时候，这篇写作就是统一的。而当一个段落中的每句话都与一个主题相联系的时候，这个段落也就有了统一性。

请注意下面这个段落是怎样通过表达一个观点来支持整篇布道的主题。

布道中的范例

因此，让每个不受上帝庇护的人都觉醒过来，远离那怒火来加入我们。毫无疑问，现在全能的上帝的怒火正笼罩在这些会众中的一大部分人头上：让每个人都逃离萨德姆城吧。“赶快逃命，不要回头看，一直逃到山上，以免你被毁灭。”

构思

使用简洁的文字，在一篇定义清楚的叙述中总结爱德华兹的技巧和你对它们有效性的评价。

写稿

以你写下的叙述作为基础，写出一个有力而紧凑的开始段落。在接下来的段落中支持你的主旨观点。

修改

通读你的评价，就好像你是第一次读到一样。删去所有与主题无关的信息。

Guide for Interpreting

Jonathan Edwards (1703—1758)

Jonathan Edwards is so synonymous with "fire and brimstone"— a phrase symbolizing the torments of hell endured by sinners—that his name alone was e–nough to make many eighteenth–century Puritans shake in their shoes.

This great American theologian and powerful Puritan preacher was born in East Windsor, Connecticut, where he grew up in an atmosphere of devout discipline.

As a young boy, Edwards is said to have preached sermons to his playmates from a makeshift pulpit he built behind his home.

A brilliant academic, he learned Latin, Greek, and Hebrew by the age of twelve, entered Yale at thirteen, and graduated four years later as class valedic–torian. He went on to earn his master's degree in theology.

<u>A Preacher Born and Raised</u> Edwards began his preaching career in 1727 as assistant to his grandfather, Solomon Stoddard, pastor of the church at Northampton, Massachusetts, one of the largest and wealthiest congregations in the Puritan world. Edwards also preached as a visiting minister throughout New England. Strongly desiring a return to the orthodoxy and fervent faith of the Puri–tan past, he became a leader of the Great Awakening, a religious revival that swept the colonies in the 1730's and 1740's.

<u>Changing Attitudes</u> The Great Awakening did not last, however, and in 1750 Edwards was dismissed from his position after his extreme conservatism alienated much of the congregation. He continued to preach and write until his death in 1758, shortly after becoming president of the College of New Jersey (now Princeton University). Edwards's highly emotional sermon "Sinners in the Hands

of an Angry God" is by far his most famous work. It was delivered to a congregation in Enfield, Connecticut, in 1741, and it is said to have caused listeners to rise from their seats in a state of hysteria.

Background for Understanding

HISTORY: EDWARDS IN THE PULPIT

You would never guess from looking at the intimidating cover of this contemporary reprint that Edwards preached this "fire and brimstone" sermon in a speaking style that was quiet and restrained. According to one account, he read the six-hour sermon in a level voice, staring over the heads of his congregation at the bell rope that hung against the back wall "as if he would stare it in two." In spite of his calm demeanor, his listeners are said to have groaned and screamed in terror.

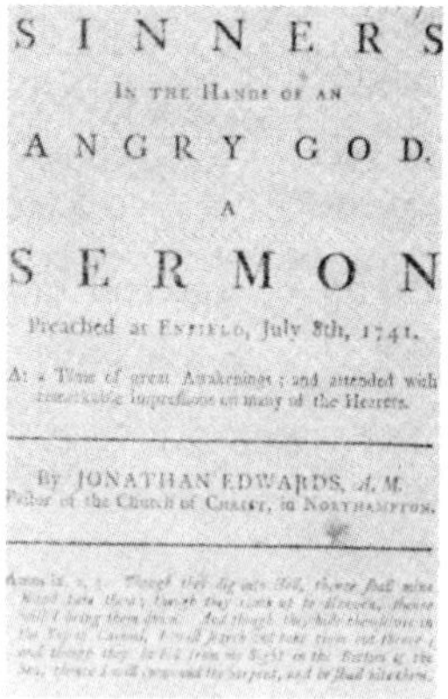
SINNERS
IN THE HANDS OF AN
ANGRY GOD.
A
SERMON
Preached at ENFIELD, July 8th, 1741.
At a Time of great Awakenings; and attended with remarkable Impressions on many of the Hearers.
By JONATHAN EDWARDS, A.M.
Pastor of the Church of CHRIST, in NORTHAMPTON.

Edwards reportedly had to stop several times and ask for silence. Without once resorting to dramatic techniques, he was able to build religious emotion to a fever pitch through effective use of vivid imagery and repetition of his main points.

Literature and your Life

CONNECT YOUR EXPERIENCE

Suppose your younger brother is involved with the "wrong crowd." Perhaps all you can do to get him back on track is paint a bleak picture of the awful future that may await him if he doesn't turn himself around. Jonathan Edwards had the same concerns about his fellow worshipers. He believed many were walking a path of certain destruction, and he desperately wanted to turn them toward repentance and heaven. Edwards achieved his goal by filling his sermons with terrifying descriptions of the horrors that awaited those who did not mend their ways.

<u>Journal Activity</u> Think about why Edwards might have chosen to use a

quiet, level tone rather than a more dramatic or emotional delivery. Explain why you think listeners might find a quiet style even more terrifying than an overly dramatic one.

THEMATIC FOCUS: THE PURITAN INFLUENCE

Is "scaring them straight" an effective way to change people's behavior for the better?

Literary Focus

SERMON

Though often associated with stern lectures or "fire and brimstone" speeches like this one, sermons can also be instructional or inspiring. A sermon is broadly defined as a speech given from a pulpit in a house of worship, usually as part of a religious service. Like its written counterpart, the essay, a sermon expresses the message or point of view its author wishes to convey to his or her audience, called a congregation. The sermon flourished as a popular literary form in colonial America.

Sinners in the Hands of an Angry god

Jonathan Edwards

This is the case of every one of you that are out of Christ: That world of misery, that lake of burning brimstone, is extended abroad under you. There is the dreadful pit of the glowing flames of the wrath of God; there is Hell's wide gaping mouth open; and you have nothing to stand upon, nor anything to take hold of; there is nothing between you and Hell but the air; it is only the power and mere pleasure of God that holds you up.

You probably are not sensible of this; you find you are kept out of Hell, but do not see the hand of God in it; but look at other things, as the good state of your bodily constitution, your care of your own life, and the means you use for your own preservation. But indeed these things are nothing; if God should withdraw his hand, they would avail no more to keep you from falling than the thin air to hold up a person that is suspended in it.

Your wickedness makes you as it were heavy as lead, and to tend downwards with great weight and pressure towards Hell; and if God should let you go, you would immediately sink and swiftly descend and plunge into the bottomless gulf, and your healthy constitution, and your own care and prudence, and best contrivance, and all your righteousness, would have no more influence to uphold you and keep you out of Hell, than a spider's web would have to stop a fallen rock. Were it not for the sovereign pleasure of God, the earth would not bear you one moment... The world would spew you out, were it not for the sovereign hand of Him who hath subjected it in hope. There are black clouds of God's wrath now hanging directly over your heads, full of the dreadful storm, and big with thunder; and were it not for the restraining hand of God, it would immediately burst forth upon you. The sovereign pleasure of God, for the present, stays his rough wind; otherwise it would come with fury, and your destruction would come like a whirlwind, and you would be like the chaff of the summer threshing floor.

The wrath of God is like great waters that are dammed for the present; they increase more and more, and rise higher and higher, till an outlet is given; and the longer the stream is stopped, the more rapid and mighty is its course, when once it is let loose. It is true, that judgment against your evil works has not been executed hitherto; the Hoods of God's vengeance have been withheld; but your guilt in the meantime is constantly increasing, and you are every day treasuring up more wrath; the waters are constantly rising, and waxing more and more mighty; and there is nothing but the mere pleasure of God, that holds the waters back, that are unwilling to be stopped, and press hard to go forward. If God should only withdraw his hand from the floodgate, it would immediately fly open, and the fiery floods of the fierceness

and wrath of God, would rush forth with inconceivable fury, and would come up–on you with omnipotent power; and if your strength were ten thousand times greater than it is, yea, ten thousand times greater than the strength of the stoutest, sturdiest devil in Hell, it would be nothing to withstand or endure it.

The bow of God's wrath is bent, and the arrow made ready on the string, and justice bends the arrow at your heart, and strains the bow, and it is nothing but the mere pleasure of God, and that of an angry God, without any promise or obligation at all, that keeps the arrow one moment from being made drunk with your blood. Thus all you that never passed under a great change of heart, by the mighty power of the spirit of God upon your souls; all you that were never born again, and made new creatures, and raised from being dead in sin, to a state of new, and before altogether unexperienced light and life, are in the hands of an angry God. However you may have reformed your life in many things, and may have had religious affections, and may keep up a form of religion in your families and closets. and in the house of God, it is nothing but His mere pleasure that keeps you from being this moment swallowed up in everlasting destruction. How–ever unconvinced you may now be of the truth of what you hear, by and by you will be fully convinced of it.

Those that are gone from being in the like circumstances with you, see that it was so with them; for destruction came suddenly upon most of them; when they expected nothing of it, and while they were saying, peace and safety: now they see, that those things on which they depended for peace and safety, were nothing but thin air and empty shadows.

The God that holds you over the pit of Hell, much as one holds a spider, or some loathsome insect over the fire, abhors you, and is dreadfully provoked: his wrath towards you burns like fire; he looks upon you as worthy of nothing else, but to be cast into the fire; he is of purer eyes than to bear to have you in his sight; you are ten thousand times more abominable in his eyes, than the most hateful venomous serpent is in ours....

O sinner! Consider the fearful danger you are in: it is a great furnace of wrath, a wide and bottomless pit, full of the fire of wrath, that you are held over in the hand of that God, whose wrath is provoked and incensed as much against you, as against many of the damned in Hell. You hang by a slender thread, with the flames of divine wrath flashing about it, and ready every moment to singe it, and burn it asunder; and you have no interest in any mediator, and nothing to lay hold of to save yourself, nothing to keep off the flames of wrath, nothing of your own, nothing that you ever have done, nothing that you can do, to induce God to spare you one moment....

When God beholds the ineffable extremity of your case, and sees your torment to be so vastly disproportioned to your strength, and sees how your poor soul is crushed, and sinks down, as it were, into an infinite gloom; he will have no compassion upon you, he will not forbear the executions of his wrath, or in the least lighten his hand; there shall be no moderation or mercy, nor will God then at all stay his rough wind; he will have no regard to your welfare, nor be at all careful lest you should suffer too much in any other sense, than only that you shall not suffer beyond what strict justice requires....

God stands ready to pity you; this is a day of mercy; you may cry now with some encouragement of obtaining mercy, But once the day of mercy is past, your most lamentable and dolorous cries and shrieks will be in vain; you will be wholly lost and thrown away of God, as to any regard to your welfare. God will have no other use to put you to, but to suffer misery; you shall be continued in being to no other end; for you will be a vessel of wrath fitted to destruction; and there will be no other use of this vessel, but to be filled full of wrath....

Thus it will be with you that are in an unconverted state, if you continue in it; the infinite might, and majesty,

and terribleness of the omnipotent God shall be magnified upon you, in the ineffable strength of your torments. You shall be tormented in the presence of the holy angels, and in the presence of the Lamb, and when you shall be in this state of suffering, the glorious inhabitants of Heaven shall go forth and look on the awful spectacle, that they may see what the wrath and fierceness of the Almighty is; and when they have seen it, they will fall down and adore that great power and majesty....

It would be dreadful to suffer this fierceness and wrath of Almighty God one moment; but you must suffer it to all eternity. There will be no end to this exquisite horrible misery. When you look forward, you shall see a long forever, a boundless duration before you, which will swallow up your thoughts and amaze your soul; and you will absolutely despair of ever having any deliverance, any end, any mitigation, any rest at all....

How dreadful is the state of those that are daily and hourly in the danger of this great wrath and infinite misery! But this is the dismal case of every soul in this congregation that has not been born again, however moral and strict, sober and religious, they may otherwise be. Oh that you would consider it, whether you be young or old! ...Those of you that finally continue in a natural condition, that shall keep you out of Hell longest will be there in a little time! Your damnation does not slumber; it will come swiftly, and, in all probability, very suddenly upon many of you. You have reason to wonder that you are not already in Hell. It is doubtless the case of some whom you have seen and known, that never deserved Hell more than you, and that heretofore appeared as likely to have been now alive as you. Their case is past all hope; they are crying in extreme misery and perfect despair; but here you are in the land of the living and in the house of God, and have an opportunity to obtain salvation. What would not those poor damned hopeless souls give for one day's opportunity such as you now enjoy!

And now you have an extraordinary opportunity, a day wherein Christ has thrown the door of mercy wide open, and stands in calling and crying with a loud voice to poor sinners; a day wherein many are flocking to him, and pressing into the kingdom of God. Many are daily coming from the east, west, north and south;

many that were very lately in the same miserable condition that you are in, are now in a happy state, with their hearts filled with love to him who has loved them, and washed them from their sins in his own blood, and rejoicing in hope of the glory of God. How awful is it to be left behind at such a day! To see so many others feasting, while you are pining and perishing! To see so many rejoicing and singing for joy of heart, while you have cause to mourn for sorrow of heart, and howl for vexation of spirit! ...

Therefore, let everyone that is out of Christ now awake and fly from the wrath to come. The wrath of Almighty God is now undoubtedly hanging over a great part of this congregation: let everyone fly out of Sodom. “Haste and escape for your lives, look not behind you, escape to the mountain, lest you be consumed.”

第2部分

Unit Two

A Nation Is Born

国家的诞生

时代故事

1750—1800

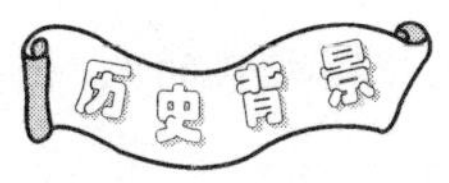

人们很容易忘记美国最早的13个州作为殖民地的时间有多长。到1750年为止，在弗吉尼亚和新英格兰生活的已是第四代和第五代欧裔美国人。总体来说，他们对英国臣民的地位还是相当满意。事实上，直到18世纪60年代早期，还没有几个美国人想到过独立的可能性。

然而，在18世纪60年代中期和70年代中期之间，人们的态度突然转变了。英王乔治三世和国会将一系列威胁殖民地人民自由的法令强加在他们身上，美国民众的愤怒随着每条法令的相继颁布而增长，最后终于爆发了战争。

理性时代 历史上的剧变总是发生在时机成熟的时候。美国革命就是这样一次剧变，欧洲作家、思想家与英王、国会共同奠定了革命的基础。18世纪经常被描绘为“启蒙时代”，或者“理性时代”。在很多17世纪的思想大师——例如科学家伽利略和伊萨克·牛顿爵士，哲学家伏尔泰和让·雅克·卢梭，政治理论家约翰·洛克——的作品的鼓舞下，启蒙时代的作家和思想家认为理性高于一切。与清教徒不同，他们并不关心来世，而是相信理性和科学具有推动人类进步的力量。他们谈论一个构成政府基础的社会契约。最重要的是，他们相信人性本善，而不是邪恶的。对于他们来说，完美社会并不只是一个空洞的梦想。

革命时期的美国政治家们本身就是启蒙时代的代表人物。如果不提及本杰明·富兰克林、托马斯·潘恩和托马斯·杰弗逊的思想和作品，那么这个时代的历史就不会完整。这些美国人不仅表达了理性时代的思想，而且在将这些思想付诸实践的伟大过程中作出了贡献。

武器的铿锵声 在美国革命之前发生了法印战争，这是英法之间为了争夺对北美洲的控制权而进行的一场斗争。这场战争于1754年爆发，持续了将近十年。1763年，官方正式宣布战争结束，战败的法国放弃了对北美洲领土的控制权。13个英国殖民地充满了欢庆的气氛。

然而，这种良好的感觉只持续了很短的时间。英国政府希望通过增加殖民地的税收来偿还战争中所欠的债务，因此于1765年通过了《印花税法案》。这个法案要求人们购买54种日常生活物品时加贴印花税票，殖民地的人民对此做出了迅速强烈的反应。他们烧毁了印花税票，殴打出售印花税票的人，并且毁掉了他们的店铺。最终，《印花税法案》被废止了。

其他的法令和反应也接踵而来。1767年通过的《汤森税法》对纸张、颜料、玻璃、铅和茶叶征税。当殖民地人民组织起来联合反抗时，英国政府解散了马萨诸塞立法院并将两个团的英国士兵派到波士顿。1770年，这些“红制服”士兵向一群嘲弄他们的民众开枪，导致五人死亡。这次被称为“波士顿大屠杀”的事件进一步激起了殖民地人民的激愤。英国国会废止了《汤森税法》中规定的税收，只保留了茶叶税，然而很快又通过了一个单独的《茶叶法案》，实际上使英国公司拥有了对茶叶的垄断。一群愤怒的波士顿人装扮成莫霍克人，把一船茶叶倒进了波士顿港湾里。作为对这次波士顿倾茶事件的惩罚，国会通过了一系列“强制法案”。因为这些法案关闭了波士顿港，禁止除年度市镇聚会以外的集会，并且坚持让英国军队驻扎到殖民地人民的家里，殖民地人民立刻称之为“不可容忍的法案”。

印刷机在反英国殖民者运动中扮演着重要的角色

1774年9月，虽然并没有公开谈及独立，然而殖民地的领导人聚集在费城，召开了“第一届大陆会议”。英国人知道自己的权威正在慢慢失去，因此指派托马斯·盖治将军就任马萨诸塞的州长。战争的舞台搭建起来了。

“传遍世界的枪声” 1775年4月19日，700名英国士兵在莱克星顿的草地上与大约70名殖民地民兵相遇。一声滑膛枪声响起（没人知道是从哪一方发出的），接着是一阵枪声，枪战中8名民兵倒地身亡。然后英国军队向西行进到康克尔德，在那里又发生了一次遭遇战。

在莱克星顿和康克尔德的两次遭遇战作为美国历史上的一个里程碑，被称做“传遍世界的枪声”。美国革命就这样开始了，没有任何挽回的余地。

一年多以后，殖民地才宣布独立。经过6年的激战，1781年10月19日，这场战争最后在弗吉尼亚的约克镇走到了尾声。华盛顿将军的军队得到了法国陆军和海军的帮助，并且征募了黑人士兵，这支军队包围了由康华里将军率领的8000人的英国军队。康华里将军看到已经没有逃跑的可能，于是投降了。

新的国家 然而，自治之路并不总是畅通无阻的。革命战争以后，《邦联条例》在新的各州之间建立了一个“友谊同盟”，但是这种安排并没有取得好的效果。后来的《联邦宪法》取代了《邦联条例》，这个《联邦宪法》要求很多折中方案，经过长期的斗争之后才得到了认可。

甚至到了那时候，还必须附加一个《权利法案》，来安抚那些害怕《宪法》带来中央集权的人们。

前期的革命者们坚持了原则，继续履行着他们的公众职责。乔治·华盛顿成为了这个国家的第一任总统。约翰·亚当斯——《独立宣言》的签署人之一，是他的继任。然后，在1800年，美国人选举了那个起草《独立宣言》的杰出政治家作为他们的总统，那就是托马斯·杰弗逊，启蒙时代的英雄之一。

抗议印花税法案

一个危机的时代 与新英格兰清教徒的个人对灵魂的探索相反，在美国革命时期创作的大部分作品都是公众写作。到独立战争的时候，在沿海城市里已经建立了近50所报社。华盛顿就职的时候，已经有了将近40份杂志，而年鉴在从马萨诸塞到佐治亚的地区都很流行。

那时整个国家的思想都聚焦在政治上。新闻工作者和印刷商们为思想的表达提供了一个论坛。1763年以后，那些思想越来越多地集中在与英国之间的关系上，更宽泛地说，集中在政府的性质上。正如这个单元中的文学作品所表明的，革命时期具有长远重要性的写作大多数都是政治作品。

作为文学的政治 在18世纪70年代和80年代这纷乱的20年中，美国政治家的公开写作和演讲不仅在重塑美国，而且在重塑世界的过程中发挥了作用。

帕特里克•亨利是一个极具吸引力的演说家，他在弗吉尼亚议院里所作的反对《印花税法案》的演讲使得有人大喊“叛国”！10年以后，他在弗吉尼亚大会上惊人的演讲表达了不断增长的渴望独立的情绪。

独立战争中的士兵

托马斯•潘恩可能在使公众观点倾向于独立的过程中发挥了最大的影响力。1776年出版的小册子《常识》席卷了整个殖民地，在3个月里卖出了10万册。

《独立宣言》是在1776年7月由托马斯•杰弗逊最早起草的。虽然一个包括本杰明•富兰克林在内的五人委员会也参与了宣言的起草，但最终完成的文件大部分都出自杰弗逊之手。除了其中对乔治三世的一些夸张的指控以外，《独立宣言》可以说是最具影响力的政治宣言之一。

革命时期产生的另一份经得起时间考验的重要文献，是1787年由一个委员会起草的《联邦宪法》。宪法的起草者为他们拥有400万人民的新国家深深感到骄傲，希望这份《宪法》能持续至少一代人的时间。结果，这份《宪法》仅仅经过27次修订，直到今天仍然是这个拥有50个州和超过两亿五千万人的超级大国的政治基础。

文化场景 虽然政治占据了革命时期的文学主流，但并不是所有知名作家都是政治家。诗歌出现在大多数的报纸上，无数单页歌谣得到了发表（单页歌谣指的是印在一张纸的单面或双面上的歌谣，谈论时事话题）。最流行的一首单页歌谣是《垂死的红制服》，根据人们的猜测，这是一名在革命战争中受了致命伤的英国军士写的。

那时的另外两名诗人是乔尔•巴罗和菲利斯•威特利，他们的作品比单页歌谣要成熟得多。巴罗是耶鲁大学1778年的毕业生，他最受人传诵的作品是《匆忙的布丁》，一首歌颂玉米粥的仿史诗颂辞。而菲利斯•威特利出生在非洲，她童年时作为一名奴隶被带到了波士顿，很早就表现出了她的文学天赋。她还是一名年轻女士时，她的一部诗集就被译成英文出版了。

另一名革命时期的作家记录了他对美国日常生活的印象，他就是米歇尔•纪饶姆•克雷弗括尔。他出生在一个法国贵族家庭，后来成为了一名雇佣兵、环游世界的旅行者和农夫。在15年的时间里，他在纽约的奥兰治县拥有一个种植园。他于1782年在伦敦发表了描写对那里生活印象的书——《一个美国农民的来信》。

在那一时期政治领域以外最著名的写作可能就是本杰明•富兰克林的作品了。殖民地的大多数家庭都熟悉他的《穷理查德的年鉴》。作为一名政治家、印刷商、作家、发明家和科学家，富兰克林确实是"启蒙时代"之子。他的《自传》虽然只包括他的早期生活，但仍然被认为是所有语言中最优秀的自传作品之一。

文化与艺术 在革命时期，美国开始建立属于自己的文化本体。从纽约到查尔斯顿的各处都建起了剧院。战后，尤其是在南方，新建了很多大学。有几名卓越的画家活跃在殖民地和新成立的共和国，其中包括：约翰•星格尔顿•考普利、吉尔伯特•斯图亚特、约翰•特拉姆布尔和查尔斯•威尔森•皮勒。培森斯•莱特是殖民地著名的蜡像雕塑家，她在战前搬到了伦敦，并在那里成为一名革命间谍。在音乐方面，威廉姆•毕灵斯创作了《新英格兰圣歌手》和一系列爱国主义赞美诗。这是一个巨变的时代——一个战斗的时代——这个时

代的遗产同时具有文化性和政治性。

美国文学的黎明 到19世纪早期，美国已经有了一小部分可以引以为荣的本国文学了。美洲土著人通过自己的口头传颂贡献了令人难忘的诗歌和传说。清教徒写下了很多有力的自省性作品。而革命时期的政治家们则创作了那个时代的政治文献。还有几个诗人和散文家在年轻的共和国的文学中留下了永久的印记。然而，那时还没有重要的长篇小说或戏剧，现代的短篇小说也仍然有待创作。

但是，在18世纪即将结束的时候，为一个伟大的国家文学做准备的原材料已经就绪，等待着人们的使用。这个国家处在领土和人口急剧增长时期的开端，而这种增长在世界历史上是独一无二的。经过了几乎整整一个世纪，美国才停止了在阿巴拉契亚山外那片广阔丰富的大陆上的边境扩张。在那个世纪中，美国文学将要爆发出一种生命力，甚至连那些富有远见的国家创建者们也会对此感到吃惊。殖民地时期结束时，美国只有一小部分值得记住的文学作品，而到19世纪结束时，一批能够流传于世的作品已经产生了。

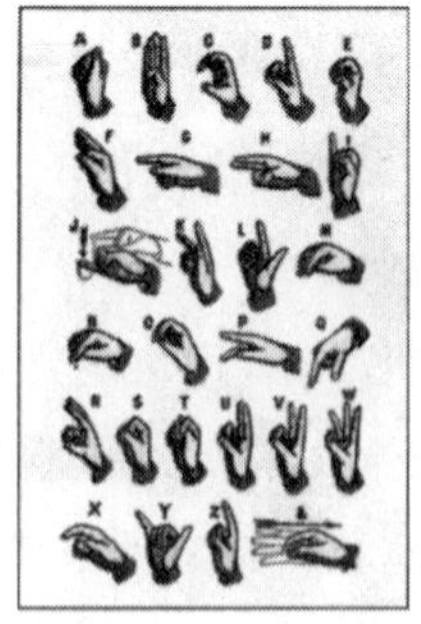

The Story of the Times
1750—1800

Historical Background

It is easy to forget how long the thirteen original states had been colonies. By 1750, there were fourth-and fifth-generation Americans of European descent living in Virginia and New England. These people were English subjects, and, on the whole, they were well satisfied with that status. In fact, as late as the early 1760's, few Americans had given much thought to the prospect of independence.

Between the mid-1760's and the mid-1770's, however, attitudes changed dramatically. King George III and Parliament imposed a number of regulations that threatened the liberties of the colonists. With each succeeding measure, the outrage in America grew, finally erupting into war.

The Age of Reason Great upheavals in history occur when circumstances are ripe. The American Revolution was such an upheaval, and the groundwork for it had been laid by European writers and thinkers as well as by the English king and Parliament. The eighteenth century is often characterized as the Enlightenment, or the Age of Reason. Spurred by the work of many seventeenth-century

thinkers — such as scientists Galileo and Sir Isaac Newton, philosophers Voltaire and Jean Jacques Rousseau, and political theorist John Locke, the writers and thinkers of the Enlightenment valued reason over faith. Unlike the Puritans, they had little interest in the hereafter, believing instead in the power of reason and science to further human progress. They spoke of a social contract that forms the basis of government. Above all, they believed that people are by nature good, not evil. A perfect society seemed to them to be more than just an idle dream.

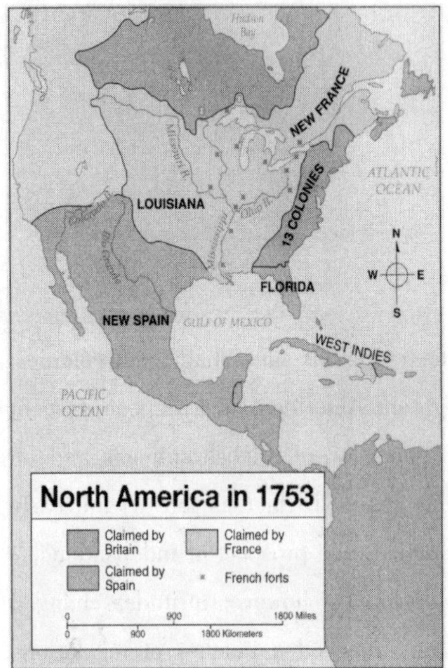

The American statesmen of the Revolutionary period were themselves figures of the Enlightenment. No history of the period would be complete without mention of the ideas and writings of Benjamin Franklin, Thomas Paine, and Thomas Jefferson. These Americans not only expressed the ideas of the Age of Reason, but they also helped to put them spectacularly into practice.

Toward a Clash of Arms The American Revolution was preceded by the French and Indian War, a struggle between England and France for control of North America. The conflict broke out in 1754 and continued for nearly a decade. When the war officially ended in 1763, defeated France gave up its claims to North American territory. There was general jubilation in the thirteen English colonies.

The good feelings were short-lived, however. The British government, wanting to raise revenue in the colonies to pay its war debt, passed the Stamp Act in 1765. Colonial reaction to the Stamp Act, which required the buying and affixing of stamps to each of 54 ordinary items, was swift and bitter. Stamps were burned. Stamp distributors were beaten and their shops destroyed. Eventually, the Stamp Act was repealed.

Other acts and reactions followed.The Townshend Acts of 1767 taxed paper, paint, glass, lead, and tea.When the colonists organized a boycott, the British dissolved the Massachusetts legislature and sent two regiments of British troops to Boston. In 1770, these Red-coats fired into a taunting mob, causing five fatalities. This so-called Boston Massacre further inflamed colonial passions. Parliament repealed the Townshend duties except for the tax on tea, but a separate Tea Act giving an English company a virtual monopoly soon greeted the colonists.Furious, a group of Bostonians dressed as Mohawks dumped a shipment of tea into Boston harbor. As punishment for this Boston Tea Party, the English Parliament passed the Coercive Acts. Because they shut down the port of Boston, forbade meetings other than annual town meetings, and insisted that British troops could be housed in colonists' homes, colonists immediately dubbed these laws the Intolerable Acts.

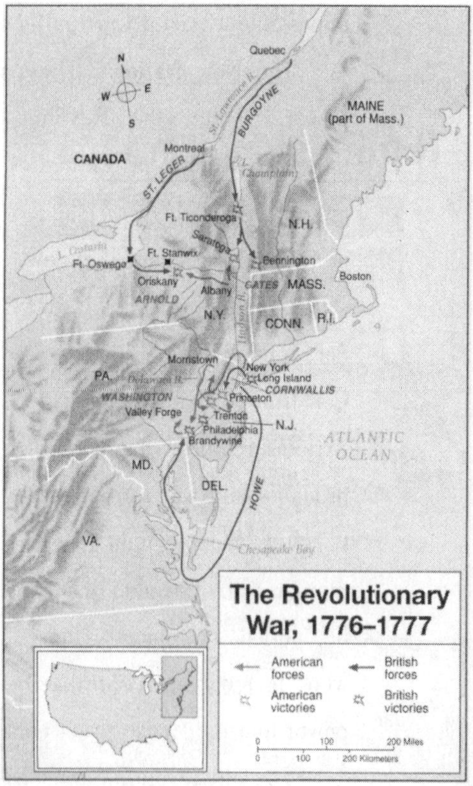

The Revolutionary War, 1776–1777

In September 1774, colonial leaders, although not speaking openly of independence, met in Philadelphia for the First Continental Congress. The British, their authority slipping away, appointed General Thomas Gage governor of Massachusetts. The stage was set for war.

"The Shot Heard Round the World" On April 19, 1775, 700 British troops met some 70 colonial minutemen on the Lexington green. A musket shot was fired (from which side, no one knows), and before the shooting that followed was over, eight Americans lay dead. The British marched west to Concord, where another skirmish took place. The encounters at Lexington and Concord, a landmark in American history, have been referred to as "the shot heard round the world." The American Revolution had begun, and there would be no turning back.

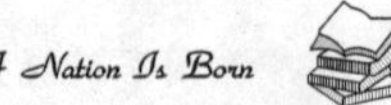

More than a year would pass before the colonies declared their independence. After six years of fighting, the war finally came to an end at Yorktown, Virginia, on October 19, 1781. Aided by the French army and the French navy, and enlisting the service of black soldiers, General Washington's army bottled up the 8,000-man British force under General Cornwallis. Seeing that escape was impossible, General Cornwallis surrendered.

The New Nation The path to self-government was not always Smooth, however. After the Revolution, the Articles of Confederation established a "league of friendship" among the new states. This arrangement did not work well. The federal Constitution that replaced the Articles required many compromises and was ratified only after a long fight. Even then, a Bill of Rights had to be added to placate those who feared the centralized power that the Constitution conferred.

The old revolutionaries, by and large, remained true to their principles and continued their public duties. George Washington became the nation's first president. John Adams, a signer of the Declaration of Independence, succeeded him in that office. Then, in 1800, Americans elected as their president the brilliant statesman who had drafted the Declaration, one of the heroes of the Enlightenment, Thomas Jefferson.

Literature of the Period

A Time of Crisis In contrast to the private soulsearching of the Puritans of

New England, much of what was produced during the Revolutionary period was public writing. By the time of the War for Independence, nearly fifty newspapers had been established in the coastal cities. At the time of Washington's inauguration, there were nearly forty magazines. Almanacs were popular from Massachusetts to Georgia.

The mind of the nation was on politics. Journalists and printers provided a forum for the expression of ideas. After 1763, those ideas were increasingly focused on relations with Great Britain and, more broadly, on the nature of government. As the literature presented in this unit testifies, the writing of permanent importance from the Revolutionary era is mostly political writing.

Politics as Literature The public writing and speaking of American statesmen in two tumultuous decades, the 1770's and 1780's, helped to reshape not only the nation but also the world.

Patrick Henry was a spellbinding orator whose speech against the Stamp Act in the Virginia House of Burgesses brought cries of "Treason!" Ten years later, his electrifying speech to the Virginia Convention expressed the rising sentiment for independence.

Thomas Paine was perhaps more influential than any other in swaying public opinion in favor of independence. His 1776 pamphlet Common Sense swept the colonies, selling 100,000 copies in three months.

The Declaration of Independence was first drafted by Thomas Jefferson in June 1776. The finished document is largely his work, although a committee of five statesmen, including Benjamin Franklin, was involved in its creation. The Declaration, despite some exaggerated charges against King George III, is one of the most influential political statements ever made.

Another revolutionary period document written by committee that has stood the test of time is the Constitution of the United States, drafted in 1787. The framers, whose new nation boasted about four million people, hoped that the Constitution would last at least a generation. It still survives, amended only 27 times, as the political foundation of a superpower of 50 states and more than 250 million people.

The Cultural Scene While politics dominated the literature of the Revolutionary period, not every writer of note was a statesman. Verse appeared in most of the newspapers, and numerous broadside ballads were published. (A broadside ballad is a single sheet of paper, printed on one or both sides, dealing with a current topic.) One of the most popular broadside ballads was called "The Dying Redcoat", supposedly written by a British sergeant mortally wounded in the Revolution.

Two other poets of the day whose works were more sophisticated than the broadside ballads were Joel Barlow and Phillis Wheatley. Barlow, a 1778 Yale graduate, is best remembered for "The Hasty Pudding," a mock-heroic tribute to cornmeal mush. Phillis Wheatley, born in Africa and brought to Boston in childhood as a slave, showed early signs of literary genius. A collection of her poems was published in England while she was still a young woman.

Another writer of the Revolutionary period recorded his impressions of everyday American life. Born into an aristocratic French family, Michel Guillaume Crevecoeur became a soldier of fortune, a world traveler, and a farmer. For fifteen years, he owned a plantation in Orange County, New York, and his impressions of life there were published in London in 1782 as Letters From an American Farmer.

Perhaps the best-known writing of the period outside the field of politics was done by Benjamin Franklin. His Poor Richard's Almanack became familiar to most households in the colonies. A statesman, printer, author, inventor, and scientist, Franklin was a true son of the Enlightenment. His Autobiography, covering only his early years, is regarded as one of the finest autobiographies in any language.

<u>Culture and Art</u> During the Revolutionary period, America began to establish a cultural identity of its own. Theaters were built from New York to Charleston. A number of new colleges were established after the war, especially in the South. Several outstanding painters were at work in the colonies and the young republic. Among them were John Singleton Copley, Gilbert Stuart, John Trumbull, and Charles Willson Peale. Patience Wright, famous in the colonies as a sculptor of wax portraits, moved to London before the war. While there, she acted as a Revolutionary spy. In music, William Billings produced The New England Psalm-Singer and a number of patriotic hymns. This was a turbulent time—a time of action—and its legacy was cultural as well as political.

<u>American Literature at Daybreak</u> By the early 1800's, America could boast a small body of national literature. The Native Americans had contributed haunting poetry and legends through their oral traditions. The Puritans had written a number of powerful, inward-looking works. The statesmen of the Revolutionary period had produced political documents for the ages. A few poets and essayists had made a permanent mark on the literature of the young republic. There were, however, no American novels or plays of importance, and the modern short story had yet to be invented.

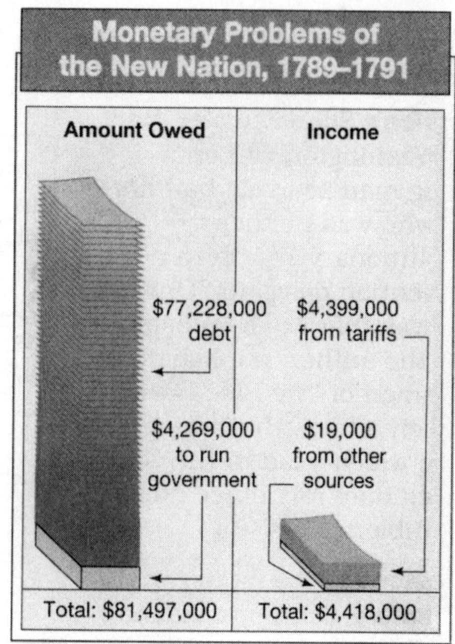

As the eighteenth century came to a close, however, the raw materials for a great national literature were at hand, waiting to be used. The nation stood on the threshold of a territorial and population explosion unique in the history of the world. It would take almost exactly a century to close the frontier on the

vast and varied continent beyond the Appalachians. During that century, American literature would burst forth with a vitality that might have surprised even the farsighted founders of the nation. The colonial age ended with a narrow volume of memorable literature. The nineteenth century would close with a library of works that form a major part of America's literary heritage.

第一课

富兰克林自传

本杰明·富兰克林 (1706—1790)

本杰明·富兰克林是最具体地表现了殖民地时期美国发展前途的美国人。凭着勤奋的工作、无私的奉献和智慧的心灵，富兰克林从贫穷中奋发，一跃成为一个富有、著名而又极富影响力的人。虽然他没有受过任何正规的教育，但他还是在文学、新闻、科学、外交、教育和哲学等各个领域作出了重要的贡献。

本杰明·富兰克林

早期生活 富兰克林出生在波士顿，他的家里一共有17个孩子，富兰克林10岁时离开了学校，在那以后他先为他的父亲工作了两年，然后就在他的哥哥——一名印刷商那里做了学徒。在富兰克林17岁的时候，他离开波士顿，去了费城，希望能开一家属于他自己的印刷店。在他奠定了作为一名印刷商的地位以后，富兰克林就开始创办一份报纸和一份名叫《穷理查德的年鉴》的年刊，在这份年刊里包

含了各种信息、评论和建议。这份《年鉴》出版于1731年至1757年期间，在当时非常流行，并使富兰克林获得了天才作家的名声。

科学人生　在富兰克林42岁时，他退出了印刷行业，并致力于科学研究。事实证明，作为科学家，他也和作为印刷商一样成功。在他的一生中，他发明了避雷针、双光眼镜和一种新型的炉子，确立了电学理论，并且对地震和洋流的科学理解作出了贡献。虽然有这些成就，但富兰克林最值得纪念的还是他的政治事业。

政治家和外交家　富兰克林在下列事件中都发挥了重要的作用：起草《独立宣言》，为法国革命战争提供援助，与英国商订和平条约，起草《美国宪法》。在他晚年，他先后出任美国驻英国和法国的大使。

甚至在华盛顿之前，富兰克林就被认为是"国家之父"。

故事背后的故事　1771年，富兰克林在65岁的时候写了他的自传的第一章，在朋友们的催促下，他又写了三章（最后一章在他逝世前不久完成），但也只将他的一生记录到了1757年至1759年。虽然他的自传并未完成，但其中包含的观点和建议不仅为人们提供了他的成就的记录，而且使人们了解了他的性格。

历史：富兰克林在费城

本杰明·富兰克林对殖民地时期费城的日常生活起到了极大的影响作用。他帮助建立了城里的公共图书馆和消防局，以及费城的第一所大学。此外，通过他的努力，费城还成为所有殖民地中第一个拥有路灯的城市。

在美国独立革命之前的时期，费城是一个重要的活动中心。宣布美国成为一个独立国家的《独立宣言》就是在这里写成并签署的。

在今天的费城，你仍然可以沿着鹅卵石路一边漫步一边参观历史遗迹。游客们和历史爱好者们只要步行就可以到达签署了《独立宣言》的"独立大厅"、"自由之钟"和贝西·罗斯的家。

联系你的经历　真实生活中的故事可以和任何虚构的戏剧故事一样令人激动。那么,畅销书的名单里经常包括名人的自传也就不是什么令人惊讶的事情了——因为我们想知道人们是怎样赢得名誉和应付困境的。诸如富兰克林之类的历史人物的自传也可以同样激动人心,因为通过他们,我们才有机会看到那些曾经塑造了我们现在世界的真实事件。

日志写作　如果你在准备写自己的自传,列出你打算选择描写的经历。

专题聚焦:自由的呼声　生活在美国独立革命时期的人们不仅仅想把英国政府赶出美国,他们还希望创造一种独特的美国生活方式。富兰克林在很多方面都足以代表"新美国人"。在他的《自传》中,他描述了想要改进完善自己的渴望,他写出自己的这个理想,来帮助别人跟随他的足迹。

自传　本杰明·富兰克林的《自传》为当时的这种新文体设定了标准。自传就是一个人对他/她自己生活的记录。自传一般以第一人称写作,作者作为"我"来讲述,所以自传是以作者的视角来表现生活中的事件。除了描述作者生活中的细节之外,自传还提供了对作者的信仰和观点的深刻了解。自传还能使人们看到作者所处的年代生活是什么样子。自传常常能提供你在历史书中无法找到的历史事件的真相。

富兰克林自传(节选)

本杰明·富兰克林

大约就在这个时候,我的脑子里酝酿了这个大胆而又艰巨的任务:达到道德上的完美境界。我希望在生活中任何时候都不犯错误,我要克服所有可能导致我犯错误的因素,无论是自然的倾向和习惯,还是我身边的人。根据我所知道的,或那时候我认为我所知道的,正确和错误的标准,我看不出为什么

做印刷工时的富兰克林

我不能一直遵循前者而同时避免后者。可是很快我就发现我承担的这个任务比我想象得更加困难。当我的注意力忙于戒备一个错误的时候，我经常因为犯了另外一个错误而大吃一惊。在我不注意的时候习惯就会占上风，而自然的倾向有时候比理智要强大得多。最后我得出了一个结论，那就是：仅仅在思想上坚信完全的道德对我们有好处，但并不足以能够阻止我们犯错误。因此我们必须先打破那些反面的习惯，养成并建立好习惯，然后才能有一种始终如一的正直品行让我们依靠。所以，为了达到这一目的，我设计了以下方法。

根据我在阅读中见到的各种列举的美德，我发现因为不同的作者在同一个名字下会包含或多或少的含义，所以这些列举的清单都比较长。比如说，“节制”这种美德，有些作者只把它限制在吃饭和饮酒的方面，而其他的作者则将它的含义扩展到对各种享受的节制，包括食欲、意愿或肉体和精神上的热爱，甚至还有我们的贪心和野心。为了清楚起见，我建议我自己多用一些美德的名字，每个名字上附加的意义少一点，而不能只用几个名字，但每个名字中有很多含义。于是我列出了13种当时我认为是必要的或值得拥有的美德，为每种美德附加了一句短短的准则，充分地表达了我为其规定的含义范围。

这些美德和它们的准则是：

1. 节制　食不可过饱，饮不得过量。
2. 沉默　避免无聊闲扯，言谈必须对人有益。
3. 秩序　生活物品要放置有序，工作时间要合理安排。
4. 果决　要做之事就下决心去做，决心做的事一定要完成。
5. 节俭　不得浪费，任何花费都要有益，不论是于人于己。
6. 勤劳　珍惜每一刻时间，去除一切不必要之举，勤做有益之事。
7. 真诚　不损害他人，不使用欺骗手段。考虑事情要公正合理，说话要依据真实情况。

8. 公正　不得损人利己，履行应尽的义务。

9. 适度　避免任何极端倾向，尽量克制报复心理。

10. 清洁　身体、衣着和居所要力求清洁。

11. 平静　戒除不必要的烦恼，即那些琐事、常见的和不可避免的不顺利的事情。

12. 纯洁　不纵欲，决不使身体虚弱，生活贫乏，不可损坏自己及他人的声誉或安宁。

13. 谦虚　以耶稣和苏格拉底为榜样。

我的目的是将所有这些美德习惯化，所以我认为不应该一次尝试所有的美德，因为这样会分散我的注意力，而是应该一次只将注意力集中在一种美德上，当我获得了这一种以后，就继续进行下一种的培养，以此类推，一直到我培养了所有的13种美德。因为有些先得到的美德可能会有助于其他一些美德的获得，所以我按照上面所示的顺序安排了这些美德。“节制”是第一个，它可以使人拥有冷静清楚的头脑，而这正是对我极其必要的，因为我要保持不断的警惕性，来防备旧习惯的持续吸引和反复不断的诱惑。在我获得并且养成这种美德之后，“沉默”就比较容易了。由于我希望在获取知识的同时能在道德上有所提高，并且考虑到在谈话中知识是利用耳朵而不是舌头来得到的，所以我希望能改掉闲聊、说双关语和开玩笑的习惯，因为这个习惯只能使我被那些琐屑而没有价值的人们接受。基于以上考虑，我把“沉默”排在了第二位。我希望这个美德和下面的“秩序”，能使我有更多的时间来专注于自己的工作和学习。而一旦“果决”成为习惯，我就能在获得下面的美德的努力过程中更加坚决。“节俭”和“勤劳”将使我从残留的债务中解脱出来，变得富裕和独立，这会使“真诚”和“公正”的实现更加容易，诸如此类，等等，等等。在我的思想中，我赞同皮萨格拉斯在他的“金色诗行”中提出的建议，那就是：每天的检查是必要的，所以我设计了下面的方法来进行每天的检查。

我做了一个小本，在这个本里我为每种美德分配了一页。我用尺子和红色的墨水在每一页中画出7列，每一列代表一周中的一天，用代表那一天的字母标明。我用13条红色的横线把这些列分开，在每一横行的开头标明一种美德的起始字母。在每一行和相应的列中，我会用一个小黑点来表示我在检查中发现的那一天我在那种美德上所犯的一个错误。

我决心依次对每种美德予以一周的严格注意。这样，在第一周里，我的全部注意力都在“节制”上，不容稍有违背，其他各项美德则平常对待，在晚上将日间疏漏标记即可。这样，如果在第一周里我能让标着“T”字的第一行里没有黑点，我想这种美德的习惯就得到了相当的加强，而与它相反的习惯则受到了减弱，那么我就敢于把我的注意力扩大到能包含下一种美德，在下一周中保持这两行里都没有黑点。如果这样一直继续到最后，我就能在13周里进行一轮完整的过程，在一年里进行4轮。这就像一个人要给一个花园除草，他不会尝试一次就根除所有的杂草，因为这超出了他的能力范围。他会一次只除一块地上的杂草，除完了第一块地里的杂草之后，再去除第二块地里的。因此，我希望我能通过依次使那些行里没有黑点，从那些页里看到我在道德上取得的进步，从而感到令人鼓舞的快乐，一直到最后，经过许多轮过程之后，我应该在13周每天的检查以后，高兴地看到一个干干净净的小本……

“秩序”的准则要求我的工作的每个部分都要有分配给它的固定时间，所以我的小本中有一页就列出了如下一天24小时中我的时间安排计划：

早晨	5	起床，洗漱，祈祷全能的上帝！计划一
问题：我今天要做什么	6	天的工作，做出一天的决定，继续进行当
好事？	7	前的学习，然后早餐。
	8	
	9	工作
	10	
	11	
中午	12	读书，或浏览我的记录，然后吃饭。
	1	
	2	
	3	工作
	4	
晚上	6	把东西归位。晚餐。音乐或娱乐，或谈话。
问题：我今天做了什么	7	一天的检查。
好事？	8	
	9	

	10	
	11	
	12	
夜	1	睡觉
	2	
	3	
	4	

我按照这个计划开始进行自我检查，在继续的过程中有时候有偶尔的中断。我惊讶地发现我所犯的错误比我以前想象的要多得多，但也很满意地看到它们在不断减少。因为我不停擦掉纸上旧的错误的记号，来为新的一轮中的新错误留出地方，我的小本上已经满是小洞了。为了避免更新小本的麻烦，我把我的美德列表和准则都转抄到了一本备忘录的象牙页上，又用能留下持久痕迹的红墨水画出行。在这些行里，我用一支黑色的铅笔标志出我犯的错误，这些标记我很容易就可以用一块湿海绵擦去。过了一段时间以后，我每一年就只进行一轮这样的过程。一直到最后，我因为忙于航行和国外的事务，有各种各样的事情妨碍我，所以我完全省去了这个过程，但是我仍然一直把我的小本带在身边。

我的关于“秩序”的计划给我带来了最多的麻烦。我发现，虽然当一个人从事的工作允许他安排自己的时间（例如一个熟练的印刷工人的工作）时，这种秩序是可行的，但对一个独立经营者来说，要精确地遵守秩序就是不可能的了，因为他必须和整个世界交往，并且根据与他有业务往来的人们各自的时间安排来接待他们。而就把物品和文件等放在固定的位置这方面的“秩序”而言，我发现这种习惯极难养成。我早先并没有这个习惯，而且由于我的超出常人的良好记忆力，我也并没意识到伴随着缺乏条理而产生的不便。因此，这一条使我花费了那么多痛苦的注意力，我在它上面犯的错误给我带来了那么多的苦恼，而我在改正时取得的进步又是那么少，并且是那么经常地故态复萌，以至于我几乎要放弃这个尝试，使自己就满足于一个在这方面有问题的性格了。就好像向我的邻居——一个铁匠——买斧子的人一样：他想要斧子的整个表面都像斧子刃一样亮，铁匠说如果这个人愿意转磨轮的话，铁匠就同意帮他把斧子磨亮。他就开始转了，因为铁匠用力把那斧子宽阔的表面重重地压在磨石上，所以转磨轮的工作非常累人。那个人不时从磨轮那里过来

看一看磨得怎么样了，最后他终于不愿再磨，而想就这样把斧子拿走。“别，”铁匠说，“继续转，继续转，我们慢慢就能把它磨亮了，就像现在，这上面只有一些小斑点了。”“是啊，”那个人说，“可是我认为我最想要的就是一把有斑点的斧子。”我相信可能很多人都会有这种情况，他们因为缺少类似我所利用的这样的方法，所以要养成好习惯、根除坏习惯非常困难。于是他们就放弃了努力，得出结论说：“一把有斑点的斧子是最好的。”有些东西伪装成理智的样子，时不时地对我建议说：我强求我自己达到这种极端的完美可能是一件道德上的蠢事，如果人们知道的话会认为我很荒谬；一个完美的人格可能会伴随着由于受到嫉妒和怨恨而带来的不便；一个善良的人应该允许自己身上存在一些错误，这样他的朋友们才能赞成他的举动。

事实上，我发现我自己在“秩序”这方面真的是积习难改，现在我老了，记忆力不好了，我深刻地感觉到了缺乏秩序的不便。然而，总体来说，虽然我从来没能达到我曾雄心勃勃地想要获得的完美境界，而是还差得很远，但是通过这些努力，我确实变得更好更快乐，而我如果没有尝试这样去做的话，我会远没有这样好这样快乐。就好像那些想通过模仿刻制的模子来获得完美的书法的人一样，经过这样的努力，他们的书法得到改善，变得漂亮和清晰，被人认为比较好了。

希望我的子孙们能知道，在上帝的保佑下，他们的祖先把他一生（一直到他79岁写成这篇自传的时候）的幸福快乐都归功于这个小小的技巧。至于在他余下的时间里会遭受什么挫折，那就是由命运掌握的了。但是，如果他受到挫折，过去幸福时光的回忆会帮助他更平静地忍受这些挫折。他把他长期的健康和现在仍然拥有的良好体格归功于“节制”；他早期自如的境况，财富的积累和所有使他成为一名有用的公民并在有学识的人中间为他获得一定声誉的知识，这些都归功于“勤劳”和“节俭”；国家对他的信任和赋予他的光荣的使命应归功于“真诚”和“公正”；而这些美德的共同

教友派会议

影响，即使是在他只能达到的不完美的境界，则使他拥有了平和的心境和令人快乐的谈话，这些使他深受身边的人们的欢迎，即使是他的年轻朋友也愿意与他相处。因此，我希望我的一些子孙能跟从这个范例，并从中受益。

文学和生活

读者反应 你对富兰克林的计划有什么看法？为什么？

主题焦点 自传反映它们写作的时代。富兰克林的《自传》中有哪些因素表现出本文写作于美国独立前夕？

小组活动 在一个小组内，做出一个美国人自身提高的计划。你会纳入哪些“美德”？比较富兰克林选择的美德和你小组做出的决定。

阅读理解

1. 用你自己的话来概述富兰克林达到道德完美境界的计划。

2. 解释富兰克林把“沉默”列入他的美德名单中的原因。

3. 在“秩序”这一美德下，富兰克林列出了一个基本的日常时间表。哪些是他每天都安排时间的活动？

4. 富兰克林计划中的哪个方面没有像他期望的那样发展？

思考

解释

1. 为什么富兰克林在文中讲述了买有斑点的斧子的人的故事？（分析）

2. 富兰克林对于达到道德完美境界的重要性的看法是怎样随时间变化的？（比较和对比）

3. 富兰克林认为他达到道德完美境界的努力所取得的长期收益是什么？（分析原因和结果）

应用

4. 分析的行为对个人的成长能够作出什么贡献？（综合）

拓展

5. 很多人都使用和富兰克林的每日活动安排表相似的日常计划。这样一个系统的好处有哪些？（工作连线）

文学聚焦

自传

自传是一个人写下的他自己一生的故事。因为作者的态度、思想和感情会影响他的自我描述，所以自传是主观的。例如，富兰克林对道德的理解就在这篇《自传》的节选中表现了出来。

1. 富兰克林表达了他性格的哪些方面？

2. 如果这不是由富兰克林写的，而是别人写的关于他的文章，那么这篇文章会有怎样的不同？

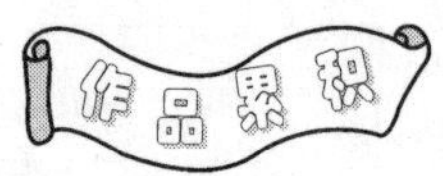

点子库

写作

1. 广告　为富兰克林的书写一条广告，登在费城的报纸上或出现在富兰克林的时代。

2. 个人改进计划　考虑几个你想要有所改进的方面，然后考虑你能做什么以便在这些方面取得改进。把你的想法在一份书面计划中写清。（健康连线）

3. 报告　《自传》对世人展示了富兰克林生活的一个侧面。将你从《自传》中所了解的内容与富兰克林作为一名政治家的事业进行比较。将你的发现写成一篇短论文。（社会研究连线）

项目

1. 海报　了解更多富兰克林在科学领域的成就。制作一张集中表现他的一些成就的海报。（社会连线）

2. 旅游指南　为到费城旅游的游客制作一本旅游指南。集中表现富兰克林的成就，并包含一些相关历史古迹的照片。

微型写作课

自传式叙述

任何人都可以写自传。你有大量的材料可供选择，包括：你的活动、友谊、家庭和学校里的事件，还有成功与失败。从你的生活中选择一次重要的经历，并写一篇关于这次经历的自传式叙述。写明为什么这个时刻值得纪念，你从中学到了什么。

写作技巧重点：表现因果关系

在你的叙述文中清楚地表现一次经历在你生活中产生的效果。注意富兰克林是怎样有意识地预期每种美德将会取得的效果的。

《自传》中的范例

而一旦"果决"成为习惯，我就能在获得下面的美德的努力过程中更加坚决。"节俭"和"勤劳"将使我从残留的债务中解脱出来，变得富裕和独立，这会使"真诚"和"公正"的实现更加容易，诸如此类，等等，等等。

构思

在头脑中列出一个你想要描写的经历的细节清单。注意发生了什么事情，你有什么感受和你可能学到了什么。尽可能包含最多的具体细节。

写稿

写出你的自传式叙述，纳入可以使读者们清楚了解这一事件及其重要性的细节。记得要表现这个事件或这次经历和你的生活之间的因果关系。使用例如"由于"、"如果……那么……"和"因此"之类的过渡词来向你的读者强调这个关系。

修改

在你作修改的时候，注意因果关系。如果一个过渡词可以使因果关系更清楚的话，就加上一个。

Guide for Interpreting

Benjamin Franklin (1706—1790)

No other colonial American more closely embodied the promise of America than Benjamin Franklin. Through hard work, dedication, and ingenuity, Franklin was able to rise out of poverty to become a wealthy, famous, and influential person. Although he never received a formal education, Franklin made important contributions in a variety of fields, including literature, journalism, science, diplomacy, education, and philosophy.

Early Years Franklin, one of seventeen children, was born in Boston. After leaving school at the age of ten, he spent two years working for his father before becoming an apprentice to his older brother, who was a printer. When he was seventeen, Franklin left Boston and traveled to Philadelphia, hoping to open his own print shop. Once he established himself as a printer, Franklin began producing a newspaper and an annual publication called Poor Richard's Almanack which contained information, observations, and advice. The Almanack, published from 1732 through 1757, was very popular and earned Franklin a reputation as a talented writer.

Man of Science When Franklin was forty-two, he retired from the printing business to devote himself to science. He proved to be as successful a scientist as he had been a printer. Over the course of his lifetime, Franklin was responsible for inventing the lightning rod, bifocals, and a new type of stove; confirming the laws of electricity; and contributing to the scientific understanding of earthquakes and ocean currents. In spite of all these achievements, Franklin is best remembered for his career in politics.

Statesman and Diplomat Franklin played an important role in drafting the

Declaration of Independence, enlisting French support during the Revolutionary War, negotiating a peace treaty with Britain, and drafting the United States Constitution. In his later years, he was ambassador first to England and then to France.

Even before Washington, Franklin was considered "the father of his country".

The Story Behind the Story Franklin wrote the first section of The Autobiography in 1771 at the age of sixty-five. At the urging of friends, he wrote three more sections—the last shortly before his death—but succeeded only in bringing the account of his life to the years 1757 to 1759. Though never completed, his Autobiography, filled with his opinions and suggestions, provides not only a record of his achievements but also an understanding of his character.

Background for Understanding

HISTORY: FRANKLIN IN PHILADELPHIA

Benjamin Franklin greatly influenced daily life in colonial Philadelphia. He helped establish the city's public library and fire department, as well as its first college. In addition, through his efforts Philadelphia became the first city in the colonies to have street lights.

Philadelphia was an important center of activity during the period leading up to the American Revolution. It was here that the Declaration of Independence, establishing the United States as an independent nation, was written and signed.

In Philadelphia today, you can still walk down cobblestone streets and visit historic sites. Independence Hall, where the Declaration of Independence was signed, the Liberty Bell, and the home of Betsy Ross are within walking distance for tourists and history enthusiasts.

Literature and your Life

CONNECT YOUR EXPERIENCE

Real-life stories can provide as much excitement as any fictional drama. It's not surprising, then, that bestseller lists frequently include the autobiographies of celebrities; we want to know how people have achieved fame and dealt with adversity. Autobiographies of historical figures, such as Franklin, can be equally gripping, allowing us a firsthand look at events that have helped shape our world.

Journal Writing List the experiences you would choose to write about if you were preparing an autobiography.

THEMATIC FOCUS: VOICES FOR FREEDOM

Beyond throwing out the British government, people living at the time of the American Revolution wanted to create a uniquely American way of life.In many ways, Franklin represents that new American.The Autobiography describes his desire to improve himself.He writes of this ambition to help others follow in his path.

Literary Focus

AUTOBIOGRAPHY

Benjamin Franklin's Autobiography set the standard for what was then a new genre. An autobiography is a person's account of his or her life. Generally written in the first person, with the author speaking as"I",autobiographies present life events as the writer views them. In addition to providing inside details about the writer's life, autobiographies offer insights into the beliefs and perceptions of the author.

Autobiographies also offer a glimpse of what it was like to live in the author's time period. Autobiographies often provide a view of historical events that you won't find in history books.

The Autobiography

Benjamin Franklin

It was about this time I conceived the bold and arduous project of arriving at moral perfection. I wished to live without committing any fault at any time; I

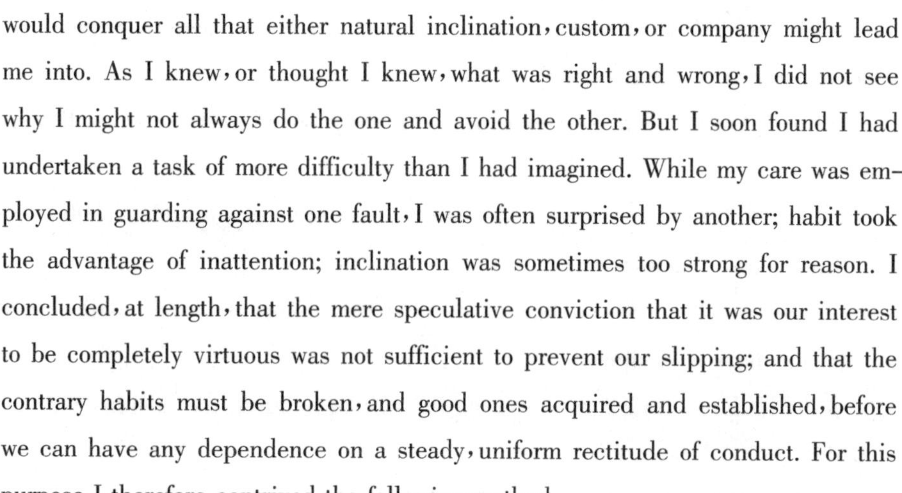

would conquer all that either natural inclination, custom, or company might lead me into. As I knew, or thought I knew, what was right and wrong, I did not see why I might not always do the one and avoid the other. But I soon found I had undertaken a task of more difficulty than I had imagined. While my care was employed in guarding against one fault, I was often surprised by another; habit took the advantage of inattention; inclination was sometimes too strong for reason. I concluded, at length, that the mere speculative conviction that it was our interest to be completely virtuous was not sufficient to prevent our slipping; and that the contrary habits must be broken, and good ones acquired and established, before we can have any dependence on a steady, uniform rectitude of conduct. For this purpose I therefore contrived the following method.

In the various enumerations of the moral virtues I had met with in my reading, I found the catalog more or less numerous, as different writers included more or fewer ideas under the same name. Temperance, for example, was by some confined to eating and drinking, while by others it was extended to mean the moderating every other pleasure, appetite, inclination, or passion, bodily or mental, even to our avarice and ambition. I proposed to myself, for the sake of clearness, to use rather more names, with fewer ideas annexed to each, than a few names with more ideas; and I included under thirteen names of virtues all that at that time occurred to me as necessary or desirable, and annexed to each a short precept, which fully expressed the extent I gave to its meaning.

These names of virtues, with their precepts, were:

1.TEMPERANCE Eat not to dullness; drink not to elevation.

2.SILENCE Speak not but what may benefit others or yourself;avoid trifling conversation.

3.ORDER Let all your things have their places; let each part of your business have its time.

4.RESOLUTION Resolve to perform what you ought; perform without fail what you resolve.

5.FRUGALITY Make no expense but to do good to others or yourself; i.e., waste nothing.

6.INDUSTRY Lose no time; be always employed in something useful; cut off all unnecessary actions.

7.SINCERITY Use no hurtful deceit; think innocently and justly, and, if you speak, speak accordingly.

8.JUSTICE Wrong none by doing injuries, or omitting the benefits that are your duty.

9.MODERATION Avoid extremes; forebear resenting injuries so much as you think they deserve.

10. CLEANLINESS Tolerate no uncleanliness in body, clothes, or habitation.

11. TRANQUILLITY Be not disturbed at trifles, or at accidents common or unavoidable.

12. CHASTITY Rarely use venery but for health or offspring, never to dulness, weakness, or injury of your own or another's peace or reputation.

13. HUMILITY Imitate Jesus and Socrates.

My intention being to acquire the habitude of all these virtues, I judged it would be well not to distract my attention by attempting the whole at once but to fix it on one of them at a time; and, when I should be master of that, then to proceed to another, and so on, till I should have gone through the thirteen; and, as the previous acquisition of some might facilitate the acquisition of certain others, I arranged them with that view, as they stand above. Temperance first, as it tends to procure that coolness and clearness of head, which is so necessary where constant vigilance was to be kept up, and guard maintained against the unremitting attraction of ancient habits and the force of perpetual temptations. This being acquired and established, Silence would be more easy; and my desire being to gain knowledge at the same time that I improved in virtue, and considering that in conversation it was obtained rather by the use of the ears than of the tongue, and therefore wishing to break a habit I was getting into of prattling, punning, and joking, which only made me acceptable to trifling company, I gave Silence the second place. This and the next, Order, I expected would allow me more time for attending to my project and my studies. Resolution, once become habitual, would keep me firm in my endeavors to obtain all the subsequent virtues; Frugality and Industry fleeing me from my remaining debt and producing affluence and independence, would make more easy the practice of Sincerity and Justice, etc., etc. Conceiving then, that, agreeably to the advice of Pythagoras in his Golden Verses, daily examination would be necessary, I contrived the following method for conducting that examination.

I made a little book, in which I allotted a page for each of the virtues. I ruled each page with red ink, so as to have seven columns, one for each day of the week, marking each column with a letter for the day. I crossed these columns with thirteen red lines, marking the beginning of each line with the first letter of one of the virtues, on which line and in its proper column I might mark, by a little black spot, every fault I found upon examination to have been committed respecting that virtue upon that day.

I determined to give a week's strict attention to each of the virtues successively. Thus, in the first week, my great guard was to avoid every the least offense against Temperance, leaving the other virtues to their ordinary chance, only marking every evening the faults of the day. Thus, if in the first week I could keep my first line, marked T. clear of spots, I supposed the habit of that virtue so much strengthened, and its opposite weakened, that I might venture extending my attention to include the next, and for the following week keep both lines clear of spots. Proceeding thus to the last, I could go through a course complete in thirteen weeks, and four courses in a year. And like him who, having a garden to weed, does not attempt to eradicate all the bad herbs at once, which would exceed his reach and his strength, but works on one of the beds at a time, and, having accomplished the first, proceeds to a second, so I should have, I hoped, the encouraging pleasure of seeing on my

pages the progress I made in virtue, by clearing successively my lines of their spots, till in the end, by a number of courses, I should be happy in viewing a clean book, after a thirteen weeks' daily examination ....

The precept of Order requiring that every part of my business should have its allotted time, one page in my little book contained the following scheme of employment for the twenty–four hours of a natural day.

THE MORNING. *Question.* What good shall I do this day?	5 6	Rise, wash, and address Powerful Goodness! Contrive day's business, and take the resolution of the day; prosecute the present study, and breakfast.
	7	
	8	
	9	Work.
	10	
	11	
NOON.	12 1	Read, or overlook my accounts, and dine.
	3	Work.
	4	
EVENING. *Question* What good have I done today?	6	Put things in their places. Supper. Music or diversion, or conversation.
	7	Examination of the day.
	8	
	9	
	10	
	11	
	12	
NIGHT.	1	Sleep.
	2	

3

4

I entered upon the execution of this plan for self-examination, and continued it with occasional intermissions for some time. I was surprised to find myself so much fuller of faults than I had imagined; but I had the satisfaction of seeing them diminish. To avoid the trouble of renewing now and then my little book, which, by scraping out the marks on the paper of old faults to make room for new ones in a new course, became full of holes, I transferred my tables and precepts to the ivory leaves of a memorandum book, on which the lines were drawn with red ink that made a durable stain, and on those lines I marked my faults with a black-lead pencil, which marks I could easily wipe out with a wet sponge. After a while I went through one course only in a year, and afterward only one in several years, till at length I omitted them entirely, being employed in voyages and business abroad, with a multiplicity of affairs that interfered; but I always carried my little book with me.

My scheme of Order gave me the most trouble; and I found that, though it might be practicable where a man's business was such as to leave him the disposition of his time, that of a journeyman printer, for instance, it was not possible to be exactly observed by a master, who must mix with the world and often receive people of business at their own hours. Order, too, with regard to places for things, papers, etc., I found extremely difficult to acquire. I had not been early accustomed to it, and, having an exceeding good memory, I was not so sensible of the inconvenience attending want of method. This article, therefore, cost me so much painful attention, and my faults in it vexed me so much, and I made so little progress in amendment, and had such frequent relapses, that I was almost ready to give up the attempt, and content myself with a faulty character in that respect, like the man who, in buying an ax of a smith, my neighbor, desired to have the whole of its surface as bright as the edge. The smith consented to grind it bright for him if he would turn the wheel; he turned, while the smith pressed the broad face of the ax hard and heavily on the stone, which made the turning of it very fatiguing. The man came every now and then from the wheel to see how

the work went on, and at length would take his ax as it was, without farther grinding. "No," said the smith, "turn on, turn on; we shall have it bright by and by; as yet, it is only speckled." "Yes," says the man, "but I think I like a speckled ax best." And I believe this may have been the case with many, who, having, for want of some such means as I employed, found the difficulty of obtaining good and breaking bad habits in other points of vice and virtue, have given up the struggle, and concluded that "a speckled ax was best"; for something, that pretended to be reason, was every now and then suggesting to me that such extreme nicety as I exacted of myself might be a kind of foppery in morals, which, if it were known, would make me ridiculous; that a perfect character might be attended with the inconvenience of being envied and hated; and that a benevolent man should allow a few faults in himself, to keep his friends in countenance.

In truth, I found myself incorrigible with respect to Older; and now I am grown old, and my memory bad, I feel very sensibly the want of it. But, on the whole, though I never arrived at the perfection I had been so ambitious of obtaining, but fell far short of it, yet I was, by the endeavor, a better and a happier man than I otherwise should have been if I had not attempted it; as those who aim at perfect writing by imitating the engraved copies, though they never reached the wished-for excellence of those copies, their hand is mended by the endeavor, and is tolerable while it continues fair and legible.

It may be well my posterity should be informed that to this little artifice, with the blessing of God, their ancestor owed the constant felicity of his life, down to his seventy-ninth year in which this is written. What reverses may attend the remainder is in the hand of Providence; but, if they arrive, the reflection on past happiness enjoyed ought to help his bearing them with more resignation. To Temperance he ascribes his long-continued health, and what is still left to him of a good constitution; to Industry and Frugality, the early easiness of his circumstances and acquisition of his fortune, with all that knowledge that enabled him to be a useful citizen, and obtained for him some degree of reputation among the learned; to Sincerity and Justice, the confidence of his country, and the honorable employs it conferred upon him; and to the joint influence of the whole mass of the virtues, even in the imperfect state he was able to acquire them, all that evenness of temper, and that cheerfulness in conversation, which makes his company still sought for, and agreeable even to his younger acquaintance. I hope, therefore, that some of my descendants may follow the example and reap the benefit.

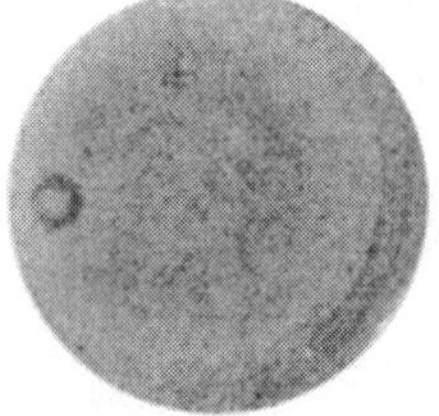

第二课

独立宣言

托马斯·杰弗逊 (1743—1826)

托马斯·杰弗逊

当你看到托马斯·杰弗逊一生中所有的成就时，你会觉得事实上他好像无所不能。他不仅帮助我们的国家赢得独立并担任了第三届总统的职务，而且还建立了弗吉尼亚大学，帮助建立公共教育系统，设计了他自己的房子，发明了一种能在楼层之间传送食品的电梯，还建立了美国货币的十进制系统。他还是一位技巧娴熟的小提琴家、艺术爱好者和杰出的作家。

杰弗逊出生在弗吉尼亚的一个富裕家庭。他进入威廉姆和玛丽学院学习并获得了法律学位。他在弗吉尼亚众议院任职时，成为一名直言不讳地保卫美国权利的斗士。当殖民地人民和英国政府之间的矛盾激化为一场革命时，杰弗逊在赢得独立的斗争中成为一名领袖。

战争结束后，杰弗逊做了几年美国驻法公使，然后又曾任职美国第一届国务卿和第二届副总统，最后于1801年成为美国总统。在他执政期间，杰弗逊授权从法国购买路易斯安那地区，使美国的国土几乎扩大了一倍。

托马斯•潘恩 (1737—1809)

托马斯•潘恩在伦敦遇到了本杰明•富兰克林，这次会面改变了他的人生——还有美国历史。潘恩于1774年从英国移居到美洲殖民地。潘恩随身带了一封富兰克林的介绍信，开始了作为一名记者的事业。1776年1月，他发表了《常识》，在其中表达了他认为美国人必须为自己的独立进行斗争的观点。这本小册子在全国范围内激起了一股革命浪潮。

托马斯•潘恩

1776年底，潘恩参加了美国军队。当时，那支军队刚刚在新泽西被英军压倒性地击败，撤退到了潘索威尼亚。他们正遭受着严寒天气、供给短缺和士气低落的折磨。那时潘恩正在写作他的第一部名为《美国的危机》的系列散文。华盛顿下令他的军队阅读潘恩的散文，然后这支军队就越过达拉维尔，在特兰顿战役中击败了和逊人。

潘恩后来的作品表达了对法国革命的支持(《人的权利》，1792)。但他对宗教组织的攻击(《理性的时代》，1794)却使美国的公众观点转而反对他，到他1809年逝世的时候，他已经身心交瘁，一蹶不振了。然而，多年以后，他再次被承认是一名革命时期的英雄。

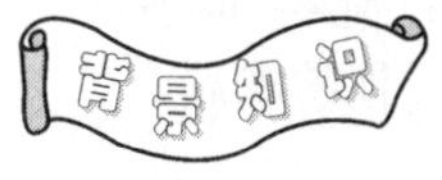

历史：杰弗逊和《独立宣言》

1776年，杰弗逊(与富兰克林、亚当斯和其他人一起)被选中来为殖民地的独立写一份宣言。“第二届大陆代表大会”所看到的宣言草案大部分出自杰弗逊之手，然而，令他失望的是，代表大会在通过这份文件之前对它进行了修改。他们删去了杰弗逊对英国政府容忍一个腐败的国会的谴责，还删去了他强烈

反对奴隶制度的部分。

除了这些修改之外，余下的部分很明显是关于叛国罪的，对于叛国罪的惩罚是死刑。由于当时的情况对殖民地人民非常不利，所以代表大会的成员要用极大的勇气来签署这份文件并把它送给乔治三世。如果殖民地人民在这场战争中失败的话，那么所有在《独立宣言》上签字的人都很可能会被处死。

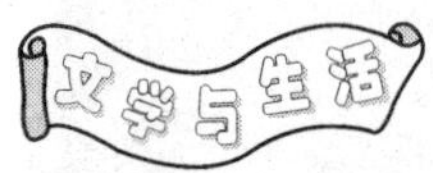

联系你的经历 当自由的呼声变为武力的时候，我们就看到了革命的征兆。现在，我们通过媒体的图像和报道来体验革命。然而，要想体验我们自己国家的独立革命，最好的方式就是阅读当时的文献，这些文献表现了使殖民地人民能够为自己赢得独立的那种精神。

日志写作 写一写你对自由这个概念的理解。有不同类型的自由吗？

专题焦点 自由的呼声 杰弗逊和潘恩都是争取美国的自由的雄辩的演说家。他们的呼声有什么相似点和不同点？

劝说文 劝说文就是说服读者用某种方式去思考或行动的写作。有说服力的作者会利用读者的感情或理智，提出自己的观点，并促使读者采取行动。

杰弗逊写作的目的是说服英王相信殖民地人民有权利宣布自己的独立。潘恩写作的目的是使美国民众相信革命的正确性并且鼓舞战场上的美国士兵们的士气。注意每个作家采用了什么技巧来说服读者接受他的观点。

独立宣言（节选）

托马斯·杰弗逊

在有关人类事务的发展过程中，当一个民族必须解除同另一个民族的联系，并按照自然法则和上帝的旨意，以独立平等的身份立于世界列国之林时，

签署《独立宣言》

出于对人类舆论的尊重，必须把驱使他们独立的原因予以宣布。

我们认为下述真理是不言而喻的：人人生而平等，造物主赋予他们若干不可剥夺的权利，其中包括生存权、自由权和追求幸福的权利。为了保障这些权利，人类才在他们中间建立政府，而政府的正当权力，则是经被统治者同意所授予的。任何形式的政府一旦对这些目标的实现起破坏作用时，人民便有权予以更换或废除，以建立一个新的政府。新政府所依据的原则和组织其权力的方式，务使人民认为唯有这样才最有可能使他们获得安全和幸福。若真要审慎地来说，成立多年的政府是不应当由于无关紧要的和一时的原因而予以更换的，过去的一切经验都说明，任何苦难，只要尚能忍受，人类还是情愿忍受，也不想为申冤而废除他们久已习惯了的政府形式。然而，当始终追求同一目标的一系列滥用职权和强取豪夺的行为表明政府企图把人民置于专制暴政之下时，人民就有权，也有义务，去推翻这样的政府，并为其未来的安全提供新的保障。这就是这些殖民地过去忍受苦难的经过，也是他们现在不得不改变政府制度的原因。当今大不列颠国王的历史，就是屡屡伤害和掠夺这些殖民地的历史，其直接目标就是要在各州之上建立一个独裁暴政，为了证明上述句句属实，现将事实公之于世，让公正的世人作出评判。

他拒绝批准对公众利益最有益、最必需的法律。

他禁止他的总督们批准迫切而极为必要的法律，要不就把这些法律搁置起来暂不生效，等待他的同意；而一旦这些法律被搁置起来，他对它们就完全置之不理。

他拒绝批准便利广大地区人民的其他法律，除非那些人民情愿放弃自己在立法机关中的代表权；但这种权利对他们有无法估量的价值，而且只有暴君才畏惧这种权利。

他把各州立法团体召集到异乎寻常的、极为不便的、远离它们档案库的地方去开会，唯一的目的是使他们疲于奔命，不得不顺从他的意旨。

他一再解散各州的议会，因为它们以无畏的坚毅态度反对他侵犯人民的权利。

他在解散各州议会之后，又长期拒绝另选新议会；但立法权是无法取消的，因此这项权力仍由一般人民来行使。其实各州仍然处于危险的境地，既有外来侵略之患，又有发生内乱之忧。

他竭力抑制我们各州增加人口；为此目的，他阻挠外国人入籍法的通过，拒绝批准其他鼓励外国人移居各州的法律，并提高分配新土地的条件。

他拒绝批准建立司法权力的法律，借以阻挠司法工作的推行。

他把法官的任期、薪金数额和支付，完全置于他个人意志的支配之下。

他建立新官署，派遣大批官员，骚扰我们人民，并耗尽人民必要的生活物质。

他在和平时期，未经我们的立法机关同意，就在我们中间维持常备军。

他力图使军队独立于民政之外，并凌驾于民政之上。

他同某些人勾结起来把我们置于一种不适合我们的体制且不为我们的法律所承认的管辖之下；他还批准那些人炮制的各种伪法案来达到以下目的：

在我们中间驻扎大批武装部队；

用假审讯来包庇他们，使他们杀害我们各州居民而仍然逍遥法外；

切断我们同世界各地的贸易；

未经我们同意便向我们强行征税；

在许多案件中剥夺我们享有陪审制的权益；

罗织罪名押送我们到海外去受审；

在一个邻省废除英国的自由法制，在那里建立专制政府，并扩大该省的疆界，企图把该省变成既是一个样板又是一个得心应手的工具，以便进而向这里的各殖民地推行同样的极权统治；

取消我们的宪章，废除我们最宝贵的法律，并且根本上改变我们各州政府的形式；

中止我们自己的立法机关行使权力，宣称他们自己有权就一切事宜为我们制定法律；

他宣布我们已不属他保护之列，并对我们作战，从而放弃了在这里的政务；

他在我们的海域大肆掠夺，蹂躏我们沿海地区，焚烧我们的城镇，残害我们人民的生命；

他此时正在运送大批外国佣兵来完成屠杀、破坏和肆虐的勾当，这种勾当早就开始，其残酷卑劣甚至在最野蛮的时代都难以找到先例。他完全不配作为一个文明国家的元首；

他在公海上俘虏我们的同胞，强迫他们拿起武器来反对自己的国家，成为残杀自己亲人和朋友的刽子手，或是死于自己的亲人和朋友的手下；

他在我们中间煽动内乱，并且竭力调唆那些残酷无情、没有开化的印第安人来杀掠我们边疆的居民。而众所周知，印第安人的作战规律是不分男女老幼，一律格杀勿论的。

在这些压迫的每一阶段中，我们都是用最谦卑的言辞请求改善。但屡次请求所得到的答复是屡次遭受损害。

一个君主，当他的品格已打上了暴君行为的烙印时，是不配做自由人民

1773年波士顿倾茶事件

的统治者的。

我们不是没有顾念我们英国的弟兄。我们时常提醒他们，他们的立法机关企图把无理的管辖权横加到我们的头上。我们也曾把我们移民来这里和在这里定居的情形告诉他们。我们曾经向他们天生的正义善感和雅量呼吁，我们恳求他们念在同种同宗的份上，弃绝这些掠夺行为，以免影响彼此的关系和往来。但是他们对于这种正义和血缘的呼声，也同样充耳不闻。因此，我们实在不得不宣布和他们脱离，并且以对待世界上其他民族一样的态度对待他们：和我们作战，就是敌人；和我们友好，就是朋友。

因此，我们，在大陆会议下集会的美利坚合众国代表，以各殖民地善良人民的名义，并经他们授权，向全世界最崇高的正义呼吁，说明我们的严正意向，同时郑重宣布：这些联合一致的殖民地从此是自由和独立的国家，并且按其权利也必须是自由和独立的国家；它们取消一切对英国王室效忠的义务；它们和大不列颠国家之间的一切政治关系从此全部断绝，而且必须断绝；作为自由独立的国家，它们完全有权宣战、缔和、结盟、通商和采取独立国家有权采取的一切行动。

为了支持这篇宣言，我们坚决信赖上帝的庇佑，以我们的生命、我们的财产和我们神圣的名誉，彼此宣誓。

文学和生活

读者反应 这篇文献激起了人们的什么感情？为什么？

主题焦点 你认为“自由的声音”和“叛国的声音”之间有什么区别？解释原因。

阅读理解

1. 第二段中列出的三个“不可让步的权利”是什么？
2. 根据杰弗逊的看法，什么时候一个政府应该被废除？
3. 列出三个证据来支持他的论断：英王的目的是“在这些州里建立一个绝对的独裁”。

4. (a) 杰弗逊声称殖民地人民在“这些压迫的每个阶段”都做了什么？(b) 英王对殖民地人民的行动是怎样反应的？

思考

解释

1. 杰弗逊列出的怨恨对他的论证产生了什么效果？（分析）

2. 为什么杰弗逊把他的攻击集中在乔治三世身上，而没有攻击英国国会或人民？（推理）

3. 18世纪对于理智的信仰是怎样反映在《独立宣言》中的？（联系）

扩展

5.《独立宣言》如果作为一篇演讲会同样有效吗？解释理由。（表演艺术连线）

美国的危机(节选)

托马斯·潘恩

这是考验人的灵魂的时代。在当前的危机中，精壮的战士和乐天的爱国者会在为国家服务的责任面前畏缩不前，但今天能坚持战斗的人应当得到全体男女的爱戴和感激。专制制度就像地狱一样，是不容易被打破的，但是我们可以堪慰的是：斗争越是艰巨，胜利就越光荣。轻易获得的东西，我们并不珍重；一切事物的价值在于它是来之不易的。上天知道怎样给它的造物定出适当的价码。如果对自由这样神圣的东西反而索价不高，那岂非咄咄怪事。凭军队来推行其专制制度的不列颠公开宣布她有权利（不但课税）而且“在一切情形下对我们进行全面约束”，如果那样约束我们还不叫奴役的话，那世上就不存在奴役这回事了。其实他们这种说法本身也是亵渎神明的，因为他们所说的那种无限权力只能属于上帝……

我和任何人一样，没有什么迷信。但我内心深处一向认为，而且现在还是这么认为，一个曾殚思竭虑，想尽一切妥善的办法，屡次真诚地寻求避免战争之灾难的民族，万能的上帝是不会听任他们横遭兵刃洗劫的。我没有那么多异教徒的思想，还不至于认为上帝会放弃对世界的主宰，把我们交给魔鬼发落。既然我并无上述想法，我也就看不出不列颠国王将能以何种理由仰对上

天求助以加害于我们：一个声名狼藉的凶手、拦路抢劫的匪徒和破门而入的强盗都会找到一个跟他一样堂皇的借口……

我不是对少数人，而是向全体呼吁；不是对这个州或那个州，而是向每一个州呼吁；呼吁你们迅速奋起，前来助战，全力以赴，共襄大业，况且生死存亡，在此一举，因而所聚兵力宁可太多，不可太少。让我们昭告后世，在这只有希望和美德才能坚持下去的隆冬季节，我城乡居民，为共同的危难而惶恐不安，纷纷挺身而出，联合退敌。且莫道几千人已经丧生，请拿出你的几万人来，不要把当前的负担推给上帝，要“用实干表现你的信心”，这样上帝才会保佑你。地不分东西，人不分贵贱，是祸是福，总会降临到你们每个人头上的。不论是远是近，是家乡还是边疆，是富人还是穷人，喜则同喜，忧则同忧。此时此刻无动于衷的心便是死的。他的孩子们将以血咒骂他的怯懦，因为他在只要付出一点便可拯救全体，使他们获得幸福的紧要关头退缩了。我爱能在危难中微笑的人；我爱能从痛苦中聚集力量的人；我爱能通过深思变得勇敢的人。临阵脱逃是小人的行径。而一位天性坚毅，行为不背良心的人，将会坚持原则，至死不渝。在我看来，我推理的思路像一线光一样笔直透明。我相信即使把全世界的财富都给我，也无法诱使我去支持一场侵略战争，因为我认为这是屠

大陆军在招募士兵

杀。但是，假如一名盗贼破门闯入我的住宅，烧毁我的财物，杀死我或威胁要杀我，或屋子里的其他人，并要我"在一切情况下受约束"于他的绝对意志，难道我要甘受其害吗?不管干这事的是国王还是平民，是我的同胞还是外国人，是单个暴徒还是一支军队，那对我有什么差别？归根到底一点差别都没有，因为，对于这些罪行，我们在一种情况下要惩罚，而在另一种情况下又要赦免，那是不公正的。

文学和生活

读者反应　你认为托马斯•潘恩关于美国革命的形象中有哪些最激动人心或令人难忘？为什么？

主题焦点　你是否感到潘恩的呼声具有迫使人接受的力量？你认为潘恩作为一名记者值得信任吗？解释理由。

阅读理解

1. 在第四段中，潘恩对什么充满信心？

2. 在最后一段中，潘恩表达了关于侵略性战争的什么观点？

思考

解释

1. 说出两种作者在这篇散文中企图激发的情感。(归类)

2. (a)这篇散文的主旨观点是什么？(b)潘恩是怎样逐渐推进他的主旨观点的？(证据支持)

应用

3. 在你看来，潘恩的散文具有怎样的说服力？用证据支持你的回答。(评价)

4. 一个一直对英国忠心耿耿的殖民地居民可能对潘恩的论证做出什么回应？(假设)

文学聚焦

劝说文

《独立宣言》和《美国的危机》都是劝说文的范例——劝说文就是试图说服读者采用某种方式方法去思考或行动的写作。在《独立宣言》中，杰弗逊列出了许多怨恨的情感来支持他的观点。而潘恩从另一个角度给出了各种信息——奇闻轶事、观点看法、事实和实例——来说服他的读者相信与英国作战是正确合理的。

1. 在《独立宣言》中，随着怨恨清单的继续，作者的指控是否变得越来越严肃呢？这种组织的效果是什么？

2. 给出两个《美国的危机》中潘恩提出的建议的例子。

3. 在你看来，潘恩在这篇散文中更多激发了读者的情感还是理智？解释原因。

4. 你认为哪篇选文更加具有说服力？为什么？

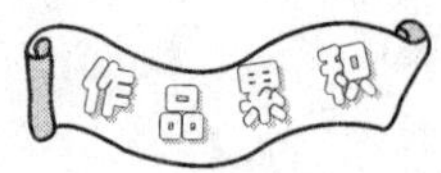

点子库

写作

1. 信件　在1776年12月的一封信中，乔治•华盛顿写道:“我疲倦得快要死了。我想这场游戏快要结束了。”给华盛顿写一封信，表达你听到潘恩的散文之后的想法。

2. 摘要大纲　摘要大纲就是对于主要观点的简练总结。为杰弗逊的《独立宣言》写一份摘要大纲。（社会研究连线）

3. 报纸故事　作为一名殖民地时期的记者，写一篇文章记录《独立宣言》的签署情况。然后写一个故事，在宣言发布之后，这个故事可能出现在一份伦敦的报纸上。

项目

1.招贴海报　根据潘恩的观点设计一份革命战争的征兵海报。像潘恩一样，你也可以嘲笑“夏天般的士兵和阳光般的爱国者”。（艺术连线）

2.关于潘恩的课堂讨论　对潘恩的早期生活进行研究。准备一些笔记小条,以便在主持一次关于潘恩对引起美国革命的贡献的讨论时使用。(社会研究连线)

微型写作课

给校长的建议

和一组同学一起选择一个你们认为应该改变的学校里的问题或情况。然后写一份给校长的建议,解释为什么这种情况需要关注,以及你们认为这种情况需要改正的原因。

写作技巧重点:使用有力的语言

有力的语言能让你的论证更加有效。使用含有肯定含义的语言来表现你希望你的读者接受的观点,使用含否定含义的语言来表现你希望你的读者反对的观点。注意潘恩是怎样利用词语的否定力量的。

构思

列出你学校里一些应该改变的状况的原因。写下细节——包括事实、例子、解释——来支持每种原因。

写稿

使用类似"高级的"和"明智的"这样的词来强调你们的建议的正确性。在适合的地方使用含有否定含义的语言来表现反对观点。然而,要记得你是在为你们的校长写作。

修改

仔细地检查你的建议,修改任何似乎不甚合理的观点。检查你是否提出了支持你的观点的证据。

Guide for Interpreting

Thomas Jefferson (1743—1826)

When you look at all the things Thomas Jefferson accomplished in his lifetime, it seems there was virtually nothing that Jefferson couldn't do. Not only did he help our nation win its independence and serve as its third president, but he also founded the University of Virginia, helped establish the public school system, designed his own home, invented a type of elevator for sending food from floor to floor, and created the decimal system for American money. He was also a skilled violinist, an art enthusiast, and a brilliant writer.

Born into a wealthy Virginia family, Jefferson attended the College of William and Mary and went on to earn a law degree. While serving in the Virginia House of Burgesses, he became an outspoken defender of American rights. When conflict between the colonists and the British erupted into a revolution, Jefferson emerged as a leader in the effort to win independence.

When the war ended, Jefferson served as the American minister to France for several years. He then served as the nation's first secretary of state and second vice president before becoming president in 1801. While in office, Jefferson nearly doubled the size of the nation by authorizing the purchase of the Louisiana Territory from France.

Thomas Paine (1737—1809)

Thomas Paine met Benjamin Franklin in London, and the introduction changed his life — and American history. Paine emigrated to the colonies from England in 1774. With a letter of introduction from Franklin, Paine began a career as a journalist. In January 1776, he published Common Sense, in which he argued that Americans must fight for independence. The pamphlet created a national mood for revolution.

Paine enlisted in the American army toward the end of 1776. At that time, the army had just suffered a crushing defeat by the British in New Jersey and had retreated into Pennsylvania. They were suffering from freezing weather, a shortage of provisions, and low morale. Paine was writing the first of a series of essays entitled The American Crisis. Washington ordered Paine's essay read to his troops before they crossed the Delaware to defeat the Hessians at the Battle of Trenton.

Paine's later works supported the French Revolution (The Rights of Man, 1792). His attack on organized religion (The Age of Reason, 1794) turned American public opinion against him, and when he died in 1809, he was a broken man. Years later, however, he was once again recognized as a hero of the Revolution.

Background for Understanding

HISTORY: JEFFERSON AND THE DECLARATION

In 1776, Jefferson was chosen (with Franklin, Adams, and others) to write a declaration of the colonies' independence. The draft presented to the Second Continental Congress was largely Jefferson's work. To his disappointment, however, Congress made changes before approving the document. They dropped Jefferson's condemnation of the British for tolerating a corrupt Parliament, and they struck out a strong statement against slavery.

Despite these changes, what remained was plainly treasonous, and the penalty for treason was death. Considering that the odds were heavily stacked against the colonists at the time, it took tremendous bravery for members of Congress to sign the document and send it off to King George III. Had the colonists failed to win the war, all who had signed the Declaration would most likely have been executed.

Literature and your Life

CONNECT YOUR EXPERIENCE

When shouts for freedom are transformed into military force, we recognize the signs of revolution. Today, we experience revolutions through images and reports in the news media. The best way to experience what our own Revolution was like, however, is to read documents that capture the spirit that enabled the colonists to win their independence.

Journal Writing Write about the concept of freedom. Are there different types of freedom?

THEMATIC FOCUS: VOICES FOR FREEDOM

Jefferson and Paine were eloquent speakers for American freedom. How are their voices similar, and how are they distinct?

Literary Focus

PERSUASION

Persuasion is writing meant to convince readers to think or act in a certain way. A persuasive writer appeals to emotions or reason, offers opinions, and urges action.

Jefferson wrote to persuade the king that the colonists were justified in declaring their independence. Paine wrote to convince American citizens of the justness of revolution and to lift the spirits of American soldiers on the battlefield. Notice the techniques each writer uses to persuade readers to share his views.

The Declaration of Independence

Thomas Jefferson

When in the course of human events, it becomes necessary for one people to dissolve the political bands which have connected them with another, and to assume among the powers of the earth, the separate and equal station to which the laws of nature and of nature's God entitle them, a decent respect to the opinions of mankind requires that they should declare the causes which impel them to the separation.

We hold these truths to be self-evident: that all men are created equal; that they are endowed by their Creator with certain unalienable rights; that among these are life, liberty and the pursuit of happiness; that to secure these rights, governments are instituted among men, deriving their just powers from the consent of the governed; that whenever any form of government becomes destructive of these ends, it is the right of the people to alter or to abolish it, and to institute new government, laying its foundation on such principles and organizing its powers in such form, as to them shall seem most likely to effect their safety and happiness. Prudence, indeed, will dictate that governments long established should not be changed for light and transient causes; and accordingly all experience hath shown, that mankind are more disposed to suffer while evils are sufferable than to right themselves by abolishing the forms to which they are accustomed. But when a long train of abuses and usurpations, pursuing invariably the same object, evinces a design to reduce them under absolute despotism, it is their right, it is their duty, to throw off such government, and to provide new guards for their future security. Such has been the patient sufferance of these colonies; and such is now the necessity which constrains them to alter their former systems of government. The history of the present king of Great Britain is a history of repeated injuries and usurpations, all having in direct object the establishment of an absolute tyranny over these states. To prove this, let facts be submitted to a candid world.

He has refused his assent to laws the most wholesome and necessary for the public good.

He has forbidden his governors to pass laws of immediate and pressing importance, unless suspended in their operation till his assent should be obtained; and when so suspended, he has utterly neglected to attend to them.

He has refused to pass other laws for the accommodation of large districts of people, unless those people would relinquish the right of representation in the legislature, a right inestimable to them and formidable to tyrants only.

He has called together legislative bodies at places unusual, uncomfortable, and distant from the depository of their public records, for the sole purpose of fatiguing them into compliance with his measures.

He has dissolved representative houses repeatedly, for opposing with manly firmness his invasions on the rights of the people.

He has refused for a long time after such dissolutions to cause others to be elected, whereby the legislative powers, incapable of annihilation, have returned to the people at large for their exercise, the state remaining in the mean time exposed to all the dangers of invasion from without, and convulsions within.

He has endeavored to prevent the population of these states; for that purpose obstructing the laws for naturalization of foreigners, refusing to pass others to encourage their migration hither, and raising the conditions of new appropriations of lands.

He has obstructed the administration of justice, by refusing his assent to laws for establishing judiciary powers.

He has made judges dependent on his will alone, for the tenure of their offices, and the amount and payment of their salaries.

He has erected a multitude of new offices, and sent hither swarms of officers to harass our people and eat out their substance.

He has kept among us in times of peace standing armies without the consent of our legislatures.

He has affected to render the military independent of, and superior to, the civil power.

He has combined with others to subject us to a jurisdiction foreign to our constitution and unacknowledged by our laws, giving his assent to their acts of pretended legislation: for quartering large bodies of armed troops among us; for protecting them by a mock trial from punishment for any murders which they should commit on the inhabitants of these states; for cutting off our trade with all parts of the world; for imposing taxes on us without our consent; for depriving us, in many cases, of the benefits of trial by jury; for transporting us beyond seas to be tried for pretended offenses; for abolishing the free system of English laws in a neighboring province, establishing therein an arbitrary government, and enlarging its boundaries, so as to render it at once an example and fit instrument for introducing the same absolute rule into these colonies; for taking away our charters, abolishing our most valuable laws, and altering fundamentally the forms of our governments; for suspending our own legislatures, and declaring themselves invested with power to legislate for us in all cases whatsoever.

He has abdicated government here, by declaring us out of his protection and waging war against us.

He has plundered our seas, ravaged our coasts, burned our towns, and destroyed the lives of our people.

He is at this time transporting large armies of foreign mercenaries to complete the works of death, desolation, and tyranny already begun with circumstances of cruelty and perfidy scarcely paralleled in the most barbarous ages, and totally unworthy the head of a civilized nation.

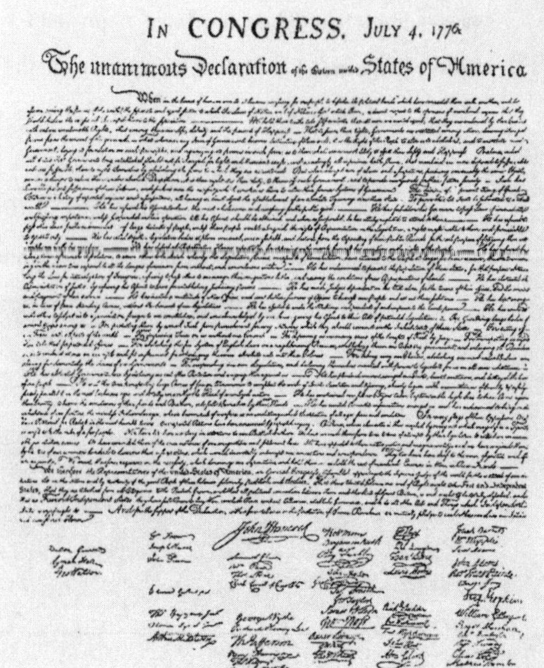

IN CONGRESS. JULY 4. 1776

The unanimous Declaration of the thirteen united States of America

John Hancock

He has constrained our fellow citizens taken captive on the high

seas to bear arms against their country, to become the executioners of their friends and brethren, or to fall themselves by their hands.

He has excited domestic insurrections amongst us, and has endeavored to bring on the inhabitants of our frontiers, the merciless Indian savages, whose known rule of warfare is an undistinguished destruction of all ages, sexes, and conditions.

In every stage of these oppressions we have petitioned for redress in the most humble terms. Our repeated petitions have been answered only by repeated injury.

A prince whose character is thus marked by every act which may define a tyrant is unfit to be the ruler of a free people.

Nor have we been wanting in attentions to our British brethren. We have warned them from time to time of attempts by their legislature to extend an unwarrantable jurisdiction over us. We have reminded them of the circumstances of our emigration and settlement here. We have appealed to their native justice and magnanimity and we have conjured them by the ties of our common kindred to disavow these usurpations which would inevitably interrupt our connections and correspondence. They too have been deaf to the voice of justice and of consanguinity. We must therefore acquiesce in the necessity which denounces our separation and hold them, as we hold the rest of mankind, enemies in war, in peace friends.

We, therefore, the representatives of the United States of America in general congress assembled, appealing to the Supreme Judge of the world for the rectitude of our intentions, do in the name and by authority of the good people of these colonies, solemnly publish and declare that these united colonies are and of right ought to be free and independent states; that they are

absolved from all allegiance to the British Crown, and that all political connection between them and the state of Great Britain is and ought to be totally dissolved; and that as free and independent states, they have full power to levy war, conclude peace, contract alliances, establish commerce, and to do all other acts and things which independent states may of right do.

And for the support of this declaration, with a firm reliance on the protection of divine providence, we mutually pledge to each other our lives, our fortunes and our sacred honor.

The Crisis, Number 1

Thomas Paine

These are the times that try men's souls. The summer soldier and the sunshine patriot will in this crisis, shrink from the service of his country; but he that stands it NOW, deserves the love and thanks of man and woman. Tyranny, like hell, is not easily conquered; yet we have this consolation with us, that the harder the conflict, the more glorious the triumph. What we obtain too cheap, we esteem too lightly; 'tis dearness only that gives everything its value. Heaven knows how to put a proper price upon its goods; and it would be strange indeed, if so celestial an article as FREEDOM should not be highly rated. Britain, with an army to enforce her tyranny, has declared that she has a right (not only to TAX) but "to BIND us in ALL CASES WHATSOEVER," and if being bound in that manner, is not slavery, then is there not such a thing as slavery upon earth. Even the expression is impious, for so unlimited a power can belong only to God...

I have as little superstition in me as any man living, but my secret opinion has ever been, and still is, that God Almighty will not give up a people to military destruction, or leave them unsupportedly to perish, who have so earnestly and so repeatedly sought to avoid the calamities of war, by every decent method which wisdom could invent. Neither have I so much of the infidel in me, as to suppose that he has relinquished the government of the world, and given us up to the care

of devils; and as I do not, I cannot see on what grounds the king of Britain can look up to heaven for help against us: a common murderer, a highwayman, or a housebreaker, has as good a pretense as he...

I turn with the warm ardor of a friend to those who have nobly stood, and are yet determined to stand the matter out: I call not upon a few, but upon all; not on tills state or that state, but on every state; up and help us; lay your shoulders to the wheel; better have too much force than too little, when so great an object is at stake. Let it be told to the future world, that in the depth of winter, when nothing but hope and virtue could survive, that the city and the country, alarmed at one common danger, came forth to meet and to repulse it. Say not that thousands are gone, turn out your tens of thousands; throw not the burden of the day upon Providence, but "show your faith by your works," that God may bless you. It matters not where you live, or what rank of life you hold, the evil or the blessing will reach you all. The far and the near, the home counties and the back, the rich and the poor, will suffer or rejoice alike. The heart that feels not now, is dead: the blood of his children will curse his cowardice, who shrinks back at a time when a little might have saved the whole, and made them happy. (I love the man that can smile at trouble; that can gather strength from distress, and grow brave by reflection.) Tis the business of little minds to shrink; but he whose heart is firm, and whose conscience approves his conduct, will pursue his principles unto death. My own line of reasoning is to myself as straight and clear as a ray of light. Not all the treasures of the world, so far as I believe, could have induced me to support

an offensive war, for I think it murder; but if a thief breaks into my house, burns and destroys my property, and kills or threatens to kill me, or those that are in it, and to "bind me in all cases whatsoever," to his absolute will, am I to suffer it? What signifies it to me, whether he who does it is a king or a common man: my countryman, or not my countryman; whether it be done by an individual villain or an army of them? If we reason to the root of things we shall find no difference; neither can any just cause be assigned why we should punish in the one case and pardon in the other.

第三课

在弗吉尼亚州大会上的演讲

帕特里克·亨利 (1736—1799)

据说帕特里克·亨利比最具天赋的演员还能轻易地使他的听众愤怒、恐惧或开怀大笑。人们最深刻地记得亨利的一句激愤的战斗口号是:“不自由,毋宁死。”他被认为是美国革命时期最有力的演说家。他鼓舞殖民地人民团结起来为赢得独立而奋斗。1765年,他被选入弗吉尼亚州的众议院,不久他就发表了他最有力的演说之一,宣称他反对《印花税法案》。虽然一些最有影响力的议员抗议他的观点,但弗吉尼亚议院还是采用了亨利的提议。

帕特里克·亨利

抗议的呼声 1775年,亨利在弗吉尼亚州的大会上发表了他最为著名的演说。那天大多数的发言者都认为殖民地应该寻求与英国的和解,亨利却大胆地敦促武装反抗英国。他的演讲在听众身上产生了强有力的影响,激发了人民的革命精神,最终导致《独立宣言》的签署。

在其后的许多年中,亨利作为弗吉尼亚州的总督和弗吉尼亚众议会的成员,一直是一名重要的政治领袖。

本杰明·富兰克林(1706—1790)

本杰明·富兰克林

虽然本杰明·富兰克林的成就覆盖了范围广阔的领域——诸如科学、文学、新闻和教育——但他最值得人们纪念的却是作为一名政治家的功绩。他是唯一一个签署了在建立这个国家过程中的4份关键性文件的美国人，这4份文件是:《独立宣言》《与法国的联盟条约》《与英国的和平协议》以及《美国宪法》。

能言善辩的外交家　富兰克林是一位独立运动中的领导人物。1776年,国会派他到法国去争取当时美国革命迫切需要的援助。富兰克林能言善辩的能力发挥了充分的作用,他达到了自己的目的——一次成为这场战争中的决定因素的关键性突破。

塑造一个国家　1783年,富兰克林签署了结束战争的《和平协议》,建立了这个新的国家。他回到家乡,成为费城立宪大会的一名代表。在那次大会上,当政治家们关于建立新政府的计划产生矛盾时,富兰克林帮助解决冲突并使《美国宪法》得以通过。

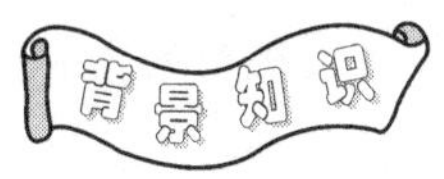

历史:帕特里克·亨利的勇敢

今天，我们很难想象像帕特里克·亨利这样的演说家要有多么大的勇气才能公开地抨击英国国王。英国是那时候世界上最强大的国家,殖民地赢得自由的可能性非常小，所以帕特里克·亨利和其他的殖民地领袖是在冒着生命的危险谴责英国国王。如果殖民地争取独立的斗争失败的话,亨利很可能会因为叛国罪而被处死。

亨利很清楚这一点。事实上,当他在1765年发表演说反对《印花税法案》的时候,就有人公开指控他犯了叛国罪。在那种情况下,亨利提到了两个因为政治原因而被杀死的领袖,并且宣称英王乔治三世能够“从这两个例子里学到什么”。他的听众听到这话,受到了极大的惊吓,以至于他们尖声叫喊了出

来，并指控他犯了叛国罪。据说亨利回答道："如果这是叛国的话，那就好好利用它吧！"

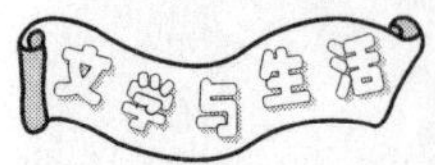

联系你的经历 你可能已经很熟悉许多著名演讲中的语句了——虽然你可能并没意识到这一点。类似马丁·路德·金的"我有一个梦想"和约翰·F.肯尼迪的"别问你的国家能为你做什么"这样的话语已经成为大多数美国人日常会话的一部分。这些话语如此出名的原因就在于它们出自曾经塑造了我们国家历史的演讲——就像你即将读到的这两篇一样。

日志写作 什么口号或箴言能抓住你这一代人的注意力呢？选择一条(从政治、音乐或广告中)并解释为什么它能有这样的影响力。

专题焦点：一个国家的诞生 亨利和富兰克林的演讲体现了宪法中"生命、自由和对幸福的追求"的什么相关观点？

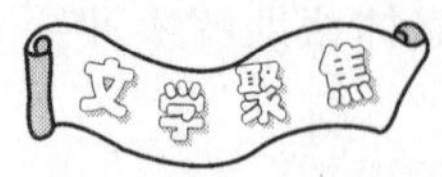

演讲 演讲从革命时期一直到现在都在美国政治中发挥了极其重要的作用。一个高水平的演说家会使用一系列技巧来强调他的要点。

重述 用不同的方法重复同一个观点。

重复 用同样的话重复一个观点。

并列 重复语法结构。

反问 反问本身答案已经确定的问题，意在激发感情。

在弗吉尼亚州大会上的演讲

帕特里克·亨利

主席先生：

我比任何人都更高度评价爱国主义，也同样高度评价刚才发言的可敬的绅士们的能力。但是不同的人经常会用不同的视角来看同一个问题。因此，我希望，如果那些绅士们像我一样愿意考虑和他们的看法背道而驰的观点的话，他们不会认为这是对他们的不敬，那么我就会自由而且毫无保留地说出我的观点。这不是一个拘泥于礼仪的时刻。大会所面临的问题对这个国家具有极其重大的意义。对我来说，我认为这是一个与自由或奴役同等重要的问题。那么，我们辩论的自由程度就应该和这个问题的重要程度相称。只有这样，我们才有希望发现真理，完成我们从上帝和国家那里承担的伟大使命。如果在这样一个时刻，我因为畏惧或怕触犯什么人而不敢说出自己的观点的话，我会认为我的罪恶就等于背叛了我的国家，并且对上帝不忠，而我敬畏上帝甚于敬畏世上所有的国王。

主席先生，沉溺于希望的幻象之中是人的天性。我们更容易对痛苦的真理视而不见，却去聆听妖女的歌声，直到她把我们都变成野兽。这难道是为自由而进行伟大艰巨的斗争的那些明智的人应该做的吗？难道我们要混同于那些人，他们长着眼睛却看不见，长着耳朵却听不见与他们当前的拯救密切相关的事情？在我看来，无论灵魂要遭受多大的痛苦，我都愿意了解全部的真相：了解最坏的可能性，并为此做好准备。

我只有一盏灯来为我指引方向，那就是经验的灯。除了根据过去的经验，我不知道还有什么方法可以来判断未来。而如果根据过去的经验判断，我想知道英国内阁在过去十年中的什么行为能使绅士们有理由抱着希望，聊以安慰自己和整个议院？是他们最近接受我们的请愿书时脸上的那种虚伪的笑容吗？先生，别相信这种笑容，它最终会证明是你脚下的陷阱。别让你自己被一个亲吻出卖。问问你自己，接受我们请愿时的微笑与这如此大规模的海、陆战争准备是否相称。在一项爱与和解的工作中难道需要有舰队和军队吗？难道我们表现得那么不愿和解，以至于他们必须动用武力来重新赢得我们的爱吗？先

帕特里克·亨利在弗吉尼亚州大会

生，让我们别再自欺欺人了。这些是战争和镇压的工具——王权采取的最后辩论手段。

主席先生，让我来问问绅士们，如果这些军队的目的不是为了迫使我们屈服的话，那他们还能意味着什么？绅士们还能为他们找到其他可能的动机吗？大不列颠在世界的这个部分有什么敌人需要召集所有这些海军和陆军吗？不，先生，没有。这些军队是为了对付我们的，他们不可能是为了对付其他任何人的。他们被派来，是为了把英国内阁长期以来一直在制造的锁链钉在我们身上，绑住我们。

我们用什么来反抗这些军队呢？我们要试试争辩吗？先生，我们已经尝试着争辩了十年了。在这个话题上我们还有什么没说过的吗？什么也没有。我们已经从每种可能的角度讨论了这个问题，但全都徒劳无功。我们要采取请求和卑微的乞求吗？我们还能找到什么没有用尽的说法吗？先生，我恳求你，让我们别再自欺欺人了。先生，我们已经竭尽所能来避免这场马上就要降临到我们头上的暴风雨了。我们进行过请愿了，我们提出过抗议了，我们也乞求过了。我们曾经匍匐在王权的宝座下，哀求它从中阻止内阁和国会的专横统治。然而，我们的请愿被忽视了，我们的抗议引起了更多的粗暴和侮辱，我们的恳求遭到了漠视，我们还被人带着轻蔑从宝座下一脚踢开！经过了所有这些事情之后，我们放任自己对于和平和解的愚蠢的希望是毫无意义的。再也没有希望的余地了。如果我们希望自由，如果我们想要保护那些我们为之长期奋斗的无价的权利不受亵渎，如果我们不想下贱地放弃那高贵的斗争，我们已经斗争了那么久，并且曾经发誓不达到我们追求的光荣目标决不放弃——我们就必须战斗！先生，我重复一遍，我们必须战斗！求助于武力和战斗之神是我们唯一的选择！

主席先生，他们对我们说，我们很弱小——我们没法对付那么可怕的一个对手。但是我们什么时候才能变得强大呢？是下周，还是明年？是要等到我们被完全解除了武装，每所房子里都有一个英国士兵在站岗的时候吗？我们要通过优柔寡断和迟钝无为来积聚力量吗？我们要朝天躺着，抱着那骗人的希望的幻影，直到敌人把我们的手脚都捆在一起，然后才找到有效抵抗的手段吗？先生，如果我们恰当地利用自然之神赋予我们的力量的话，我们就并不弱小。三百万由自由的神圣思想武装起来的人民，在我们拥有的这样一片土地上，是无论我们的敌人派来什么样的军队都无法征服的。除此以外，先生，我们将不会独自作战。有一位公正的上帝统辖着国家的命运，他会让朋友们挺身而出，帮助我们作战。先生，战争并不只是偏向强大的一方，它也会偏向警觉的、积极的、勇敢的那一方。此外，先生，我们别无选择。就算我们卑贱到想要从这场斗争中退却，现在也已经太晚了。除非我们屈服并且甘受奴役，否则我们就无从退却。为我们制造的锁链已经完工了，在波士顿的平原上能够听到那叮当的响声。战争是无法避免的——那就让它来吧！先生，我再说一遍，让它来吧！

先生，想为这件事情找个借口是没有用的。绅士们可能会叫喊："和平，和平"——但是不可能有和平！战争实际上已经开始了！我们将在下一阵从北方席卷而来的狂风中听到武器铿锵作响的声音！我们的兄弟们已经在战场上了！我们为什么还无所事事地站在这里？绅士们希望的到底是什么？他们将拥有什么？难道生命是那么可贵，和平是那么甜蜜，以至于我们愿意用锁链和奴役的代价去交换吗？全能的上帝啊，禁止这种事情吧！我不知道其他人会做出什么选择，但是就我而言，不自由，毋宁死！

文学和生活

读者反应 你对帕特里克·亨利有什么样的印象？根据这篇演讲判断，你认为他应该拥有强有力的演说家的声誉吗？解释原因。

主题焦点 在一个生死攸关的关键时刻，类似亨利的这样一篇政治演说能起到多么重要的作用？

课堂民意测验 亨利认为和没有自由的生命相比，牺牲更加可取。进行一次投票的民意测验，看看你们班里的同学是否同意他的看法。

阅读理解

1. 亨利是怎样表明他判断未来的方法的？

2. (a)亨利说在美国建立英国的军事建筑是为了什么原因？(b)殖民地人民必须采取什么行动？

3. 亨利说"下一阵从北方席卷而来的狂风"会带来什么？

思考

解释

1. 你认为亨利为什么从对他之前的发言者的看法开始？(推断)

2. 为什么亨利认为与英国妥协不是一个可行的解决方法？(证据支持)

3. 亨利是怎样回答殖民地人民还没做好战斗准备的反对意见的？(分析)

4. 亨利把殖民地人民的情况比喻成什么？(分析)

应用

5. 在今天，什么样的情况或条件可能会促使一名政治家做出这样一篇正式的、戏剧性的演讲？(联系)

拓展

6. 把亨利的演讲和今天的政治演讲做一个比较。哪些演讲者(如果有的话)能达到和亨利同样的影响力？(社会研究连线)

在立宪大会上的演讲

本杰明·富兰克林

总统先生：

我承认，目前我对这部《宪法》并不完全满意；不过，先生，我也不能肯定我是否会永远不满意；因为在我漫长的一生中，我曾经历过很多次因为了解更充分或考虑更周详而不得不改变想法的情况，甚至是在重要的问题上，当我发现自己本来以为正确的想法并非如此的时候，我也会改变的。因此，随着年龄的增长，我越发易于怀疑自己对别人做出的判断。实际上，大多数的人以及大多数宗教教派都认为自己掌握着全部的真理，无论其他人在任何方面和自己持不同意见，那都是错误的……有很多人认为他们自己几乎和他们的教派一样绝对正确，但很少有人能像一位法国夫人表达得那么自然，这位夫人在和她姐妹的一次小小争执中说道："我发现在所有的人里只有我自己总是正确的(Je ne trouve que moi qui aie toujours raison)。"

虽然我有着这些想法和情绪，先生，我还是同意这个《宪法》，包括它的种种缺陷——如果确实有的话；因为我认为对于我们而言，一个共同的政府是必要的，而只有在管理完善的条件下能造福于人民的政府才是唯一适合的政府形式；此外，我还相信这个政府在若干年的过程中很有可能管理完善，并且像其他形式的政府以前经历过的那样，这个政府只可能在人民堕落到不能接受其他形式而需要专制的政府的时候，因为专制暴政而完结。同样，我也怀疑我们是否能拥有任何一个其他的“立宪大会”，能制定出一部更好的《宪法》；因为，当你将一群人召集在一起以利用他们的集体智慧时，你无法避免同时聚集了他们所有的成见、情绪、观点中的错误、地方利益和自私的观点。我们怎么能期待从这样的一个集会中产生完美的成果呢？因此，先生，令我感到震惊的是，我发现这个宪法系统竟然能这样接近于完美；我认为它也会使我们的敌人感到震惊的，因为他们正在满怀信心地等着听说我们的会议像巴别城的建筑者们召开的会议那样混乱不堪，我们的各州即将分裂，从此以后再相见也只是为了割断彼此的喉咙。在这样的考虑下，先生，我赞同这个《宪法》，因为我不能期望更好的，也因为我不能确定这不是最好的。我为公众的利益放弃我关于这部《宪法》中的错误的观点。我从来没在国外透露过关于这些观点的一言半语。它们在这几堵墙里产生，也会在这里消亡。如果我们中的任何人在回到我们各自的立宪议会后，要去报告他对于这《宪法》的反对意见，并且努力争取支持他的拥护者的话，我们就会阻止公众接受他的观点，因为他的这种行为会使我们失去所有来自外国以及我们自己的有益结果和巨大的优势，这些结果和优势本来会自然地从我们真正的或表面的一致意见中产生而来。任何政府在追求和保证人民的幸福过程中的力量和效率都依赖于意见，对于那个政府的利益的共同意见，也依赖于它的管理者们的智慧和一致。因此，我希望，作为人民的一部分，为了我们自己，也为了我们的后代，我们应该全心全意团结一致，在我们的影响力所能及的范围内推介这个宪法体制，并且把我们今后的思想和努力都集中起来使这个体制得到良好的管理。

总体来说，先生，我忍不住要表达一个愿望，我希望在这种情况下，这次大会的每个对此还持反对意见的成员能和我一起稍稍怀疑一下自己是否绝对正确，然后，为了表明我们的意见一致，在这份文件上签下自己的名字。

文学和生活

读者反应 基于富兰克林的论证，你会同意通过《美国宪法》吗？为什么？

主题焦点 富兰克林是怎样利用他作为一名外交家的经历来说服他的听众的？

阅读理解

1. 富兰克林给出了哪三个同意宪法的理由？
2. 富兰克林关于什么“从没在国外说过一个字”？
3. 富兰克林认为代表们的一致同意会带来什么好处？

思考

解释

1. 富兰克林通过第一段中的他的“坦白”取得了什么效果？（解释）
2. 为什么富兰克林承认宪法中的“错误”？（推断）
3. 富兰克林为“公共利益”压抑自己的“观点”的目的是什么？（分析）

评价

4. 富兰克林的演讲的整体结构产生了怎样的效果？解释原因。（评价）

拓展

5. 富兰克林在他的《自传》节选中详细描述了他试图达到道德完美境界的努力。将那篇文章中所描述的年轻的富兰克林和发表这篇演讲的这个富兰克林进行对比。（文学连线）

文学聚焦

演讲

在演讲中，亨利和富兰克林使用了很多不同的技巧来强调他们的观点，包括：反问，重复观点，重复和并列。

1. (a)找出一个亨利使用了一系列反问的例子。(b)这些反问要达到什么目的？

2. 找到一个亨利使用了重复技巧的例子。

3. (a)从富兰克林的演讲中找出三个重复观点的例子。(b)这种重复观点有什么效果？

4. 从富兰克林的演讲中找出一个并列的例子。这有什么效果？

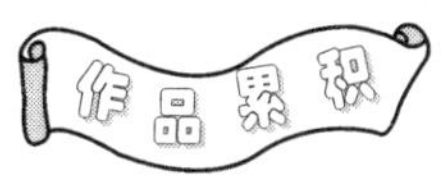

点子库

写作

1. 日记　作为弗吉尼亚众议院的一名议员，你刚刚听到了亨利强有力的演说。写一篇日记记录你的感受。

2. 演讲　想象你是弗吉尼亚州大会上的一名发言者，你不同意帕特里克·亨利的看法。写一篇演讲稿，反驳亨利的每一个观点。

3. 评论　评论员理查德·比曼认为：亨利有一种不同寻常的"理解（当时）政治事件的中心意义和重点的能力。（他是）美国曾经产生的最有力、最有效、并且一般来说有建设性的地方政治家。"利用这篇演讲中的证据，写一篇简短的文章来对比曼的评价做出回应。

项目

1. 著名演讲展示　收集不同历史时期的演讲，以及相关照片或图片。制作一个强调这些演讲中的重点段落的展示。

2. 多媒体报告　利用图片、地图和音乐作一次多媒体报告，为你班里的同学重现美国革命时期。（技术连线）

微型写作课

对演讲进行评价

帕特里克·亨利有能力在很短的时间内作一篇感人的演讲。选择一篇由有能力的现代演说家作出的演讲——例如：马里奥·库莫、罗纳尔多·里根或杰西·杰克森——写一篇评论文章，评价演讲者用来引导他的听众同意其观点的方法。

写作技巧重点：预先估计问题

如果想想你的听众可能会问的问题或反对观点，你就可以提前处理这些问题，由此减少听者脑海中的问题。注意亨利是怎样利用这些反问来预先估计听众的反对观点的。

演讲中的范例

我们用什么来反抗这些军队呢？我们要试试争辩吗？先生，我们已经尝试

着争辩了十年了。在这个话题上我们还有什么没说过的吗？什么也没有。

通过总结可能的反对意见并在有人提出之前就做出回应，亨利控制了他的辩论的发展方向。

构思

反复读几遍你所选择的演讲，概括出演讲者的主要观点，或注意他/她使用的有说服力的技巧。然后用评论的眼光来分析演讲者是否有效地支持了自己的主要观点和使用了说服性的技巧。

写稿

把你的每一段集中在一个观点上。例如：可以有一段集中评论演讲者对听众情感的激发。

修改

预先估计你的评论家可能提出的问题。想象你是一个持不同意见的读者，重读你的文章，注意你可能反驳的观点或你可能提出的问题。然后回到文章中，对这些可能出现的反对意见做出回应。

Guide for Interpreting

Patrick Henry (1736—1799)

It was said that Patrick Henry could move his listeners to anger, fear, or laughter more easily than the most talented actor. Remembered most for his fiery battle cry "Give me liberty or give me death," Henry is considered the most powerful orator of the American Revolution. He helped to inspire colonists to unite in an effort to win their independence. Shortly after his 1765 election to the Virginia House of Burgesses, Henry delivered one of his most powerful speeches, declaring his opposition to the Stamp Act. Over the protests of some of the most influential members, the Virginia House adopted Henry's resolutions.

Voice of Protest In 1775, Henry delivered his most famous speech at the Virginia Provincial Convention. While most of the speakers that day argued that the colony should seek a compromise with the British, Henry boldly urged armed resistance to England. His speech had a powerful impact on the audience, feeding the Revolutionary spirit that led to the signing of the Declaration of Independence.

In the years that followed, Henry continued to be an important political leader, serving as governor of Virginia and member of the Virginia General Assembly.

Benjamin Franklin (1706—1790)

Although his achievements spanned a wide range of areas — including science, literature, journalism, and education — Benjamin Franklin is most remembered as a statesman. He is the only American to sign the four documents that established the nation: the Declaration of Independence, the treaty of alliance with France, the peace treaty with England, and the Constitution.

A Persuasive Diplomat Franklin was a leader in the movement for inde-

pendence. In 1776, Congress sent him to France to enlist desperately needed aid for the American Revolution. Franklin's persuasive powers proved effective, as he was able to achieve his goal—a pivotal breakthrough that may have been the deciding factor in the war.

Helping Forge a Nation In 1783, Franklin signed the peace treaty that ended the war and established the new nation. He returned home to serve as a delegate to the Constitutional Convention in Philadelphia. There, as politicians clashed over plans for the new government, Franklin worked to resolve conflicts and ensure ratification of the Constitution.

Background for Understanding

HISTORY: PATRICK HENRY'S BRAVERY

Today, it's hard for us to imagine the bravery it took for speakers like Patrick Henry to publicly denounce the British king. England was the most powerful country in the world, and the odds were overwhelmingly against the colonies' winning their freedom. By criticizing the king, Patrick Henry and other colonial leaders were putting their lives on the line. If the colonies' efforts to win their independence had failed, Henry could have been executed for treason.

Henry was quite aware of this. In fact, he had openly been accused of treason when he delivered his speech in opposition to the Stamp Act in 1765. On that occasion, Henry had referred to two leaders who had been killed for political reasons and declared that King George III of Britain might "profit by their example." This shocked the members of the audience so much that they screamed out, accusing him of treason. Henry is reported to have replied, "If this be treason, make the most of it!"

Literature and your Life

CONNECT YOUR EXPERIENCE

You're probably already familiar with lines from many famous speeches—

even though you may not be aware of it. Lines like Martin Luther King's "1 have a dream" and John F. Kennedy's "Ask not what your country can do for you" have become a part of most Americans' vocabularies. The reason why those lines have become so famous is that they come from speeches — like the two you're about to read—that have shaped our nation's history.

Journal Writing What slogans or mottoes capture the attention of your generation? Choose one — from politics, music, or advertisements — and explain why it works.

THEMATIC FOCUS: A NATION IS BORN

What ideas about "life, liberty, and the pursuit of happiness" that the Constitution promises are planted in the speeches of Henry and Franklin?

Literary Focus

SPEECHES

Speeches have played an important role in American politics — from the Revolutionary period to the present. An effective speaker uses a variety of techniques to emphasize important points:

- Restatement: repeating an idea in a variety of ways
- Repetition: restating an idea using the same words
- Parallelism: repeating grammatical structures
- Rhetorical question: asking a question whose answer is self-evident; intended to stir emotions.

Speech In the Virginia Convention

Patrick Henry

Mr. President:

No man thinks more highly than I do of the patriotism, as well as abilities, of the very worthy gentlemen who have just addressed the house. But different men often see the same subject in different lights; and, therefore, I hope it will not be thought disrespectful to those gentlemen, if, entertaining, as I do, opinions of a character very opposite to theirs, I shall speak forth my sentiments freely and without reserve. This is no time for ceremony. The question before the house is one of awful moment to this country. For my own part, I consider it as nothing less than a question of freedom or slavery. And in proportion to the magnitude of the subject ought to be the freedom of the debate. It is only in this way that we can hope to arrive at truth, and fulfill the great responsibility which we hold to God and our country. Should I keep back my opinions at such a time, through fear of giving offense, I should consider myself as guilty of treason toward my country, and of an act of disloyalty toward the Majesty of Heaven, which I revere above all earthly kings.

Mr. President, it is natural to man to indulge in the illusions of hope. We are apt to shut our eyes against a painful truth, and listen to the song of that siren till she transforms us into beasts. Is this the part of wise men, engaged in a great and arduous struggle for liberty? Are we disposed to be of the number of those who having eyes see not, and having ears hear not, the things which so nearly concern their temporal salvation? For my part, whatever anguish of spirit it may cost, I am willing to know the whole truth; to know the worst and to provide for it.

I have but one lamp by which my feet are guided, and that is the lamp of experience. I know of no way of judging of the future but by the past. And judging by the past, I wish to know what there has been in the conduct of the British ministry for the last ten years to justify those hopes with which gentlemen have been pleased to solace themselves and the house? Is it that insidious smile with which our petition has been lately received? Trust it not, sir; it will prove a snare to your feet. Suffer not yourselves to be betrayed with a kiss. Ask yourselves how this gracious reception of our petition comports with those

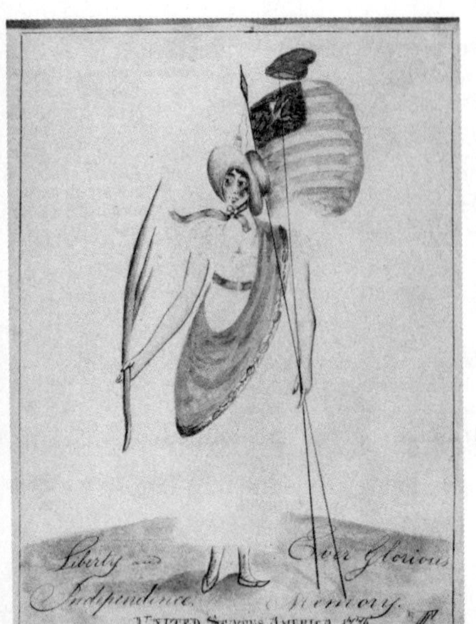

warlike preparations which cover our waters and darken our land. Are fleets and armies necessary to a work of love and reconciliation? Have we shown ourselves so unwilling to be reconciled that force must be called in to win back our love? Let us not deceive ourselves, sir. These are the implements of war and subjugation—the last arguments to which kings resort.

I ask gentlemen, sir, what means this martial array, if its purpose be not to force us to submission? Can gentlemen assign any other possible motive for it? Has Great Britain any enemy in this quarter of the world, to call for all this accumulation of navies and armies? No, sir, she has none. They are meant for us: they can be meant for no other. They are sent over to bind and rivet upon us those chains which the British ministry have been so long forging.

And what have we to oppose to them? Shall we try argument? Sir, we have been trying that for the last ten years. Have we anything new to offer upon the subject? Nothing. We have held the subject up in every light of which it is capable; but it has been all in vain. Shall we resort to entreaty and humble supplication? What terms shall we find which have not been already exhausted? Let us not, I beseech you, sir, deceive ourselves longer. Sir, we have done everything that could be done to avert the storm which is now coming on. We have petitioned; we have remonstrated; we have supplicated; we have prostrated ourselves before the throne, and have implored its interposition to arrest the tyrannical hands of the ministry and Parliament. Our petitions have been slighted; our remonstrances have produced additional violence and insult; our supplications have been disregarded; and we have been spurned with contempt from the foot of the throne! In vain, after these things, may we indulge the fond hope of peace and reconciliation. There is no longer any room for hope. If we wish to be free, if we mean to preserve inviolate those inestimable privileges for which we have been so long contending, if we mean not basely to abandon the noble struggle in which we have been so long engaged, and which we have pledged ourselves never to abandon until the glorious object of our contest shall be obtained—we must fight! I repeat it, sir, we must fight! An appeal to arms and to the God of Hosts is all that is left us!

They tell us, sir, that we are weak — unable to cope with so formidable an adversary. But when shall we be stronger? Will it be the next week, or the next year? Will it be when we are totally disarmed, and when a British guard shall be stationed in every house? Shall we gather strength by irresolution and inaction? Shall we acquire the means of effectual resistance by lying supinely on our backs and hugging the delusive phantom of hope until our enemies shall have bound us hand and foot? Sir, we are not weak, if we make a proper use of those means which the God of nature hath placed in our power. Three millions of people, armed in the holy cause of liberty, and in such a country as that which we possess, are invincible by any force which our enemy can send against us. Besides, sir, we shall not fight our battles alone. There is a just God who presides over the destinies of nations and who will raise up friends to fight our battles for us. The battle, sir, is not to the strong alone; it is to the vigilant, the active, the brave. Besides, sir, we have no election; if we were base enough to desire it, it is now too late to retire from the contest. There is no retreat but in submission and slavery! Our chains are forged! Their clanging may be heard on the plains of Boston! The war is inevitable—and let it come! I repeat it, sir, let it come!

It is in vain, sir, to extenuate the matter. Gentlemen may cry, "Peace, peace" — but there is no peace. The war is actually begun! The next gale that sweeps from the north will bring to our ears the clash of resounding arms! Our brethren are already in the field! Why stand we here idle? What is it that gentlemen wish? What would they have? Is life so dear, or peace so sweet, as to be purchased at the price of chains and slavery? Forbid it, Almighty God! I know not what course others may take; but as for me, give me liberty or give me death!

Speech in the Convention

Benjamin Franklin

Mr. President,

I confess, that I do not entirely approve of this Constitution at present; but,

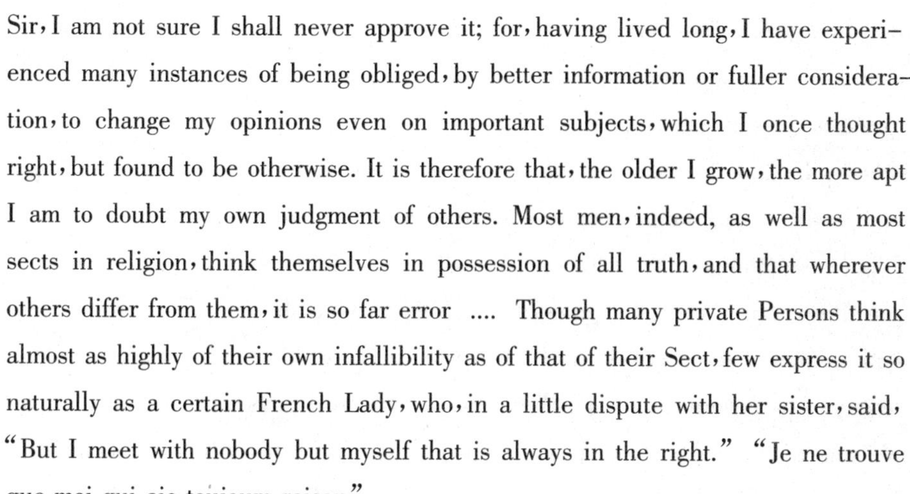

Sir, I am not sure I shall never approve it; for, having lived long, I have experienced many instances of being obliged, by better information or fuller consideration, to change my opinions even on important subjects, which I once thought right, but found to be otherwise. It is therefore that, the older I grow, the more apt I am to doubt my own judgment of others. Most men, indeed, as well as most sects in religion, think themselves in possession of all truth, and that wherever others differ from them, it is so far error .... Though many private Persons think almost as highly of their own infallibility as of that of their Sect, few express it so naturally as a certain French Lady, who, in a little dispute with her sister, said, "But I meet with nobody but myself that is always in the right." "Je ne trouve que moi qui aie toujours raison".

In these sentiments, Sir, I agree to this Constitution, with all its faults, —if they are such; because I think a general Government necessary for us, and there is no form of government but what may be a blessing to the people, if well administered; and I believe, farther, that this is likely to be well administered for a course of years, and can only end in despotism, as other forms have done before it, when the people shall become so corrupted as to need despotic government, being incapable of any other. I doubt, too, whether any other Convention we can obtain, may be able to make a better constitution; for, when you assemble a number of men, to have the advantage of their joint wisdom, you inevitably assemble with those men all their prejudices, their passions, their errors of opinion, their local interests, and their selfish views. From such an assembly can a perfect production be expected? It therefore astonishes me, Sir, to find this system approaching so near to perfection as it does; and I think it will astonish our enemies, who are waiting with confidence to hear, that our councils are confounded like those of the builders of Babel, and that our States are on the point of separation, only to meet hereafter for the purpose of cutting one another's throats. Thus I consent, Sir, to this Constitution, because I expect no better, and because I am not sure that it is not the best. The opinions I have had of its errors I sacrifice to the public good. I have never whispered a syllable of them abroad. Within these walls

they were born, and here they shall die. If every one of its, in returning to our Constituents, were to report the objections he has had to it, and endeavour to gain Partisans in support of them, we might prevent its being generally received, and thereby lose all the salutary effects and great advantages resulting naturally in our favour among foreign nations, as well as among ourselves, from our real or apparent unanimity. Much of the strength and efficiency of any government, in procuring and securing happiness to the people, depends on opinion, on the general opinion of the goodness of that government, as well as of the wisdom and integrity of its governors. I hope, therefore, for our own sakes, as a part of the people, and for the sake of our posterity, that we shall act heartily and unanimously in recommending this Constitution, wherever our Influence may extend, and turn our future thoughts and endeavors to the means of having it well administered.

On the whole, Sir, I cannot help expressing a wish, that every member of the Convention who may still have objections to it, would with me on this occasion doubt a little of his own infallibility, and, to make manifest our unanimity, put his name to this Instrument.

第四课

穷理查德的年鉴

本杰明·富兰克林（1706—1790）

本杰明·富兰克林

本杰明·富兰克林从十几岁到42岁退休，一直从事印刷行业。他的哥哥是一名印刷商，富兰克林最初在那里做学徒。16岁的时候，他不仅做印刷工作，而且还为他哥哥的报纸写一部分文章。富兰克林用“沉默好狗”做笔名，对波士顿的日常生活和政治进行了讽刺。在他的印刷生涯中诞生了他对美国文学的最受人欢迎和经久不衰的贡献之一——《穷理查德的年鉴》。富兰克林于1731至1757年期间出版的这份年刊里包含了各种信息、评论和建议，很受当时读者的欢迎。

“写作”的声誉　就像在为他哥哥的报纸所写的文章里署名“沉默好狗”一样，富兰克林也为他的《年鉴》创造出了一个假想的作者/编者：饶舌的里查德·桑德斯（和他的妻子布瑞吉特）来发表他的作品，但大家都知道富兰克林就是作者。尽管他用笔名出版，但《年鉴》还是为他赢得了天才作家的声誉。

成功的秘诀　和大多数年鉴一样，富兰克林的年历里也包含了日历的实

用信息,包括太阳、月亮还有天气。

《穷理查德的年鉴》的一个特色是有大量的简单朴素的格言和评论,其中有很多一直到今天还被广泛地引用。正是这些格言和它们典型的道德暗示使《年鉴》成为当时最畅销的书。富兰克林在他的年历中大多数页码的顶上或下面都印上一条格言，这些充满智慧而又简短的语言使他能表达很多道德内容,而同时又能取悦他的读者。

富兰克林在1758年开始出售这本年历,一直到1796年,只是名字不同。虽然现在我们不再每年有《穷理查德的年鉴》,但是富兰克林写出来的那些曾经使这本年鉴的每一页都生动活泼的格言却流传下来,成为美国文化的经典部分。

历史:谚语的传统

本杰明·富兰克林的大多数格言都是从没有作者的传统民间俗话改编而来的,这些就是我们所说的谚语。富兰克林认为好的散文最重要的两个特征就是清楚和简洁,所以重写了很多谚语,精心制造了简短、直接、机智又能给人以教益的格言。

谚语的历史几乎和语言本身的历史一样久远。谚语有很多不同的目的,在不同类型的情况下使用——有逗人笑的,有教育人的,有表示赞同的,有羞辱人的,有表达观点的,也有为谈话增加色彩的。

谚语作为从日常经验中提取出来的民间智慧的简洁表达,存在于所有的社会中。它们反映一种文化的世界观,表达对于命运、季节、自然界、工作和成就、爱、死亡和其他普遍经验的感受。这些值得纪念的点点智慧流传了几个世纪,可能就因为它们反映了关于人类本性不变的真理吧。

联系你的经历　“没有付出,没有收获。”“错进,错出。”你在汽车保险杠、T恤衫和广告牌上看到这样的短句。虽然这样的大众智慧的片断更可能从娱乐媒体中而不是一本年历中产生，但它们仍然折射出了现代社会的价值观，就像富兰克林的格言折射出了殖民地时期美国的价值观一样。

日志写作 想出至少三条现代格言。它们表达了美国文化的哪些方面？在你的日志中写出你的回答。

专题聚焦：定义美国民族 富兰克林的格言具有极大的影响力，甚至早期的美国硬币上都刻着"莫管闲事"，据说这是一句由富兰克林提出的警句。他的格言帮助塑造了整个民族的形象，这个国家的人们高度评价辛勤工作和常识情理。

格言

你可能会发现《穷理查德的年鉴》中的很多机智的谚语和格言你都已经很熟悉了。格言就是简明扼要的话，表述明智的或机智的评论或者普遍真理。有各种技巧使得格言容易记忆。有些含有韵律或重复的单词或发音，其他的则使用并列的结构来表达对比的含义。例如："没有付出，没有收获"这句格言中就使用了押韵、重复和并列结构。

穷理查德的年鉴（节选）

本杰明·富兰克林

傻瓜准备宴席，聪明人来享受。

选朋友要慎重，换朋友更要慎重。

你把商店管好，商店管你吃饱。

早睡早起，健康、富有、又聪明。

三个人中死了两个才能保守住秘密。

天助自助者。

一个烂苹果会让整堆苹果烂掉。

一个公开的敌人可能是个祸根，可是一个伪装的朋友更加糟糕。

今日事，今日毕。

一个真正的朋友是一笔最好的财产。

大船因为一道小缝沉没。

没有不需付出的收获。

小心不养成坏习惯比改正坏习惯要容易得多。

说得好不如做得好。

你爱生命吗？那就别浪费时间，因为生命就是由时间构成的。

把你受到的伤害写在尘土里，把你得到的收益刻在石头上。

脚下一滑可以很快康复，可舌头一滑（说错话）可能永远无法弥补。

如果你的头是蜡做的，那就别在阳光下走。

一个好的范例就是最好的布道。

饥饿就是最好的下饭菜。

没受过教育的天才就像矿井里的银子一样。

因为少了一个钉子，我们失去了一块马蹄铁；因为少了一块马蹄铁，我们失去了一匹马；因为少了一匹马，我们失去了骑手。

匆忙出差错。

智慧的门永远不会关闭。

爱你的邻居，但也不要拆掉你的篱笆。

依靠希望生活的人会饿死。

文学和生活

读者反应　你的朋友或家人曾经引用过富兰克林的哪些格言？

主题焦点　富兰克林的哪些格言表现了直到现在还被美国人广泛持有的价值观？

小组活动　请你班里的同学讲一讲他们从家里或朋友那里学到的民族或文化谚语。把这些谚语写在黑板上，并标明它们起源的国家。有没有和富兰克林的格言反映同样价值观的呢？

阅读理解

1. 本杰明•富兰克林所说的“最好的财富”是什么？

2. 找出两条讨论教育问题的格言。

3. 关于改掉坏习惯，富兰克林给出了什么建议？

4. 用你自己的话解释这里的三条格言。

思考

解释

1. 解释“选朋友要慎重，换朋友更要慎重。”和“把你受到的伤害写在尘土里，把你得到的收益刻在石头上”两句格言之间的联系。(联系)

2. 用你自己的话说出至少两个在富兰克林的格言中明显反复出现的主题。(分析)

3. 根据这些格言，你会怎样描述富兰克林的生活哲学？(推断)

应用

4. 如果你需要从《穷理查德的年鉴》中选择一条格言作为你的人生箴言，你会选择哪一条？为什么？(联系)

文学聚焦

格言

为了使这些格言中所表达的观点更容易记忆，富兰克林使用了重复、并列和押韵。

1. 在下面的格言中找出富兰克林使用的技巧，然后说明它们的意思：

a. 脚下一滑可以很快康复，可舌头一滑(说错话)可能永远无法弥补。

b. 早睡早起，让人健康、富有、又聪明。

2. 解释为什么格言要比简单表达它的意思更有影响力。

3. 使用富兰克林的技巧，写一条现代生活的格言。

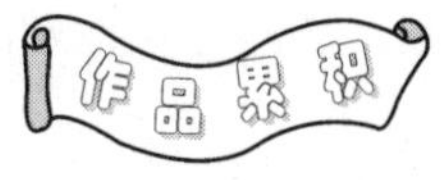

点子库

写作

1. 个人叙述　叙述你生活中和富兰克林的某一条格言有关系的一个片断或场景，总结你从这次经历中所学到的经验教训。

2. 杂志文章　写一篇帮助人们获得成功的友谊的文章，包括怎样保持好朋友的建议。使用至少四条富兰克林的格言来支持你的观点。

3. 民间故事　写出一个原创的民间故事或语言，作为支持《年鉴》中的一条格言的例证。

项目

1. 指导手册　做一本名叫《穷理查德的生活指南》的手册。参考《穷理查德的年鉴》中全部格言，并按不同标题把相关格言分类，例如："做生意的指导"和"充分利用每一天"。在标题中总结穷理查德的建议，引出每一章。

2. 纸板游戏　根据《穷理查德的年鉴》创造一种游戏。设计游戏规则和一块游戏纸板。一种可供选择的方式：做出游戏卡片，上面标明主题，例如："友谊"和"教育"。

微型写作课

格言网页

想象你要制作一个格言的网页，这个网页应该适应青少年的需要。为《穷理查德的年鉴》中的格言写一篇吸引人的介绍，然后制作两到三个链接，例如"穷理查德谈友谊"，以便你的用户可以点击这个链接，浏览相关的格言。

写作技巧重点：适合媒体的风格

为了达到为因特网写作的目的，你要考虑到人们怎样从不同的媒体中获得信息，然后为这种媒体选择一种适合的风格。媒体向其听众或观众发布新闻或任何信息的方式决定了它的风格：

广播

利用简洁生动的语言快速传播重点事实。

电视

对视觉形象和影视片段进行解释或补充的文字。

新闻杂志

对一个事件的多方面进行深层次的剖析。

在你制作网页时，记住即将从中获取信息的人们和他们如何获取信息这两方面决定了你的风格。

构思

根据你对你的观众的了解来决定怎样最好地表现富兰克林的格言。总览全部的格言，确定要包含的链接并为它们命名，然后选择要列入各个链接的格言。

写稿

考虑人们是怎样使用因特网的：他们通过快速的浏览来决定一个网页是否能引起他们的兴趣。制作一个使人感兴趣又包含大量信息的网页。

修改

确保你写作风格的每一个方面都能适应因特网的快速步伐的需要。如果你看到这个网页的话，会有兴趣点击链接吗？对你发现的弱项进行返工。

Guide for Interpreting

Benjamin Franklin (1706—1790)

From his teen years until his retirement at forty-two, Benjamin Franklin worked as a printer. Franklin got his start as an apprentice to his brother, a Boston printer. By the time he was sixteen, he was not only printing, but writing parts of his brother's newspaper. Using the name "Silence Dogood," Franklin satirized daily life and politics in Boston. His printing career gave birth to one of Franklin's most popular and enduring contributions to American culture, Poor Richard's Almanack. This annual publication, which Franklin published from 1732 through 1757, contained information, observations, and advice that was very popular with readers of his day.

<u>The "Write" Reputation</u> Just as he had signed "Silence Dogood" to the letters he wrote for his brother's paper, Franklin created for the Almanack a fictitious author/editor, the chatty Richard Saunders (and his wife, Bridget). It was, however, well known that Franklin was the author. Despite the fact that he published under a pseudonym, the Almanack earned him a reputation as a talented writer.

<u>Secret to Success</u> Like most almanacs, Franklin's contained practical information about the calendar, the sun and moon, and the weather.

Poor Richard's Almanack also featured a wealth of homespun sayings and observations, many of which are still quoted today. It was these aphorisms, with their characteristic moral overtones, that made the Almanack a bestseller. Franklin put an aphorism at the top or bottom of most pages of his almanacs. The wit and brevity of these sayings allowed Franklin to include many moral messages in very little space, while also entertaining his readers.

Franklin sold the almanac in 1758, and it continued publication under a different name until 1796. While Poor Richard's Abnanack is no longer with us, the aphorisms that enlivened its pages under Franklin live on as classic bits of Americana.

Background for Understanding

SOCIAL STUDIES: THE PROVERB TRADITION

Most of Benjamin Franklin's aphorisms are adapted from anonymous traditional or folk sayings, known as proverbs. Franklin, who believed that clarity and brevity were two of the most important characteristics of good prose, rewrote many proverbs, crafting short, direct, witty sayings that taught a lesson.

Proverbs are nearly as old as language itself. They have many different purposes and are used in different types of situations — to amuse, to educate, to sanction, to shame, to make a point, or to add color to a conversation.

As expressions of basic principles of folk wisdom drawn from he daily experiences of a group of people, proverbs exist in all societies. They reflect a particular culture's view of the world and convey feelings about fate, the seasons, the natural world, work and effort, love, death, and other universal experiences. These memorable bits of wisdom have survived centuries, perhaps because they reflect unchanging truths about human nature.

Literature and your Life

CONNECT YOUR EXPERIENCE

"No pain, no gain." "Garbage In, Garbage Out" You see sayings like these on bumper stickers, T-shirts, and billboards. Though such snippets of pop-wisdom are more likely to originate in entertainment media than an almanac, they mirror modern social values, just as Franklin's aphorisms reflect the values of colonial America.

Journal Writing Think of at least three contemporary aphorisms. What do

they say about our culture? Write your answers in your journal.

THEMATIC FOCUS: DEFINING AN AMERICAN

Franklin's aphorisms were so influential that even this early United States coin was stamped "mind your business", a motto supposedly suggested by Franklin. His sayings helped shape the nation's image as a country of people who prized hard work and common sense.

Literary Focus

APHORISMS

You may find that you are already familiar with many of the witty sayings, or aphorisms, from Poor Richard's Almanack. An aphorism is a short, concise state-ment expressing a wise or clever observation or a general truth. A variety of de-vices make aphorisms easy to remember. Some contain rhymes or repeated words or sounds; others use parallel structure to present contrasting ideas. The aphorism "no pain, no gain" for instance, uses rhyme, repetition, and parallel structure.

Poor Richard's Almanack

Benjamin Franklin

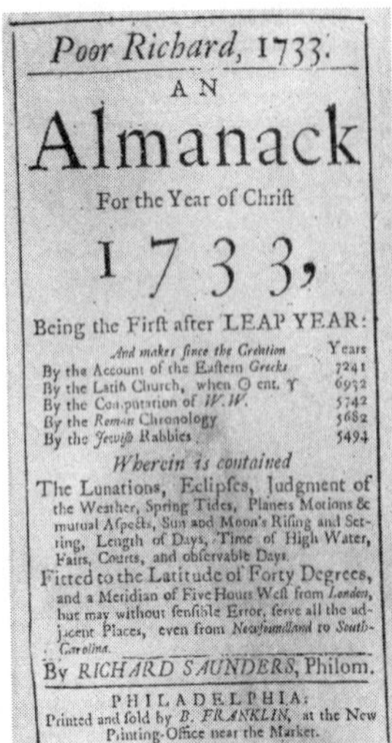

Poor Richard, 1733.

AN

Almanack

For the Year of Chrift

1733,

Being the Firft after LEAP YEAR:

And makes ſince the Creation	Years
By the Account of the Eaſtern *Greeks*	7241
By the Latin Church, when ☉ ent. ♈	6932
By the Computation of *W.W.*	5742
By the *Roman* Chronology	5682
By the *Jewiſh* Rabbies	5494

Wherein is contained

The Lunations, Eclipfes, Judgment of the Weather, Spring Tides, Planets Motions & mutual Afpects, Sun and Moon's Rifing and Setting, Length of Days, Time of High Water, Fairs, Courts, and obfervable Days.

Fitted to the Latitude of Forty Degrees, and a Meridian of Five Hours Weft from *London*, but may without fenfible Error, ferve all the adjacent Places, even from *Newfoundland* to *South-Carolina*.

By *RICHARD SAUNDERS*, Philom.

PHILADELPHIA:
Printed and fold by *B. FRANKLIN*, at the New Printing-Office near the Market.

Fools make feasts, and wise men eat them.

Be slow in choosing a friend, slower in changing.

Keep thy shop, and thy shop will keep thee.

Early to bed, early to rise, makes a man healthy, wealthy, and wise.

Three may keep a secret if two of them are dead.

God helps them that help themselves.

The rotten apple spoils his companions.

An open foe may prove a curse; but a pretended friend is worse.

Have you somewhat to do tomorrow, do it today.

A true friend is the best possession.

A small leak will sink a great ship.

No gains without pains.

Tis easier to prevent bad habits than to break them.

Well done is better than well said.

Dost thou love life? Then do not squander time; for that's the stuff life is made of.

Write injuries in dust, benefits in marble.

A slip of the foot you may soon recover, but a slip of the tongue you may never get over.

If your head is wax, don't walk in the sun.

A good example is the best sermon.

Hunger is the best pickle.

Genius without education is like silver in the mine.

For want of a nail the shoe is lost; for want of a shoe the horse is lost; for want of a horse the rider is lost.

Haste makes waste.

The doors of wisdom are never shut.

Love your neighbor; yet don't pull down your hedge.

He that lives upon hope will die fasting.

第五课

从新白宫里写给女儿的信

阿比盖尔·史密斯·亚当斯 (1744—1818)

妻子、母亲、作家、第一夫人、革命家、女权运动先驱——阿比盖尔·史密斯·亚当斯拥有所有这些身份，而且还不止于此。作为美国第二任总统约翰·亚当斯聪明坦率的妻子和第六任总统约翰·昆西·亚当斯的母亲，阿比盖尔·亚当斯是当时最有影响的美国妇女之一。

阿比盖尔·史密斯·亚当斯

因为在美国革命中和革命后负有的政治职责，约翰·亚当斯在那十年中的大多数时间都不在家。因此，阿比盖尔成为一名热心的通信者，她给她的丈夫和亲戚们写信，与他们讨论各种问题，包括妇女权益和她对奴隶制的反对，等等。在战争期间，她甚至还随时向她的丈夫报告英国部队行动的最新消息。

约翰·亚当斯被选为美国总统之后，他和阿比盖尔成为住在白宫里的第一对夫妇。这封阿比盖尔写给她女儿的信描述了他们临时的家，抓住了这个新国家的生活本质。

阿比盖尔·亚当斯逝世22年之后，人们发表了她的信件。今天，人们普遍认为她是美国妇女运动的先驱。

米歇尔·纪饶姆·让·德·克雷弗科尔 (1735—1813)

法国贵族米歇尔·纪饶姆·让·德·克雷弗科尔是第一位把美国比喻为一个融合一切的熔炉的作家，他用编年史的形式记录了他作为一名欧洲移民在美国的经历。他理想化的描绘证实了很多人认为美国是一个充满繁荣希望的国家的看法。

米歇尔·纪饶姆·让·德·克雷弗科尔

克雷弗科尔在殖民区旅行了十年之后，在纽约的奥兰治县结婚并定居在一个农场上，在那里他开始用写作描绘他在美国的经历。1780年，他坐船来到伦敦，两年以后他的《一个美国农民的信》在那里出版。这本书被翻译成几种语言，为克雷弗科尔赢得了声誉。

在法国停留一段时间之后，他于1783年作为法国领事回到美国，却发现他的农场被烧毁，他的妻子被杀死，而他的孩子则被送走和他们的养父母住在一起。当1789年法国革命开始后，他被迫回到巴黎。后来他逃到了诺曼底，在那里他继续描写那个曾经接纳过他而他却再也无法见到的国家。

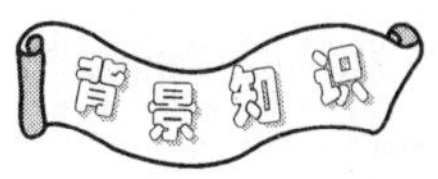

历史：克雷弗科尔的理想化的美国

当米歇尔·纪饶姆·让·德·克雷弗科尔出版了《一个美国农民的信》，他描述了饱受压迫、渴望更好的生活的欧洲人想象中的国家。然而，美国的生活却远远不是田园诗般闲适的，但这不是欧洲人想要听到的事实。

因为这个国家需要的是勤奋的工人，而不是那些追求悠闲生活的人，因此很自然有些美国领导人对克雷弗科尔的热烈的描述可能产生的效果感到担忧。乔治·华盛顿说那些信“实在太过恭维”。而作为对这本书的回应，智慧诙谐的富兰克林则于1784年写作并且发表了（首先是用法文）《给要移居美国的人的忠告》。富兰克林在文章开始就警告说虽然“在那个国家没有什么人像欧洲的穷人一样过得那么凄惨”，但是那里也没有很多富人。他继续写道，“美国是一个劳动的国家”，它需要的是有献身精神的技术工人，那些希望过上悠闲生活的人不必来到美国。

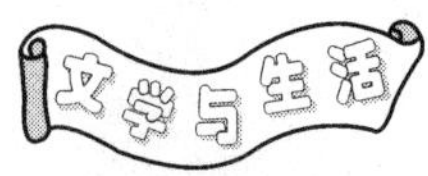

联系你的经历 当你想联系一个朋友的时候，你很可能会打个电话或发送一封电子邮件。在我们这个高科技的世界里，使用纸和笔的人越来越少了。然而，就在不久以前，通信还是远距离交流的唯一途径。

日志写作 如果写信是你唯一可以选择的交流方式，那么你的生活将会发生什么样的变化？

主题焦点：定义美国人 信件是早期的美国人发送和接收个人、职业和政治信息的生命线。在一个建立在自由思想的基础之上的国家里，信件是一个与个人读者和公众读者交流观点和看法的重要手段。克雷弗科尔和亚当斯的信告诉我们在国家的初期做一个美国人意味着什么？

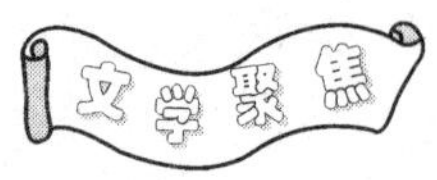

私人信和公开信（书信） 像亚当斯这样的私人信件多为对话式的并且只写给收信人自己看。而与之不同的是，克雷弗科尔的《一个美国农民的信》虽然假设是一个叫做詹姆斯的美国农民写给他的朋友F.B.先生的，但实际上却是为众多读者所写的公开信。这种被称做“书信”的文学作品是为大众创作的，但却采用个人信件的形式写作。

从新白宫里写给女儿的信

阿比盖尔·史密斯·亚当斯

我亲爱的孩子：

我上周日到达了这里，没有碰到什么值得注意的事情，只是我们在走出巴尔的摩的时候迷了路，我们先顺着福来德里克路走了8—9英里，然后就不得不在树林里又走了8英里，我们在树林里走了两个小时，也没找到一个向导或是一条小路。幸运的是，我们碰到了一个独自游荡的黑人，雇他做了向导，这才从困境中解脱了出来。然而，在巴尔的摩，在你到达“城市”之前，你所能看见的只有森林。这名义上的“城市”，也只是没有玻璃窗的小屋散布在树林中而已，而你在树林里走上几英里也看不见任何人烟。如果城市里的建筑是紧凑完整的话，那么应该是足够国会和相关人员住的，但是，按照它们目前的完工情况和分散的状况，我看它们不能带来什么大的安慰。从我的窗口可以看见流向亚历山德拉的河，看着船只来来往往。房子的面积宏大，需要大约30个佣人来打扫和整理房间，做房子里和马厩里的日常活计。这可真是和总统的工资非常相称的一栋建筑啊。整栋房子的照明，从厨房到客厅和寝室，确实是一个沉重的负担。为了不每天冻得发抖，我们必须生火，这又是一个非常令人振奋的安慰。摇铃能在这大城堡里帮助我们，使我们不用各处奔走，而这里的摇铃却极度缺乏，整栋房子里没有一个摇铃，你能得到的只是许诺而已。这里的生活是那么不方便，以至于我不知道应该做

在修建白宫的工地上

什么事或是应该怎么做了。乔治镇和城里的很多夫人都来拜访了我，昨天我回访了15位——乔治镇看起来是那样的一个地方，天哪，和它相比我们的米尔顿就是漂亮的了。

不过让我们别做比较了——如果他们能给我安一些摇铃，再给我足够生火用的木头，我就会很高兴了。无论在什么地方生活三个月，我几乎都能让自己知足。但是，你能相信我们被森林包围着却没有木头用，只因为我们找不到人来砍伐和运送木材吗？布里斯勒和一个人达成协议，由那个人为他供应木头。他只弄到了一小部分，只有几捆，而其中的大多数都被用来在我们搬来之前烘干房子的墙壁了。昨天那个人告诉他，他也没法找人砍伐和运送木头了。他试过用煤，但是我们找不到人为我们制造和安装炉子。实际上，我们进入了一个"新的国家"。

你千万不要把我信里的内容告诉别人，而且，如果有人问你我认为这里怎么样，你就说我写信告诉你这里的情况很好，事实也是这样。房子是可以居住的，但是没有一套房间是完全建成的，而除了抹墙之外的所有内部装修都是在布里斯勒来了以后才做的。我们没有篱笆、院子或其他房子外面的设施，我把那间很大的还没装好的会见室作为了一间晾衣服的房间。主楼梯现在还没建好，今年冬天是建不好了。有六个房间现在很舒服了，两个分给了总统和肖先生，两个楼下的房间，一个做了普通的起居室，一个做了招待室。椭圆形房间在楼上，设计做绘画室，里面有深红色的家具。现在这是一个很不错的房间了，但是到它完全装好的时候，它会非常漂亮。在以往的12年中，如果人们早就把它作为未来政府所在地而改进的话，如果在新英格兰肯定会这样，那么现在的种种不便就不会存在。这是一个美丽的地方，有进行各种改善的潜力，我看它看得越多，我就越喜欢它。

在我坐下来给你写信之后，有一个从蒙特福依来的佣人拜访了我，他带来了古斯提斯市长的一封短信，还有路易斯夫人送给我的一条鹿腿和一封亲切的祝贺我到达这个城市的贺信，还有华盛顿夫人的问候和邀请我去蒙特福依的口信。如果健康状况允许的话，我会在离开这个地方之前去拜访他们的。

爱你的妈妈　阿比盖尔•亚当斯

1800年11月21日于华盛顿

文学和生活

读者反应 在亚当斯对于白宫和华盛顿特区周围地区的描述中，有什么地方使你感到惊讶？

主题焦点 对于我们理解我们国家的第一批领导人努力建立一个集中的国家政府时面对的困难，亚当斯的信件提供了什么样的帮助？

阅读理解

1. 亚当斯是怎样描述华盛顿的市区和周围环境的？

2. 描述白宫中生活区域的状况。

思考

解释

1. 你认为亚当斯为什么不让她的女儿把她的抱怨告诉别人？（推断）

2. 你怎样描述亚当斯对她的新家的感受？（归类）

评价

3. 在亚当斯生活的时代，能写出既有趣又能传达丰富的信息的信件会受到人们的高度评价。你认为亚当斯是一个好的写信人吗？解释你的回答。（评价；证据支持）

一个美国农民的信（节选）

米歇尔·纪饶姆·让·德·克雷弗科尔

在这个伟大的美国庇护所里，欧洲的穷人们通过某些方式、由于不同的原因而聚集到了一起。他们为什么要询问彼此是哪个国家的人呢？唉，他们中有三分之二的人都没有国家。一个四处流浪、辛苦工作还要忍饥挨饿的可怜人，他的生活就是不断的悲伤和忍受折磨或者令人痛苦的贫穷，那个人能说英国或者任何其他国家是他的祖国吗？一个国家不给他面包，那里的土地没有给他任何收成，他在那里只能遇到富人的白眼、法律的严厉、监狱和惩罚，

他在这个行星的广阔表面上没有一寸土地？不！他们受到各种动机的驱使来到了这里。这里的所有东西都使他们获得新生：新的法律，新的生活模式，新的社会系统。在这里，他们变成了人，而在欧洲他们就像那么多无用的植物，缺乏肥沃的土壤和清新的雨露，他们枯萎了，被贫困、饥饿和战争摧毁了。然而现在因为移植带来的力量，像所有其他的植物一样，他们生根发芽、蓬勃生长了！

以前，在他们的国家里，在任何重要公民的名单中他们都没有一席之地，却只被列入穷人的名单里。而在这里他们则被承认为正式的公民。是什么无形的力量造成了这个惊人的变化呢？是这里的法律和他们的勤劳。这法律，这宽容的法律从他们到达伊始就保护着他们，在他们身上印着居留的标记；他们靠自己的劳动获得充足的报酬，而这些报酬积累起来就使他们获得了土地，土地使他们拥有了自由人的资格，伴随着那种资格而来的就是人们有可能赢得的所有利益。这就是我们的法律每天发挥的伟大作用。这些法律从何而来？从我们的政府。我们的政府从何而来？它产生于王权批准认可的那些人最初的精神和强烈愿望中。

一个贫穷的欧洲移民对一个使他一无所有的国家有什么留恋的呢？对他而言仅有的牵绊就是对于那种语言的掌握和几个和他自己一样穷的亲属的爱。现在他的祖国是给他土地、面包、保护和尊严的那个国家；“哪里有面包，哪里就是祖国”是所有移民的箴言。那么，美国人，这个新的民族，到底是什么民族呢？他既不是欧洲人，也不是欧洲人的后代，因此他是你在任何其他国家都不可能见到的各种民族的奇特混合。我可以向你指出一个家庭，他们的祖父是一个英国人，他的妻子是荷兰人，他们的儿子娶了一个法国妻子，而现在他们的四个儿子则分别娶了四个不同国籍的妻子。一个美国人就是抛弃了他自己所有古老的成见和态度，而从他接受的新的生活方式中、他服从的新的政府中和他拥有的新身份中获得了新的态度和思想。我们伟大的“养母”将他收入膝下，他就成为一个美国

抽烟的美国农民

人。在这里，各个国家的人们都融入了一个新的民族，而他们的劳动和后代终有一天会在世界上引起巨大的变化。美国人就是西方的朝圣者，他们带来了大量很久以前起源于东方的艺术、科学、活力和勤奋，现在他们将要完成这个循环。美国人曾经一度散居在欧洲各处，在这里他们被纳入一个历史上最优秀的社会系统中，从此以后，由于他们所处的截然不同的风气的力量，这个系统将会变得与众不同。因此，对这个国家，美国人应该怀有比他自己或他祖先出生的那个国家更深厚的爱。在这里，他的辛勤劳动与他获得的报偿是平等的，他的劳动是建立在自然和自利的基础之上的，难道还需要更大的诱惑吗？他的妻子和孩子们，以前徒然地向他要求一小点儿面包，而现在，他们变得圆润欢畅，快乐地帮助他们的父亲清理田地，从那些田地里将长出茂盛的庄稼，为他们所有的人提供食物和衣服。既没有专横的王子，富裕的男修道院长，也没有有权有势的统治者来要求他交出一部分收成。在这里，宗教只要求他付出一点儿，自愿付给牧师的一小部分工资和对上帝的奉献，他怎么能拒绝这些呢？美国人是一个新人，按照新的原则做事，因此他必须接受新的观点，形成新的思想。他从不自觉的懒散、卑屈的依赖、贫困和无用的劳动转变为一种性质完全不同的辛劳，获得充足的赖以为生的报酬——这就是美国人。

文学和生活

读者反应　如果你是一个18世纪的欧洲人，这篇文章能促使你移居美国吗？为什么？

主题焦点　克雷弗科尔的观点适合今天的美国吗？为什么？

阅读理解

1. 克雷弗科尔将移民美国以前的贫困的欧洲人比喻为什么？

2. 将卑贱的欧洲农民转变为受尊敬的美国公民的“无形的力量”的根源是什么？

思考

解释

1. 克雷弗科尔在描述美国的过程中多次回归到哪个主题上？（分析）

2. 你怎么总结克雷弗科尔对美国人的定义？（得出结论）

评价

3. 克雷弗科尔暗示说自利是一种有价值的品质，因为这能促使人们更勤奋地工作。现代社会普遍将自利作为一种值得称赞的品质吗？为你的回答做出解释。（评价）

私人和公开信（书信）

阿比盖尔·亚当斯的私人信提供了一个观察新国家里的生活的有趣视角。这些信最初只是写给她的家人看的。而与之不同的是，克雷弗科尔则通过书信的形式面对广大的读者——也就是经常写给一个虚构人物的公开信。

1. 如果亚当斯的信是写给公众读者的话，指出至少两个不同的方面。

2. 公开信的形式是怎样帮助克雷弗科尔说服他的读者接受他的观点的？解释理由。

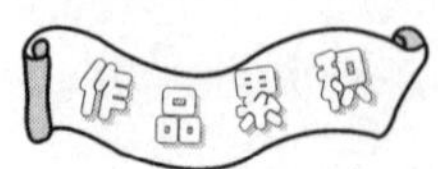

点子库

写作

1. 描述性的信件　写一封信，为一个从没见过你家的朋友描述你的家，使他的脑海里生成一幅图像。

2. 思考散文　克雷弗科尔将美国看做一个具有光明前景的国家。你怎样看这个国家？写一篇简短的散文，思考美国对你意味着什么。

3. “融合一切的熔炉”公开信　在一封公开信中，赞扬美国城市中的民族多元化。你的写作意图是说服公众相信文化的多元化是大有裨益的。

项目

1. 美国人的解释　美国人是什么？用你自己选择的形式对克雷弗科尔的问题做出回答。考虑利用一首诗或照片剪辑来表达你的回答。

2. 广告宣传运动　制作一个广告宣传来吸引18世纪晚期的移民。利用克雷弗科尔在他的信中给出的描述。(传媒连线)

微型写作课

私人信件

如果你能给生活在过去的人写信，你会怎样对他讲述现代的生活呢？从美国历史中选择一个你感兴趣的人物。写一封私人信件，为他讲述从他生活的时代到现在，一个与他有关的地方发生了什么变化。就像一个外国笔友一样，你的收信人也生活在另一个国度——过去的国度——也需要帮助才能理解你的世界。

写作技巧重点：必要的环境/背景知识

当为一个与你自己的文化不同的人写作时，你需要提供必要的环境和背景知识——一个读者要理解你提到的事情所必需的信息。别以为读者对于像“工作和学校”这样的词语的理解会和你自己的理解一样。

例如，阿比盖尔·亚当斯作为妇女权益的拥护者，会对妇女问题的进步很感兴趣，例如带薪产假，但是为了理解这一概念，她需要妇女在家庭和工作中的角色变化的相关信息。

构思

为你的信选定一个合适的主题。列出你要提到的发展变化。然后确定你的读者要理解你的观点所需的背景信息。

写稿

在写信的时候时刻想着你写信的对象，记得这是一封私人信件，是你们两人之间一对一的交流形式。

修改

重读你的信，问问你自己你的收信人是否能理解你提到的事物。对一个不熟悉20世纪的美国的人，你是否提供了必要的环境和背景知识？

Guide for Interpreting

Abigail Smith Adams (1744—1818)

Wife, mother, writer, first lady, revolutionary, women's rights pioneer — Abigail Smith Adams was all these and more. As the intelligent, outspoken wife of John Adams, the second president of the United States, and the mother of John Quincy Adams, the sixth president, Abigail Adams was one of the most influential American women of her time. John Adams's political duties during and after the Revolution kept him from home for the better part of ten years. Abigail, therefore, became an avid correspondent, penning hundreds of letters to her husband and relatives, discussing everything from women's rights to her opposition to slavery. During the war, she even kept her husband posted oil the movements of British troops.

When John Adams was elected president of the United States, he and Abigail became the first couple to live in the White House. This letter to her daughter, which describes their temporary home, captures the essence of life in the new nation.

Twenty-two years after Abigail Adams's death, her letters were published. Today, she is widely recognized as a pioneer of the American women's movement.

Michel-Guillaume Jean de Crèvecoeur (1735—1813)

The first writer to compare America to a melting pot, French aristocrat Michel-Guillaume Jean de Crèvecoeur chronicled his experiences as a European immigrant in America. His idealistic descriptions confirmed many people's vision of America as a land of great promise.

After spending ten years traveling the colonies, Crevecoeur married and settled on a farm in Orange County, New York, where he began writing about his experiences in America. In 1780, he sailed to London, where his Letters From an

American Farmer was published two years later. This book, which was translated into several languages, made Crevecoeur famous.

After visiting France, he returned to America in 1783 as a French Consul to find his farm burned, his wife killed, and his children sent to live with foster parents. When the French Revolution began in 1789, he was obliged to return to Paris. He later fled to Normandy, where he continued to write about the adoptive country he would never again see.

Background for Understanding

HISTORY: CREVECOEUR'S AMERICA IDEALIZED

When Michel-Guillaume Jean de Crevecoeur published Letters From an American Farmer, he captured the imagination of downtrodden Europeans hungry for a better life. Life in America, however, was far from idyllic, but that was not what Europeans wanted to hear.

Because the country needed hard workers, not those seeking an easy life, it is no wonder that some American leaders worried about the effects of Crèvecoeur's glowing descriptions. George Washington called the Letters "rather too flattering," and the wise and witty Ben Franklin responded by writing and publishing (first in France) Advice to Such as Would Remove to America in 1784. Franklin begins by warning that even though "there are in that country few people so miserable as the poor of Europe" neither are there many rich. "America is a land of labor," he continues, and what it needs are dedicated, skilled workers. Those interested in a life of leisure need not apply.

Literature and your Life

CONNECT YOUR EXPERIENCE

When you want to get in touch with a friend, you probably pick up the phone or send an e-mail. In our high-tech world, fewer and fewer people reach for pen and paper. Not too long ago, however, letters were the only means of com-

municating over distances.

Journal Writing How might your life change if letter writing were the only communication option available to you?

THEMATIC FOCUS: DEFINING AN AMERICAN

Letters were the lifeline through which early Americans sent and received personal, professional, and political information. In a country founded on free thought, letters were an important means of sharing ideas and opinions with both private and public readers. What do the letters of Crèvecoeur and Adams tell us about what it meant to be an American during our nation's early years?

Literary Focus

PRIVATE AND PUBLIC LETTERS (EPISTLES)

Personal or private letters, like Adams's, tend to be conversational and intended only for the reader (s) to whom they are addressed. Crèvecoeur's Letters, on the other hand, while supposedly written by an American farmer named James to his friend Mr. F. B., are actually public letters intended for a wide audience. Called epistles, these works of literature are created for general publication but written in the form of personal letters.

Letter to Her Daughter From the New White House

Abigail Adams

Washington, 21 November, 1800

My Dear Child:

I arrived here on Sunday last, and without meeting with any accident worth noticing, except losing ourselves when we left Baltimore and going eight or nine miles on the Frederick road, by which means we were obliged to go the other eight through woods, where we wandered two hours without finding a guide or the path. Fortunately, a straggling black came up with us, and we engaged him as a guide to extricate us out of our difficulty; but woods are all you see from Baltimore until you reach the city, which is only so in name. Here and there is a small cot, without a glass window, interspersed amongst the forests, through which you travel miles without seeing any human being. In the city there are buildings enough, if they were compact and finished, to accommodate Congress and those attached to it; but as they are, and scattered as they are, I see no great comfort for them. The river, which runs up to Alexandria, is in full view of my window, and I see the vessels as they pass and repass. The house is upon a grand and superb scale, requiring about thirty servants to attend and keep the apartments in proper order, and perform the ordinary business of the house and stables; an establishment very well proportioned to the President's salary. The lighting of the apartments, from the kitchen to parlors and chambers, is a tax indeed; and the fires we are obliged to keep to secure us from daily agues is another very cheering comfort. To assist us in this great castle, and render less attendance necessary, bells are wholly wanting, not one single one being hung through the whole house, and promises are all you can obtain. This is so great an inconvenience, that I know not what to do, or how to do. The ladies from Georgetown and in the city have many of them visited me. Yesterday I returned fifteen visits—but such a place as Georgetown appears—why, our Milton is beautiful.

But no comparisons—if they will put me up some bells and let me have wood enough to keep fires, I design to be pleased. I could content myself almost anywhere three months; but, surrounded with forests, can you believe that wood is not to be had because people cannot be found to

cut and cart it? Briesler entered into a contract with a man to supply him with wood. A small part, a few cords only, has he been able to get. Most of that was expended to dry the walls of the house before we came in, and yesterday the man told him it was impossible for him to procure it to be cut and carted. He has had recourse to coals; but we cannot get grates made and set. We have, indeed, come into a new country.

You must keep all this to yourself, and, when asked how I like it, say that I write you the situation is beautiful, which is true. The house is made habitable, but there is not a single apartment finished, and all withinside, except the plastering, has been done since Briesler came. We have not the least fence, yard, or other convenience without and the great unfinished audience room I make a drying-room of, to hang up the clothes in. The principal stairs are not up, and will not be this winter. Six chambers are made comfortable; two are occupied by the President and Mr. Shaw; two lower rooms, one for a common parlor, and one for a levee room. Upstairs there is the oval room, which is designed for the drawing room, and has the crimson furniture in it. It is a very handsome room now; but, when completed, it will be beautiful. If the twelve years, in which this place has been considered as the future seat of government had been improved, as they would have been if in New England, very many of the present inconveniences would have been removed. It is a beautiful spot, capable of every improvement, and, the more I view it, the more I am delighted with it.

Since I sat down to write, I have been called down to a servant from Mount Vernon, with a billet from Major Custis, and a haunch of venison, and a kind, congratulatory letter from Mrs.Lewis, upon my arrival in the city, with Mrs. Washington's love, inviting me to Mount Vernon, where, health permitting, I will go before I leave this place.

Affectionately, your mother

Abigail Adams

Letters from an American Farmer

Michel. Guillaume Jean de Crevecoeur

In this great American asylum, the poor of Europe have by some means met together, and in consequence of various causes; to what purpose should they ask one another what countrymen they are? Alas, two thirds of them had no country. Can a wretch who wanders about, who works and starves, whose life is a continual scene of sore affliction or pinching penury, can that man call England or any other kingdom his country? A country that had no bread for him, whose fields procured him no harvest, who met with nothing but the frowns of the rich, the severity of the laws, with jails and punishments; who owned not a single foot of the extensive surface of this planet? No! Urged by a variety of motives, here they came. Everything has tended to regenerate them; new laws, a new mode of living, a new social system; here they are become men: in Europe they were as so many useless plants, wanting vegetative mold and refreshing showers;they withered, and were mowed down by want, hunger, and war; but now by the power of transplantation, like all other plants they have taken root and flourished!

Formerly they were not numbered in any civil lists of their country, except in those of the poor; here they rank as citizens. By what invisible power has this surprising metamorphosis been performed? By that of the laws and that of their industry. The laws, the indulgent laws, protect them as they arrive, stamping on them the symbol of adoption; they receive ample rewards for their labors; these accumulated rewards procure them lands; those lands confer on them the title of freemen, and to that title every benefit is affixed which men can possibly require. This is the great operation daily performed by our laws. From whence proceed these laws? From our government. Whence the government? It is derived from the original genius and strong desire of the people ratified and confirmed by the crown ....

What attachment can a poor European emigrant have for a country where he

had nothing? The knowledge of the language, the love of a few kindred as poor as himself, were the only cords that tied him: his country is now that which gives him land, bread, protection, and consequence: Ubi panis ibi patria is the motto of all emigrants. What then is the American, this new man? He is either a European, or the descendant of a European, hence that strange mixture of blood, which you will find in no other country. I could point out to you a family whose grandfather was an Englishman, whose wife was Dutch, whose son married a French woman, and whose present four sons have now four wives of different nations. He is an American, who, leaving behind him all his ancient prejudices and manners, receives new ones from the new mode of life he has embraced, the new government he obeys, and the new rank he holds. He becomes an American by being received in the broad lap of our great Alma Mater. Here individuals of all nations are melted into a new race of men, whose labors and posterity will one day cause great changes in the world. Americans are the western pilgrims, who are carrying along with them that great mass of arts, sciences, vigor, and industry which began long since in the east; they will Finish the great circle. The Americans were once scattered all over Europe: here they are incorporated into one of the finest systems of population which has ever appeared, and which will hereafter become distinct by the power of the different climates they inhabit. The American ought therefore to love this country much better than that wherein either he or his forefathers were born. Here the rewards of his industry follow with equal steps the progress of his labor; his labor is founded on the basis of nature, self-interest; can it want a stronger allurement? Wives and children, who before in vain demanded of him a morsel of bread, now, fat and frolicsome, gladly help their father to clear those fields whence exuberant crops are to arise to feed

and to clothe them all; without any part being claimed, either by a despotic prince, a rich abbot, or a mighty lord. Here religion demands but little of him; a small voluntary salary to the minister, and gratitude to God; can he refuse these? The American is a new man, who acts upon new principles; he must therefore entertain new ideas, and form new opinions. From involuntary idleness, servile dependence, penury, and useless labor, he has passed to toils of a very different nature, rewarded by ample subsistence—This is an American.

第3部分

Unit Three

A 国家的发展

A Growing Nation

时代故事

1800—1870

1831年，法国人亚力克希斯·德·托克维尔被派到美国来考察美国监狱，然而他最后描写的东西却有趣得多：一个喧闹的新国家，那里充满乐观追求命运的人们。他在《论美国的民主》中说，美国人“对于人类的可完美性抱有活跃的信念”，他们相信“今天在他们看来很好的东西可能明天就会被更好的东西取代”。

1831年吸引了德·托克维尔的那种喧闹的精神在接下来的几十年中就发展成了一个充满变化的“明天”：到1870年为止，个人主义、急剧的人口和经济增长以及美国内战都使得这个国家的精神日趋成熟。而在这个时代，美国文学也成熟了起来。1831年，德·托克维尔写道：“美国没有产生几个知名作家……（英国文学）的光线仍然能够射入那个新世界的森林中。”而到了1870年，美国却已经产生了很多“知名作家”：鄂文、库柏、布莱恩特、坡、爱默生、梭罗、霍桑、梅尔维尔、迪金森，还有惠特曼——他们身上的那种毫无疑问的美国之光最终射入而且远远超越了那“新世界的森林”。

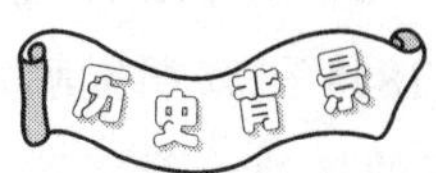

1800年，美国由聚集在东海岸附近的16个州构成。1803年，托马斯·杰弗逊签署了路易斯安那购买合同，将国家的领土扩大了一倍。这个国家的迅速

成长引起了民族自豪感和自我意识的高涨。

国内民主的成长:1800–1840 随着国家的扩张,美国人开始拥有了更多直接控制政府的权利。由于对于选举权的财产要求开始被取消,1828年安德鲁·杰克逊当选“人民的总统”,预示着普通人时代的开始。然而,那个时代的民主进步仅限于男性白人身上。政治方面对于妇女的注意还远远不足,而多数美国黑人仍然保持着奴隶身份。这一时期最悲惨的政策之一就是“印第安人迁移”,美洲土著人的部落土地被没收,被迫向西迁移——在1838年的“血泪之路”上,1.5万名切落基人中的4000人在从佐治亚向俄克拉何马艰苦跋涉的路途中失去了生命。

世界舞台上的年轻国家 1812年的战争使欧洲人相信美国将要继续留在世界舞台上。在1823年的“门罗政策”中,詹姆斯·门罗总统警告欧洲不要干涉新成立的拉丁美洲国家事务。19世纪30年代,因为从墨西哥接管得克萨斯的问题,美国卷入了一场战争。1836年,墨西哥军队进行了著名的阿拉莫袭击,在那次袭击中,所有的得克萨斯抵抗者都被杀死了。1845年,美国合众国接纳了得克萨斯,由此引发了与墨西哥之间的战争(1846–1848),最终美国战胜,获得了包括加利福尼亚在内的更多的领土。不久之后,1849年的“掘金热潮”使得成千上万人涌向这片充满希望的土地。

西进之路与经济增长 从某种意义上说,随着新领土的开辟和交通运输的改善,美国历史的全过程就可以被看做一次不断向西行进的盛装游行。1825年在纽约建成的爱丽运河引发了一阵修建运河的浪潮。而在19世纪50年代,“铁马”——铁路——开始占领了美国远距离旅行方式的首要地位,到了1869年,铁路线将东西海岸联系了起来。

送给印第安部落首领的冠军奖牌

技术进步促进了社会变化。在东北部到处新工厂林立。钢犁和收割机使在广阔的草地上的耕种变得可行,从而鼓励了人们在边境地区定居。电报则帮助实现了跨越长距离的几乎是即时的交流。1844年,发明家萨缪尔·F. B.·摩尔斯从华盛顿发往巴尔的摩的一条信息可以作为这个时代的箴言:“上帝创造了什么啊!”

变化的狂风 即使最乐观的观察者也很确定,19世纪中期的美国在面对光明希望的同时也面临着问题。新的繁荣引发了激烈的竞争，产生了使用童工和工作条件不安全的工厂。1840年，多数妇女还不能投票选举或申请法律诉讼。而19世纪40、50年代则爆发了争取提高妇女权利的运动，其中最著名的是1848年的赛内卡瀑布大会。最重要的是，存在了几个世纪的奴隶制度使这个国家分裂为两方面。废止派反对奴隶制度，而州权利的拥护者们则认为联邦政府不能使各州屈从于它的意志，在19世纪50年代，他们之间的矛盾尖锐化了，这不断聚集的风暴最终于1861年爆发成了战争。但这其实是从第一个带着锁链的奴隶被带到这片大陆上起开始，积蓄了250年的风暴。

美国文学时代的到来 1800年以前，美国作家的作品并没有很多人重视——甚至在美国也没有，然而那种情况很快就开始改变了。这个时期的作家们将要标榜美国的声音——个人化、特殊、大胆——以及它的基本主题：个人对于标榜自己的渴求。

浪漫主义 虽然19世纪早期的作家之间存在着毫无疑问的差异，但是他们——华盛顿•鄂文、詹姆斯•菲尼莫•库柏、威廉姆•库仑•布莱恩特和埃德加•爱伦•坡——都可以被算做浪漫主义作家。浪漫主义是19世纪一个影响了欧洲和美国的文艺运动。浪漫主义作家认为想象高于理智，直觉高于事实。第一个在世界范围内赢得声誉的美国作家是华盛顿•鄂文，他的《纽约的历史》(1809)在文学史中留下了印记，这并不是一个枯燥的历史事件记录，而是随作者意愿改变事实的喧闹而欢乐的故事。

浪漫主义作家们往往陶醉于自然。鄂文的《锐普•凡•温克尔》和《睡谷的传说》使人们对他所热爱的哈德森河谷产生了浓厚的兴趣。詹姆斯•菲尼莫•库柏的《四个皮长袜的故事》描述了纳提•巴姆博在纽约北部偏远的森林中的功绩。纳提•巴姆博是一个绝对正直的人，他认为自然比文明要好，他为后来无数的美国英雄设立了一个模范。

浪漫主义写作经常强调人类经历中奇妙幻想的方面。痛苦的天才埃德加•爱伦•坡因为他那些令人难以忘怀的诗作和充满悬念的故事，直到今天仍然非常受读者欢迎，正如一位传记作家说过的，他笔下的人物“不是很古怪就

是生活在另一个世界里的人”。

新英格兰文艺复兴：1840–1855 1837年，拉尔夫·沃尔多·爱默生，一位曾经在波士顿做过牧师的作家，做出了他著名的演说《美国学者》，他在演说中呼吁美国的知识分子独立于欧洲之外。爱默生认为美国作家们应该开始用新的方法来阐释他们自己的文化了。仿佛是对于爱默生呼吁的回应，在1840年至1855年之间，在波士顿及周围地区发生了一次惊人的文学发展运动。这次“新英格兰的繁荣”中产生了很多伟大的作家和不朽的作品。

先验主义 这些作家中的大部分，如果不是全部的话，都受到了最初由德国人伊曼努尔·康德表述的先验主义哲学的影响。在他的《实践理性批判》(1788)中，康德将先验定义为人类通过直觉获得的理解。美国的先验主义与爱默生有着紧密的联系，同时也吸收了其他思想家的观点：希腊哲学家柏拉图，法国数学家帕斯卡，瑞典神秘主义者和科学家斯韦登博格，还有反物质主义的佛教思想。先验主义者们相信大多数基本真理都存在于感官经验之外，正如爱默生所说的，是“超灵魂……一个共通的、善良的普遍存在”。

瓦尔登湖 先验主义哲学最有影响力的作品出自爱默生和他的年轻朋友及门徒——亨利·大卫·梭罗，他退出了社会，独自住在瓦尔登湖畔。梭罗在他对于这次经历的记述《瓦尔登湖》的开头写道：“当我写出以下这些文章时……我住在马萨诸塞的康科德县的瓦尔登湖边，在我自己建造的小房子里，在森林中独自生活，离最近的邻人也有一英里远，只靠我双手的劳动来赚钱生活。”《瓦尔登湖》发表于1854年，其中包含18篇散文，谈论的话题包括从红蚂蚁和黑蚂蚁之间的战争到个人与社会的关系等。梭罗对于自然的评论表现了他的个人主义、简单和对不公正的消极抵抗等生活哲学。

运输矿石的火车

罪恶的可能性 并不是每个人都拥有和先验主义者一样的乐观看法。内森尼尔·霍桑和荷曼·梅尔维尔表达了比较黑暗的看法，按照霍桑所说的，他们代表了那些挖掘到我们共同本性深处，发现那里并不总是闪光的，而是经常“有些幽暗”的人。霍桑的祖先对他的清教徒影响总是存在于他的意识之中。他的杰作《红字》(1850)中的故事背景是17世纪的波士顿，表达了关于罪恶、隐藏的罪行、虚伪和谦卑的主题。而在《七道山墙的房子》中，他则深入考察了17世纪的巫术、精神错乱和一个传说中的诅咒。

霍桑可以说是梅尔维尔的良师益友。梅尔维尔的长篇小说《白鲸》(1851)受到了否定的评论，他在抑郁之中与那位年长于他、也更加成功的作家成为朋友。这两个人都从比较悲观的角度观察人类生活，但是他们的性格却大相径庭。霍桑虽然倾向于独处，但他稳定沉静，是一个没有幻觉的精明的人。与他相反的是，梅尔维尔是一个总是与世界对立的人，他的性格扭曲而神秘。在他事业中的大部分时间，他都对自己的命运充满怒气，就像《大白鲸》中的阿哈勃船长对那条使他残废的白鲸感到怒不可遏一样。

在阿姆赫斯特的家里 当梭罗在瓦尔登湖边种豆子的时候，爱米丽•迪金森正在马萨诸塞州阿姆赫斯特旁边的小镇里成长。她令人震惊而又高度集中的诗作使她跻身于美国最伟大的诗人之列——虽然不是在她有生之年里。在一生的后半期中，狄金森隐遁于世，她并不是为了发表而写作，甚至也不是写给家人，而是出自一种个人的需要，她需要努力解决关于死亡、不朽和灵魂的问题——那些传统宗教没有解决的问题。

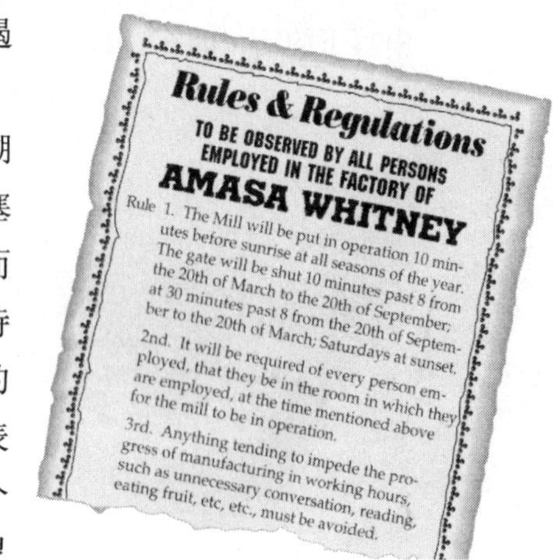
Rules & Regulations
TO BE OBSERVED BY ALL PERSONS EMPLOYED IN THE FACTORY OF
AMASA WHITNEY

Rule 1. The Mill will be put in operation 10 minutes before sunrise at all seasons of the year. The gate will be shut 10 minutes past 8 from the 20th of March to the 20th of September; at 30 minutes past 8 from the 20th of September to the 20th of March; Saturdays at sunset.

2nd. It will be required of every person employed, that they be in the room in which they are employed, at the time mentioned above for the mill to be in operation.

3rd. Anything tending to impede the progress of manufacturing in working hours, such as unnecessary conversation, reading, eating fruit, etc, etc., must be avoided.

工厂工作规章制度公告

新英格兰以外 同时，那位典范美国诗人却正在乡村四处流浪，打零工挣钱来继续写诗。1855年，纽约人沃尔特•惠特曼发表了他的创新诗集——《草叶集》，骄傲地从布鲁克林到宇宙四处传播他那“粗野的呐喊”。大多数美国读者对这位革命性诗人不规则的形式和直率的语言不屑一顾，但是爱默生的慧眼能够辨别新颖的创作，他对惠特曼的作品大加褒扬。在1800年至1870年之间的所有诗人中，惠特曼会对美国文学产生最持久的影响——虽然《草叶集》的第一版只卖出了不到20本。

壁炉旁的诗人 以上那些是20世纪的学者们筛选出的那个时代的文学巨匠。然而，在1850年，美国的读者们很可能会指出另外4个新英格兰的作家，他们被称做“壁炉旁的诗人”：亨利•沃兹华兹•朗费罗，一位哈佛大学教授和

极其受欢迎的诗人；约翰·格林里夫·威替尔，来自一个勤奋工作的教友派农民家庭；詹姆斯·拉塞尔·洛维尔，出生在富有高贵的家庭里；还有奥利佛·温德尔·赫尔密斯，诗人兼医师，他是这群诗人自评的桂冠诗人。

繁盛之后 随着战争阴云的不断聚集，东北部创造性的爆发开始趋于平息了。反对奴隶制的作家，诸如爱默生、梅尔维尔、威替尔和洛维尔，在内战中强烈支持北部的斗争。梭罗和霍桑在战争结束前就逝世了。惠特曼在战争中做了一名护士，并将战争诗歌收入了他后来版本的《草叶集》。迪金森在她的诗作中根本不提战争。奥利佛·温德尔·赫尔密斯精力充沛天性快乐，他比那著名的一代中的其他人都长寿。他成为“树上的最后一片叶子”，这是他自己在1831年发表的一首描写梅尔维尔的祖父——一位革命战争退伍老兵的诗中写下的话，那时这位诗人和他的国家都还年轻。

The Story of the Times
1800—1870

In 1831, the Frenchman Alexis de Tocqueville, sent to report on America's prisons, ultimately wrote about something far more interesting: a bustling new nation full of individuals optimistically pursuing their destinies. His Democracy in America observed that Americans had "a lively faith in the perfectibility of man," believing "what appears to them today to be good may be superseded by something better tomorrow."

The bustling spirit that had enchanted De Tocqueville in 1831 would make for a turbulent "tomorrow" in the decades to come: By 1870, industrialism, explosive population and economic growth, and the Civil War had all aged the nation's spirit. American literature also matured during this time. In 1831, De Tocqueville wrote, "America has produced very few writers of distinction .... The literature of England still darts its rays into the forests of the New World." By 1870, America had produced many "writers of distinction": Irving, Cooper, Bryant, Poe, Emerson, Thoreau, Hawthorne, Melville, Dickinson, and Whitman—all of whom eventually shone their unmistakably American light into and far beyond "the forests of the New World".

Historical Background

In 1800, the United States consisted of sixteen states clustered near the east

coast. In 1803, Thomas Jefferson doubled the nation's size by signing the Louisiana Purchase. The rapid growth of the nati on inspired an upsurge in national pride and self-awareness.

<u>The Growth of Democracy at Home: 1800–1840</u> As the nation expanded, Americans began to take more direct control of their government. The 1828 election of Andrew Jackson, "the People's President," ushered in the era of the common man, as property requirements for voting began to be eliminated. The democratic advances of the time, however, were confined to white males. Scant political attention was paid to women, and most African Americans remained enslaved. One of the most tragic policies of this period was "Indian removal," the forced westward migration of Native Americans from confiscated tribal lands — as in the 1838 "Trail of Tears," in which 4,000 of 15,000 Cherokee perished on the trek from Georgia to Oklahoma.

<u>Young Nation on the World Stage</u> The War of 1812 convinced Europeans that the United States was on the world stage to stay. In the Monroe Doctrine of 1823, President James Monroe warned Europe not to intervene in the new Latin American nations. In the 1830's, the U.S. became embroiled in a conflict over the secession of Texas from Mexico; in 1836, the Mexican Army made its famous assault on the Alamo, in which every Texan defender was killed. When Texas was admitted to the Union in 1845, the resulting war with Mexico (1846 –1848) ended in a U.S. victory, which added more territory to the nation, including California. Soon after, the Gold Rush of 1849 drew hundreds of thousands to this new land of promise.

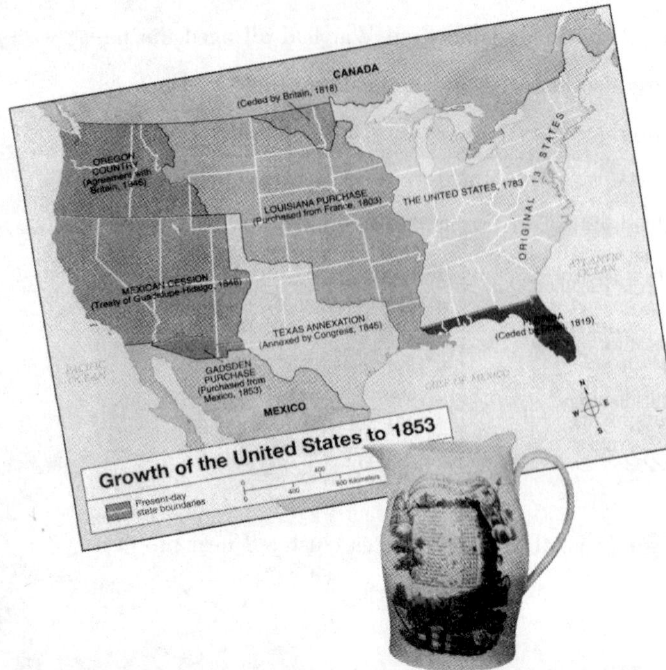

The Way West and Economic Growth In a sense, the entire course of American history can be seen as a pageant rolling ever westward, as new territories opened up and transportation improved. The Erie Canal, completed in New York in 1825, set off a wave of canal building. In the 1850's, the "iron horse"—the railroad—began to dominate long-distance American travel; by 1869, rail lines linked east and west coasts.

Advances in technology spurred social change, Factories sprang up all over the Northeast. The steel plow and reaper encouraged frontier settlement by making farming practical on the vast, sod-covered grasslands. The telegraph facilitated almost instant communication across great distances. Inventor Samuel F.B. Morse's message from Washington to Baltimore in 1844 could serve as the motto for this era: "what hath God wrought!"

Winds of Change It was evident to even the most cheerful observer that the United States at mid-century faced trouble as well as bright promise. The new prosperity unleashed fierce competition, leading to the creation of factories scarred by child labor and unsafe working conditions. In 1840, most women could not vote or file a lawsuit. The 1840's and 1850's saw an outburst of efforts promoting women's rights, notably the 1848 Seneca Falls Convention. Above all, the centuries-old institution of slavery bitterly divided the nation. The conflict between abolitionists, who opposed slavery, and the advocates of states' rights, who argued that the federal government could not bend states to its will, sharpened in the 1850's. The gathering storm finally burst into war in 1861, but it was a storm that had been building for 250 years, ever since the first slave was brought in chains to this continent.

Literature of the Period

American Literature Comes of Age Before 1800, American writers were not widely read-not even in America, but that situation soon began to change. The writers of this period would define the American voice—personal, idiosyncratic, bold—and its primary theme: the quest of the individual to define him or herself.

Romanticism Despite their unmistakable differences, the writers of the early nineteenth century—Washington Irving, James Fenimore Cooper, William Cullen Bryant, and Edgar Allan Poe—can all be described as Romantics. Romanticism is an artistic movement that dominated Europe and America during the nineteenth century. Romantic writers elevated the imagination over reason and intuition over fact. Washington Irving, the first American to be read widely overseas, made his mark with his History of New York (1809), which is not a dry historical record but a rollicking narrative that alters facts at will.

The Romantics reveled in nature. Irving's "Rip Van Winkle" and "The Legend of Sleepy Hollow" sparked an interest in his beloved Hudson River Valley. James Fenimore Cooper's four Leatherstocking Tales feature the exploits of Natty Bumppo in the frontier forests of upstate New York. A man of absolute moral integrity, Natty Bumppo preferred nature over civilization, establishing the pattern for countless American heroes to come.

Romantic writing often accented the fantastic aspects of human experience. The tortured genius Edgar Allan Poe remains popular to this day for his haunting poems and suspenseful stories whose characters, as one biographer has said, "are either grotesques or the inhabitants of another world than this."

New England Renaissance: 1840–1855 In 1837, Ralph Waldo Emerson, a former Boston minister, delivered his famous oration "The American Scholar", calling for American intellectual independence from Europe. Emerson believed that American writers should begin to interpret their own culture in new ways. As if in response to Emerson's call, an impressive burst of literary activity took place in and around Boston between 1840 and 1855. This "flowering of New Eng-

ATTENTION
SOUTHERN MEN!
DOWN WITH
THE ABOLITION PRESS
MEET AT
SCHNEIDER'S
At 8 o'clock This Night.

place in and around Boston between 1840 and 1855. This "flowering of New England" would produce an array of great writers and enduring literature.

<u>Transcendentalism</u> Most, if not all, of these writers were influenced by the Transcendental philosophy originally expressed by the German Immanuel Kant. In his Critique of Practical Reason (1788), Kant defines the transcendental as the understanding a person gains intuitively. Closely associated with Emerson, American Transcendentalism drew on other thinkers as well: the Greek philosopher Plato, the French mathematician Pascal, the Swedish mystic and scientist Swedenborg, and the anti-materialism of Buddhist thought. The Transcendentalists believed that the most fundamental truths lie outside the experience of the senses, residing instead, as Emerson put it, in the "Over-Soul ... a universal and benign omnipresence."

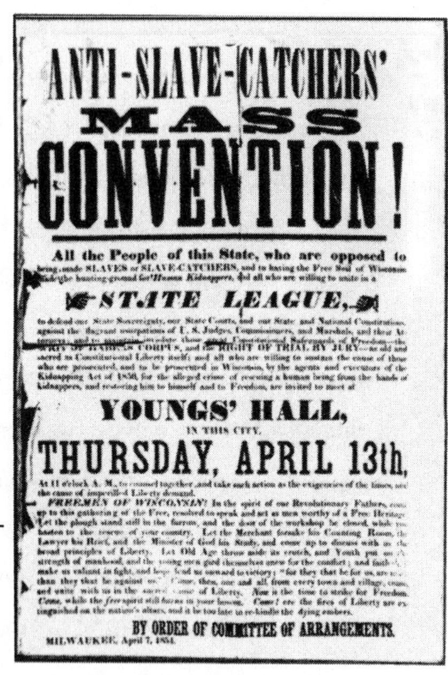

<u>Walden</u> The most influential expression of Transcendental philosophy came from Emerson and his younger friend and protege, Henry David Thoreau, who withdrew from society to live by himself on the shores of Walden Pond. Thoreau begins Walden, his account of this experience, by writing, "When I wrote the following pages... I lived alone, in the woods, a mile from any neighbor, in a house which I had built myself, on the shore of Walden Pond, in Concord, Massachusetts, and earned my living by the labor of my hands only." Published in 1854, Walden consists of eighteen essays about matters ranging from a battle between red and black ants to the individual's relation to society. Thoreau's observations of nature reveal his philosophy of individualism, simplicity, and passive resistance to injustice.

<u>The Possibility of Evil</u> Not everyone shared the Transcendentalists' optimistic views. Nathaniel Hawthorne and Herman Melville expressed the darker vision of those who, in Hawthorne's words, "burrowed into the depths of our com-

mon nature" and found the area not always shimmering, but often "dusky". Hawthorne's Puritan heritage was never far from his consciousness. His masterpiece, The Scarlet Letter (1850), set in Boston in the seventeenth century, deals with sin, concealed guilt, hypocrisy, and humility. In The House of the Seven Gables, he delves into seventeenth-century witchcraft, insanity, and a legendary curse.

Hawthorne became a kind of mentor to Melville. Depressed about the negative critical response to his novel Moby-Dick (1851), Melville befriended the older, more successful writer. Both men saw human life in grim terms, but their personalities were quite different. Hawthorne, despite a tendency toward solitude, was stable and self-possessed, a shrewd man without illusions. Melville, by contrast, was a man at odds with the world, a tortured and cryptic personality. For a large part of his career, he raged against his fate, much as Captain Ahab in Moby-Dick unleashed his fury against the white whale that had maimed him.

At Home in Amherst While Thoreau was planting beans next to Walden Pond, Emily Dickinson was growing up in the nearby town of Amherst, Massachusetts. Her startling, intensely focused poetry catapulted her into the company of the greatest American poets—although not in her lifetime. A recluse for the second half of her life, Dickinson did not write for publication, or even for her family, but rather from a personal need to wrestle with questions about death, immortality, and the soul-questions unresolved by conventional religion.

Beyond New England Meanwhile, the quintessential American poet was tramping about the countryside, laboring at odd jobs to finance his poetry. In 1855, New Yorker Walt Whitman published his groundbreaking series of poems, Leaves of Grass, proudly broadcasting his "barbaric yawp" from Brooklyn to the universe. Most American readers ignored the irregular forms and frank language of this revolutionary poet, but Emerson knew an American original when he saw one and praised Whitman's work. Of all the poets of the period between 1800 and 1870, Whitman would have the most lasting effect on American literature—despite the fact that the first edition of Leaves sold fewer than twenty copies.

Fireside Poets Those were the literary giants of the period, as singled out by twentieth-century scholars. In 1850, however, the American reading public would probably have pointed instead to four other New England writers, known as the Fireside Poets: Henry Wadsworth Longfellow, a Harvard professor and tremendously popular poet; John Greenleaf Whittier, from a hardworking Quaker farm family; James Russell Lowell, born to wealth and position; and Oliver Wendell Holmes, a poetphysician and the unofficial laureate of the group.

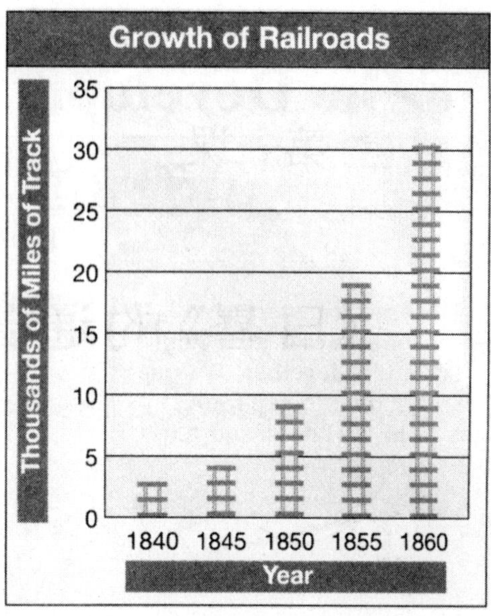

After the Flowering As the war clouds gathered, the great burst of creativity in the Northeast began to subside. Antislavery writers, such as Emerson, Melville, Whittier, and Lowell, strongly supported the northern effort in the Civil War. Thoreau and Hawthorne died before the war ended. Whitman worked as a nurse in the war and incorporated war poems in his later editions of Leaves of Grass. Dickinson ignored the war in her poetry. Oliver Wendell Holmes, energetic and cheerful, outlasted the rest of his renowned generation. He became "the last leaf upon the tree", to quote words he himself had written about Melville's grandfather, an old Revolutionary War veteran, in a poem published in 1831, when the poet and his country were still young.

第一课

《日晷》的通告

玛格丽特·福勒 (1810—1850)

玛格丽特·福勒个性刚强，她对很多女人的自甘低于男人一等表示轻蔑，激励女性发展自己的才能。她想象男性和女性之间的一种平等的伙伴关系，这种关系将存在于从婚姻生活到最高级别的政府管理和商业生活等各个层面。她写道："我们要让所有对男性开放的道路也同样对女性开放。"

玛格丽特·福勒

一位有影响的知识女性 福勒的事业是从作为一名教师开始的，她先后在波士顿和普罗维登斯从事教学工作。之后，她停止教学，转而组织了一系列女性公众讨论小组，讨论具有知识性和思想性的问题。她与拉尔夫·沃尔多·爱默生和其他一些新英格兰的作家和思想家建立了联系，而他们当时正在进行一个名为"先验主义"的哲学和文学运动，这一运动重点强调人文和自然之间的联系。当他们开始出版自己的期刊《日晷》时，福勒担任了编辑工作，同时也对出版发行作出了贡献。

不幸的结局　为了完成一生的夙愿，她于1846年去欧洲旅行。在1850年回国途中，她在纽约的火岛附近遭遇轮船失事，与她的丈夫和儿子一起淹死了。

拉尔夫·沃尔多·爱默生 (1803—1882)

拉尔夫·沃尔多·爱默生

拉尔夫·沃尔多·爱默生是他所在的时代最有影响力的作家和哲学家之一。1836年他发表了散文《自然》，标志着先验主义的开端。爱默生、福勒、亨利·大卫·梭罗和其他与这一运动有关的人组成了一个讨论群体，被称做"先验主义俱乐部"。这个小组定期在爱默生在马萨诸塞州康科德的家里聚会，讨论他们关于自然、个人主义和人类精神的观点。

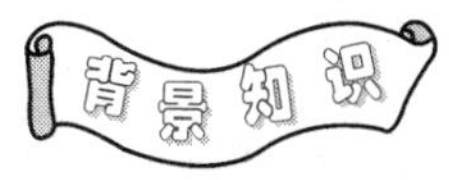

文学：玛格丽特·福勒和《日晷》

19世纪30年代，被称做"先验主义"的文学和哲学运动在新英格兰具有一定影响，它的主要发言人是拉尔夫·沃尔多·爱默生。随着这个运动的发展，参与其中的人们开始寻求更多的听众来宣传他们的观点。他们决定出版一份期刊，定名为《日晷》，并选择了玛格丽特·福勒和拉尔夫·沃尔多·爱默生作为联合主编。他们对福勒的选择是既不同寻常又非常明智的——不同寻常，是因为人们从来没听说过一名女性编辑；但这又是明智的，因为只有通过福勒的操作、组织和推动，才能使这份期刊获得成功。

《日晷》每年出版四次。经过无数次的拖延之后，福勒本人又写了几篇文章，才完成了第一期，使它在1840年7月问世。在《日晷》出版的4年中，许多作家都因它而成名，其中就包括亨利·大卫·梭罗。福勒承担了很大部分的工作，两年之后，她因为压力太大而辞去了编辑的职务。之后，由于饱受资金问题的困扰，又失去了福勒有组织的领导，这份期刊仅仅维持了两年。

联系你的经历 你是否曾经和一群朋友合作，进行一个发展更多听众或观众的项目呢？你们可能表演了一出戏剧，制作了一份简讯，或者画了一幅墙画。无论你们的目的是什么，你都很可能感受到与大家交流观点并为共同目标工作的兴奋。这就是1840年造就了《日晷》的那种精神。

日志写作 假设你要制作一份简讯，记下你关于所选主题的想法。

专题聚焦：炉火和营火 19世纪中期，在探险界的先锋们向西方进发的时候，知识界的先锋，例如先验主义者们，却在探索着哲学和文学领域中的思想观点。先验主义者们希望激励别人改变态度、价值观和言行。一份期刊怎样能对一个国家的性质产生这样的影响力？

通告 政治家和作家们依靠通告来宣传他们想让公众了解的事件或新书。通告就是一个公开通知，一份正式宣言。通告的主要目的是吸引公众的兴趣，但它也可以达到其他的目的。例如，在《〈日晷〉的通告》中，爱默生和福勒想赢得他们的听众的支持，使人们对这份期刊产生期待，并向作家们征集稿件。他们也概述了这份期刊的哲学思想。

《日晷》的通告

玛格丽特·福勒 和 拉尔夫·沃尔多·爱默生

我们请国人注意这个新的产物。虽然我们为保证这份期刊能受到大家的欢迎而颇下了一番苦功，但它可能不会看起来很出人意料。本期刊物的编辑无须为自己的热心参与而自责，相反，他们应记起大家曾多次聚集在一起为之工作，多么急切地渴望它的面世，以及因无人综合集中众多自愿来稿而一拖再拖。编辑们是迫于朋友们的压力才参与这项工作的，总是有些勉强。朋友们不断督促着期刊的工作，他们认为期刊代表着一种新的精神，是神圣的事业。

编辑们没有毛遂自荐地来做这个工作，他们不能说自己有权选择或决定孕育了这份期刊的那种精神或其内容。从这方面而言，他们还是很愉快地服从了那股思想的潮流。这股潮流在过去的几年里，使新英格兰的很多真诚的人对文学提出了新的要求，他们反对我们宗教和教育传统中的那种严厉，因为这种严厉正在把我们变成石头，它拒绝希望，只会向后看，只要求未来和过去一样，它怀疑进步，认为新观点和青年的梦想是最令人恐怖的东西。

这期刊物的编者们不愿对这种恐慌采取什么行动——他们甚至连一句责备的话都不愿浪费在这里。他们知道在这个国家的年轻人和成年人中都有一部分人没有感到这种恐慌，他们在私下里或公开地宣誓拥护真理和自由；他们热爱真实到了不在乎虚名的程度；他们拥有一种那么诚挚而深刻的信仰，以至于他们从不怀疑自己信仰的永恒目标，从不动摇其在心中的神圣位置。在发挥前人思想的探索下，他们重新定义了“必要”、“朴素”、“真实”和“人性”——他们曾经拥有的思想，使他们可以掌握过去和现在的历史。

任何人只要和新英格兰无论什么社会阶级的人稍做交谈，就会提及一场革命的进步。参加这场革命的那些人没有外部的组织，没有标志，没有信条，也没有名字。他们不投票选举，不印刷传单，甚至不聚集在一起开会。他们互不认识，也不知道彼此的名字。他们只是因为共同的对真理及其结果的热爱才团结到一起。他们的情况各不相同。在这些真理的追随者中，有一些身世良好，也有很多人衣不蔽体、怀才不遇、天生缺陷——和其他人一样身上带着遗传的缺点的印记。没有盛会，没有宣传，在孤独荒凉的地方，在艰苦的劳动中，在灵魂的懊悔中，在贫困的生活中；在一条尘土飞扬的大道上随着队伍艰难跋涉；或是受雇于人，在别人的田地里辛苦劳作。有薪金微薄向几

介绍观察自然的书籍的插页

个孩子教授基础知识的老师；有偏远地区小教堂里的牧师；有寄人篱下的孤单妇女、女管家和年轻使女。无论富裕贫穷，无论相貌美丑，没有音乐会或任何形式的宣告，他们毫不声张地信仰一个新的希望，在他们的同伴中，他们表现出的对自然和人类创造精神的坚定信念超出了法律或大众观点所能允许的程度。

每个人都能感受到这时代的精神，只是不同的人感受有所不同——因为每个人都把这种时代精神与自己的性格和习惯相融合——对一个人来说，这精神的形式是国家某些方面的变革；对另一个人来说，是人们不同职业和行业习惯的改善；对第三个人来说，是文学艺术的新领域的开拓；对第四个人来说，是哲学思想的深刻思考；而对第五个人来说，则是一个人孤单的祈祷。无论以哪种形式出现，它都是对惯例的反抗和对原则的探索。它在所有的运动中都是和平的，而在最低级的运动中已经取得了一个胜利。当然，它引起了所有受到它批评和谴责的人的反对，但是，它是那样的充满自信，以至于它没有包含任何反对意见，因此它也没有建筑任何外部防御来抵抗难以预料的敌人。它有着和“命运”一样的脚步，像橡树或河流一样地存在，因为它必须以这种形式存在。

在文学领域里，这种影响在新书中不如在较高水平的评论文章中表现得多。医治所有浅薄狭隘的良方就是将人类的记录和自然相比较，这种比较立刻就会让人类的记录自惭形秽，并且激发人们进行新的努力和尝试。当我们看到这一点的时候，我们就会奇怪人们怎么会认为任何一本书都值得保存。在所有的生活中有些东西或多或少是无法用语言表达的，但是注意观察的人就会比其他人写得更好一些。每一种思想都有它束缚人的一面，同时也有提高人的一面，而且它的意志力越强，它就越拒绝成为思想的对象。因此，伟大的思想往往从我们的指缝间滑过，而人们写下一个栩栩如生的词句的过程是足以令人惊奇的。如果我们的期刊能够与时代的脉搏同步，那么它现在就无法确定自己的进程。它无法按照条理预先列出它将要讨论的观点。所有的评论都应该是诗意的，无法预料的，并且像每一个新思想取代从前的旧思想一样不断更替，为整个世界带来新的视角。它的眉头不会谨慎地皱起，相反，它是安详、快乐、充满爱心的。它要讨论世间的万物，它的最终听众也将是世间的众生。

我们的计划中所包含的远不止评论文章，如果不是这样，我们的评论文章也将空洞无物。所有高尚的事物都指向生活。我们不希望讨论非常美好的或不同寻常的事情，或用不同的形式来重复几个观点，但是，我们将尽我们所能去表达一种精神，这种精神把人们提升到一个较高的层次，使他们重获宗教的情感，为他们带来有价值的目标和纯洁的快乐，清洗他们心灵的眼睛，使生活更有条理更有目标，使人们不再带着忧郁的心情去观赏自然风景，并在实际生活和思想的力量之间取得平衡。

不过也许我们把这个小故事讲得太庄重了。关于一次真正的行动，即使是几页纸的写作，也总会有大的争论。所有的事情都看起来与它密切相关并对它起到促进作用——星星中间太阳的轨道，苹果树中流动的汁液——每件事、每个景象都似乎对它产生影响。

我们的方式是与我们提到的目的相对应的。因为我们并不希望多生产刊物，而是希望报告生活，所以我们稿件的主要来源不是有经验的作家，更多则是来源于生活中的言论和朋友们出于友谊而对我们奉献的作品集。我们希望能从以下各个角落中提取思想和感情：从个人思想的美好的最深处；从人们心灵的经历和希望中，这些心灵正在挣脱所有的旧形式，而在所有新的形式中寻求能满足它们无法平息的渴望；从天才们的秘密告白中，除了对志同道合的人，他们不敢把自己的秘密告诉任何其他人；从热烈神秘的笃信上帝的人的谈话中；从染着斑斑泪迹的充满悲伤和热情的日记中；从年轻诗人的手稿中；从尝试评价传统艺术作品的年轻人的记录中，生活就能从这些有生命力的思想和感情中表达出来。

就这样，通过辛勤的劳动和良好的意图，我们把我们的《日晷》带到了这个世界上。我们希望这份刊物能和那个仪器一样具有那种无人不知的快乐天性，那种不是测量时间而是测量阳光的快乐。让它成为悲吟和争辩的嘈杂声中一个快乐而理智的声音。或者说，为了符合我们所选择的这个形象，让它成为一个这样的日晷：不是钟表的死气沉沉的刻度盘，甚至也不像普通花园中的日晷，而是像那样一个花园中的日晷：在那个花园的花草果树中，一个睡着的人突然醒来，日晷告诉他的不是僵死的时间，而是已经到达和将要来临的生命和成长的状态。

文学和生活

读者反应　你想读一读即将发行的《日晷》中的文章吗？为什么？

主题焦点　这篇文章的作者们是怎样总结他们所处时代的特征的？他们对于国家的未来是充满希望还是感到灰心？

阅读理解

1. 创办这份期刊的主意最初是从哪里产生的？解释理由。
2. 谁参加了进步的“革命”？是什么使他们团结在一起？
3. 谁将为《日晷》写稿？他们写作的主题是什么？

思考

解释

1.《日晷》创始者们的精神特征是什么？(推断)

2. 为什么“追随者”这个词用来描述《日晷》期望中的读者们是合适的？(分析)

3. (a)作者笔下的“普通花园”和“那样一个花园”有什么区别？(b)为什么《日晷》是这份新期刊的合适的名字。(区分；证据支持)

应用

4.《〈日晷〉的通告》中的哪种技巧对今天的读者最有效？(应用)

扩展

5. 将宣传一种新产品的广告或一部新电影的预告片与《〈日晷〉的通告》做比较。你发现它们之间有什么相似点和不同点？(媒体连线)

文学聚焦

通告

通告使公众预知一个即将发生的事件。当福勒和爱默生宣布第一期《日晷》的出版时，他们发布信息的方式使潜在的读者们急切地盼望读到这本期刊。

1. 作者们是怎样使读者对《日晷》产生急切的期待之情的？

2. 列出两个《〈日晷〉的通告》赞扬其读者的例子。

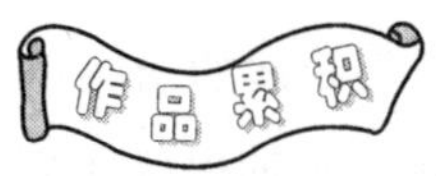

点子库

写作

1. 通告信　给一个朋友写信，通知他/她一个项目或一件事。在你的信中使你的朋友感到这个项目是专为他/她设计的。

2. 有说服力的信条　关于某个事件选定一个你坚信不疑的观点，写一篇文章表达你的信条或信念，同时说服别人接受你的观点。

3. 说服性的短文　你觉得读哲学作品能像改变爱默生和福勒一样改变你的言行或改善你的生活吗？在一篇短文中，就支持或反对这一观点进行辩论。

项目

1. 期刊评审　对其他学校发行的期刊进行研究。收集样本并将它们与你学校发行的期刊做比较。将你的研究结果报告给学校的管理机构。

2. 文章展示　收集表达观点激动人心或条理清楚的文章。把它们按主题分组，并为你班里的同学安排一次展示。

微型写作课

一份学生杂志的提议

这是一个为适应一些读者的特别目的而做出的提议——为赢得他们对一个项目的支持。假设你和一些同学想在你的学校里创办一份杂志，写一篇提议来说服学校管理机构允许你们开始发行这份杂志。

写作技巧重点：一个清楚一致的目的

为了说服学校的管理者们分配给你们资金或对你们进行指导，你需要清楚一致地说明情况。请注意爱默生和福勒是怎样表明《日晷》的目标的。

《通告》中的范例

我们不希望讨论非常美好的或不同寻常的事情，或用不同的形式来重复几个观点，但是，我们将尽我们所能去表达一种精神，这种精神把人们提升到一个较高的层次，使他们重获宗教的情感，为他们带来有价值的目标和纯洁的快乐，清洗他们心灵的眼睛，使生活更有条理有目标，使人们不再带着忧郁的心情去观赏自然风景，并在实际生活和思想的力量之间取得平衡。

构思

在头脑中为你的杂志确定一个焦点。把你的目标用一句简洁的话写下来。调查你所需的资源需要多少成本。这些信息说明你已经把你的提议仔细全面地考虑过了。

写稿

陈述你的杂志的目标，并用一套观点来支持它。逐条列出成本，并强调创办这份杂志的必要性，以使所需的花费合理化。

修改

你提出的每个事实都应该与你的主要目标相关。在必要的时候，加入细节以表现其中的关联性。请一个同学看看你的计划是否清楚、一致和合理。根据他的意见进行修改。

Guide for Interpreting

Margaret Fuller (1810—1850)

A strong individual, Margaret Fuller scorned the inferior lot of most women and urged women to develop their talents. She envisioned an equal partnership for men and women that would extend from married life to the highest ranks of government and business. She wrote, "We would have every path laid open to woman as to man".

<u>An Influential Intellectual</u> Fuller began her career as a teacher, first in Boston and later in Providence. She gave up teaching to conduct a series of public discussion groups for women on intellectual topics. She developed an association with Ralph Waldo Emerson and other New England writers and thinkers who were involved in a philosophical and literary movement, known as Transcendentalism, that emphasized humanity's connection to nature. When they launched their magazine The Dial, Fuller both edited and contributed to the publication.

Her activities attracted the attention of Horace Greeley, the editor of the New York Tribune, who invited her to be a columnist for his paper. Her critical pieces for the Tribune and her book Woman in the Nineteenth Century (1845) established her reputation as a social critic.

<u>A Tragic End</u> Fulfilling a lifelong wish, she traveled to Europe in 1846. Returning in 1850, she drowned, with her husband and son, in a shipwreck off Fire Island, New York.

Ralph Waldo Emerson (1803—1882)

Ralph Waldo Emerson was one of the most influential writers and philosophers of his time. The publication in 1836 of his essay "Nature" marks the be-

ginning of Transcendentalism. Emerson, Fuller, Henry David Thoreau, and others associated with the movement formed a discussion circle known as the Transcendental Club. The group met regularly at Emerson's house in Concord, Massachusetts, to discuss their ideas related to nature, individuality, and the human spirit.

Background for Understanding

LITERATURE: MARGARET FULLER AND THE DIAL

In the 1830's in New England, the literary and philosophical movement known as Transcendentalism took hold, with Ralph Waldo Emerson as its main spokesperson. As the movement grew, those involved in it sought a wider audience for their ideas. They decided to publish a journal, which they called The Dial, and chose Margaret Fuller and Ralph Waldo Emerson to be co-editors. Their choice of Fuller was both remarkable and wise — remarkable because a woman editor was unheard of, but wise because it was only through Fuller's practicality, organization, and drive that the magazine succeeded.

The Dial was to be published four times a year. After numerous delays in getting started, Fuller herself wrote several articles necessary to fill the first issue, which appeared in July 1840. In the four years that it was published, The Dial was instrumental in establishing the reputations of a number of authors, including Henry David Thoreau. Much of the work was done by Fuller, and after two years, she gave up the editorship because of the strain. Beset with funding problems, and without Fuller's organized leadership, the magazine lasted another two years.

Literature and your Life

CONNECT YOUR EXPERIENCE

Have you ever collaborated with a group of friends on a project intended for a wider audience? Maybe you produced a play, created a newsletter, or painted a mural. Whatever your purpose, you probably got caught up in the excitement of sharing ideas and working toward a common goal. This was the spirit that produced The Dial in 1840.

Journal Writing　Record your thoughts about the topic you'd choose if you were to produce a newsletter.

THEMATIC FOCUS: FIRESIDE AND CAMPFIRE

As adventurous pioneers moved west in the mid-nineteenth century, intellectual pioneers, such as the Transcendentalists, were exploring ideas in philosophy and literature. The Transcendentalists hoped to encourage others to change their attitudes, values, and behaviors.How can a magazine make such an impact on a nation's identity?

Literary Focus

ANNOUNCEMENT

Politicians and writers depend on announcements to publicize events or books they want to make known to the public. An announcement is a public notice, an official and formal declaration. The main purpose of announcements is to attract interest, but they can also serve various other goals. For example, in "The Announcement of The Dial," Emerson and Fuller wanted to win over their audience, build expectations about the publication, and solicit articles from writers. They also outlined the philosophy of the journal.

The Announcement of the Dial

Margaret Fuller and Ralph Waldo Emerson

We invite the attention of our countrymen to a new design. Probably not quite unexpected or unannounced will our Journal appear, though small pains have been taken to secure its welcome. Those, who have immediately acted in editing the present Number, cannot accuse themselves of any unbecoming forwardness in their undertaking, but rather of a backwardness, when they remember how often in many private circles the work was projected, how eagerly desired, and only postponed because no individual volunteered to combine and concentrate the freewill offerings of many cooperators. With some reluctance the present conductors of this work have yielded themselves to the wishes of their friends, finding something sacred and not to be withstood in the importunity which urged the production of a Journal in a new spirit.

As they have not proposed themselves to the work, neither can they lay any the least claim to an option or determination of the spirit in which it is conceived, or to what is peculiar in the design. In that respect, they have obeyed, though with great joy, the strong current of thought and feeling, which, for a few years past, has led many sincere persons in New England to make new demands on literature, and to reprobate that rigor of our conventions of religion and education which is turning us to stone, which renounces hope, which looks only backward, which asks only such a future as the past, which suspects improvement, and holds nothing so much in horror as new views and the dreams of youth.

With these terrors the conductors of the present Journal have nothing to do, —not even so much as a word of reproach to waste. They know that there is a portion of the youth and of the adult population of this country, who have not shared them; who have in secret or in public paid their vows to truth and freedom; who love reality too well to care for names, and who live by a Faith too earnest and profound to suffer them to doubt the eternity of its object, or to shake themselves free from its authority. Under the fictions and customs which occupied others, these have explored the Necessary, the Plain, the True, the Human, — and so gained a vantage ground, which commands the history of the past and the present.

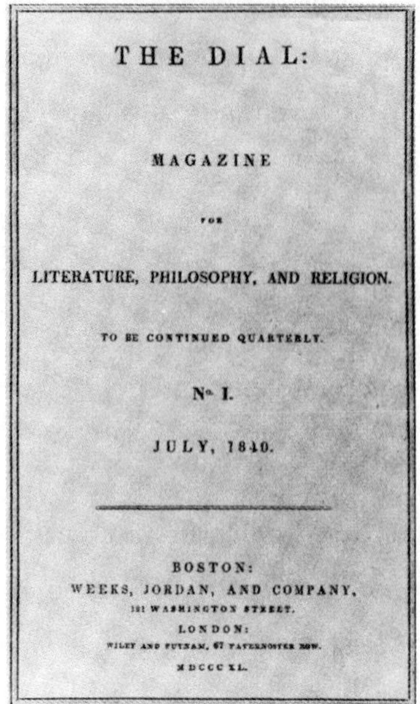
THE DIAL:

MAGAZINE

FOR

LITERATURE, PHILOSOPHY, AND RELIGION.

TO BE CONTINUED QUARTERLY.

No. I.

JULY, 1840.

BOSTON:
WEEKS, JORDAN, AND COMPANY,
121 WASHINGTON STREET.
LONDON:
WILEY AND PUTNAM, 67 PATERNOSTER ROW.
MDCCCXL.

No one can converse much with different classes of society in New England, without remarking the progress of a revolution. Those who share in it have no external organization, no badge, no creed, no name. They do not vote, or print, or even meet together. They do not know each other's faces or names. They are united only in a common love of truth, and love of its work. They are of all conditions and constitutions. Of these acolytes if some are happily born and well bred, many are no doubt ill dressed, ill placed, ill made—with as many scars of hereditary vice as other men. Without pomp, without trumpet, in lonely and obscure places, in solitude, in servitude, in compunctions and privations, trudging beside the team in a dusty road, or drudging a hireling in other men's cornfields, schoolmasters, who teach a few children rudiments for a pittance, ministers of small parishes of the obscurer sects, lone women in dependent condition, matrons and young maidens, rich and poor, beautiful and hard-favored, without concert or proclamation of any kind, they have silently given in their several adherence to a new hope, and in all companies do signify a greater trust in the nature and resources of man, than the laws or the popular opinions will well allow.

This spirit of the time is felt by every individual with some difference,—to each one casting its light upon the objects nearest to his temper and habits of thought;—to one, coming in the shape of special reforms in the state; to another, in modifications of the various callings of men, and the customs of business; to a third, opening a new scope for literature and art; to a fourth, in philosophical insight; to a fifth, in the vast solitudes of prayer. It is in every form a protest against usage, and a search for principles. In all its movements, it is peaceable, and in the very lowest marked with a triumphant success. Of course, it rouses the opposition of all which it judges and condemns, but it is too confident in its tone to comprehend an objection, and so builds no outworks for possible defense against contingent enemies. It has the step of Fate, and goes on existing like an oak or a river, because it must.

In literature, this influence appears not yet in new books so much as in the higher tone of criticism. The antidote to all narrowness is the comparison of the record with nature, which at once shames the record and stimulates to new attempts. Whilst we look at this, we wonder how any book has been thought worthy to be preserved. There is somewhat in all life untranslatable into language. He who keeps his eye on that will write better than others, and think less of his writing, and of all writing. Every thought has a certain imprisoning as well as uplifting quality, and, in proportion to its energy on the will, refuses to become an object of intellectual contemplation. Thus what is great usually slips through our fingers, and it seems wonderful how a lifelike word ever comes to be written. If our Journal share the impulses of the time, it cannot now prescribe its own course. It cannot foretell in orderly propositions what it shall attempt. All criticism should be poetic; unpredictable; superseding, as every new thought does, all foregone thoughts, and making a new light on the whole world. Its brow is not wrinkled with circumspection, but serene, cheerful, adoring. It has all things to say, and no less than all the world for its final audience.

Our plan embraces much more than criticism; were it not so, our criticism would be naught. Everything noble is directed on life, and this is. We do not wish to say pretty or curious things, or to reiterate a few propositions in varied forms, but, if we can, to give expression to that spirit which lifts men to a higher platform, restores to them the religious sentiment, brings them worthy aims and pure pleasures, purges the inward eye, makes life less desultory, and, through raising men to the level of nature, takes away its melancholy from the landscape, and reconciles the practical with the speculative powers.

But perhaps we are telling our little story too gravely. There are always great arguments at hand for a true action, even for the writing of a few pages. There is nothing but seems near it and prompts it, —the sphere in the ecliptic, the sap in the apple tree, —every fact, every appearance seem to persuade to it.

Our means correspond with the ends we have indicated. As we wish not to multiply books, but to report life, our resources are therefore not so much the Pens of practiced writers, as the discourse of the living, and the portfolios which friendship has opened to us. From the beautiful recesses of private thought; from the experience and hope of spirits which are withdrawing from all old forms, and seeking in all that is new somewhat to meet their inappeasable longings; from the secret confession of genius afraid to trust itself to aught but sympathy; from the conversations of fervid and mystical pietists; from tear-stained diaries of sorrow and passion; from the manuscripts of young poets; and from the records of youthful taste commenting on old works of art; we hope to draw thoughts and feelings, which being alive can impart life.

And so with diligent hands and good intent we set down our Dial on the earth. We wish it may resemble that instrument in its celebrated happiness, that of measuring no hours but those of sunshine. Let it be one cheerful rational voice amidst the din of mourners and polemics. Or to abide by our chosen image, let it be such a Dial, not as the dead face of a clock, hardly even such as the Gnomon in a garden, but rather such a Dial as in the Garden itself, in whose leaves and flowers and fruits the suddenly awakened sleeper is instantly apprised not what part of dead time, but what state of life and growth is now arrived and arriving.

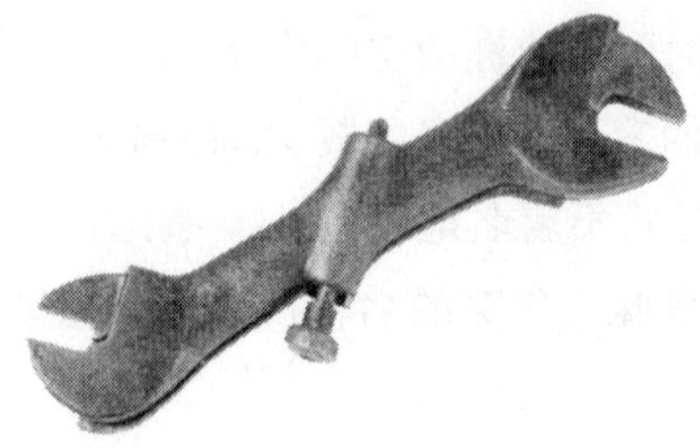

第二课

魔鬼和汤姆·沃克

华盛顿·鄂文 (1783—1859)

华盛顿·鄂文的父母以美国第一任总统的名字为他命名，而他成为第一位获得国际声誉的美国作家。

华盛顿·鄂文

一个美国青年 鄂文出生在一个富裕的家庭里，在16岁的时候开始学习法律。虽然他曾经计划做一名律师，但后来他却发现自己对旅行和写作更感兴趣。他用了很多时间在欧洲全境和纽约的哈德森峡谷旅行，同时阅读欧洲的文学作品。鄂文还以“乔纳森·老式”的笔名写作讽刺散文。在鄂文24岁时，他和哥哥开始不署名地发行一本杂志：《萨尔马巩蒂》（一种辣味开胃菜的名称），这份杂志里刊登的是关于纽约社会的幽默短文和散文。

1809年，他使用假名“第德里克·尼克伯克”发表了第一部重要作品，《从世界开端到荷兰王朝结束时的纽约历史》。这部书是对殖民地时期的纽约的幽默描述，受到了读者的欢迎，鄂文因此而成名。

在欧洲的旅行 1815年至1832年之间，鄂文居住在欧洲。他在那里四处旅行，了解欧洲的风俗、传统和民间文化。受到欧洲民间传统文化的启发，鄂文将两个德国传统故事改编为发生在哈德森峡谷中的特征明显的美国故事，创作了他最出名的故事中的两个:《睡谷的传说》和《瑞普•凡•温寇》。鄂文用笔名“杰弗瑞•克雷恩”在杂志《素描本》(1820)中发表了这两个故事后，全欧洲和美国的作家和评论家都做出了热烈的回应。

鄂文的故事在世界上取得的成功标志着特征明显的美国文学传统的开端。

一个爱国的美国人 鄂文在欧洲居住的时期中，完成了另外3本书，其中包括《旅行者的故事》《魔鬼和汤姆•沃克》就收录在这本书中。当有人因为他长期居住国外而对他的爱国心提出质疑时，鄂文回答道:“我在尽全力为我的国家效劳。无论我写了什么，都是以一个美国人的感情写成并作为一个美国人的写作发表的。那难道是对我的国家的背弃吗？我还能怎样为我的国家效劳——回到家里乞求别人给我一个职位，而我根本没有那些职位所需的那种才能或经验——如果我能对这世界有所贡献的话，那就是通过我的笔。”虽然鄂文回到美国之后仍然继续发表作品，但人们主要是因为他在欧洲创作的几个人物而记住了他。

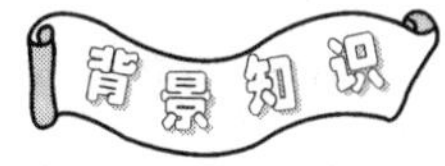

文学:浮士德传说

《魔鬼和汤姆·沃克》是浮士德传说的一个变体——讲述一个人为了俗世的利益而对魔鬼出卖自己灵魂的故事。这个传说起源于一个真实的人物，一个生活在16世纪早期的德国，名叫浮士德的四处游荡的学者和魔术师。浮士德传说的第一个印刷版本，《浮士德》，出版于1587年。那个故事讲述了浮士德和魔鬼签订条约，来交换世上的知识和权利。

在其后的许多年里，出现了浮士德传说的不同变体版本，其中包括:1640年由英国剧作家克里斯托弗·玛罗创作的戏剧，约哈恩·歌德创作的两部分的戏剧性长诗(1808，1832)，查尔斯·高诺德1859年的歌剧和托马斯·曼1947年的长篇小说。所有的版本都讲述了一个用灵魂来交换经验、知识或财宝的人。

但是不同的改编结尾不同——在有些故事中，主人公最终受到了诅咒；而在其他的故事中，他则得到了拯救。

联系你的经历 在我们的社会里，我们经常会看到政治竞争者们不计一切代价地争取胜利，经商的人用不诚实的手段赚钱，而奥运会上的运动员为了赢得金牌而对规则进行变通。而这个故事中的主人公为了获得巨大的财富做出了更加极端的选择：虽然他知道最终会为自己的决定付出代价，他还是和魔鬼做了一笔交易。

日志写作 从现代的新闻中找出受到金钱、权力或名誉的欲望驱使的人的例子。

专题聚焦：炉火和营火 这是一个以德国传说为基础的故事，其中的哪些细节使它变成一个有明显美国特色的故事，从而反映它所处时代的特征？

无所不知的叙述者 《魔鬼和汤姆·沃克》的讲述者不是作为故事的某个人物，而是以一个无所不知的叙述者，置身事外，讲述所有人物的思想和感情。当一个故事由无所不知的叙述者讲述出来时，读者就不再限于一个人物的思想和视角，而是能够了解所有人物的思想感情。这种叙述者甚至可以对故事中的事件进行评论。

魔鬼和汤姆·沃克（节选）

华盛顿·鄂文

离马萨诸塞州的波士顿几英里以外的地方，有一条深水湾，它从查尔斯海湾蜿蜒几英里深入陆地内部，最终汇到一片浓荫覆盖的沼泽里。这条水湾的一边是一片美丽幽深的小树林，而对岸的地面则从水边突然急剧上升，形成了一个高高的山脊，那上面零散地长着几棵年纪很老、树形巨大的橡树。根据以前的故事传说，在其中一棵大树下面有海盗基德埋下的一大笔财宝。这条水湾使人可以很容易地在夜里用一条小船秘密地把那笔钱运到山脚下；那个地方地势的高度则可以使人清楚地瞭望四周，确保没有人在附近；而那些容易辨认的树则成为这个地方极佳的标志，让人容易再次找到这里。另外，那个老故事还说，魔鬼在这个藏钱的地方出没，并且把它置于自己的监控之下；不过人们也都知道他总是和埋藏的财宝打交道，尤其是来历不明的钱。

无论那是不是真的，反正基德没再回来挖出他的财宝，他在波士顿被抓住后不久就被送到了英国，在那里因为海盗的罪名被绞死。

1727年左右，就是那次地震席卷了新英格兰，使很多高大的罪人双膝跪下的时候，在这个地方附近住着一个瘦削、贪婪的家伙，名叫汤姆•沃克。他有一个和他自己一样贪婪的妻子，他们甚至贪婪到了阴谋互相欺骗的程度。无论什么东西，只要到了这个女人手里，就会被她藏起来。只要母鸡一咯咯叫，她就会警觉地去把那新下的蛋拿起来。她的丈夫则不停地四处窥探，想找出她的秘密金库。他们为到底哪些应该是共同的财产进行了多次激烈的争吵。他们住在一栋外观凄惨、远离其他邻居的房子里，整栋房子都笼罩在一种饥饿的气氛里。房子附近散乱地长着几棵萨文树，象征着土地的贫瘠；房子的烟囱里从来没有冒出烟来；也从没有旅行者在门前逗留。一匹悲惨的马，肋骨像烤架上的铁条一样清晰可见，它在一块地周围四处漫步，地上一层薄薄的苔

魔鬼和汤姆•沃克

藓几乎盖不住那铺满圆石的凹凸不平的地面，逗弄折磨着它的饥饿，有时候它把头探到篱笆外面，可怜地看着过路人，似乎是在哀求人们把它从这片饥荒的土地上解救出去。

这所房子和里面住的人全都一样名声不佳。汤姆的妻子是个高高的悍妇，脾气暴躁，声音响亮，胳膊强壮。人们经常听到她和她丈夫舌战的声音，而他的脸上有时也表现出他们的矛盾并不仅限于口头争斗的迹象。然而，没人敢于介入他们之间。那孤独的旅行者在这种可怕的喧闹和抓打面前退缩进自己的一角，斜眼看着这不和的一家；然后急忙离开，如果他是个单身汉的话，就会为自己的独身感到庆幸。

有一天，汤姆•沃克去了一个很远的地方。他回家的时候抄了一条近道，穿过那个沼泽。像大多数近道一样，这也是一条选择并不明智的路线。那个沼泽被巨大阴暗的松树和铁杉浓密地覆盖着，其中有些树有90英尺高，这使得沼泽里即使在中午也一片黑暗，成为附近所有猫头鹰的栖息地。沼泽里到处是深坑和泥沼，被杂草和苔藓遮盖住了一部分，那绿色表面经常欺骗了旅行者，让他们陷入充满黑色的、令人窒息的湿泥的深渊；那里还有黑色的停滞不动的池塘，那是蝌蚪、牛蛙和水蛇的住处；松树和铁杉的树干一半淹没在沼泽中，一半腐烂，看上去就像在泥泞中睡觉的短吻鳄。

汤姆已经在这片危险的森林中小心翼翼地择路而行了很长时间了；他踏着一簇簇的灯芯草和草根——那些在深深的沼泽中的不稳定的立足点；或是像一只猫一样顺着倒下的树干慢慢前进；他不时被水鸟突然的尖叫声或两旁某个单独的池塘中传来的野鸭叫声吓得惊跳起来。最后他到了一块坚实的土地，这块地像半岛一样延伸进沼泽的深深的腹地里。这曾经是印第安人与最早的殖民者交战时的一个堡垒。他们在这里建起了一个自认为固若金汤的要塞，把它作为他们的女人和孩子的避难所。现在那印第安古堡只剩下了几条堤防，慢慢下降到了和周围的土地一样的高度，而且它的一部分已经被森林里的橡树和其他树淹没了，它们的绿荫和沼泽地里黑沉沉的松树和铁杉形成了鲜明的对比。

当汤姆•沃克到达那个古堡的时候，天色已经很晚了，他在那里停了一下，稍事休息。除了他以外，没有人会愿意在这个孤独、阴郁的地方逗留，因为根据从印第安战争时期流传下来的故事，一般人都对这地方印象很坏，他们说野蛮人在这里下了咒语，为魔鬼奉献祭品。

然而，汤姆·沃克可不是会被这类恐惧困扰的人。他坐在一棵倒在地上的铁杉的树干上休息，他一边听着树蛙仿佛预示着什么的叫声，一边用他的手杖在脚旁的一个松软的黑土堆中戳戳挖挖。就在他无意识地翻土的时候，他的手杖戳到了一个坚硬的东西。他把它从土里挖出来，嗬！一个被劈开了的头盖骨就摆在了他面前，一把印第安战斧还深深地夹在骨头中间，斧上的锈迹显示着那致命的一击与现在相隔的时间。在这个印第安战士最后的落脚点曾经发生了一场激烈的战斗，而这就是那场战斗的一个可怕的纪念品。

汤姆·沃克家的银茶壶

“哈！”汤姆·沃克一边说，一边踢了它一脚，想把上面沾着的土弄掉。

“别碰那骨头！”一个粗暴的声音说。汤姆抬起眼睛，看到一个高大的黑男人坐在他正对面的一个树桩上。他不禁大吃一惊，因为他既没听到也没看到任何人走近；然而让他更加迷惑不解的是，借着仅有的一点微光，他看到这个陌生人既不是黑人也不是印第安人。确实，他穿着一件式样简单的好像印第安人的衣服，身上还缠绕着一条红色的腰带或肩带。但是他的脸既不是黑色也不是古铜色，而是一种暗淡的黝黑色，上面还蒙着一层黑灰，就好像他经常在火堆旁或是铁匠铺里干活一样。他有一头乱蓬蓬又黑又粗的头发，从头上向四面八方伸出来，他的肩上还背着一把斧子。

他瞪着一双大红眼睛怒视了汤姆一会儿。

“你在我的土地上干什么？”这个黑人用一种粗暴的声音咆哮着说。

“你的土地！”汤姆冷笑了一声说，“这土地不是你的，也不是我的，它属于迪肯·皮伯蒂。”

“让迪肯·皮伯蒂去……死吧。”那陌生人说，“要是他不多注意自己犯下的罪行，而老是注意他周围的人的罪行的话，他就会死了。看看那边，看看迪肯·皮伯蒂过得怎么样。”

汤姆顺着陌生人手指的方向望过去，看到一棵大树，没有茂盛的枝叶，树的中心都被虫子蛀烂了，他看到这棵大树几乎被人完全劈开了，以至于一阵大风就可能把它吹倒。在这棵树的树皮上就刻着迪肯·皮伯蒂的名字，他是一

个地位显赫的人，因为和印第安人精明地做交易而迅速发家致富。现在汤姆向四周看看，看到多数的大树上都刻着殖民地里显赫的人的名字，都是用斧子刻上去的。一直被他坐在身下的这棵大树很显然刚刚被砍倒，上面刻着克朗宁西尔德的名字。他想起一个有权有势的富人就叫这个名字，那个人粗俗地显示自己的财富，可大家都悄悄传说他的这笔财富是做海盗得来的。

“他就要被烧掉了。”那黑男人胜利地咆哮着说，“你看我很可能有一大堆冬天用的柴火了。”

“可是你有什么权利，”汤姆说，“砍下迪肯·皮伯蒂的木材呢？”

“很久以前就有的权利，”那个人说，“在你的白脸种族中的任何一个人踏上这里的土壤之前很久，这林地就属于我了。”

“那么，原谅我的冒昧，请问，你是谁？”汤姆说。

“噢，我有很多名字。在有些国家里，我是荒野中的猎人，而在其他国家里，我又是黑色掘矿人。在这个地区人们叫我黑色伐木人，那些红色人把这个地方奉献给我，为了我，他们时不时地烤一个白人来献上味道香甜的祭品。现在因为红色人已经被你们这些白色的野蛮人消灭了，我就只好去主持对教友会教徒和非浸礼会教徒的迫害，从中取乐了。我就是奴隶贸易者的伟大保护神和发起者，也是撒勒姆女巫们的主人。”

“那么，如果我没弄错的话，你说的所有的话的要点就是，”汤姆坚定地说，“你就是大家通常说的‘老魔鬼’喽。”

“没错，随时效劳！”这个黑男人答道，同时似乎彬彬有礼地点了一下头。

根据传说，这就是这次会谈的开始，不过这种气氛几乎类似于亲密，所以人们很难相信。人们认为，在这样一个荒凉萧瑟的地方见到这样一个异乎寻常的人物，无论什么人都会失去勇气的。可是汤姆是个意志坚强的人，他可不那么容易被吓倒；而且他和一个悍妇老婆共同生活了那么久，以至于他连魔鬼都不害怕了。

据说在这个开端之后，在汤姆回家的路上，他们一起进行了一场诚恳的长谈。那个黑男人告诉他在离沼泽不远的山脊上的橡树下，海盗基德曾经埋下了大笔的财富。这些都在他的控制之下并且受他力量的保护，因此除非能赢得他的好感，否则任何人都不能找到这笔财富。由于他对汤姆产生了一种特别的好感，所以他提出把这笔财富送给汤姆，只是汤姆必须答应他一些条件。虽然汤姆从来没有公开透露过这些条件的内容，但是人们可能很容易猜测出来。这些条件一定很难完成,因为汤姆要求给他时间考虑。然而,他并不是一个眼前摆着财宝还会纠缠小事的人。当他们走到沼泽边缘的时候,陌生人停下了——汤姆说:“你凭什么让我相信刚才你告诉我的都是真的呢?”“这就是我的标记。”黑男人一边说,一边把他的手指按在汤姆的前额上。这样说完,他就转身走向沼泽的草丛中,而且据汤姆说,他看起来好像一直向下、向下、向下,走进地下,到只露出头和肩膀的时候还一直向下,直到完全消失得无影无踪。

当汤姆到家的时候,他发现自己的前额上有一个手指的黑色印记,看上去就好像烙上去的一样,无论用什么都擦不掉。

而他妻子告诉他的第一条新闻就是阿布萨罗姆•克朗宁西尔德,那个有钱的海盗,突然死去了。报纸上用常见的那种华丽辞藻宣告了他的死:“一个伟大的人坠入了以色列。”

汤姆想起了他的黑朋友刚刚砍倒准备烧掉的那棵树。“让那海盗被烤死吧,”汤姆说,“谁在乎他!”现在他确信刚才的所见所闻并不是幻觉了。

他本来并不想把这个秘密告诉他的妻子;但是因为这是个让人心里颇不轻松的秘密,所以他还是愿意和她一起来承担。当汤姆提到那埋藏的黄金时,她内心所有的贪婪都一下苏醒了过来,她催促丈夫答应那个黑男人的条件,以便得到那笔能让他们终生富有的财宝。无论汤姆多么愿意把自己出卖给魔鬼,他都决心不让他妻子从中受惠。因此,出于单纯的反抗精神,他直接拒绝了妻子的要求。他们在这个问题上进行了多次激烈的争吵,但是她劝说得越多,汤姆就越下定决心不让她满意。

最后她决定自己去和魔鬼做交易,并且独占所有的财宝。凭着和她丈夫一样的无所畏惧的性格,她在一个夏日的白天快要结束的时候,出发去了那个旧印第安堡垒。她在那里停留了很多个小时,当她回来的时候,她沉闷地不愿回答问题。但她提到在黄昏时遇到了一个黑男人,他正在砍一棵大树的树根。然而,他很生气,不愿意和她达成任何协议。她还要带着礼物再去一次,请求他的原谅,但是她没有说那礼物是什么。

第二天晚上她又出发去了沼泽地,围裙里沉甸甸地装满了东西。汤姆等啊等,但是她还是没回来。夜已经深了,可她还没出现。早晨、中午、夜晚再次降临,但是她仍然没回来。现在汤姆开始为她的安全感到担心了,尤其是当他发现她把银茶壶、银汤匙和所有能带走的值钱东西都装在围裙里带走了的时候，他就更加担心了。又一个夜晚过去了，又一个清晨来临了，但是汤姆还是没见到他的妻子。一句话，她从此就杳无音信了。

虽然有很多人自作聪明地说自己知道她最终的命运，但实际上没人知道到底发生了什么。这是被很多历史学家弄成谜团的事件之一。有人说她在沼泽地绕来绕去的迷宫里迷了路，陷入了某个深坑或泥沼；其他的人则更加无情地暗示说，她带着家里的财物逃到了其他地方；而还有些人猜测说，她的脾气使她陷入了一片阴沉的泥塘，后来人们在泥塘上发现了她的帽子。作为这种说法的证明，据说有人看见一个身材巨大的黑男人，肩上背着斧子，在那天深夜的时候从沼泽里出来，拿着一捆系在方格围裙里的东西，脸上很明显带着胜利的表情。

然而，最新的也是最有可能的说法是：汤姆·沃克为他妻子和他的财产的命运感到非常焦虑，最后他终于出发去那个印第安堡垒寻找。在那个夏日的整个下午，他在那个阴森的地方四处搜寻，但是没有看到他妻子的任何踪迹。他不停地呼唤她的名字，可是没有任何人听到，在他从沼泽边尖叫着飞奔而过时，只有沼泽中的水鸟回应他的叫声，还有旁边的水塘中传来牛蛙令人沮丧的呱呱的叫声。据说，最后在黄昏刚刚降临，猫头鹰开始叫嚣，蝙蝠四处飞腾的时候，他注意到一群盘旋在一棵柏树周围的吃腐肉的乌鸦的喧闹声。他抬头向上望去，看到了一个方格围裙系成的包裹挂在树枝间，一只秃鹫停在近旁，好像在看守这包裹一样。他高兴得跳了起来，因为他认出那是他妻子的围裙，以为里面装着他家里的值钱东西。

“让我拿到那财产，”他安慰自己说，“没有那女人也可以过活。”

当他爬上树的时候，那秃鹫展开宽阔的翅膀，尖叫着滑入了森林黑沉沉的阴影里。汤姆一把抓住了方格围裙，却看到了悲惨的景象，那里面除了一副心肝以外什么也没有！

根据最可信的传说，这些就是汤姆的妻子唯一的遗物了。她很可能试图用她习惯对待汤姆的方式来对待那个黑男人，可是虽然人们通常认为一个泼妇相当于魔鬼，但是在这件事上看起来她却得到了最坏的结局。然而，她肯定死得很英勇，因为据说汤姆注意到在树周围深深地印着很多脚掌裂开的脚印。他还发现一把把的头发，看起来好像是从伐木人的那蓬又黑又粗的头发上拔下来的一样。根据经验，汤姆很了解他妻子的勇猛。当他看到这场激烈打斗留下的迹象时，他耸了耸肩，“哎呀，”他自言自语地说，“老魔头肯定赢得不容易！”

虽然失去财产，但是汤姆因失去妻子使自己得到了安慰，因为他是一个不屈不挠的人。他甚至有一点感激那黑色伐木人，因为他认为伐木人为他做了一件好事。因此，他希望能和他进一步熟识起来，可是在一段时间里却没有成功。那“老黑腿”表现得很矜持，无论人们怎样认为，他都不是能够随叫随到的。他知道在对牌局深有把握的时候应该怎样出牌。

据传说，最后，当一再的拖延使汤姆的急切心情达到顶峰，只要能得到魔鬼答应给他的财宝，他什么条件都准备同意的时候。一天晚上，他碰到了那黑男人，他穿着平常的伐木人的衣服，肩上背着斧子，沿着沼泽一边闲逛一边哼着小曲。对于汤姆和他拉交情的话，他假装表现得非常冷淡，简单地回答了一两句，就又接着哼他的小曲了。

然而，汤姆还是慢慢地把他引入了正题，他们开始就汤姆获得海盗的财宝的交换条件讨价还价。有一个条件是不用说的，人们普遍知道在所有魔鬼给人好处的情况下都会有这个条件。但是，还有其他的条件，虽然不是那么重要，但他还是顽固地毫不让步。他坚持由他发现的这笔钱应该用来为他做事。因此，他建议汤姆把这笔钱用在黑色交通上，也就是说，他应该装备一条运奴船。然而，汤姆坚决地拒绝了这个条件。虽然他的良心已经足够坏了，但就是魔鬼本人也无法引诱他成为一个奴隶贩子。

魔鬼发现汤姆在这一点上是那么神经敏感，他就没有再坚持，而是转而建议汤姆当一个高利贷者。魔鬼把高利贷者视为他特别的臣民，所以极其迫切地想增加他们的人数。

对于这个建议，汤姆毫不拒绝，因为这正合他的胃口。

“下个月你要在波士顿开一家经纪所。”黑男人说。

“如果你想的话，我明天就开。”汤姆·沃克说。

“你要按每个月两厘的利息借给别人钱。”

“哎呀，我会要四厘！”汤姆·沃克回答道。

“你要勒索债券，取消抵押的赎回权，把商人们逼到破产……”

“我会把他们逼到魔……鬼那去！”汤姆•沃克叫道。

“那你就是用我的钱放高利贷的人了。”黑腿高兴地说，“你想什么时候要这笔钱？”

“今天夜里。”

“成交！”魔鬼说。

“成交！”汤姆•沃克说。就这样他们握了握手，做成了这笔交易。

几天以后，汤姆•沃克就坐在了波士顿一间账房的桌子后面。

他的名声很快就传开了，人们都知道他手头总是有现钱，而且出于好意乐于借钱给别人。大家应该都记得贝尔舍总督执政的时候，那时候钱特别紧缺。那是一个靠金钱建立信誉的时期。政府的纸币在全国泛滥；著名的大陆银行建立了；兴起了一股投机的热潮；人们因为扩充新的殖民地区和在荒野中建立城市的计划而几近疯狂；地产经纪人带着标有镇区的地图四处奔走，虽然没人知道这些地方到底在哪儿，但每个人都愿意把它们买下。总而言之，在这个国家里不时爆发的投机高温已经发展到了令人惊恐的程度，每个人都梦想着白手起家牟取暴利。与通常的情况一样，这阵高温消退了；美梦和那想象中的财富一起幻灭了；那些病人却被留在了悲惨的困境中，结果是，“艰难时代”的喊声在整个国家里回响。

就在这大众痛苦不断增长的时候，汤姆•沃克在波士顿成为一名成功的高利贷者。他的门前很快就挤满了上门的顾客。急需用钱的和敢于冒险的人，孤注一掷的投机商，做着美梦的地产经纪人，挥霍无度的贸易家，丧失信用的商人，简而言之，所有不惜采用一切手段、牺牲来借钱的人都疯狂涌向了汤姆•沃克。

就这样汤姆变成了需要用钱的人的共同朋友，所作所为就像是一个“患难之交”；那也就是说，他总是坚持要有高昂的利息和足够价值的抵押品。他条件的苛刻和借钱人的困难是成正比的。他积累了大批的债券和抵押，逐渐把他的顾客压榨得越来越干瘪，最后，当他们干得像海绵一样的时候，他就把他们从自己门前赶走。

他用这种方法不停地挣钱，变成了一个有钱有势的人，他的三角帽甚至抬到了“交易所”的上面。像通常的情况一样，他为了炫耀，给自己造了一栋大房子；然而由于他的吝啬，那房子的大部分却没有盖完，也没有家具。在虚荣心最高涨的时候，他甚至给自己配了一辆马车，但是他几乎要把拉车的马饿死了；而当那些没上油的轮子在车轴上尖叫悲吟时，你会觉得你听到了他压榨的那些借债人的灵魂的呼喊。

然而，当汤姆慢慢变老的时候，他开始越来越多地思考。在得到了这一世的好东西之后，他开始为下一世的那些东西担忧了。他懊悔地想起他和他的黑朋友所做的交易，绞尽脑汁想找出摆脱那些条件的办法。因此，他突然之间变成了一个狂热的信徒。他高声地勤奋祈祷，仿佛天堂是靠着肺部的力量达到的一样。事实上，人们总是可以从他周日祈祷的叫嚷声中判断出来他在哪些周里犯了最多的罪。那些一直谦卑信仰上帝的基督徒们感到了强烈的自责，因为他们看到自己在这件事上那么突然地被一个刚刚信仰基督的人超过了。汤姆在宗教的事情上和他在金钱的事情上一样严格：他是所有邻居的严厉的监督者和批评者，他似乎认为他们被记录下来的每项罪过会变成他自己的一个功劳。他甚至谈到了恢复对教友会教徒和再洗礼教徒的迫害的适宜性。简单说，汤姆对宗教的热衷变得和他的财富一样众人皆知。

尽管汤姆热衷地重视宗教信仰的形式，但他心里仍然隐隐担心那魔鬼终有一天会来取回他应得的东西。因此，据说为了不让魔鬼在他不知不觉中把他带走，他总是在外衣口袋里装着一本小圣经。他还在账房桌子上放着一本很大的对开本的圣经。人们来找他做生意的时候经常发现他在读圣经，在这种时候，他就会把那副绿色的眼镜夹在书里做个标记，然后转过身来做他那高利贷的生意。

有人说汤姆在老年的时候变得有一点儿精神错乱，他幻想自己的末日快要来临了，于是把自己的马重新钉好蹄铁、上好鞍辔，然后把它四脚朝上埋了起来；因为他以为在最后一天，世界会天地颠倒，在那种情况下，他就能看到他的马站得好好地等他爬上去，而他决心最差也要和他那老朋友赛一赛跑。然而，这很可能只是老太太们的寓言而已，假如他真的采取了这样一个预防措施的话，那也是完全多余的，至少那个权威的古老传说是这么讲的。在那个传说

美洲秃鹫

里,他的故事是这样结尾的:

三伏天里一个闷热的下午,一场黑色的伴有雷暴的大风正在逼近,汤姆戴着他那白色的亚麻布帽,穿着印度丝绸的晨袍,坐在他的账房里。他正要取消一个抵押的赎回权,这样他就把一个不幸的地产投机商完全毁掉了。虽然他曾经对那人表示了最伟大的友谊,然而当那可怜的地产经纪人哀求他再宽限几个月的时候,他却变得暴躁愤怒,不肯再等一天。

“我的家庭会被毁掉,带到教区去的。”那地产经纪人说。

“慈善事业就是从家里开始的,”汤姆回答道,“在这么困难的时候,我得照顾好我自己。”

“你已经从我身上赚了那么多钱了。”那投机商说。

汤姆失去了耐心和虔诚——“要是我赚了一分钱的话,”他说,“就让魔鬼来把我抓走。”

就在那时,从街门那儿传来了三下响亮的敲门声。他走出去看是谁在那儿。一个黑男人牵着一匹黑马,那马不耐烦地嘶鸣着刨地。

“汤姆,你的时间到了。”那黑家伙粗声说道。汤姆向后退缩着,但是太晚了。他把他的小圣经留在了外衣的口袋里,而他的大圣经则被埋在了桌上那些他就要取消赎回权的抵押文件下面:从来没有一个罪人像他那样毫无防备地被带走。那黑男人把他像个婴儿一样轻轻放到马鞍上,给了那马一鞭子,它就驮着汤姆在暴风雨中疾驰而去。职员们把钢笔夹在自己的耳朵后面,透过窗户用视线追随着他。汤姆•沃克就这样走了,顺着大街飞驰而去。他那白色的帽子上下跳动着,他的晨袍在风中摆动,而他座下的马则每次跃起都在硬路面上敲击出火花来。当职员们转回视线来寻找那个黑男人时,他已经消失得无影无踪了。

汤姆•沃克再也没有回来终结那抵押的赎回权。一个住在那个沼泽边的农民说,在那次风暴最厉害的时候,他听到路上有一阵响亮的马蹄嗒嗒声和人的嗥叫声。他跑到窗边,看见在一匹马上有一个像我刚才描述过那样的人影,那匹马像疯了一般穿过田野、越过山丘、向下朝着那个印第安古堡奔去,冲进了长满黑暗铁杉的沼泽地。而不久以后,一个闪电击向了那个方向,似乎使整片森林都燃起了熊熊烈火。

波士顿的好人们摇摇头、耸耸肩膀,不过因为从殖民地最早的定居开始,他们就习惯了各种形式的女巫、小妖精和魔鬼的把戏,所以他们并不像我们预料的那样受到了惊吓。人们指定了受托人来管理汤姆的财产，然而，他却没有留下任何可以进行管理的遗产。当人们查看他的保险箱时，发现他所有的债券和抵押都变成了灰烬。他那装着金银的铁箱子现在满是碎屑和刨花；在他的马厩里两副骨架取代了他那快要饿死的马，而第二天他的大房子就起了火，烧成了灰烬。

这就是汤姆•沃克和他那些不义之财的下场。请所有吝啬的做金钱生意的人都牢记这个故事。它的真实性是不容置疑的。他从橡树下挖出基德的财宝的那个大洞今天还能看得见；而在暴风雨的夜里，人们经常能看见一个穿着晨袍、带着白色帽子、骑在马背上的身影在附近的沼泽和印第安古堡出现，那无疑是那高利贷者的受折磨的鬼魂。事实上，这个故事已经变成了一句格言，就是在新英格兰地区非常盛行的那句话的起源："魔鬼和汤姆•沃克"。

文学和生活

读者反应 你认为汤姆•沃克应该受到那样的命运惩罚吗？为什么？

主题焦点 这个故事从哪些方面说有典型的美国特征？

小组活动 很多故事中，主人公都受到了一个教训：他达成的协议会伴随着难以预料的高昂代价。和你的小组成员一起想出电影中的三个例子，它们中的人物也受到了类似的教训。然后把你们的选择和汤姆•沃克的选择做比较。

阅读理解

1. 描述汤姆•沃克第一次和魔鬼见面的情景。

2. 解释为什么汤姆起初不同意和魔鬼做交易。

3. 描述汤姆对于失去妻子的反应。

4. (a)汤姆•沃克和魔鬼最终达成的是什么协议？(b)当他开始为这个协议感到懊悔时，他做了什么事？

思考

解释

1. 对于沃克家的房子和马的描述表现了他们的什么方面？(推断)

2. 故事里的什么细节暗示了虽然汤姆的情况改变了，但他的本性还是没有变化？(证据支持)

3. (a)当鄂文说到汤姆变成了一个“狂热的信徒”时，他是什么意思？(b)汤姆对于宗教的做法和他对于金融买卖的做法有什么相似之处？(解释)

4. 鄂文希望他的读者从这个故事中吸取什么教训？(得出结论)

评价

5. 汤姆·沃克为了金钱出卖了自己的灵魂。你认为如果他是为了知识而出卖自己的灵魂，那么他会不会成为一个比较令人同情的人物？(评价)

扩展

6. 鄂文暗示说贷款给别人的人是贪婪的，一个银行家将会对这种暗示作出什么回答？今天的什么因素将会使汤姆·沃克无法在贷款的生意上取得成功？(职业连线)

文学聚焦

无所不知的叙述者

通过一个无所不知的叙述者，作者可以揭示许多人物的思想和感情，由此从不止一个视角表现事件。在这个故事里，鄂文使用了一个讲故事的人的声音，好像是他把从不同时期收集来的记录编在一起成为这个故事。

1. 举出故事里汤姆·沃克在某些情况下的思想和视角。

2. 从故事中找到一个叙述者揭露了汤姆·沃克的妻子的思想或隐瞒起来的计划的地方。

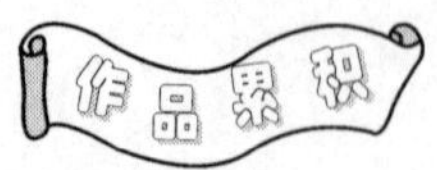

点子库

写作

1. 通信　在汤姆·沃克被魔鬼带走之前，以汤姆的名义给你的侄女写封信。在信里警告她小心与魔鬼做交易的危险。

2. 改写结尾　如果汤姆·沃克的妻子也和魔鬼做了交易，那么会发生什么事情呢？在这个假设的基础上为这个故事写一个新的结尾。

3. 分析　一个评论家曾经说:“华盛顿•鄂文写散文最大的天赋就是他能在最可怕的环境中找到幽默。”写一篇短文,阐明并讨论这个故事中的幽默因素所取得的效果。

项目

1. 纸板游戏　设计一个纸板游戏教低年级的学生认识贪婪和莽撞决定的后果。把你的游戏展示给同学们看。(艺术连线)

2. 展览　浮士德的传说启发了戏剧、歌剧、甚至还有一部百老汇的音乐剧。对这些艺术作品做研究,并制作一个展览,展出你研究的结果。如果可能的话,包含这些表演的磁带、CD和录像片断。(媒体连线)

微型写作课

更新一个故事

鄂文故事中的信息与今天的世界仍然有关系。为这个故事创作一个更新的版本,设计新的故事情节和人物细节,把它们放在今天的世界背景中,通过一种吸引现代读者的方式来传递这个故事的信息。

写作技巧重点:适应读者

在你写故事的时候,注意使用今天的读者熟悉和喜欢的语言和细节。注意文中的词汇和语句结构,它们会吸引鄂文生活的时代的读者,但现在看来却很过时了。

日志中的范例

“那么,原谅我的冒昧,请问,你是谁?”汤姆说。

在你更新了的版本中，你很可能会让汤姆•沃克用一种适合现代读者的方式来说话。此外,在你设计情节和情景的细节时,你应该时刻想到你的读者的兴趣和背景。

构思

把原版故事的情节列出来。考虑更新你列出的每个情节的最好方法。比如说:汤姆•沃克碰到魔鬼的地方可能不是在树林里,而是在一个购物中心。

写稿

把你的故事写出来。你的人物的话语、服饰和行为都应该清楚地表现出这个故事发生在现代。把当前流行的食品、衣服和表演包含在你的故事里。

修改

确定你写的故事在原来的成分和更新的细节之间取得了平衡。检查并保证故事中的斗争和信息是一样的，但是你已经把语言和情景改在今天的世界中。

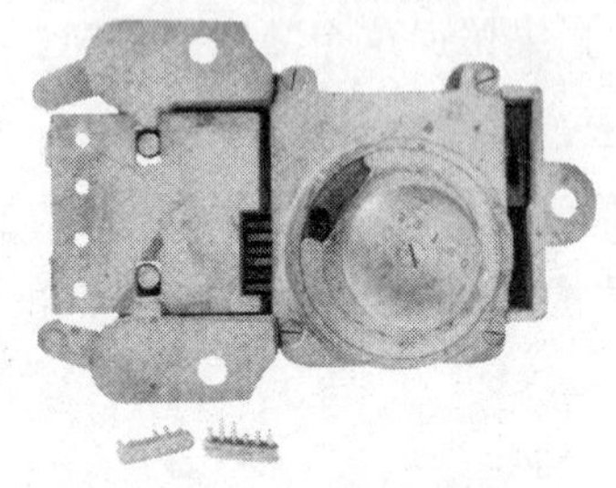

Guide for Interpreting

Washington Irving(1783—1859)

Named after the first American president, Washington Irving became the first American writer to achieve an international reputation.

<u>An American Youth</u> Born into a wealthy family, Irving began studying law at the age of sixteen. Though he had planned to be a lawyer, he found he was more interested in travel and writing. He spent much time traveling throughout Europe and New York's Hudson Valley and reading European literature. Irving also wrote satirical essays using the pen name Jonathan Oldstyle. When Irving was twenty-four, he and his brother began publishing a magazine anonymously, Salmagundi (the name of a spicy appetizer), which carried humorous sketches and essays about New York society.

In 1809, he published his first major work, A History of New York From the Beginning of the World to the End of the Dutch Dynasty, using the pseudonym Diedrich Knickerbocker. The book, a humorous examination of New York during colonial times, was well received and made Irving famous.

<u>Tour of Europe</u> From 1815 to 1832, Irving lived in Europe. There he traveled extensively and learned about European customs, traditions, and folk lore. Inspired by the European folk heritage, Irving created two of his most famous stories, "The Legend of Sleepy Hollow" and "Rip Van Winkle", transforming two traditional German tales into distinctly American stories set in the Hudson Valley. When Irving published these two stories in the Sketchbook (1820), under the pseudonym Geoffrey Crayon, writers and critics throughout Europe and the United States responded enthusiastically.

The international success of Irving's stories marked the beginning of a dis-

tinctly American literary heritage.

A Devoted American While in Europe, Irving completed three other books, including Tales of a Traveller, which contains "The Devil and Tom Walker." When his patriotism was questioned because of his time abroad, Irving responded: "I am endeavoring to serve my country. Whatever I have written has been written with the feelings and published as the writing of an American. Is that renouncing my country? How else am I to serve my country—by coming home and begging an office of it: which I should not have the kind of talent or the business habits requisite to fill? —If I can do any good in this world it is with my pen." Although Irving continued to publish after returning to the United States, he is remembered mainly for a few characters he created while in Europe.

Background for Understanding

LITERATURE: THE LEGEND OF FAUST

"The Devil and Tom Walker" is a variation of the Faust legend—a tale about a man who sells his soul to the Devil for earthly benefits. The legend was inspired by a real person, a wandering scholar and conjurer named Faust, who lived in early sixteenth century Germany. Faustbach, the first printed version of a Faust legend, was published in 1587. That story proposed that Faust had made a pact with the Devil for knowledge and power on Earth.

Over the years, many variations of the Faust legend have appeared, including a 1604 play by English dramatist Christopher Marlowe, a two-part dramatic poem (1808, 1832) by Johann Goethe, an 1859 opera by Charles Gounod, and a 1947 novel by Thomas Mann. Each retelling involves a person who trades his soul for experience, knowledge, or treasure. Adaptations do not share the same ending—in some, the protagonist is doomed; in others, he is redeemed.

Literature and your Life

CONNECT YOUR EXPERIENCE

In our society, it's not uncommon to see political candidates who fight to win at any cost, business executives who make money in a dishonest way, and Olympic athletes who bend the rules to get the gold. The main character in this story goes to even greater extremes to achieve his goal of great wealth: He makes a pact with the Devil—even though he knows that he will eventually have to pay for this decision.

Journal Writing Give examples of people in today's news who are driven by their need for money, power, or fame.

THEMATIC FOCUS: FIRESIDE AND CAMPFIRE

What details make this story, based on a German legend, a distinctly American tale that reflects the characteristics of its time?

Literary Focus

OMNISCIENT NARRATOR

"The Devil and Tom Walker" is told not by a participant in the story but by an omniscient (all-knowing) narrator who stands outside the action and relates the thoughts and feelings of all the characters. When a story is told by an omniscient narrator, the reader is not limited to the thoughts and perspective of a single character but may know the thoughts and feelings of any character. The narrator may even comment on the events of the story.

The Devil and Tom walker

Washington Irving

A few miles from Boston in Massachusetts, there is a deep inlet, winding several miles into the interior of the country from Charles Bay, and terminating in

a thickly wooded swamp or morass. On one side of this inlet is a beautiful dark grove; on the opposite side the land rises abruptly from the water's edge into a high ridge, on which grow a few scattered oaks of great age and immense size. Under one of these gigantic trees, according to old stories, there was a great amount of treasure buried by Kidd the pirate. The inlet allowed a facility to bring the money in a boat secretly and at night to the very foot of the hill; the elevation of the place permitted a good look-out to be kept that no one was at hand; while the remarkable trees formed good landmarks by which the place might easily be found again. The old stories add, moreover, that the Devil presided at the hiding of the money, and took it under his guardianship; but this it is well known he always does with buried treasure, particularly when it has been ill-gotten.

Be that as it may, Kidd never returned to recover his wealth; being shortly after seized at Boston, sent out to England, and there hanged for a pirate.

About the year 1727, just at the time that earthquakes were prevalent in New England, and shook many tall sinners down upon their knees, there lived near this place a meager, miserly fellow, of the name of Tom Walker. He had a wife as miserly as himself: they were so miserly that they even conspired to cheat each other. Whatever the woman could lay hands on, she hid away; a hen could not cackle but she was on the alert to secure the new-laid egg. Her husband was continually prying about to detect her secret hoards, and many and fierce were the conflicts that took place about what ought to have been common property. They lived in a forlorn-looking house that stood alone, and had an air of starvation. A few straggling savin trees, emblems of sterility, grew near it; no smoke ever curled from its chimney; no traveler stopped at its door. A miserable horse, whose ribs were as articulate as the bars of a gridiron, stalked about a field, where a thin carpet of moss, scarcely

covering the ragged beds of puddingstone, tantalized and balked his hunger; and sometimes he would lean his head over the fence, look piteously at the passerby, and seem to petition deliverance from this land of famine.

The house and its inmates had altogether a bad name. Tom's wife was a tall termagant fierce of temper, loud of tongue, and strong of arm. Her voice was often heard in wordy warfare with her husband; and his face sometimes showed signs that their conflicts were not confined to words. No one ventured, however, to interfere between them. The lonely wayfarer shrunk within himself at the horrid clamor and clapperclawing eyed the den of discord askance; and hurried on his way, rejoicing, if a bachelor, in his celibacy.

One day that Tom Walker had been to a distant part of the neighborhood, he took what he considered a shortcut homeward, through the swamp. Like most shortcuts, it was an ill-chosen route. The swamp was thickly grown with great gloomy pines and hemlocks, some of them ninety feet high, which made it dark at noonday, and a retreat for all the owls of the neighborhood. It was full of pits and quagmires, partly covered with weeds and mosses, where the green surface often betrayed the traveler into a gulf of black, smothering mud; there were also dark and stagnant pools, the abodes of the tadpole, the bullfrog, and the watersnake; where the trunks of pines and hemlocks lay half-drowned, half-rotting, looking like alligators sleeping in the mire.

Tom had long been picking his way cautiously through this treacherous forest; stepping from tuft to tuft of rushes and roots, which afforded precarious footholds among deep sloughs; or pacing carefully, like a cat, along the prostrate trunks of trees; startled now and then by the sudden screaming of the bittern, or the quacking of a wild duck, rising on the wing from some solitary pool. At length he arrived at a piece of firm ground, which ran out like a peninsula into the deep bosom of the swamp. It had been one of the strongholds of the Indians during their wars with the first colonists. Here they had thrown up a kind of fort, which they had looked upon as almost impregnable, and had used as a place of refuge for their squaws and children. Nothing remained of the old Indian fort but a few embankments, gradually sinking to the level of the surrounding earth, and already

overgrown in part by oaks and other forest trees, the foliage of which formed a contrast to the dark pines and hemlocks of the swamp.

It was late in the dusk of evening when Tom Walker reached the old fort, and he paused there awhile to rest himself. Anyone but he would have felt unwilling to linger in this lonely, melancholy place, for the common people had a bad opinion of it, from the stories handed down from the time of the Indian wars; when it was asserted that the savages held incantations here, and made sacrifices to the evil spirit.

Tom Walker, however, was not a man to be troubled with any fears of the kind. He reposed himself for some time on the trunk of a fallen hemlock, listening to the boding cry of the tree toad, and delving with his walking staff into a mound of black mold at his feet. As he turned up the soil unconsciously, his staff struck against something hard. He raked it out of the vegetable mold, and lo! a cloven skull, with an Indian tomahawk buried deep in it, lay before him. The rust on the weapon showed the time that had elapsed since this deathblow had been given. It was a dreary memento of the fierce struggle that had taken place in this last foothold of the Indian warriors.

"Humph!" said Tom Walker, as he gave it a kick to shake the dirt from it.

"Let that skull alone!" said a gruff voice. Tom lifted up his eyes, and beheld a great black man seated directly opposite him, on the stump of a tree. He was exceedingly surprised, having neither heard nor seen anyone approach; and he was still more perplexed on observing, as well as the gathering gloom would permit, that the stranger was neither Negro nor Indian. It is true he was dressed in a rude half-Indian garb, and had a red belt or sash swathed round his body; but his face was neither black nor copper color, but swarthy and dingy, and begrimed with soot, as if he had been accustomed to toil among fires and forges. He had a shock of coarse black hair, that stood out from his head in all directions, and bore an ax on his shoulder.

He scowled for a moment at Tom with a pair of great red eyes.

"What are you doing on my grounds?" said the black man, with a hoarse growling voice.

"Your grounds!" said Tom with a sneer, "no more your grounds than mine; they belong to Deacon Peabody."

"Deacon Peabody be d—d," said the stranger, "as I flatter myself he will be, if he does not look more to his own sins and less to those of his neighbors. Look yonder, and see how Deacon Peabody is faring."

Tom looked in the direction that the stranger pointed, and beheld one of the great trees, fair and flourishing without, but rotten at the core, and saw that it had been nearly hewn through, so that the first high wind was likely to blow it down. On the bark of the tree was scored the name of Deacon Peabody, an eminent man, who had waxed wealthy by driving shrewd bargains with the Indians. He now looked round, and found most of the tall trees marked with the name of some great man of the colony, and all more or less scored by the ax. The one on which he had been seated, and which had evidently just been hewn down, bore the name of Crowninshield: and he recollected a mighty rich man of that name, who made a vulgar display of wealth, which it was whispered he had acquired by buccaneering.

"He's just ready for burning!" said the black man, with a growl of triumph. "You see I am likely to have a good stock of firewood for winter."

"But what right have you," said Tom, "to cut down Deacon Peabody's timber?"

"The right of a prior claim," said the other. "This woodland belonged to me long before one of your white-faced race put foot upon the soil."

"And pray, who are you, if I may be so bold?" said Tom.

"Oh, I go by various names. I am the wild huntsman in some countries; the black miner in others. In this neighborhood I am known by the name of the black woodsman. I am he to whom the red men consecrated this spot, and in honor of

whom they now and then roasted a white man, by way of sweetsmelling sacrifice. Since the red men have been exterminated by you white savages, I amuse myself by presiding at the persecutions of Quakers and Anabaptists; I am the great patron and prompter of slave dealers, and the grandmaster of the Salem witches."

"The upshot of all which is, that, if I mistake not," said Tom, sturdily, "you are he commonly called Old Scratch."

"The same, at your service? replied the black man, with a half-civil nod.

Such was the opening of this interview, according to the old story; though it has almost too familiar an air to be credited. One would think that to meet with such a singular personage, in this wild, lonely place, would have shaken any man's nerves; but Tom was a hard-minded fellow, not easily daunted, and he had lived so long with a termagant wife, that he did not even fear the Devil.

It is said that after this commencement they had a long and earnest conversation together, as Tom returned homeward. The black man told him of great sums of money buried by Kidd the pirate, under the oak trees on the high ridge, not far from the morass. All these were under his command, and protected by his power, so that none could find them but such as propitiated his Favor. These he offered to place within Tom Walker's reach, having conceived an especial kindness for him; but they were to be had only on certain conditions. What these conditions were may easily be surmised, though Tom never disclosed them publicly. They must have been very hard, for he required time to think of them, and he was not a man to stick at trifles where money was in view. When they had reached the edge of the swamp, the stranger paused—"What proof have I that all you have been telling me is true?" said Tom. "There is my signature," said the black man, pressing his finger on Tom's forehead. So saying, he turned off among the thickets of the swamp, and seemed, as Tom said, to go down, down, down, into the earth, until nothing but his head and shoulders could be seen, and so on, until he totally disappeared.

When Tom reached home, he found the black print of a finger, burnt, as it were, into his forehead, which nothing could obliterate.

The first news his wife had to tell him was the sudden death of Absalom

Crowninshield, the rich buccaneer. It was announced in the papers with the usual flourish, that "A great man had fallen in Israel."

Tom recollected the tree which his black friend had just hewn down, and which was ready for burning, "Let the freebooter roast," said Tom, "who cares?" He now felt convinced that all he had heard and seen was no illusion.

He was not prone to let his wife into his confidence; but as this was an uneasy secret, he willingly shared it with her. All her avarice was awakened at the mention of hidden gold, and she urged her husband to comply with the black man's terms and secure what would make them wealthy for life. However Tom might have felt disposed to sell himself to the Devil, he was determined not to do so to oblige his wife; so he flatly refused, out of the mere spirit of contradiction. Many and bitter were me quarrels they had on the subject, but the more she talked, the more resolute was Tom not to be damned to please her.

At length she determined to drive the bargain on her own account, and if she succeeded, to keep all the gain to herself. Being of the same fearless temper as her husband, she set off for the old Indian for towards the close of a summer's day. She was many hours absent. When she came back, she was reserved and sullen in her replies. She spoke something of a black man whom she had met about twilight, hewing at the root of a tall tree. He was sulky, however, and would not come to terms: she was to go again with a propitiatory offering, but what it was she forbore to say.

The next evening she set off again for the swamp, with her apron heavily laden. Tom waited and waited for her, but in vain; midnight came, but she did not make her appearance: morning, noon, night returned, but still she

did not come. Tom now grew uneasy for her safety, especially as he found she had carried off in her apron the silver teapot and spoons, and every portable article of value. Another night elapsed, another morning came; but no wife. In a word, she was never heard of more.

What was her real fate nobody knows, in consequence of so many pretending to know. It is one of those facts which have become confounded by a variety of historians. Some asserted that she lost her way among the tangled mazes of the swamp, and sank into some pit or slough; others, more uncharitable, hinted that she had eloped with the household booty, and made off to some other province; while others surmised that the tempter had decoyed her into a dismal quagmire, on the top of which her hat was found lying. In confirmation of this, it was said a great black man, with an ax on his shoulder, was seen late that very evening coming out of the swamp, carrying a bundle tied in a checked apron, with an air of surly triumph.

The most current and probable story, however, observes that Tom Walker grew so anxious about the fate of his wife and his property, that he set out at length to seek them both at the Indian fort. During a long summer's afternoon he searched about the gloomy place, but no wife was to be seen. He called her name repeatedly, but she was nowhere to be heard. The bittern alone responded to his voice, as he flew screaming by; or the bullfrog croaked dolefully from a neighboring pool. At length, it is said, just in the brown hour of twilight, when the owls began to hoot, and the bats to flit about, his attention was attracted by the clamor of carrion crows hovering about a cypress tree. He looked up, and beheld a bundle tied in a checked apron, and hanging in the branches of the tree, with a great vulture perched hard by, as if keeping watch upon it. He leaped with joy; for he recognized his wife's apron, and supposed it to contain the household valuables.

"Let us get hold of the property," said he, consolingly to himself, "and we will endeavor to do without the woman."

As he scrambled up the tree, the vulture spread its wide wings, and sailed off screaming into the deep shadows of the forest. Tom seized the checked apron, but woeful sight! found nothing but a heart and liver tied up in it!

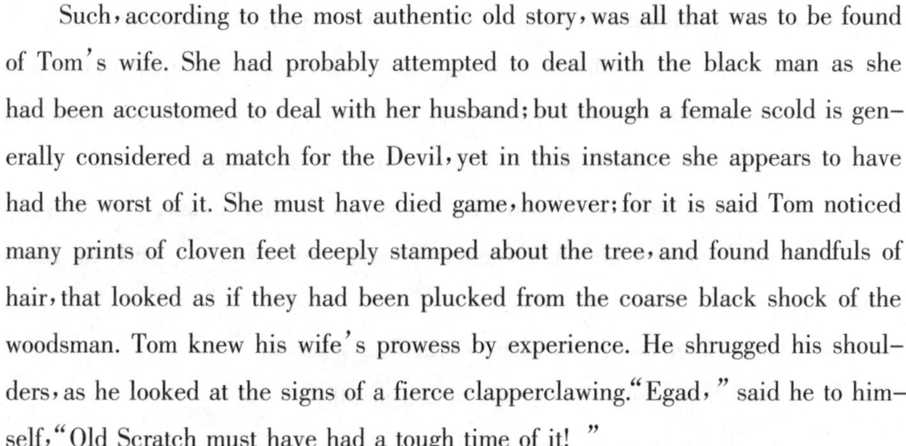

Such, according to the most authentic old story, was all that was to be found of Tom's wife. She had probably attempted to deal with the black man as she had been accustomed to deal with her husband; but though a female scold is generally considered a match for the Devil, yet in this instance she appears to have had the worst of it. She must have died game, however; for it is said Tom noticed many prints of cloven feet deeply stamped about the tree, and found handfuls of hair, that looked as if they had been plucked from the coarse black shock of the woodsman. Tom knew his wife's prowess by experience. He shrugged his shoulders, as he looked at the signs of a fierce clapperclawing. "Egad," said he to himself, "Old Scratch must have had a tough time of it! "

Tom consoled himself for the loss of his property, with the loss of his wife, for he was a man of fortitude. He even felt something like gratitude towards the black woodsman, who, he considered, had done him a kindness, He sought, therefore, to cultivate a further acquaintance with him, but for some time without success; the old blacklegs played shy, for whatever people may think, he is not always to be had for calling for: he knows how to play his cards when pretty sure of his game.

At length, it is said, when delay had whetted Tom's eagerness to the quick, and prepared him to agree to anything rather than not gain the promised treasure, he met the black man one evening in his usual woodsman's dress, with his ax on his shoulder, sauntering along the swamp, and humming a tune. He affected to receive Tom's advances with great indifference, made brief replies, and went on humming his tune.

By degrees, however, Tom brought him to business, and they began to haggle about tile terms on which the former was to have the pirate's treasure. There was one condition which need not be mentioned, being generally understood in all cases where the Devil grants favors; but there were others about which, though of less importance, he was inflexibly obstinate. He insisted that the money found through his means should be employed in his service. He proposed, therefore, that Tom should employ it in the black traffic; that is to say, that he should fit out a slave ship. This, however, Tom resolutely refused: he was bad enough in all con-

science, but the Devil himself could not tempt him to turn slave-trader.

Finding Tom so squeamish on this point, he did not insist upon it, but proposed, instead, that he should turn usurer; the Devil being extremely anxious for the increase of usurers, looking upon them as his peculiar people.

To this no objections were made, for it was just to Tom's taste.

"You shall open a broker's shop in Boston next month," said the black man.

"I'll do it tomorrow, if you wish," said Tom Walker.

"You shall lend money at two per cent a month."

"Egad, I'll charge four! " replied Tom Walker.

"You shall extort bonds, foreclose mortgages, drive the merchant to bankruptcy—"

"I'll drive him to the Devil," cried Tom Walker.

"You are the usurer for my money!" said the blacklegs with delight. "When will you want the rhino?"

"This very night."

"Done! " said the Devil.

"Done! " said Tom Walker. So they shook hands and struck a bargain.

A few days' time saw Tom Walker seated behind his desk in a counting-house in Boston.

His reputation for a ready-moneyed man, who would lend money out for a good consideration, soon spread abroad. Everybody remembers the time of Governor Belcher, when money was particularly scarce. It was a time of paper credit. The country had been deluged with government bills; the famous Land Bank had been established; there had been a rage for speculating; the

people had run mad with schemes for new settlements, for building cities in the wilderness; land jobbers went about with maps of grants, and townships, and El Dorados, lying nobody knew where, but which everybody was ready to purchase. In a word, the great speculating fever which breaks out every now and then in the country, had raged to an alarming degree, and everybody was dreaming of making sudden fortunes from nothing. As usual the fever had subsided; the dream had gone off, and the imaginary fortunes with it; the patients were left in doleful plight, and the whole country resounded with the consequent cry of "hard times."

At this propitious time of public distress did Tom Walker set up as usurer in Boston. His door was soon thronged by customers. The needy and adventurous, the gambling speculator, the dreaming land jobber, the thriftless tradesman, the merchant with cracked credit, in short, everyone driven to raise money by desperate means and desperate sacrifices, hurried to Tom Walker.

Thus Tom was the universal friend of the needy, and acted like a "friend in need"; that is to say, he always exacted good pay and good security. In proportion to the distress of the applicant was the hardness of his terms. He accumulated bonds and mortgages; gradually squeezed his customers closer and closer, and sent them at length, dry as a sponge, from his door.

In this way he made money hand over hand, became a rich and mighty man, and exalted his cocked hat upon Change. He built himself, as usual, a vast house, out of ostentation; but left the greater part of it unfinished and unfurnished, out of parsimony. He even set up a carriage in the fullness of his vainglory, though he nearly starved the horses which drew it; and as the ungreased wheels groaned and screeched on the axletrees, you would have thought you heard the souls of the poor debtors he was squeezing.

As Tom waxed old, however, he grew thoughtful. Having secured the good things of this world, he began to feel anxious about those of the next. He thought with regret on the bargain he had made with his black friend, and set his wits to work to cheat him out of the conditions. He became, therefore, all of a sudden, a violent churchgoer. He prayed loudly and strenuously, as if heaven were to be taken by force of lungs. Indeed, one might always tell when he had sinned most

during the week, by the clamor of his Sunday devotion. The quiet Christians who had been modestly and steadfastly traveling Zionward, were struck with self-reproach at seeing themselves so suddenly outstripped in their career by this new-made convert. Tom was as rigid in religious as in money matters; he was a stern supervisor and censurer of his neighbors, and seemed to think every sin entered up to their account became a credit on his own side of the page. He even talked of the expediency of reviving the persecution of Quakers and Anabaptists. In a word, Tom's zeal became as notorious as his riches.

Still, in spite of all this strenuous attention to forms, Tom had a lurking dread that the Devil, after all, would have his due. That he might not be taken unawares, therefore, it is said he always carried a small Bible in his coat pocket. He had also a great folio Bible on his countinghouse desk, and would frequently be found reading it when people called on business; on such occasions he would lay his green spectacles in the book, to mark the place, while he turned round to drive some usurious bargain.

Some say that Tom grew a little crackbrained in his old days, and that fancying his end approaching, he had his horse newly shod, saddled and bridled, and buried with his feet uppermost; because he supposed that at the last day the world would be turned upside down, in which case he should find his horse standing ready for mounting, and he was determined at the worst to give his old friend a run for it. This, however, is probably a mere old wives' fable. If he really did take such a precaution, it was totally superfluous; at least so says the authentic old legend, which closes his story in the following manner.

One hot summer afternoon in the dog days, just as a terrible black thunder-gust was coming up, Tom sat in his counting house in his white linen cap and India silk morning gown. He was on the point of foreclosing a mortgage, by which he would complete the ruin of an unlucky land speculator for whom he had professed the greatest friendship. The poor land jobber begged him to grant a few months' indulgence. Tom had grown testy and irritated, and refused another day.

"My family will be ruined and brought upon the parish," said the land jobber. "Charity begins at home," replied Tom; "I must take care of myself in these hard times."

"You have made so much money out of me," said the speculator.

Tom lost his patience and his piety— "The Devil take me," said he,"if I have made a farthing! "

Just then there were three loud knocks at the street door. He stepped out to see who was there. A black man was holding a black horse, which neighed and stamped with impatience.

"Tom, you're come for," said the black fellow, gruffly. Tom shrunk back, but too late. He had left his little Bible at the bottom of his coat pocket, and his big Bible on the desk buried under the mortgage he was about to foreclose: never was sinner taken more unawares. The black man whisked him like a child into the saddle, gave the horse the lash, and away he galloped, with Tom on his back, in the midst of the thunderstorm. The clerks stuck their pens behind their ears, and stared after him from the windows. Away went Tom Walker, dashing down the streets, his white cap bobbing up and down, his morning gown fluttering in the wind, and his steed striking fire out of the pavement at every bound. When the clerks turned to look for the black man he had disappeared.

Tom Walker never returned to foreclose the mortgage. A countryman who lived on the border of the swamp, reported that in the height of the thunder-gust he had heard a great clattering of hoofs and a howling along the road, and running to the window caught sight of a figure, such as I have described, on a horse that galloped like mad across the fields, over the hills and down into the black hemlock swamp towards the old Indian fort; and that shortly after a thunderbolt falling in that direction seemed to set the whole forest in a blaze.

The good people of Boston shook their heads and shrugged their shoulders, but had been so much accustomed to witches and goblins and tricks of the Devil, in all kind of shapes from the first settlement of the colony, that they were not so much horror struck as might have been expected. Trustees were appointed to take charge of Tom's effects. There was nothing, however, to administer upon. On searching his coffers all his bonds and mortgages were found reduced to cinders. In place of gold and silver his iron chest was filled with chips and shavings; two skeletons lay in his stable instead of his half-starved horses, and the very next day his great house took fire and was burned to the ground.

Such was the end of Tom Walker and his ill-gotten wealth. Let all griping money brokers lay this story to heart. The truth of it is not to be doubted. The very hole under the oak trees, whence he dug Kidd's money, is to be seen to this day; and the neighboring swamp and old Indian fort are often haunted in stormy nights by a figure on horseback, in morning gown and white cap, which is doubtless the troubled spirit of the usurer. In fact, the story has resolved itself into a proverb, and is the origin of that popular saying, so prevalent throughout New England, of "The Devil and Tom Walker".

第三课

穿越大裂谷

麦里韦泽·李维斯 (1774—1809)

麦里韦泽·李维斯和威廉姆·克拉克带领着一队全心追随他们的退役士兵一起完成了一次为期两年，全长8000英里的探险考察，他们穿越了美国在购买路易斯安那时获得的未经勘探的领土。在1804年至1806年之间，李维斯和克拉克沿密苏里河从圣路易斯行进到密苏里河的源头，然后越过落基山脉，到达了太平洋海岸。当他们回到圣路易斯时，他们带回了关于太平洋西北地区的很有价值的信息。

麦里韦泽·李维斯

李维斯的探险是由托马斯·杰弗逊总统赞助的，但总统也给他和他的队伍布置了相当严格的任务：在地图上标出一条通往太平洋的通路，收集他们探险沿途地区的科学信息，探查路易斯安那区域的边界，并为美国索回奥雷根地区。

李维斯为了准备这次旅行，花了很多时间在费城学习科学分类的知识。在他分类整理沿途碰到的植物、动物和矿物时，这些知识给了他很大的帮助。作为对李维斯自然科学的兴趣的补充，克拉克拥有高超的绘制地图的技术，并绘制了他们穿越的地区的详细草图。他们还遇到了不同的印第安民族，并与这些边缘地区的土著居民交换礼物和信息。

约翰·威斯利·鲍威尔 (1834—1902)

约翰·威斯利·鲍威尔作为一名联邦士兵参加了内战，并在施洛战役中失去了一条胳膊。虽然如此，鲍威尔仍然成为第一个在科罗拉多河和大峡谷中航行并进行勘探的人。

约翰·威斯利·鲍威尔

作为一名地质学家，鲍威尔于1869年在科罗拉多河上进行了一次为期3个月的大胆而又充满危险的航行。在斯密斯索尼亚学院和国会的资助下，鲍威尔带领着一支由10个人和4条船组成的队伍进行探险。在进入峡谷之前的一刻沉思中，鲍威尔将他面临的经历描述为“一段等待完成的未知旅程；一条等待探索的未知河流”。这支探险队伍的成员乘小船进入了大峡谷，他们面对的是狂暴的急流、高耸的瀑布和危险尖利的岩石群。一次，在大峡谷中，鲍威尔的探险队分裂了。被这条河吓坏了的那一部分人走上了陆路，就此丧了命。鲍威尔和其他留在了河上的人则活了下来，并完成了这次探险。

后来，鲍威尔又进行了其他探险，勘测了落基山脉和绿河的峡谷。19世纪70年代，他指导了联邦对西部公共领土土地的一次地理勘测，以促使政府制定利用这些土地的计划。

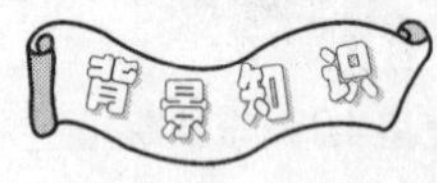

历史：购买路易斯安那

1803年，美国从法国人那里一次性买进的土地使美国控制的领土面积增加了一倍。由于法国正在寻找金钱来支持它和其他欧洲国家的战争，所以它将地图上用红色标出的土地以1500万美元的总价卖给了美国——一英亩还不到三美分。这就是著名的购买路易斯安那行动，这片土地的获得开始了一个西进运动的时期，这个时期持续了几乎一个世纪。

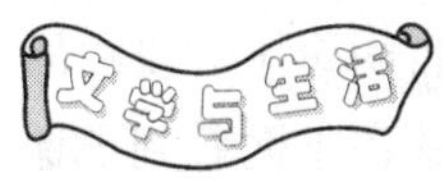

联系你的经历 如果你曾经进行过户外探险活动——例如远足、登山或水上木筏漂流——你就会知道亲身体验自然的魅力和力量是多么令人兴奋。想象一下像麦里韦泽·李维斯、约翰·威斯利·鲍威尔和其他穿越西部地区的先行者一样勘测新的领土会是什么感觉。

专题聚焦:炉火和营火 这些记录提供了第一手的视点,使人们看到像李维斯和鲍威尔这样的探险家们在旅途中所经历的快乐、恐惧和艰辛。如果你处在他们的地位,你会有什么样的反应?

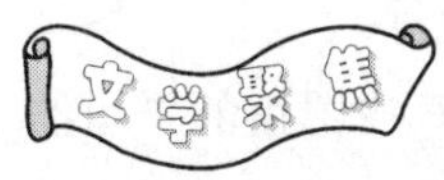

描绘 游记可能写得引人入胜,也可能乏味无趣,而经常是描绘造成了这两者间的区别。描绘就是捕捉到视觉、听觉、嗅觉、味觉和身体感觉的写法。例如,当鲍威尔写道"这条河永不停息地雷鸣般咆哮着"的时候,他就生动地描绘了那条河的声音。通过描绘,作者能使读者在想象中看到栩栩如生的图像。

在你的阅读中,使用如下所示的图表来记录表现每种感觉的描绘细节。

视觉	听觉	嗅觉	身体感觉	味觉

日志写作 想象一个美丽的地方。然后写一篇简短的描述,使用语言表现出你所看到、听到、摸到或闻到的。

穿越大裂谷

麦里韦泽·李维斯

1805年8月17日 星期六

这天早晨我很早就起了床,派德鲁叶和那个印第安人顺河而下,让席尔兹

去打猎，我又让麦克尼尔把我们剩下的肉煮熟，为我们和酋长准备了一顿不甚丰盛的早餐。在德鲁叶出发了两个小时左右，一个沿着河独自闲逛了一段距离的印第安人回来了，并且报告说白人们要回来了，因为他就在下面看到了他们。他们所有的人都表现出激动和狂喜，酋长不停地重复他友爱的拥抱。听到这条消息，我和那些印第安人表现出一样的高兴。不久之后，克拉克船长就和翻译卡波诺，还有那个印第安妇女一起到达了这里，后来我们发现那个妇女是卡米沃特酋长的姐妹。那些人相见的场面真的很感人，尤其是萨卡嘎维阿和一个印第安妇女的见面更是令人感动，那个印第安妇女曾经和她同时被囚禁，后来从米内塔勒斯逃走并回到了她的族人中间。中午时分，独木舟也都到达了这里，我们再一次充满喜悦，因为我们所有的人都聚在了一起，并且他们还带来了一个振奋人心的希望，那就是如果从水上航行不妥当的话，那么我们也有希望不久就得到足够多的马匹，使我们能从陆路进行我们的旅行。

现在我们在河左岸分岔路的交叉点下方一块有很好的草皮覆盖的平坦的地方支起了帐篷。我们在这里卸下了独木舟里的东西，并且把我们的行李都安放在岸上，我们又用一张大帆支起了一个天篷，并在地上插了一些柳树枝，以便在我们和印第安人谈话的时候他们可以坐在柳树枝的树荫下。我们认为最好这天傍晚就和印第安人进行谈话，所以大约下午四点左右，我们把他们叫到了一起，通过拉布士、卡波诺和萨卡嘎维阿的翻译，我们向他们充分地解释了我们到国家的这个边远地区来的目的。在解释的过程中我们特别注意把他们纳入我们的良好祝愿和我们政府的关心范围之中。我们使他们意识到，他们的每种货物、他们的安全防卫和生活的舒适都要依靠于我们的政府，我们还告诉他们我们政府的强大和政府对他们友好的态度。我们也向他们解释了我们为什么要深入这个地区的原因，那就是探查并发现一条能更直接地把商品带给他们的通路。由于在我们回家之前没人能与他们进行交易，所以他们尽可能地为我们提供帮助，使我们尽快完成旅行回家，这是对我们双方都大有益处的。

李维斯在密苏里河

文学和生活

读者反应 你认为李维斯与印第安人谈判的方法怎么样？解释原因。

主题焦点 李维斯知道有一天他的旅行日记会被公之于众。这一点可能对他的写作产生什么影响？

阅读理解

1. 总结李维斯记录的第一段的大意。
2. 为什么李维斯和其他人相聚的时候会那么高兴？

思考

解释

1. 李维斯在向印第安人解释这次探险的原因时态度是坦白的吗？解释你的理由。（推断）

2. 李维斯在和印第安人谈判之后分发了礼物。他为什么要这样做？（分析）

3. 李维斯对印第安人的兴趣完全是为了得到他们的帮助吗？解释你的理由。（得出结论）

评价

4. 作为一名谈判家，李维斯能得到你的怎样的评价？解释你的理由。（评估）

地球上最壮观的景象

约翰·威斯利·鲍威尔

科罗拉多大峡谷是一个由很多个峡谷组成的大峡谷，它是千万个峡谷的合成体。同样地，这个峡谷的每道峭壁也是合成的结构，一道峭壁也是由很多道峭壁组成，但却绝没有丝毫重复。这些几乎数不清的峡谷中的每一个峡谷本身就是一个美的世界。在大峡谷中有几千个峡谷像尼亚加拉瀑布下的那个峡谷一样，还有成千个和约瑟麦茨一样。所有这些峡谷联合在一起组成了大峡谷，这地球上最壮观的景象。就算将华盛顿山脉从海平线的高度连根拔起，再把它头朝下扔到大峡谷里去，也不会使大峡谷里的水溢到峭壁之外。就算把蓝里奇山拔起来投到大峡谷里去，也不会把峡谷塞满。

大峡谷中的雕刻是雨水和河水的杰作。这片广阔的峡谷迷宫剖开了科罗拉多河流过的高原地区，而这迷宫也是水的杰作。每条河流挖通了它自己的峡谷，每条小溪也同样为自己凿通谷道。当一场大雨降临这片土地时，涓涓细流雕刻出了峡谷——但是每场大雨只刻出一点。虽然大雨间隔的时间很长，峡谷上方的天空在一年中的大多数日子里都是晴朗无云的，但是，岁月悠悠，大雨带来的断断续续的细流在世纪的累积中就能发挥神奇的作用。

虽然峡谷中体现出来的冲蚀作用是广阔的，但这却只是这个地区巨大冲蚀作用的一小部分，因为在山岩之间被冲走的石块数量比用来填满峡谷所需的数量要大得多。使这整个地区的所有部分很可能都降低了1000英尺以上，而且某些地区有超过3万英尺的岩石被冲走了。总计起来，就相当于一个面积超过20万平方英里的地区平均有6000英尺的地面被冲蚀了。想象一块占地面积20万平方英里，厚度为一英里的石头，云朵向它投下暴雨，把它击成细沙，这些细沙被细流带入小溪，又被小溪冲进河里，最后被科罗拉多河带进了大海。我们认为是山脉在它们的山眉处形成了云朵，其实却是云朵造成了山脉。巨大的陆地块是被地球内部的地质力量从海下举起来的，而正是这种力量塑造了地球。然后那些四处漂浮的云朵以及蕴含着暴风雨、装扮如彩虹的云朵就用巨大的力量和高超的技巧雕刻出了山谷和峡谷，造出了小山、悬崖和山脉。云朵是真正卓越的艺术家。

在冬季，大峡谷的某些特征着重表现了出来。下面黑色的片麻岩，条纹斑驳的石英岩和绿色的或凹壁上的砂岩共同组成了雄伟的红色石壁的基础。耸起的石灰石高高居于带状的砂岩的柱上。在冬天，这一切都被白雪覆盖。从下面向上望去，这些变换的部分似乎逐渐升入了天空，而石壁与蓝色的天空之间看不到分隔的平面。天空成为整个景观的一个组成部分，在石壁之间支起了一个宽阔的圆顶，为大峡谷染上了苍穹的蓝色。就这样，在一个广阔的建筑中，天与地融为了一体。

经常在雨季，当云朵在峡谷中嬉戏时，又会产生另一种效果。云朵们从一些峡谷里爬出来，又迂回溜进了其他的峡谷。整个天空似乎有了生命，不像在

科罗拉多大峡谷

平原上空那样，总在风的推动下朝一个方向移动，而是像那些峡谷的小径一样复杂多变。这样一来，那些小云朵似乎变成了一个个人，有着自己的意志和灵魂，每个人都在做着不同的事情——它们就是一大群各持己见的云朵，随着埋藏自己心里的目的四处飘荡。在这想象中，云朵属于天空，当它们留在峡谷中的时候，天空就也降到谷道之中，抓住山崖，把它们举向无法丈量的高空，因为那高空仍然还在遥远的地方。就这样，它们将石壁无限放大了。

无论是语言的符号还是语言本身都无法充分描绘大峡谷的奇观。在试图描写它的特征时，文字艺术的能力就不堪重负了。语言和插图结合起来也无法完成这个任务。结合在一起造成了大峡谷这个自然界中最壮观的景象的那些元素是多种多样而又变化万千的。这个巨人般的奇观是经过人类无法计算的漫长岁月，由风雨雕琢出无穷的细致特征而最终形成的。要描述它，这与描述天空中的繁星或由橡树、松树、杨树、山毛榉、菩提树、山楂树、郁金香、百合花、玫瑰花、蕨类、苔藓和地衣等植物装饰而成的种种美丽的森林具有相同的难度。除了形态的元素以外，还有颜色，因为在这里，岩石的颜色可以与天空的颜

色相匹敌,大峡谷有着与彩虹一样丰富的色彩。然而形态和颜色仍然无法完全概括大峡谷所有的非凡特质,这里还是音乐的世界。这条河永不停息地雷鸣般咆哮着,暴风雨之神在岩石上演奏时,它意气飞扬激情澎湃,而当无垠的蓝天开始显露时,它又轻柔低沉地轻唱着退去。伴着美妙的音乐,大潮涨落,永不停息地升起又消逝。而当水流跃入岩石间的激流中或在巨大的瀑布中跳跃时,在旁边的峡谷谷道中,又能听到其他的曲调。所以,大峡谷就成了一个歌曲的世界。无穷的音乐在河流中激扬,无尽的音乐在溪流中翻腾,无边的音乐在潺潺流过岩石的细流中低唱。它们合在一起就是各种旋律组成的交响乐章。所有这些就是水的音乐。地球上那坚硬的地基被造成了一把壮观的竖琴,而天上的云朵就用强大的暴风雨或轻柔的细雨在这把竖琴上演奏。

形态、颜色和声音的壮丽和优美在大峡谷中得到了统一——它的形态甚至那些山脉也无法与之媲美,它的颜色可与日落争辉,而它的声音则跨越了从暴风雨到叮当作响的雨滴、从奔流到喷珠洒玉的泉水的全部音域。但还不止这些:它还是一片广大的地域。如果一个山谷是平坦的地面的话,它就可以成为一个国家。一小时又一小时,一天又一天,一周又一周,一月又一月,你也只能看到它的部分,一年还几乎不够看到它的全部。它的颜色虽然在任何一个时刻已经多种多样又繁复难辨,却还要随着日升日落而不断变化。飘过的云朵引起光影的浮现和消翳,变幻的季节也用变换的色彩留下自己的足迹。你无法一眼将大峡谷尽收眼底,仿佛它是一个毫无变化的景观,拉起一道帘子就可以看到,相反,你需要月复一月地在它的迷宫中跋涉,才能看尽它的景色。这是一个比阿尔卑斯山和喜马拉雅山还难以穿过的地区,但是如果力量和勇气足够完成这一使命的话,经过一年的艰苦跋涉,你就可以大概了解它那独一无二的壮观了。

文学和生活

读者反应　你喜欢读这篇文章吗?为什么?

主题焦点　鲍威尔写了很多关于大峡谷的情况,但却几乎只字未提他的旅程。你认为这表现了他的什么品质?

阅读理解

1. 列出鲍威尔详尽描写的大峡谷的四个方面。

2. 鲍威尔描述了两个因为季节产生的特殊视觉效果。这两个效果是什么？

3. 除了视觉以外，鲍威尔还描写了哪种感觉？

思考

解释

1. 当鲍威尔写道要描述大峡谷“语言和插图结合起来也无法完成这个任务”时，他想要表达的是什么观点？（解释）

2. 你认为对于鲍威尔来说探索大峡谷意味着什么？（得出结论）

评价

3. 鲍威尔的描绘取得了怎样的效果？用证据来支持你的回答。（批评）

扩展

4. 一幅大峡谷的图画可能表现哪些文字描述所不能表现的方面？而哪些方面是文字描述能包含图画却不能的？（美术连线）

文学聚焦

描绘

麦里韦泽•李维斯和约翰•威斯利•鲍威尔细致入微的写作都是关于西部未知领土的探险，然而他们之间的相似点也仅止于此。描绘——对于人类能感觉到的事物的文字描写——就是他们之间的不同之处。鲍威尔通过使用生动的描绘，使我们看到听到了大峡谷所有的“无穷变化”。例如，鲍威尔将峡谷的色彩比喻为彩虹，将河流的声音比喻为优美的音乐。与他相反，李维斯虽然传达了很多信息，但他却没有创作一幅我们能够看到的画面。

1. 从鲍威尔的文章中找出三个描绘性的段落，解释是什么造成了这种效果。

2. 李维斯虽然不像鲍威尔那样擅长描绘，但他的写作中也包含了一些描绘性的成分。从李维斯的作品中找到一个帮助读者看到他的营地的段落。

3. 基于每位作家使用的描绘比例，你能猜出每篇文章的写作目的是什么？

为什么？

4. 你认为哪篇文章更有效果？为什么？

5. 你更喜欢哪篇文章？解释理由。

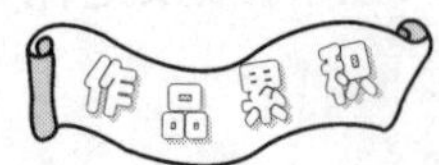

点子库

写作

1. 摘要　去掉描述性的语言，鲍威尔的根本要点是什么？写一篇简短的总结，对《地球上最壮观的景象》中的主要细节做一摘要。

2. 旅游广告　写一份到大峡谷观光游览的广告。你写出的标题和文章要能吸引读者们在下个假期里去探索那“地球上最壮观的景象”。（职业连线）

3. 新闻报道　想象你是一名记者，1805年8月17日你也在麦里韦泽·李维斯当时所处的现场。写一篇新闻报道那天的事件。

项目

1. 探险地图　李维斯和克拉克于1804年4月离开密苏里河的圣路易斯。画一张地图显示他们的探险路线，标明重要的地点和日期。（社会研究连线）

2. 研究报告　大峡谷是亘古以来地质力量作用的产物，写一篇关于大峡谷的地质发展史的研究报告。

微型写作课

描绘一个自然奇观

你是否曾经见到一个自然的奇观——它使你震惊得目瞪口呆，试图搜索一些词句来描绘它？选择一个你亲眼见到、从研究中知道或在电影中看到的自然奇观。例如，你可能会选择“老信徒”——一棵红木树，或一座正在爆发的火山。写一篇简短的描绘，在写作的过程中使用以下技巧。

写作技巧重点：利用过渡词表现地点

在写描绘文章的时候，利用过渡词来表现你采用的细节之间的关系。以下是一些表现地点关系的过渡词：

在后面，挨着，在前面，在地下，在上方，在下方，在右边，在左边，在北方，向西方，在里面，在外面，附近，在……之间。

使用这些词和词组作为坐标，使你的读者保持方向感。

构思

想象你要描绘的自然奇观。画出一份草图，并且记下一些你用来描绘它的细节——景象、声音、气味。

写稿

决定你要首先描绘的特征，然后从那一点按照逻辑关系和空间关系继续下去。利用你的草图来确定方位。

修改

重读你的文章，看它是否准确地表现出了你要描绘的对象。添加或修改感官细节，使你的描绘更加清楚。同时找出一些地方，添加过渡词使空间关系更容易理解。

Guide for Interpreting

Meriwether Lewis (1774—1809)

Along with William Clark and a team of hearty former soldiers, Meriwether Lewis completed a two-year, 8,000-mile expedition across the uncharted territory that the United States acquired in the Louisiana Purchase. Between 1804 and 1806, Lewis and Clark traveled from St.Louis up the Missouri River to its source, then across the Rocky Mountains to the Pacific coast. When they returned to St. Louis, they brought back valuable information about the Pacific Northwest.

Lewis's efforts were sponsored by President Thomas Jefferson, who gave him and his team a rigorous assignment-map a passage to the Pacific Ocean, collect scientific information about the regions they traveled, trace the boundaries of the Louisiana territory, and claim the Oregon territory for the United States.

In preparation for his journey, Lewis spent time in Philadelphia learning about scientific classification. These skills served him well as he documented the plants, animals, and minerals he encountered during his journey.To complement Lewis's naturalist interests, Clark provided strong map skills and created detailed sketches of the regions they crossed, The men also encountered a variety of Indian nations, trading gifts and information with these natives of the frontier.

John Wesley Powell (1834—1902)

As a Union soldier fighting in the Civil War, John Wesley Powell lost an arm at the Battle of Shiloh. Despite this injury, Powell was the first to navigate and chart the Colorado River and the Grand Canyon.

Powell was a geologist who conducted a daring and dangerous three-month journey on the Colorado River in 1869.Financed by the Smithsonian Institution and Congress, Powell led a party of ten men and four boats. In a reflective moment before he entered the canyon, Powell described the experience ahead of him as "an unknown distance yet to run; an unknown river yet to explore." Entering the Grand Canyon by boat, the members of the expedition party faced raging rapids, towering waterfalls, and dangerously sharp rock formations. Once in the canyon, Powell's expedition party split. Those that became terrified of the river went overland at "Separation Rapids" and perished. Powell, and the others who remained on the river, survived and completed the expedition.

Powell later conducted other expeditions surveying the Rocky Mountains and the canyons of the Green River. In the 1870's, he directed a federal geographic survey of western lands in the public domain, urging the government to develop plans for using the land.

Background for Understanding

HISTORY: THE LOUISIANA PURCHASE

In 1803, the United States doubled the amount of territory it controlled with a single purchase of land from the French. Looking for money to finance its wars against other European nations, France sold the land shown in red on the map to the United States for a total price of $15 million—less than three cents an acre. Known as the Louisiana Purchase, the acquisition began an era of westward expansion that lasted nearly a century.

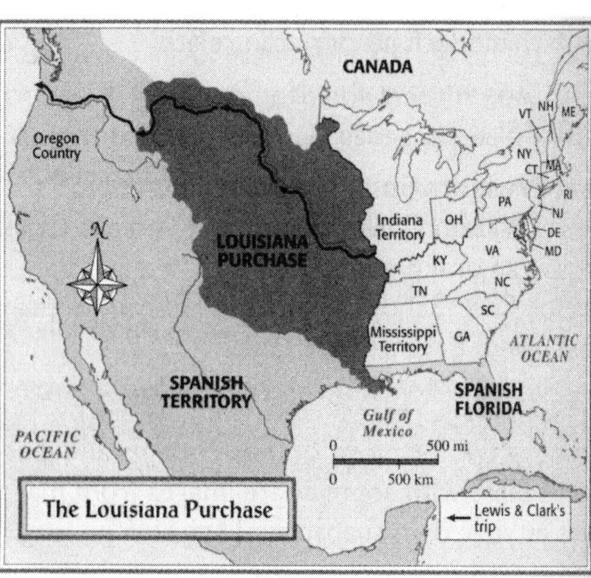

The Louisiana Purchase

Literature and your Life

CONNECT YOUR EXPERIENCE

If you've ever had an outdoor adventure—like backpacking, mountain climbing, or white-water rafting—you know how exciting it can be to gain first-hand experiences with the beauty and power of nature. Just imagine what it would have been like to chart new territory like Meriwether Lewis and John Wesley Powell and the other adventurers who blazed a trail across the western frontier.

Journal Writing Picture a beautiful place. Then write a short description of it using language that captures what you see, hear, feel, or smell.

THEMATIC FOCUS: FIRESIDE AND CAMPFIRE

These accounts provide a firsthand view of the joys, terrors, and hardships that adventurers like Lewis and Powell experienced during their travels. How would you have reacted in their place?

Literary Focus

DESCRIPTION

Travel writing can either be fascinating or dry as a bone. Often, description makes the difference, Description is writing that captures sights, sounds, smells, tastes, and physical sensations. For example, Powell vividly captures the sound of the river when he writes that "the river thunders in perpetual roar." Through descriptions, a writer can bring a scene to life in readers' minds.

As you read, use a graphic organizer like this one to record descriptive details appealing to each sense.

Sights	Sounds	Smells	Physical Sensations	Tastes

Crossing the Great Divide

Meriwether Lewis

Saturday, August 17th, 1805

This morning I arose very early and dispatched Drewyer and the Indian down me river. Sent Shields to hunt. I made McNeal cook the remainder of our meat which afforded a slight breakfast for ourselves and the Chiefi Drewyer had been gone about 2 hours when an Indian who had straggled some little distance down the river returned and reported that the white men were coming, that he had seen them just below. They all appeared transported with joy, and the chief repeated his fraternal hug. I felt quite as much gratified at this information as the Indians appeared to be. Shortly after Capt. Clark arrived with the Interpreter Charbono, and the Indian woman, who proved to be a sister of the Chief Cameahwait. The meeting of those was really affecting, particularly between Sah–ca–ga– we–ah and an Indian woman, who had been taken prisoner at the same time with her, and who had afterwards escaped from the Minnetares and rejoined her nation. At noon the canoes arrived, and we had the satisfaction once more to find ourselves all together, with a flattering prospect of being able to obtain as many horses shortly as would enable us to prosecute our voyage by land should that by water be deemed unadvisable.

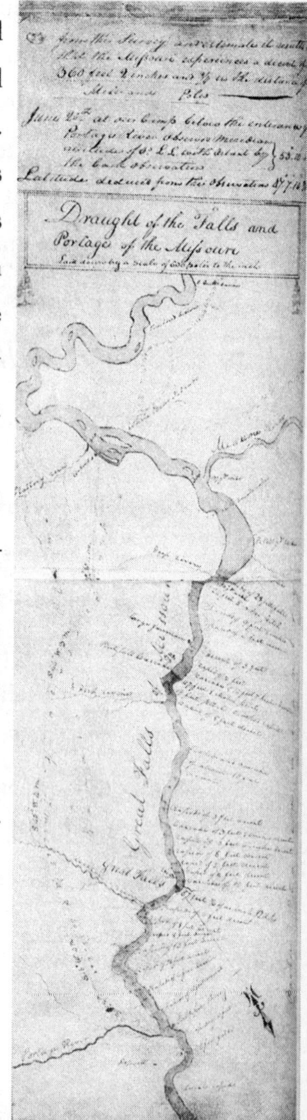

We now formed our camp just below the junction of the forks on the Lard side in a level smooth bottom covered with a fine turf of greensward. Here we unloaded our canoes and arranged our baggage on shore; formed a canopy of one of our large sails and planted some willow brush in the ground to form a shade for the

Indians to sit under while we spoke to them, which we thought it best to do this evening. Accordingly about 4 P.M. we called them together and through the medium of Labuish, Charbono and Sah-ca-ga-we-ah, we communicated to them fully the objects which had brought us into this distant part of the country, in which we took care to make them a conspicuous object of our own good wishes and the care of our government. We made them sensible of their dependence on the will of our government for every species of merchandise as well for their defense and comfort, and apprised them of the strength of our government and its friendly dispositions towards them. We also gave them as a reason why we wished to penetrate the country as far as the ocean to the west of them was to examine and find out a more direct way to bring merchandise to them. That as no trade could be carried on with them before our return to our homes that it was mutually advantageous to them as well as to ourselves that the should render us such aids as they had it in their power to furnish in order to hasten our voyage and of course our return home.

The Most Sublime Spectacle on Earth

John Wesley Powell

The Grand Canyon of the Colorado is a canyon composed of many canyons. It is a composite of thousands, of tens of thousands, of gorges. In like manner, each wall of the canyon is a composite structure, a wall composed of many walls, but never a repetition. Every one of these almost innumerable gorges is a world of beauty in itself. In the Grand Canyon there are thousands of gorges like that below Niagara Falls, and there are a thousand Yosemites. Yet all these canyons unite to form one grand canyon, the most sublime spectacle on the earth. Pluck up Mt. Washington by the roots to the level of the sea and drop it headfirst into the Grand Canyon, and the dam will not force its waters over the walls. Pluck up the Blue Ridge and hurl it into the Grand Canyon, and it will not fill it.

The carving of the Grand Canyon is the work of rains and rivers. The vast labyrinth of canyon by which the plateau region drained by the Colorado is dissected is also the work of waters. Every river has excavated its own gorge and every creek has excavated its gorge. When a shower comes in this land, the rills carve canyons—but a little at each storm; and though storms are far apart and the heavens above are cloudless for most of the days of the year, still, years are plenty in the ages, and intermittent rill called to life by a shower can do much work in centuries of centuries.

The erosion represented in the canyons, although vast, is but a small part of the great erosion of the region, for between the cliffs blocks have been carried away far superior in magnitude to those necessary to fill the canyons. Probably there is no portion of the whole region from which there have not been more than a thousand feet degraded, and there are districts from which more than 30,000 feet of rock have been carried away. Altogether, there is a district of country more than 200,000 square miles in extent from which on the average more than 6,000 feet have been eroded. Consider a rock 200,000 square miles in extent and a mile in thickness, against which the clouds have hurled their storms and beat it into sands and the rills have carried the sands into the creeks and the creeks have carried them into the rivers and the Colorado has carried them into the sea. We think of the mountains as forming clouds about their brows, but the clouds have formed the mountains. Great continental blocks are upheaved from beneath the sea by internal geologic forces that fashion the earth. Then the wandering clouds, the tempest-bearing clouds, the rainbow — decked clouds, with mighty power and with wonderful skill, carve out valleys and canyons and fashion hills and cliffs and mountains. The clouds are the artists sublime.

In winter some of the characteristics of the Grand Canyon are emphasized. The black gneiss1 below, the variegated quartzite, and the green or alcove sandstone form the foundation for the mighty red wall. The banded sandstone entablature is crowned by the tower limestone. In winter this is covered with snow. Seen from below, these changing elements seem to graduate into the heavens, and no plane of demarcation between wall and blue firmament can be seen. The heavens constitute a portion of the facade and mount into a vast dome from wall to wall, spanning the Grand Canyon with empyrean blue. So the earth and the heavens are blended in one vast structure.

When the clouds play in the canyon, as they often do in the rainy season, another set of effects is produced. Clouds creep out of canyons and wind into other canyons. The heavens seem to be alive, not moving as move the heavens over a plain, in one direction with the wind, but following the multiplied courses of these gorges. In this manner the little clouds seem to be individualized, to have wills and souls of their own, and to be going on diverse errands — a vast assemblage of self-willed clouds, faring here and there, intent upon purposes hidden in their own breasts. In the imagination the clouds belong to the sky, and when they are in the canyon the skies come down into the gorges and cling to the cliffs and lift them up to immeasurable heights, for the sky must still be far away. Thus they lend infinity to the walls.

The wonders of the Grand Canyon cannot be adequately represented in symbols of speech, nor by speech itself. The resources of the graphic art are taxed beyond their powers in attempting to portray its features. Language and illustration combined must fail. The elements that unite to make the Grand Canyon the most sublime spectacle in nature are multifarious and exceedingly diverse. The Cyclopean forms which result from the sculpture of tempests through ages too long for man to compute, are wrought into endless details, to describe which would be a task equal in magnitude to that of describing the stars of the heavens or the multitudinous beauties of the forest with its traceries of foliage presented by oak and pine and poplar, by beech and linden and hawthorn, by tulip and lily and rose, by

fern and moss and lichen. Besides the elements of form, there are elements of color, for here the colors of the heavens are rivaled by the colors of the rocks. The rainbow is not more replete with hues. Bu form and color do not exhaust all the divine qualities of the Grand Canyon. It is the land of music. The river thunders in perpetual roar, swelling in floors of music when the storm gods play upon the rocks and fading away in soft and low murmurs when the infinite blue of heaven is unveiled. With the melody of the great tide rising and falling, swelling and vanishing forever, other melodies are heard in the gorges of the lateral3 canyons, while the waters plunge in the rapids among the rocks or leap in great cataracts. Thus the Grand Canyon is a land of song. Mountains of music swell in the rivers, hills of music billow in the creeks, and meadows of music murmur in the rills that ripple over the rocks. Altogether it is a symphony of multitudinous melodies. All this is the music of waters. The adamant foundations of the earth have been wrought into a sublime harp, upon which the clouds of the heavens play with mighty tempests or with gentle showers.

The glories and the beauties of form, color, and sound unite in the Grand Canyon—forms unrivaled even by the mountains, colors that vie with sunsets, and sounds that span the diapason4 from tempest to tinkling raindrop, from cataract to bubbling fountain. But more: it is a vast district of country. Were it a valley plain it would make a state. It can be seen only in parts from hour to hour and from day to day and from week to week and from month to month. A year scarcely suffices to see it all. It has infinite variety, and no part is ever duplicated. Its colors, though many and complex at any instant, change with the ascending and declining sun; lights and shadows appear and vanish with the passing clouds, and the changing seasons mark their passage in changing colors. You cannot see the Grand Canyon in one view, as if it were a changeless spectacle from which a curtain might be lifted, but to see it you have to toil from month to month through its labyrinths. It is a region more difficult to traverse than the Alps or the Himalayas, but if strength and courage are sufficient for the task, by a year's toil a concept of sublimity can be obtained never again to be equaled on the hither side of Paradise.

第四课

厄舍府的倒塌

埃德加·爱伦·坡(1809—1849)

埃德加·爱伦·坡

当埃德加·爱伦·坡逝世的时候，鲁弗斯·格瑞斯沃德写了一篇挖苦这位古怪作家的讣告。他宣称坡曾经被学校开除，他既没有好朋友也没有好品德，还空前地剽窃了别人的作品。有些人对这篇不同寻常的讣告感到怀疑，推测是坡自己编写了这篇讣告，以使人们记住他的名字。

坡的一生几乎和他的小说一样黑暗凄凉。

痛苦的童年 坡于1809年出生在波士顿，父母是贫穷的流浪演员。在坡出生后不久，他的父亲就抛弃了这个家庭。一年以后，他的母亲就去世了。约翰·爱伦——一个弗吉尼亚富商接纳了小埃德加，但他们并未正式地收养他。爱伦一家让坡接受教育，然而，由于坡的养父拒绝为他偿还他在弗吉尼亚大学欠下的大笔赌债，这个年轻人被迫离开了学校。

开创文学事业 1827年，坡使用一个假名字参了军，然后他发表了他的第一部诗集：《泰莫雷恩和其他诗歌》。两年之后，他又出版了第二部诗集：《阿尔·阿拉夫》。1830年，约翰·爱伦帮助坡在西点军校里谋得了一个职位，然而，不到一年坡就因为违反学校纪律而被学校开除，这次开除使他和他的养父之间产生了不可弥补的裂痕。

不幸的结局 在他短暂一生的后半期，坡在纽约、里奇蒙德、费城和巴尔的摩追寻他的文学事业，靠写作和为几家杂志做编辑来勉强度日。他发表了第三部诗集：《诗》(1831)，因为这本诗集并没能给他带来金钱或名誉上的任何收益，所以他开始转向写小说和文学评论文章。他的五篇短篇小说于1832年在报纸上发表，1838年他发表了他唯一的一部长篇小说：《亚瑟·戈登·皮姆的故事》。虽然他的短篇小说使他受到了一定程度的承认，他的诗《渡鸦》也受到了读者的热情欢迎，但他一直没能摆脱贫困。1849年，在他深爱的妻子弗吉尼娅死后两年，坡孤独不幸地在巴尔的摩逝世。

文化遗产 在他死后的许多年里，坡的作品一直吸引着人们的注意。坡作为侦探小说的开创者而闻名于世，他的心理恐怖小说也成为许多现代作家模仿的对象。有些学者严厉地批评坡的写作，而其他的学者则热情地赞扬他对于生动的形象和声音效果的使用，还有他对于人类发生了改变的心理状态和人类本性的黑暗面的不倦探索。虽然坡在评论家眼中的地位并不确定，但是他的作品却受到了一代代美国读者的热烈欢迎。

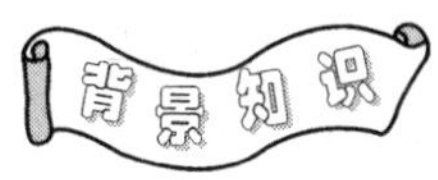

文学：作为编辑的坡

1839年，坡住在费城，成为《伯顿绅士》杂志的一名合作编辑，这份期刊刊登散文、小说、评论、诗歌，还有各种关于航海、打猎和板球的文章。坡写的文章覆盖了所有的题目范围。他解说双杠运动、对斯通亨格的神秘事件进行沉思、还评论了80多本不同主题的书。

就是在这本杂志中，坡于1839年首次发表了《厄舍府的倒塌》。

联系你的经历 感觉到焦虑是很自然的事情。我们都很熟悉经历一件可

怕的事的时候双手颤抖或胃部痉挛的感觉。然而，在一些极端的情况下，“神经紧张”可能会成为一个人人格中毁灭性的部分。压力甚至能导致情感上的崩溃，就像下面这个故事中的主人公的情况一样。

日志写作　写一段话，描述使你感到紧张的事情或情况。在你看来，紧张和害怕之间有什么不同吗？

专题聚焦：想象的阴影　使埃德加•爱伦•坡深感兴趣的是：一个人处在压力下时，他的想象力对黑暗能有多么大的影响力。在下面的故事中，读者想象的阴影对于故事中的恐怖气氛起到了什么作用？

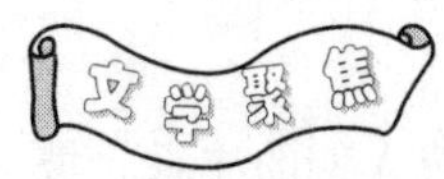

单一效果　坡是第一位把短篇小说定义为一个单独的文体的作家，他还主张短篇小说应该拥有与诗歌和长篇小说一样的地位。在坡的定义（见他为霍桑的《讲了两遍的故事》写的评论）中，他主张短篇小说的写作应该是为了取得“一个唯一或单一的效果”。他认为一篇短篇小说中的每个人物、事件和细节都应该为这个效果服务。坡说如果一个作者的“第一句话不是为了带出这个效果，那么他的第一步就失败了”。

厄舍府的倒塌（节选）

埃德加•爱伦•坡

一天晚上，那疑病症患者突然告诉我玛德琳小姐已经不在人世了，然后他说出了他的想法：他想把她的遗体在这栋大厦的无数个地下室中的一间保存两周（在最终下葬之前）。此时，我难以抑制地想起了这本书里那野蛮的仪式和它有可能对这患者产生的影响。然而，他对这异常行为所做的解释却让我感到不便与其争论。（他是这样告诉我的）这位哥哥之所以做出了这个决定，是因为他考虑到病死的人有不同寻常的特点，也考虑到主治医生的催促，还有他们偏远的家族墓地的荒芜。我不愿否认，当我想起我到达这栋大厦的那天在楼梯上碰到的那个人的凶恶面容时，我就丝毫也不想反对这个在我看来是不损害任何人并且很自然的想法了。

在厄舍的请求下，我答应亲自帮助他安排那临时的坟墓。尸体已经装在了棺材里，我们两个人把它搬到了合适的地方。我们放棺材的地下室(因为那地下室已经很久没有打开过了，我们的火炬在沉重的空气中半明半暗，使我们几乎无法看清什么东西)又小又潮湿，没有一扇可以进光的窗户，它在深深的地下，就在我睡觉的房间的正下方。很显然，在久远的封建时代，这个地下室曾经被用做罪恶的地牢。在后来的日子里，它又被用来存放火药或其他极其易燃的物品，因为地板的一部分和我们曾经通过的一条长拱道的内部都被人细心地用铜包了起来。那扇大铁门也受到了类似的保护，当它在铰链上移动时，由于巨大的重量而发出了非同寻常的尖锐刺耳的声音。

我们把那沉重的棺材放到这可怕的地方后，把还没钉好的棺材盖打开了一些，看着放在里面的人的脸。这兄妹两人之间令人惊讶的相像第一次引起了我的注意，厄舍可能猜到了我的想法，喃喃地说了几句话，从中我得知那死去的人和他是孪生兄妹，他们之间一直存在着一种令人难以理解的灵犀。然而，我们并没长时间地注视那死人——因为我们看着她的时候不由得感到一种敬畏。使这位小姐正当青春就迈进坟墓的疾病的症状表现为全身僵硬，在死者的胸部和脸上留下了一抹嘲弄的淡红色，死者可怕的嘴唇上也有一抹可疑的微笑。我们把棺材盖盖好，钉好螺丝，关紧了那扇大铁门，然后就疲惫地回到了几乎同样黑暗的大厦厅堂。

现在，在痛苦悲伤中经过了一些日子以后，我朋友神志混乱的表现开始明显起来。他平常的样子不见了，他平常做的事情也被忽略遗忘了。他从一个房间闲逛到另一个房间，脚步急促、不规则而且漫无目的。他苍白的脸上甚至染上了一层更加惨白的颜色——而他眼中明亮的光芒却彻底熄灭了。他声音中一度偶尔出现的咕噜再也听不到了，取而代之的是一种成为他说话习惯的颤音，仿佛他正处在极度的恐惧之中。的确在有些时候我

埃德加·爱伦·坡的小说充满了神秘和焦虑

认为他一直精神不安，是因为他心里承受着一个沉重秘密的压迫，而他正在努力积累勇气来把这秘密透露出来。然而，我有时又情愿把这一切都归咎于他那令人费解的疯狂的奇特行为，因为我见到他几个小时眼神空洞地瞪着前方，表情极其专注，似乎在倾听想象中的声音。因此他的状况很自然地使我感到恐惧——实际上是感染了我。我觉得他的那种幻想似乎在以某种不确定的方式与节奏对我产生着影响。

尤其是我们把玛德琳小姐放到地下室以后的第七或第八天的晚上，我在上床睡觉时完全体验到了这种感觉。我一直没有丝毫的睡意——而时间却在一小时一小时地慢慢流逝。我试图用理智驱赶那控制着我的紧张情绪。我努力说服自己相信我所感觉到的来自只不过是房间里阴沉的家具所产生的令人昏乱的影响——那黑沉沉的破破烂烂的帏帐在即将来临的暴风雨中扭曲着随风飘摇，一阵阵地，并且发出令人不安的沙沙声。然而，我的一切努力都毫无作用。一阵难以抑制的颤抖渐渐蔓延了我的全身，终于，一种梦魇般的毫无缘由的惊恐降临到我心里。我深吸了一口气，挣扎了一下，从这惊恐中挣脱出来。我坐起身来，努力地想透过房间里浓重的黑暗看出去，同时倾听着——我不知道出于什么原因，除非是一种直觉的预感促使我这样做——倾听着某些在暴风雨的间隔中不时传来的低沉缥缈的声音，但是我不知道它们从何而来。我的身心都被强烈的恐惧占据了。这恐惧无法解释但却难以忍受，我飞快地穿上衣服(因为我感觉到那天夜里我再也不可能入睡了)，快步地在房间里走来走去，想借此使自己从那可悲的状态中解脱出来。

我还没有这样走上几个来回，我房间旁的楼梯上传来轻轻的脚步声就引起了我的注意，我马上就听出来那是厄舍的脚步声。过了一会儿，他轻轻地敲敲我的门，然后手里拿着一盏灯走了进来。他的脸和平时一样苍白得没有血色——但除此之外，他的眼睛里却有着一种疯狂的喜悦——他的全部举止中都带着一种很明显的压抑着的歇斯底里。他的神态把我吓坏了——然而任何事情都比我忍受了那么久的孤独要好，我甚至欢迎他的到来，从中感到一种解脱。

“你没看见它吗？”他沉默着向周围凝视了一会儿，然后突然说道：“那么你没看见它吗？——但是，留下来！你必须留下来。”他说完这些话，又仔细地调暗了那盏灯，然后就快步走到一扇窗户前，一下把它推开，面对着暴风雨。

一阵暴怒的狂风猛扑进来，几乎把我们掀翻在地。实际上，那个夜晚虽然有暴风雨，但却是极其美丽，在它的恐怖和美丽之中还蕴含着一种狂野的奇特。显然有一阵旋风在我们附近的地区积聚起了力量，因为那风的方向不断地发生着猛烈的变化。虽然云层格外厚重（那云层低得仿佛压到了大厦的角楼上），我们还是能看到那些云朵拼命从各个角度猛冲，却不涌往远方，虽然云层厚重但我们还是看到了这个情景——然而我们却看不见月亮或星星，连任何它们光芒的闪耀都见不到。但是那些翻腾着的水蒸气的下面和围绕在我们身边的世间万物都闪耀着非自然的光芒，那光芒来自于一层淡淡地发着光的气体，这气体清晰可见，围绕并且遮蔽了整栋大厦。

“你千万不要——你不应该看到这个。”我一边战栗着对厄舍说，一边微微用力把他从窗边领到一把椅子那里。“这些使你迷惑的景象只不过是普通的电学现象而已——或者也可能产生于那个小湖里恶臭的沼气。让咱们关上这扇窗户——空气非常冷，对你的身体很危险。这儿有一本你最喜欢的冒险故事，我来朗读，你来听——咱们一起度过这个糟糕的夜晚吧。”

我拿起的那本古老的书是伦瑟洛特·卡宁爵士的《疯狂的旅程》，但是当我说这是厄舍最喜欢的书时，我更多的是出于伤心的玩笑而不是诚心诚意。因为，说实话，在这本笨拙而毫无想象力的冗长的书里没有什么能使我那骄傲的理想主义者朋友感兴趣的内容。然而，这是当时我手边唯一的一本书，而且我心里有一种模糊的希望，我希望我将要朗读的极度愚蠢的故事能使那疑病症患者从他不安的兴奋中解脱出来（因为精神混乱症表现为混乱的奇特行为）。事实上，如果我能准确判断我朋友倾听故事时表现出的那种紧张与快活的话，那么我就会庆幸自己成功地做出了这个选择。

我读到了故事里著名的那一部分，主人公伊瑟瑞德发现要和平地进入隐士的居所是不可能的，就利用暴力破门而入。人们应该记得，故事里的叙述是这样的：

“伊瑟瑞德天生有一颗勇敢的心，此外，因为他喝下去的酒发挥的效力，他现在浑身充满力量。他不愿意继续和那隐士谈判下去，因为那隐士顽固而且满含恶意地不同意他的请求。他感到雨点落在他的肩上，恐怕暴风雨就要到来了，于是高举起他的狼牙棒，用戴着铁手套的手很快把门上的木板打破了。随即他用力地把门拉了下来，把它撕裂砸碎，以至于那干燥的木头发出的空洞惊人的声音在整片森林里回响。”

读完这句话，我吓了一跳，并停顿了一会儿，因为我好像（虽然我立刻就

认定是我兴奋的幻觉欺骗了我)——我好像听到从大厦深处隐隐传来一种声音,它和伦瑟洛特·卡宁爵士特别描述的撕裂砸碎木头的声音那样相似,以至于我觉得它就是那种声音的回响。毫无疑问,正是这种巧合引起了我的注意,因为在窗框嘎嘎的响声和越发猛烈的暴风雨的混杂噪音中,这种声音本身并没有什么值得我感兴趣或使我受到惊扰的。我继续朗读那故事:

“然而,当那勇敢的战士伊瑟瑞德冲进门去时,却愤怒惊讶地发现那里根本没有那邪恶隐士的踪迹,取而代之的是一条体形庞大,身上长满鳞片的龙。它盘踞在银制的地板上,守护着一座金子的宫殿。墙上挂着一个闪闪发光的黄铜盾牌,上面刻着两句话:

进入这里的人,已成为征服者;

杀死巨龙的人,将赢得盾牌。

“伊瑟瑞德高举起他的狼牙棒,向巨龙的头上打去,那头就掉在他身前,结束了微弱的呼吸,同时发出了一声令人毛骨悚然的刺耳的尖叫,那叫声是闻所未闻的尖利,以至于伊瑟瑞德举起双手捂住了耳朵。”

在这里我再次突然地停住了,感到一阵强烈的惊愕——因为这次我无疑听到了(虽然我无法说出它是从哪个方向传来的)一声低沉的尖叫声或吱嘎的声音,那声音听起来很远,但又长又刺耳,而且非常不同寻常——和我想象中那故事里巨龙发出的反常的叫声几乎丝毫不差。

我当然被这不同寻常的巧合所烦扰,心里缠绕着千差万别的感觉,其中惊愕和极度的恐惧占了上风。但我仍然注意保持自己神志的足够清醒,以保证不激起我同伴敏感的紧张情绪。虽然我可以确定在过去的几分钟里他的行为发生了奇怪的变化,但我仍然无法判断他是否听到了那种声音。在我的正前方他渐渐地把椅子转了过去,这样他的脸就对着房间的门,而我就只能看到他脸的一部分。我看到他的嘴唇在颤抖着,仿佛在无声地喃喃自语。他的头垂到了胸前——但是我知道他并没有睡着,因为我从他的侧面看到他的一只眼睛大睁着。他身体的动作也表明他没

美洲渡鸦

有睡着——他轻轻地摇来摇去，动作连贯单一。我很快注意到了他的这些表现，于是重新开始朗读伦瑟洛特·卡宁爵士的故事，故事是这样继续的：

“现在，那战士从巨龙可怕的怒火下逃脱之后，想起他已经打破了附在那黄铜盾牌上的魔法，于是把巨龙的尸体从他面前的路上移开，勇敢地踏上城堡中银子做的路，走向那挂在墙上的盾牌。然而他还没走到那里，那盾牌就掉在他脚下的银地板上，发出了一声巨大可怕的轰响。”

这个音节刚一从我的嘴唇中发出，我就听到一声清晰空洞、好像金属发出的反响，那声音响亮却又低沉，就好像在那一刻真有一个黄铜盾牌沉重地落在银地板上。我完全失去了自制，不由得跳了起来，但是厄舍那有规律的摇动却丝毫没受影响。他的眼神定定地向前方瞪视，脸上的表情像石头般僵硬。然而，当我把手放在他的肩膀上时，他的全身都剧烈地颤抖了一下，嘴唇抖动着现出一个病态的微笑。我看到他低声快速地发出含混不清的喃喃自语，就好像没有意识到我的存在一样。我弯下腰靠近他，终于明白了他话语中可怕的含义。

“没听到吗？——是的，我听到了，我已经听了很久、很久、很久，很多分钟、很多小时、很多天了。——可是我不敢——哦，可怜可怜我吧，我是一个那么可悲的人！——我不敢——我不敢说！我们把她活着放进了坟墓里！我不是说过我的感觉很敏锐吗？现在我告诉你她在那空洞的棺材里第一次微弱地移动时我就听到了。我听到了——很多很多天以前——可是我不敢——我不敢说！现在——今晚——伊瑟瑞德——哈！哈！——隐士的门的破裂声，巨龙垂死的叫声，盾牌的铿锵声——还不如说是她的棺材裂开的声音，她那监狱的铁铰链的摩擦声，和她在地下室包铜的拱道里挣扎的

哈伯船长

声音！哦！我要逃到哪里去？她不是很快就会到这里来吗？她不是正在赶来责备我的匆忙吗？我难道没听见她踩在楼梯上的脚步声吗？我难道分辨不出她心脏沉重可怕的跳动声吗？疯子！”——说到这里他猛地跳了起来，尖叫着喊出每一个词，就好像他要喊出他的灵魂一样。——“疯子！我告诉你她现在就站在那扇门外面！”

那说话人的话语里超人的精力中仿佛含有一种魔咒的力量，就在这时，他指着的那扇古老巨大的大门的两扇笨重的乌木门扇慢慢地打开了。这是猛吹进来的一阵风造成的——然而在打开的门外确实站着厄舍家的玛德琳小姐那高高的朦胧身影。她的白色长袍上沾着血迹，她那瘦弱的身上到处都显示出痛苦挣扎的迹象。她颤抖着站在门口前后摇晃了一会儿——然后，随着一声低沉痛苦的叫声，她沉重地向里倒在了她哥哥的身上。在她死前最后的剧痛中，他也倒在地板上变成了一具尸体，死在他曾经预料到的恐惧之中。

我惊恐地从那个房间、那栋大厦里逃了出来。在我穿越那条古旧的堤道时，暴风雨仍然充分地表现着它的狂怒。突然有一道明亮的光照在路上，我转过身，想看看这样一道异常的光束是从哪里发出来的，因为在我身后的只有那栋大厦和它的阴影。光芒是那轮正在下落的血红色的满月发出来的，现在它从那道裂缝中强烈地照射出来。那裂缝一度是难以辨认的，我曾经说过它从呈“之”字形大厦的房顶一直延伸到地基。就在我回头瞪视着它时，这道裂缝迅速地变宽了——那里传来了旋风的狂暴声音——整个月亮立刻出现在我的视野里——当我看到那些巨大的墙猛地破碎倒下时，我的大脑眩晕了——我听到一阵长时间的骚乱和喊声，仿佛成千上万个大浪发出的声音一样——然后我脚下的那深深的阴暗的湖水就阴沉而安静地淹没了“厄舍大厦”的碎片。

文学和生活

读者反应 故事中的什么形象一直留在你的脑海里？为什么？

主题焦点 这个故事的讲述者一直没能摆脱罗德里克幻想的世界。你被卷入故事中幻想的世界了吗？这个故事对你的想象产生了什么影响？解释原因。

阅读理解

1. 讲述者发现玛德琳的死尸有什么令人惊讶的地方？

2. (a)讲述者在朗读《疯狂的旅程》过程中听到了什么声音？(b)厄舍怎样解释这些声音？(c)厄舍解释之后马上发生了什么事情？

思考

解释

1. 评论家们认为玛德琳和罗德里克实际上是同一个人的肉体和精神的两部分。故事中有什么证据支持这个说法？(证据支持)

2. 叙述者没能帮助厄舍，反而发现自己被厄舍的状态感染了。这件事有什么重要性？(分析)

3. 关于与外部世界保持联系的重要性，这个故事传达了什么信息？用证据支持你的回答。(得出结论)

评价

4. 坡的故事表明人类的想象力可以产生对现实的错误概念。你同意这个说法吗？为什么？(评价)

文学聚焦

单一效果

在坡对于短篇小说的定义中，他主张短篇小说的写作应该是为了取得一个单一效果，一篇短篇小说中的每句话、每个细节、人物和事件都应该为这个效果服务。虽然这个理论最初是为短篇小说而设定的，但坡也将它应用到了诗歌中。

1. 解释在《厄舍府的倒塌》中下列事件或细节是怎样为取得一种不断增长的恐怖感的效果服务的：

a. 暴风雨和其他自然现象的描述。

b. 故事最后玛德琳的外貌描写。

点子库

写作

1. 信件　给一个电影专业的学生写一封信，解释为什么你认为她/他能从对坡充满悬念的作品的分析中获益。

2. 讣告　详细解释故事中的细节，为罗德里克·厄舍写一篇讣告。这篇讣告包含他死亡的环境，简短的生平介绍和关于葬礼安排的信息。

项目

报告　研究欧洲和美洲的哥特派小说，写一篇报告，总结这种文体的重要作品。

微型写作课

广播节目介绍

埃德加·爱伦·坡的作品以其生动的戏剧性效果而著称。选择《厄舍府的倒塌》，考虑你怎样介绍这篇作品在广播中的戏剧性朗读。你的目标是为远离坡作品中的世界的听众创造理解的环境。你的介绍应该既能引起听众的兴趣，又能为他们提供必需的背景信息。

写作技巧重点：适应媒体需要

在为一个广播节目写一篇有效的介绍时，你应该注意你的写作要适应媒体的需要。遵循下列要点：

· 使用声音效果来获得你希望为听众创造的气氛，因为他们不能看到人物、动作、背景或灯光。

· 写出对于广播节目的听众来说是清楚而且观点明确的句子，使他们不可能误解你的词句或观点。

构思

先通读你选择介绍的坡的作品。记下可能对听众的理解有帮助的词语或短语。添加你自己的解释性注释和可能的声音效果。最后，把你的注释加以组织，成为一篇有效的介绍。

写稿

通过指出或说明作品中难以理解的因素，诸如一个主题或环境，来指导你的听众。不要透露主要的情节细节或破坏可以吸引听众的悬念。在写稿时参考你已经写好的注释。

修改

大声朗读你的介绍，感觉一下听起来的效果。在适当的地方简化句子，使它们更加简单。把复杂的长句变成较短的句子。

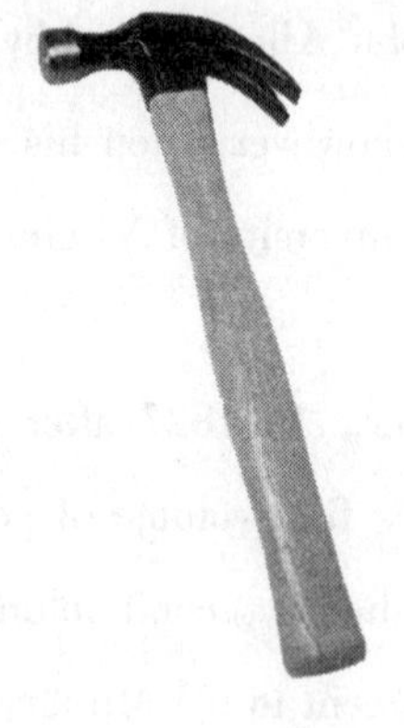

Guide for Interpreting

Edgar Allan Poe (1809—1849)

When Edgar Allan Poe died, Rufus Griswold wrote a slanderous obituary of the eccentric writer. He claimed that Poe had been expelled from college, that he had neither good friends nor good qualities, and that he committed unparalleled plagiarism. Suspicious of this unconventional obituary, some have speculated that Poe orchestrated the death notice himself to keep his name alive.

Poe's own life was almost as dark and dismal as the fiction he produced.

A Troubled Childhood Poe was born in Boston in 1809, the son of impoverished traveling actors. Shortly after Poe's birth, his father deserted the family; a year later, his mother died. Young Edgar was taken in –though never formally adopted — by the family of John Allan, a wealthy Virginia merchant. The Allans provided for Poe's education; however, when his stepfather refused to pay Poe's large gambling debts at the University of Virginia, the young man was forced to leave the school.

Building a Literary Career In 1827, after joining the army under an assumed name, Poe published his first volume of poetry, Tamerlane and Other Poems. Two years later, he published a second volume, Al Aaraaf In 1830, John Allan helped Poe win an appointment to the Military Academy at West Point. Within a year, Poe was expelled for academic violations, and his dismissal resulted in an irreparable break with his stepfather.

An Unhappy Ending During the second half of his short life, Poe pursued a literary career in New York, Richmond, Philadelphia, and Baltimore, barely supporting himself by writing and working as an editor for several magazines. After a third volume of poetry, Poems (1831), failed to bring him money or acclaim, he turned to fiction and literary criticism Five of his short stories were published in newspapers in 1832, and in 1838 published his only novel, The Narrative of Arthur Gordon Pym. Though his short stories gained him some recognition and his poem "The Raven" (1845) was greeted with enthusiasm, he could never escape from poverty. In 1849, two years after the death of his beloved wife, Virginia, Poe died in Baltimore alone and unhappy.

A Legacy In the years since his death, Poe's work has been a magnet for attention. Poe is widely known as the inventor of the detective story, and his psychological thrillers have been imitated by scores of modern writers. Some scholars have harshly Criticized Poe's writing; others have celebrated his use of vivid imagery and sound effects and his tireless exploration of altered mental states and the dark side of human nature. Despite Poe's uncertain status among critics, however, his work has remained extremely popular among generations of American readers.

Background for Understanding

LITERATURE: POE AS AN EDITOR

In 1839, Poe lived in Philadelphia and became co-editor of Burton's Gentleman's Magazine, a journal that published essays, fiction, reviews, and poems, as well as various articles on sailing, hunting, and cricket. Poe's articles ran the gamut of topics. He explained the parallel bars, mused about the mysteries of Stonehenge, and reviewed more than eighty books on a variety of topics.

It was in this magazine that Poe first published "The Fall of the House of Usher" in 1839.

Literature and your Life

CONNECT YOUR EXPERIENCE

It's natural to feel anxiety. We're all familiar with the trembling hand or the fluttering stomach that can accompany a dreaded event. In extreme circumstances, however, "nerves" can become a destructive part of a person's personali-

ty. Stress can even lead to emotional breakdowns, as is the case for characters in both the poem and the story that follow.

<u>Journal Writing</u> Write a paragraph about some event or situation that makes you feel nervous. In your opinion, is there any difference between nervousness and fear?

THEMATIC FOCUS: SHADOWS OF THE IMAGINATION

Edgar Allan Poe was fascinated by the dark reaches the imagination can inhabit when a person is under great stress. How do shadows of the reader's imagination contribute to the atmosphere of terror in the following story and poem?

Literary Focus

SINGLE EFFECT

Poe was the first writer to define the short story as a distinct literary genre and to argue that it deserved the same status as a poem or novel. In Poe's definition (which appeared in his review of Hawthorne's Twice-Told Tales), he asserted that a story should be constructed to achieve "a certain unique or single effect."He believed that every character, incident, and detail in a story should contribute to this effect Poe said that if a writer's "very initial sentence tend not to the outbringing of this effect, then he has failed in his first step."

The Fall of The House of Usher

Cdgar Allan poe

I could not help thinking of the wild ritual of this work, and of its probable influence upon the hypochondriac, when, one evening, having informed me abruptly that the lady Madeline was no more, he stated his intention of preserving her corpse for a fortnight (previously to its final interment), in one of the numerous vaults within the main walls of the building. The worldly reason, however, assigned for this singular proceeding, was one which I did not feel at liberty to dispute. The brother had been led to his resolution (so he told me) by consideration of the unusual character of the malady of the deceased, of certain obtrusive and eager inquiries on the part of her medical men, and of the remote and exposed situation of the burial ground of the family. I will not deny that when I called to mind the sinister countenance of the person whom I met upon the staircase, on the day of my arrival at the house, I had no desire to oppose what I regarded as at best but a harmless, and by no means an unnatural precaution.

At the request of Usher, I personally aided him in the arrangements for the temporary entombment. The body having been encoffined. we two alone bore it to its rest. The vault in which we placed it (and which had been so long unopened that our torches, half smothered in its oppressive atmosphere, gave us little opportunity for investigation) was small, damp, and entirely without means of admission for light; lying, at great depth, immediately beneath that portion of the building in which was my own sleeping apartment. It had been used. apparently, in remote feudal times, for the worst purposes of a donjon-keep, and, in later days. as a place of deposit for powder, or some other highly combustible substance, as a portion of its floor, and the whole interior of a long arch way through which we reached it, were carefully sheathed with copper. The door, of massive iron had been, also, similarly protected. Its immense weight caused an unusually sharp, grating sound, as it moved upon its hinges.

Having deposited our mournful burden upon trestles within this region of horror, we partially turned aside the yet unscrewed lid of the coffin, and looked upon the face of the tenant. A striking similitude between the brother and sister now first arrested my attention; and Usher, divining, perhaps, my thoughts, murmured out some few words from which I learned that the deceased and himself had

been twins, and that sympathies of a scarcely intelligible nature had always existed between them.Our glances, however, rested not long upon the dead — for we could not regard her unawed.The disease which had thus entombed the lady in the maturity of youth, had left, as usual in all maladies of a strictly cataleptical character, the mockery of a faint blush upon the bosom and the face, and that suspiciously lingering smile upon the lip which is so terrible in death. We replaced and screwed down the lid, and, having secured the door of iron, made our way, with toil, into the scarcely less gloomy apartments of the upper portion of the house.

And now, some days of bitter grief having elapsed, an observable change came over the features of the mental disorder of my friend. His ordinary manner had vanished. His ordinary occupations were neglected or forgotten. He roamed from chamber to chamber with hurried unequal, and object-less step. The pallor of his countenance had assumed, if possible, a more ghastly hue — but the luminousness of his eye had utterly gone out. The once occasional huskiness of his tone was heard no more; and a tremulous quaver, as if of extreme terror, habitually characterized his utterance. There were times, indeed, when I thought his unceasingly agitated mind was laboring with some oppressive secret, to divulge which he struggled for the necessary courage. At times, again, I was obliged to resolve all into the mere inexplicable vagaries of madness, for I beheld him gazing upon vacancy for long hours, in an attitude the profoundest attention, as if listening to some imaginary sound. It was no wonder that his condition terrified-that it infected me. I felt creeping upon me, by slow yet uncertain degrees, the wild influences of his own fantastic yet impressive superstitions.

It was, especially, upon retiring to bed late in the night of the seventh or eighth day after the placing of the lady Madeline within the donjon that I experienced the full power of such feelings. Sleep came not near my couch-while the hours waned and waned away. I struggled reason off the nervousness which had dominion over me. I endeavored to believe that much if not all of what I felt, was due to the bewildering influence of the gloomy furniture of the room — of the dark and tattered draperies, which, tortured into motion by the breath of rising tempest, swayed fitfully to and fro upon the walls, and rustled uneasily about the decorations of the bed. But my efforts were fruitless. An irrepressible tremor gradually pervaded my frame; and, at length, there sat upon my very heart an incubus of utterly causeless alarm. Shaking this off with a gasp and a struggle, I uplifted myself upon the pillows, and, peering earnestly within the intern darkness of the chamber, hearkened—I know not why, except that an instinctive spirit prompted me—to certain low and indefinite sounds which came, through the pauses of the storm, at long intervals, I knew not whence Overpowered by an intense sentiment of horror, unaccountable yet unendurable, I threw on my clothes with haste (for I felt that I should sleep no more during the night), and endeavored to arouse myself from the pitiable condition into which I had fallen by pacing rapidly to and fro through the apartment.

I had taken but few turns in this manner, when a light step on an adjoining staircase arrested my attention. I presently recognized it as that of Usher. In an instant afterward he rapped, with a gentle touch, at my door, and entered, bearing a lamp. His countenance was, as usual, cadaverously wan — but, moreover, there was a species of mad hilarity in his eyes — an evidently restrained hysteria in his whole demeanor. His air appalled me — but anything was preferable to the solitude which I had so long endured, and I even welcomed his presence as a relief.

"And you have not seen it?" he said abruptly, after having stared about him for some moments in silence — "you have not then seen it? but, stay! you shall." Thus speaking, and having carefully shaded his lamp, he hurried to one of the casements, and threw it freely open to the storm.

The impetuous fury of the entering gust nearly lifted us from our feet. It was, indeed, a tempestuous yet sternly beautiful night, and one wildly singular in its terror and its beauty. A whirlwind had apparently collected its force in our

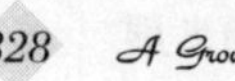

vicinity; for there were frequent and violent alterations in the direction of the wind; and the exceeding density of the clouds (which hung so low as to press upon the turrets of the house) did not prevent our perceiving the lifelike velocity with which they flew careering from all points against each other, without passing away into the distance. I say that even their exceeding density did not prevent our perceiving this—yet we had no glimpse of the moon or stars, nor was there any flashing forth of the lightning. But the under surfaces of the huge masses of agitated vapor, as well as all terrestrial objects immediately around us, were glowing in the unnatural light of a faintly luminous and distinctly visible gaseous exhalation which hung about and enshrouded the mansion.

"You must not—you shall not behold this!" said I, shuddering, to Usher, as I led him, with a gentle violence, from the window to a seat. "These appearances, which bewilder you, are merely electrical phenomena not uncommon—or it may be that they have their ghastly origin in the rank miasma of the tarn. Let us close this casement: the air is chilling and dangerous to your flame. Here is one of your favorite romances. I will read, and you shall listen: and so we will pass away this terrible night together."

The antique volume which I had taken up was the Mad Trist of Sir Launcelot Canning; but I had called it a favorite of Usher's more in sad jest than in earnest; for, in truth, there is little in its uncouth and unimaginative prolixity which could have had interest for the lofty and spiritual ideality of my friend. It was, however, the only book immediately at hand; and I indulged a vague hope that the excitement which now agitated the hypochondriac, might find relief (for the history of mental disorder is full of similar anomalies) even in the extremeness of the folly which I should read. Could I have judged, indeed, by the wild overstrained air of vivacity with which he hearkened, or apparently hearkened, to the words of the tale, I might well have congratulated myself upon the success of my design.

I had arrived at that well-known portion of the story where Ethelred, the hero of the Trist, having sought in vain for peaceable admission into the dwelling of the hermit, proceeds to make good an entrance by force. Here, it will be remembered, the words of the narrative run thus:

"And Ethelred, who was by nature of a doughty heart, and who was now mighty withal, on account of the powerfulness of the wine which he had drunken, waited no longer to hold parley with the hermit, who, in sooth, was of an obstinate and maliceful turn, but feeling the rain upon his shoulders, and fearing the rising of the tempest, uplifted his mace outright, and, with blows, made quickly room in the plankings of the door for his gauntleted hand; and now pulling there with sturdily, he so cracked, and ripped, and tore all asunder, that the noise of the dry and hollow-sounding wood alarumed and reverberated throughout the forest."

At the termination of this sentence I started and, for a moment, paused; for it appeared to me (although I at once concluded that my excited fancy had deceived me)—it appeared to me that, from some very remote portion of the mansion, there came, indistinctly to my ears, which might have been. in its exact similarity of character, the echo (but a stifled and dull one certainly) of the very cracking and ripping sound which Sir Launcelot had so particularly described. It was, beyond doubt, the coincidence alone which had arrested my attention; for, amid the rattling of the sashes of the casements, and the ordinary commingled noises of the still increasing storm, the sound, itself, had nothing, surely, which should have interested or disturbed me. I continued the story:

"But the good champion Ethelred, now entering within the door, was sore enraged and amazed to perceive no signal of the maliceful hermit; but, in

the stead thereof, a dr agon of a scaly and prodigious demeanor, and of a fiery tongue, which sate in guard before a palace of gold, with a floor of silver; and upon the wall there hung a shield of shining brass with this legend enwritten:

Who entereth herein, a conqueror hath bin;

Who slayeth the dragon, the shield he shall win.

And Ethelred uplifted his mace, and struck upon the head of the dragon, which fell before him, and gave up his pasty breath, with a shriek so horrid and harsh, and withal so piercing, that Ethelred had fain to close his ears with his hands against the dreadful noise of it, the like whereof was never before heard."

Here again I paused abruptly, and now with a feeling of wild amazement–for there could be no doubt whatever that, in this instance, I did actually hear (although from what direction it proceeded I found it impossible to say) a low and apparently distant, but harsh, protracted, and most unusual screaming or grating sound—the exact counterpart of what my fancy had already conjured up for the dragon's unnatural shriek as described by the romancer.

Oppressed, as I certainly was, upon the extra ordinary coincidence, by a thousand conflicting sensations, in which wonder and extreme terror were predominant, I still retained sufficient presence of mind to avoid exciting, by an observation, the sensitive nervousness of my companion. I was by no means certain that he had noticed the sounds in question; although, assuredly, a strange alteration had, during the last few minutes, taken place in his demeanor.From a position fronting my own, he had gradually brought round his chair; so as to sit with his face to the door of the chamber; and thus I could but partially perceive his features, although I saw that his lips trembled as if he were murmuring inaudibly. His head had dropped upon his breast—yet I knew that he was not asleep, from the wide and rigid opening of the eye as I caught a glance of it in profile. The motion of his body, too, was at variance with this idea—for he rocked from side to side with a gentle yet constant and uniform sway. Having rapidly taken notice of all this, I resumed the narrative of Sir Launcelot, which thus proceeded:

"And now, the champion, having escaped from the terrible fury of the dragon, be thinking himself of the brazen shield, and of the breaking up of the enchantment which was upon it, removed the carcass from out of the way before him, and approached valorously over the silver pavement of the castle to where the shield was upon the wall; which in sooth tarried not for his full coming, but fell down at his feet upon the silver floor, with a mighty great and terrible ringing sound."

No sooner had these syllables passed my lips, than — as if a shield of brass had indeed, at the moment, fallen heavily upon a floor of silver — I became aware of a distinct, hollow, metallic, and clangorous, yet apparently muffled, reverberation. Completely unnerved, I leaped to my feet; but the measured rocking. movement of Usher was undisturbed. I rushed to the chair in which he sat. His eyes were been fixedly before him, and throughout his whole countenance there reigned a stony rigidity. But, as I placed my hand upon his shoulder, there came a strong shudder over his whole person; a sickly smile quivered about his lips; and I saw that he spoke in a low, hurried, and gibbering murmur, as if unconscious of my presence. Bending closely over him I at length drank in the hideous import of his words.

"Not hear it? — yes, I hear it, and have heard it Long-long-long — many minutes, many hours, many days, have I heard it—yet I dared not—oh, pity me, miserable wretch that I am! — I dared not — I dared not speak! We have put her living in the tomb! Said I not that my senses were acute? I now tell you that I heard her first feeble movement in the hollow coffin. I heard them—many, many days ago—yet I dared not—I dared not speak! and now—tonight—Ethelred — ha! ha! the breaking of the hermit's door. and the death cry of the dragon, and the clangor of the shield — say, rather, the rending of her coffin, and the grating of the iron hinges of her prison, and her struggles within the coppered archway of the vault! Oh! wither shall I fly?

Will she not be here anon? Is she not hurrying to upbraid me for my haste? Have I not heard her footstep on the stair?. Do I not distinguish that heavy and horrible beating of her heart? Madman! here he sprang furiously to his feet, and shrieked out his syllables, as if in the effort he were giving up his soul—"Madman! I tell you that she now stands without the door! "

As if in the superhuman energy of his utterance there had been found the potency of a spell, the huge antique panels to which the speaker pointed threw slowly back, upon the instant, their ponderous and ebony jaws. It was the work of the rushing gust—but then without those doors there did stand the lofty and enshrouded figure of the lady Madeline of Usher. There was blood upon her white robes, and the evidence of some bitter struggle upon every portion of her emaciated frame. For a moment she remained trembling and reeling to and fro upon the threshold—then, with a low moaning cry, fell heavily inward upon the person of her brother, and in her violent and now final death agonies, bore him to the floor a corpse, and a victim to the terrors he had anticipated.

From that chamber, and from that mansion, I fled aghast. The storm was still abroad in all its wrath as I found myself crossing the old causeway. Suddenly there shot along the path a wild light, and I turned to see whence a gleam so unusual could have issued; for the vast house and its shadows were alone behind me. The radiance was that of the full, setting, and bloodred moon, which now shone vividly through that once barely discernible fissure, of which I have before spoken as extending from the roof of the building, in a zigzag direction, to the base. While I gazed, this fissure rapidly widened—there came a fierce breath of the whirlwind—the entire orb of the satellite burst at once upon my sight—my brain reeled as I saw the mighty walls rushing asunder—there was a long tumultuous shouting sound like the voice of a thousand waters—and the deep and dank tarn at my feet closed sullenly and silently over the fragments of the "House of Usher".

第五课

自 然

拉尔夫·沃尔多·爱默生 (1803—1882)

个人主义，独立，对自然奇迹的欣赏力——这些只是在拉尔夫·沃尔多·爱默生的帮助下扎根于我们民族性中的几条原则。虽然有时候人们认为他的观点值得争论，但他仍然对他所处时代的年轻人有着巨大的影响力，他的观点直到今天还对人们有所启示。

拉尔夫·沃尔多·爱默生

在爱默生的一生中，他的头脑一直处于不停的运转中，不断地产生新的想法，不断定义和重新定义他对于世界的观点。无论是在散文、演讲还是在诗歌里，他都具有天生的表达这些观点的口才，这使他成为美国文学史上被人引用最多的作家之一。

在新英格兰的童年 爱默生出生在波士顿，他的父亲是一位牧师。在爱默生8岁的时候，他的父亲去世了，于是他投奔了一位才华横溢但为人古怪的姑姑——玛丽·穆迪·爱默生，正是她鼓励了爱默生的独立思想。爱默生14岁

时进入哈佛大学学习，在那里他开始记日记，这个习惯他坚持了一生。在哈佛神学院结束了研究生学习之后，他成为波士顿第二教堂的牧师。

找到自己的位置 爱默生的牧师事业并没有持续很长时间。由于他为自己年轻妻子的逝世感到极度悲伤，同时又对他所看到的教会对精神的束缚感到不满，爱默生在3年之后辞去了牧师的职位。然后他去了欧洲，在那里他结识了英国作家托马斯•卡莱尔、塞缪•泰勒•寇瑞智和威廉姆•沃兹华兹。爱默生回到美国之后，定居在马萨诸塞州的康科德，他再次结婚，并且开始了一生的写作和演讲的事业。

独立的思想家 爱默生说话时声音柔和，从来没有姿态或情绪上的过激表现。

在爱默生镇静稳重的举止下埋藏着的是一种永不停息、高度个人主义、反对屈服的思想。

“优秀的人，”他曾经写道，“不能太服从法律。”

1841年，爱默生出版了《散文》，一部基于他的日记和演讲中的材料的文集，这使他首次在全国范围内声誉大振。他又继续出版了几部散文集，包括：《散文（第二卷）》(1844)，《典型的人》(1849)和《生活的指导》(1860)。

虽然爱默生主要因为散文和演讲而著称，但他认为自己本质上是一名诗人。“我天生就是一名诗人，”他曾经写道，“毫无疑问是低级的，但还是一名诗人。这是我的本性，也是我的职业。”他出版了两本成功的诗集，《诗》(1847)和《“国际劳动节”及其他》(1867)。和他的散文一样，爱默生的诗也表达了他对于个人主义和人类与自然之间的精神联系的信仰。

哲学：爱默生和先验主义俱乐部

19世纪30~40年代，爱默生和一小群志同道合的文化界朋友定期在他的书房聚会，讨论哲学、宗教和文学。这群人中有：爱默生的门徒亨利·大卫·梭罗、教育家布朗松·阿尔科特、女权主义作家玛格丽特·福勒和以前是牧师而后来成为作家的乔治·瑞普利。这群体被称为“先验主义俱乐部”，他们发展了一个哲学系统，强调直觉、个人主义和自我依靠。

1836年，爱默生发表了《自然》，这篇长长的散文成为先验主义俱乐部非正式的信念宣言。

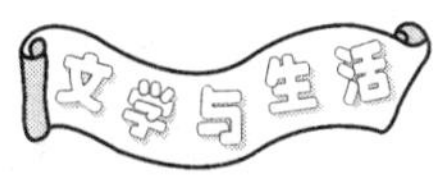

联系你的经历 “成为你自己”、“追随你的梦想”这些话是不是很熟悉？我们大部分人都会面临这样的选择：是听从大众的意见还是遵从自己的判断。在《依靠自己》里，爱默生以强硬的语气表明了自己的观点，那就是遵从自己的判断。

日志写作 描述你面临听从他人还是走自己的路这种选择的时期。

专题聚焦：人类精神和自然世界 爱默生在自然中发现了灵性和深刻的意义。对于自然世界的研究能够怎样揭示人类精神的方面？

先验主义 先验主义是由爱默生发起的一次文化运动，当时大部分作家都受到了这个运动的影响。先验主义者们认为人类感官只能感觉到物质的现实世界。对于先验主义者们来说，生命的基本实质是感官所不能触及的，只有通过直觉才能对它有所理解和领会。因此，先验主义者们把注意力集中在人类的精神方面，他们也对自然世界与人类之间的关系深感兴趣。通过对自然的认真观察，他们相信人类精神可以通过自然世界反映出来。这导致了他们信念的中心结论：各种形式的生命体——上帝、自然和人类——都通过一种共同的灵魂，或者说超灵魂，在精神方面联合在一起。

自然(节选)

拉尔夫•沃尔多•爱默生

自然就像一个舞台布景，它既适合喜剧，也同样适合悲剧。对于身体健康的人来说，空气就是一剂拥有不可思议效力的补品。在阴沉天空下的暮色中，当我穿行在一片荒芜的坑坑洼洼的雪地里时，我并没有想到任何特别好的运

气，但就在这时我的心中涌起一阵极度的喜悦，我快乐得几乎接近了恐惧的边缘。同样，在森林里，一个人抛掉他所经历过的岁月，就像一条蛇蜕掉自己的皮一样，因此无论在生命的哪个时期，他都是一个孩子。在森林里人们拥有永恒的青春。在这些上帝的花园里，笼罩着端庄神圣的气氛，常年举行着欢宴，园里的客人即使过了一千年也找不到厌倦的理由。在森林里，理智和信仰回归到我们心中。在那里，我感觉生活中的任何不幸都无法降临到我的身上——没有自然不能修补的耻辱和灾难(除了我的眼睛以外)。站在赤裸的土地上——我的头脑沐浴在无忧无虑的空气中，上升到无限的空间里——所有卑贱的自私自利的想法都消失无踪了。我变成了一个透明的眼球：我空如无物，但我却将万物都纳入眼中，那共同生命的暗流在我全身循环流动。我是上帝的一部分。在那时，最亲近的朋友的名字听起来也觉得陌生而并不重要了：所有的人都是兄弟，都是朋友，谁是主人谁是仆人就只是微不足道的干扰而已了。我热爱那不受遏抑的永恒的美。我从荒野中发现的东西比街道上或村庄中发现的还要亲切自然。在宁静的自然中，尤其是在远方的地平线上，人类看到了和他自己的本性同样美丽的东西。

人们从荒野和森林中体会到的最大的快乐暗示了人类和植物之间的一种神秘的联系。我并不是独自一人无人回应的。它们向我点头，我也向它们致意。风雨中树枝的摇曳对我来说既陌生又熟悉，它使我感到惊奇，但却并不是从未见过，那感觉就像当我认为我的思想公正或行为正确时，我的心中产生了一个更高尚的想法或一种更优秀的情感。

然而我们可以确定的是产生这种喜悦的力量并不存在于自然之中，而是在人的心里，或者在这两者之间的和谐统一中。对于这些喜悦加以大力节制是非常必要的。因为自然并不总是穿着节日的盛装，相反，昨天还在仙女的嬉戏中散发芳香闪烁光芒的景象，今天就被忧伤笼罩。自然总是会染上精神的

落日余晖

颜色。对于一个遭受灾难的人来说，他内心的火焰中就蕴含着忧伤。一个刚刚失去了亲近朋友的人会从自然风景中感受到一种轻视。而天空在那些卑贱的人头顶上，也会显得不那么庄严宏大。

文学和生活

读者反应 你经历过的哪些事情曾经使你“快乐得几乎接近了恐惧的边缘”？

主题焦点 你在今天的美国文化中能为爱默生对自然的崇敬找到什么证据？解释理由。

阅读理解

1. 根据爱默生的观点，在哪里“理智和信仰回归到我们心中”？

2. 当爱默生站在那里，头脑“上升到无限的空间里”的时候，他的心理发生了什么变化？

3. 什么是“人们从荒野和森林中体会到的最大的快乐”？

思考

解释

1. 爱默生说在森林里“一个人抛掉他所经历过的岁月”，他实际的意思是什么？（分析）

2. 爱默生把自己描绘成一个“透明的眼球”所表达的是什么思想？（解释）

3. 在这篇散文中找到证据，支持先验主义者关于人类精神和自然世界是一个整体的观点。（证据支持）

评价

4. 爱默生具有多强的说服力？你接受他关于自然的观点吗？解释原因。（评估）

扩展

5. 爱默生对自然的态度和科学家的态度有什么不同？（科学连线）

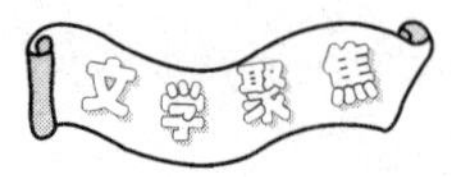

先验主义

爱默生的写作向读者介绍了先验主义，这次文化运动宣称对于基本现实的认识是超出人类有限的感官之外的，是通过直觉而不是感官经验获得的。先验主义者关注人类精神，人类和自然之间的精神联系和对于人类潜能的乐观信念。他们哲学思想的中心就是各种形式的生命都是通过一个共同的灵魂，或者叫超灵魂，联合在一起的。

1. 《自然》揭示了先验主义者对于自然的态度的哪些方面？

2. 从《自然》中找出表达了先验主义者对超灵魂的信念的两个段落。

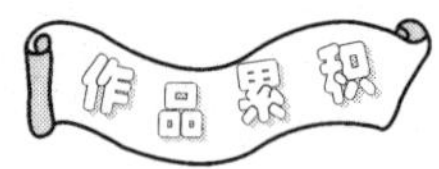

点子库

写作

1. 关于自然的诗　写一首诗，表达你与自然接触时的经历、感觉或情感。

2. 广告　假设你要组成一个与“先验主义俱乐部”类似的组织。你将会怎样去吸引会员？写一篇广告词，为人们提供相关信息并说服人们参加这个组织。

项目

艺术　用艺术范例来说明你从《自然》中随意选择的一个生动的词组。画一幅画、选择一段音乐或编演一段舞蹈。（艺术连线，音乐连线，表演艺术连线）

微型写作课

写给编辑的信

如果爱默生生活在今天的话，他很可能会成为一个自然保护主义者。选择一个现在的环境问题，决定你的观点和立场。给本地报纸的编辑写一封信，表达你的观点，并使用推理、事实或实例来支持你自己的观点。你的例子越个人化，你的信就会越有说服力。

写作技巧重点：详细阐述使你的写作个人化

在一篇写作中详细阐述或发展观点的一种方法就是利用个人的经历或观察。例如，如果你在写一篇关于本地湖水污染问题的文章，那么你可以描绘你小时候是怎样在湖里游泳的，然后指出你最近去湖边的时候注意到再没有人在湖里游泳了。与你的读者分享这样的经历不仅可以通过你亲身体验的实例来加强你写作的说服力，而且可以使你和读者之间建立一种个人的联系感。

构思

列出你要写的要点。记下可以用来支持每一个要点的个人经历或观察。此外，你还可以收集可用做证据支持的其他事实和统计数据。

写稿

在信的开头就直接陈述你的观点，然后用你的亲身经历和观察，还有你收集到的事实和统计数据来支持你的观点。在整封信里，尽可能直接一语中的。

修改

让一个同学读这封信，并提出能使这封信更个人化、直接和有说服力的建议。

Guide for Interpreting

Ralph Waldo Emerson (1803—1882)

Individuality, independence, and an appreciation for the wonders of nature—these are just a few of the principles that Ralph Waldo Emerson helped to in-grain in our nation's identity. Although his ideas were sometimes considered controversial, he had a tremendous influence on the young people of his time, and his beliefs have continued to respire people to this day.

Throughout his life, Emerson's mind was constantly in motion, generating new ideas and defining and redefining his view of the world. His natural elo-quence in expressing these ideas—in essays, lectures, and poetry—makes him one of the most quoted writers in American literature.

A New England Childhood The son of a Unitarian minister, Emerson was born in Boston. When Emerson was eight, his father died. The boy turned to a brilliant and eccentric aunt, Mary Moody Emerson, who encouraged his indepen-dent thinking. At fourteen, Emerson entered Harvard, where he began the journal he was to keep all his life. After postgraduate studies at Harvard Divinity School, he became pastor of the Second Church of Boston.

Finding His Niche Emerson's career as a minister was short-lived. Grief-stricken at the death of his young wife, and dissatisfied with what he saw as the spiritual restrictions in Unitarianism, Emerson resigned after three years. He then went to Europe, where he met the English writers Thomas Carlyle, Samuel Taylor Coleridge, and William Wordsworth. On his return to the United States, Emerson settled in Concord, Massachusetts. He married again and began his life long ca-reer of writing and lecturing.

An Independent Thinker Emerson was a soft-spoken man, given to neither physical nor emotional excess.

Beneath Emerson's calm, sober demeanor existed a restless, highly individualistic mind that resisted conformity.

"Good men," he once wrote, "must not obey the laws too well."

Emerson first achieved national fame in 1841, when he published Essays, a collection based on material from his journals and lectures. He went on to publish several more volumes of essays, including Essays, Second Volume (1844), Representative Men (1849), and The Conduct of Life (1860).

Though Emerson was known mostly for his essays and lectures, he considered himself primarily a poet. "I am born a poet," he once wrote, "of a low class without doubt, yet a poet. That is my nature and my vocation." He published two successful volumes of poetry, Poems (1847) and May-Day and Other Pieces (1867). Like his essays, Emerson's poems express his beliefs in individuality and in humanity's spiritual connection to nature.

Background for Understanding

PHILOSOPHY: EMERSON AND THE TRANSCENDENTAL CLUB

During the 1830's and 1840's, Emerson and a small group of like-minded intellectual friends gathered regularly in his study to discuss philosophy, religion, and literature. Among them were Emerson's protégé Henry David Thoreau, as well as educator Bronson Alcott, feminist writer Mar garet Fuller, and ex-clergyman and author George Ripley. The group, known as the Transcendental Club, developed a philosophical system that stressed intuition, individuality, and self-reliance.

In 1836, Emerson published "Nature," a lengthy essay that became the Transcendental Club's unofficial statement of belief.

Literature and your Life

CONNECT YOUR EXPERIENCE

"Be true to yourself", "Follow your dream". Do these words sound familiar? Most of us have faced the choices these sentiments address: whether to conform

to what's expected or to step out of the crowd and follow our own judgment. In "Self-Reliance" Emerson states his views on the matter in uncompromising terms, coming down squarely in favor of nonconformity.

<u>Journal Writing</u> Describe a time when you had to choose whether to follow others or to blaze your own trail.

THEMATIC FOCUS: THE HUMAN SPIRIT AND THE NATURAL WORLD

Emerson found spirituality and profound meaning in nature. How can a study of the natural world reveal the human spirit?

Literary Focus

TRANSCENDENTALISM

Transcendentalism was an intellectual movement founded by Emerson that affected most of the writers of his day. The Transcendentalists believed that the human senses can know only physical reality. To the Transcendentalists, the fundamental truths of existence lay outside the reach of the senses and could be grasped only through intuition. As a result, the Transcendentalists focused their attention on the human spirit. They also had a deep interest in the natural world and its relationship to humanity. Through the careful observation of nature, they believed that the human spirit is reflected in the natural world. This led them to the conclusion that formed the heart of their beliefs: All forms of being — God, nature, and humanity — are spiritually united through a shared universal soul, or Over-Soul.

Nature

Ralph Waldo Emerson

Nature is a setting that fits equally well a comic or a mourning piece. In good health, the air is a cordial of incredible virtue. Crossing a bare common, in snow puddles, at twilight, under a clouded sky, without having in my thoughts any occurrence of special good fortune, I have enjoyed a perfect exhilaration. I am glad to the brink of fear. In the woods, too, a man casts off his years, as the snake his slough, and at what period soever of life is always a child. In the woods is perpetual youth. Within these plantations of God, a decorum and sanctity reign, a perennial festival is dressed, and the guest sees not how he should tire of them in a thousand years. In the woods, we return to reason and faith. There I feel that nothing can befall me in life—no disgrace, no calamity (leaving me my eyes), which nature cannot repair. Standing on the bare ground—my head bathed by the blithe air and uplifted into infinite space—all mean egotism vanishes. I become a transparent eyeball; I am nothing; I see all; the currents of the Universal Being circulate through me; I am part or parcel of God. The name of the nearest friend sounds then foreign and accidental: to be brothers, to be acquaintances, master or servant, is then a trifle and a disturbance. I am the lover of uncontained and immortal beauty. In the wilderness, I find something more dear and connate than in the streets or villages. In the tranquil landscape, and especially in the distant line of the horizon, man beholds somewhat as beautiful as his own nature.

The greatest delight which the fields and woods minister is the suggestion of an occult relation between man and the vegetable. I am not alone and unacknowledged. They nod to me, and I to them. The waving of the boughs in the storm is new to me and old. It takes me by surprise, and yet is not unknown. Its effect is like that of a higher thought or a better emotion coming over me, when I deemed I was thinking justly or doing right.

Yet it is certain that the power to produce this delight does not reside in nature, but in man, or in a harmony of both.It is necessary to use these pleasures with great temperance. For nature is not always tricked in holiday attire, but the same scene which yesterday breathed perfume and glittered as for the frolic of the nymphs is overspread with melancholy today. Nature always wears the colors of the spirit. To a man laboring under calamity. the heat of his own fire hath sadness in it. Then there is a kind of contempt of the landscape felt by him who has just lost by death a dear friend. The sky is less grand as it shuts down over less worth in the population.

第六课

瓦尔登湖

亨利·大卫·梭罗(1817—1862)

亨利·大卫·梭罗

亨利·大卫·梭罗从童年时就被他在马萨诸塞州康科德的邻居们认为是一个怪人。他很少遵守规则,他独立自主,意志坚强,对于自己的学习却不十分专注,但他母亲对自然的热爱以及对他的激励使他坚持接受教育。梭罗进入了康科德学院,这是一所为进入大学做准备的学院。5年以后,他被哈佛大学录取,在那里他用自己独特的方式进行学习。虽然哈佛大学的校规要求学生穿黑色衣服,但梭罗却穿绿色的衣服。

质疑权威 梭罗总是对他所面对的规则提出质疑。当他因为反对体罚制度而被迫辞去了他的第一份教职时,梭罗和哥哥约翰在康科德开办了他们自己的学校。这所学校办得相当成功,但后来因为约翰得病,他们不得不将其关闭。

1842年,梭罗搬进了康科德另一位著名的居民——拉尔夫·沃尔多·爱默生——的家里。他在那里住了两年,做各种奇怪的工作来付自己的食宿费。梭罗住在那里的时候,深深地被爱默生的先验主义信仰所吸引,不久,梭罗就成

为了爱默生的密友和忠诚的信徒。梭罗决定不再回头去教书，也拒绝从事其他的职业，于是他献身于通过经历来检验先验主义理论。通过简化自己的需要，梭罗得以把自己的下半生都奉献给对人类和自然之间的精神联系的探索和写作，并用以支持自己的政治和社会信仰。

在瓦尔登湖畔 有两年时间(1845–1847)，梭罗独自住在康科德郊外瓦尔登湖边自己建起的小木屋里。梭罗在这个时期的经历为他的杰作《瓦尔登湖》提供了素材。梭罗把他在瓦尔登湖畔的经历浓缩为一年，用四季作为这部书的结构框架。《瓦尔登湖》是一部将自然观察、社会批评和哲学思想独特地融合在一起的著作，被人们普遍认为是先验主义作品中的最优秀著作。梭罗的这部著作写作仔细、设计精心，反映了他一生为之奋斗的精神。

当梭罗44岁死于肺结核时，他的作品还并没有多少人承认。然而，自他死后，他的声誉就稳步上升。他的作品启发了作家、环保主义者还有社会和政治领袖，他使一代代读者意识到人类精神可能达到的高度和社会的局限性。

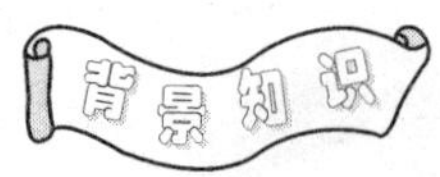

历史：梭罗与墨西哥战争

墨西哥战争是1846至1848年间发生在墨西哥与美国之间的战争。这场战争的起因是关于得克萨斯州和墨西哥之间的边界争执，以及墨西哥拒绝将加利福尼亚和新墨西哥卖给美国。梭罗和其他很多美国人认为波尔克总统在国会通过之前就有意地引起了双方之间的矛盾，因此他们强烈反对这场战争。为了表示自己的反对，梭罗拒绝纳税，并因此被迫在监狱里度过了一夜。在这次经历之后，梭罗写了《论公民的不服从》，激励人民反抗他们不同意的政府政策。

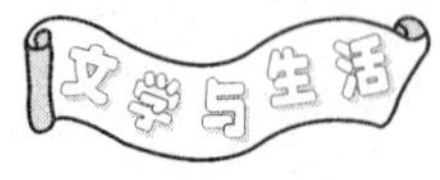

联系你的经历 在今天的世界里，我们依靠无数现代的便利事物生活——移动电话、电脑、电视。不久以前，所有这些事物还都只存在于人类的

想象之中。虽然我们中的大多数人从来都不会想到这一点，但还是有些人在考虑这些科技的进步是真的使生活更美好——还是只不过使生活更复杂。

日志写作 谈谈你认为生活在森林中而没有任何现代的便利会是什么感觉。

专题聚焦：人类精神与自然世界 梭罗生活的时代是一个现代化带来生活的快速变化的时代。正如《瓦尔登湖》中描述的经历所揭示的一样，梭罗认为人们需要简化自己的生活，重新与自然建立联系。

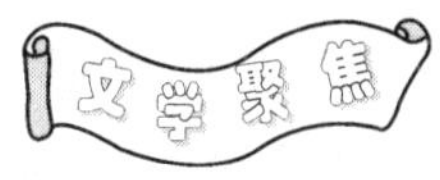

风格 风格指的是作家把自己的观点用文字表达出来的方式。在《瓦尔登湖》的写作中，梭罗的风格是与他的写作目的密切相关的，他的写作目的是鼓励人们检查自己的生活方式并进行思考。为了达到自己的目的，梭罗对文章中的段落进行组织，使得所有的句子一起积蓄至一个高潮。

爱默生很赞赏梭罗的风格，与爱默生一样，大多数当代的读者和评论家都为梭罗的写作中的力量和活力感到惊讶。在他最有效的段落中，句子产生的效果可以与把钉子钉进木头里的锤子相比。

瓦尔登湖(节选)

亨利•大卫•梭罗

我生活的地方和我生活的目的(节选)

在我们生命的某个季节里，我们习惯于把每个地方都考虑为可能建一栋房子的地点。就这样，我遍察了我现在居住的地方周围方圆20英里之内的地方。在想象中，我已经陆续买下了所有的农场，包括其中所有需要购买的东西，而且我还知道它们的价格。我从每个农民的房屋前走过，品尝他的野苹果，和他谈论农事，无论他出什么价格，我都按他的出价买下他的农场。我甚至出了个更高的价——买下农场中全部的东西，只是不要契约——我把他的承诺就作为契约，因为我非常喜欢谈话——培养谈话，我相信在某种程度上也培养了他，然后在我享受了足够长时间之后就退出谈话，让他继续下去。这

样的经历使我的朋友们把我称做一类地产经纪人。无论我坐在哪里，我就可能住在哪里，整片土地就随之从我所在之处辐射出去。一栋周围没有土地的房子算什么房子？——最好还是一块乡村土地。我发现很多房子所在的地点很难迅速改善，有些人可能会认为那些地方离村庄太远，而在我看来却是村庄离它们太远。我说过，我有可能住在那里，而且我确实在那里住过，一小时，一个夏天还有一个冬天的时间；我看到了我可以怎样让一年年流逝，在搏斗中度过冬天，看到春天的来临。在这个地区里的未来住户们，无论他们将把自己的房子建在哪里，他们可以确定的是我已经为他们的到来做好了准备。一个下午就足够我把那些土地安排成果树林和牧场，并决定哪些漂亮的橡树或松树应该留在门前，从哪里看去每棵枯萎的树都应该有最好的效果。然后我就让那土地躺在那里，间或休耕，因为一个人的富有是和他能放下不管的事情的数目成正比的。

我的想象走得如此之远，以至于在想象中我甚至拥有了几个农场的优先取舍权——那优先取舍权是我最想要的——可是我的手指却从没碰触过真正拥有的土地。我最接近真正拥有土地的一次就是我买下了豪洛威尔的土地。我已经开始整理种子，并且收集材料打算做一辆手推车，用来装运产品了。然而就在那块地的主人把契约交给我之前，他的妻子——每个男人都有那样一个妻子——改变了主意，想要保留那块地，于是他提出给我十美元来和我解除合约。现在，说实话，我在这世界上也只有十美分，而我的算术知识却已经不够我来判断我拥有了的是那十美分，还是一个农场，还是十美元，还是所有这些。然而，我还是让他既保留了那十美元，也保留了他的农场，因为我已经进行得足够

初春晨景

远了；或者不如说，出于慷慨起见，我按我购买的价格把它卖给了他。此外，因为他不是个富人，我又把那十美元作为礼物送给了他，而同时，我仍然拥有我的十美分、种子和做一辆手推车的材料。我发现这样我就成为一个富人，而我的贫困又丝毫无损。然而我保留了那风景，从那时起我每年都不用手推车就收获了那土地的产物。提到那风景：

“我是我看到的一切的统治者，

我在那里的权利无人可以质疑。”

我曾经多次见到一个诗人在享受了一个农场最有价值的部分之后离开，而那急性子的农民却认为他只得到了几个野苹果。唉，那拥有土地的人不知道在很多年里当一个诗人把他的土地写进诗里的时候，那诗就是最值得赞赏的无形的藩篱，已经把他的土地围在栏中了，他的土地的乳汁已经被挤出脱脂，诗人获得了所有的奶油，留给农民的却只是脱去了奶油的牛奶而已。

对于我来说，豪洛威尔真正的诱人之处就是：它完完全全与世隔绝。它离村庄有两英里远，离最近的邻居有半英里远，和公路之间还隔着一片宽阔的田地；它的边界一直延伸到河边，地的主人说这边界受到春天霜雾的保护，不过那对我来说却不算什么。房子和仓库都灰暗破旧，篱笆也废弃已久，这在我和那最后住在这里的人之间设下了那样的间隔。苹果树的树心中空，树身长满青苔，被野兔啃咬得伤痕累累，这让我清楚地知道我将会有什么样的邻居。但最重要的是：我第一次沿河旅行留给我的回忆。那时我看到这栋房子被遮掩在一小片浓密的红枫林后，我能听见房子里的狗叫声从林子那边传来。我急于将它购买下来，等不及房主搬走那些岩石，砍伐掉那些树身已空的苹果树，铲除那些牧场中新近跃起的赤杨幼树，一句话，等不及它的任何收拾了。为了能享受这些特别的风景，我准备在这块土地上坚持下来，就像阿特拉斯一样，把整个世界担到我的肩膀上——我从没听说他为此得到了什么补偿——我做所有那些事情，没有其他的动机或理由，只是为了我能把它买下，并能不受打扰地拥有它。因为我一直都很清楚，只要我能把它放在一边不管的话，它就会出产大量我所希望的收成。可是事情最后却变成了我说过的结果。

因此，关于在一大块土地上耕作（我曾经一直耕种一个花园），我能说的就是我已经把种子准备好了。很多人认为时间越长种子就越好，我毫不怀疑时间能把好种子和坏种子区分开。当我最后播种的时候，我就不太可能会失望了。但是我要对我的朋友们说，只说一次：尽可能生活得自由而不受束缚。

受到一个农场的束缚和受到国家监狱的束缚并没有什么不同。

老卡托的《乡村逸叙》是我的"栽培者",他说过下面的话,而我见过的唯一的译本却把这一段翻译得完全言不及义:"当你想到要得到一个农场时,把这想法这样转变一下,不要贪婪地把它买下,也不要不遗余力地去看着它,不要以为把它全部走过一遍就足够了。如果这块地很好的话,你越经常去那里,它就会带给你越多的快乐。"我想我不会贪婪地把它买下,但是我会在有生之年一次次地到那里游赏,并且首先要埋葬在那里,使它能在最后给我更多快乐……

我不是要写一首忧郁的颂诗,而是要像清晨的公鸡站在鸡窝上那样热情地鸣叫,只为让我的邻人们醒过来。

当我第一次住进我林中的住所,也就是说,开始昼夜都待在那里的时候,恰巧是在美国独立日,也就是1845年7月4日。那时候我的房子还没做好过冬的准备,只能遮挡雨水。它没有涂灰泥,也没有烟囱,墙是用粗糙的风吹雨淋褪了色的木板做成的,墙上有宽宽的裂缝,所以晚上在屋里很凉快。笔直的、砍伐得来的、白色的间柱,新近才刨得平坦的门户和窗框使屋子看起来干净宽敞。尤其是在清晨,屋子的木料浸透了露水,以至于我幻想着到了中午那木料里会渗出甜蜜的树胶来。在我的想象中,它在一天中都或多或少地保留了这种清晨的特质,使我想起我前一年曾经见过的某栋山里的房子。那是一座宽敞的没有涂灰泥的木屋,适合接待一位从此经过的神,还可以让一位女神在里面拖曳着她的衣服。从我住处经过的风就像从山脊上扫过的风一样,中间夹杂着大自然断续的旋律,或者不如说,只有其中天国的部分。晨风不断吹拂,创造的诗篇从未被打断,但却没有什么人能听到。

我到森林里去是因为我想要从容地生活,去面对生活的本质,看看我是否无法学到生活要教给我的东西,并且在我死去的时候不会发现我不曾生活过。我不想过不是生活的生活,因为生活是那样可贵,我也不愿一味顺从,除非那是十分必要的。我想要深入生活,吸出生活中所有的精髓,强壮得像斯巴达克人一样生活,彻底打败所有不属于生活的东西,割出一条宽阔的通路并且除去所有杂草,把生活逼到一个角落里,把它降到最低的条件,并且,如果最终证明它是低劣的话,那么为什么要获得它全部真正的低劣并把这低劣公之于众呢;或者如果它是高尚的,那么就要通过经历来了解它,并且在我下一次旅行中能够真正地利用它。因为在我看来,大多数人对于生活都处在一种奇怪的不肯定的状态中，不知道它到底是属于魔鬼还是属于上帝，而且多少有些鲁莽地得出了结论，认为人生最重要的目的就是要“赞扬上帝并永远因他而幸福”。

我们仍然像蚂蚁一样卑贱地生活，虽然寓言告诉我们说我们很久以前就变成人了。像小人国里的人，我们和长脖子仙鹤作战，这真是错上加错，脏抹布之上更抹脏：我们最优美的德性在这里成了多余的本可避免的劫数。我们的生活在琐碎中消耗掉了。一个诚实的人几乎不需要数超出他的十个手指的数，或者在极端的情况下他可能加上他的十个脚趾，剩余的就都合并在一起。简单，简单，简单！我说，让你的事情只有两件或三件，而不是一百或一千件；用数十个数来代替数一百万，把你的账目保持在最简单的程度。在这个文明社会的变化无常的大海中，乌云、风暴、流沙和一千零一件要考虑的事项是那样繁杂，以至于如果一个人不到海底为自己建造港口，那么他就要完全靠算账来生活，他必须成为一个巨大的计算器，而实际上就是这种人获得了成功。简单，简单。如果一天只需要吃一顿饭，那么就不吃三顿；不要有一百个菜，有五个就行了；把其他的事情也按照比例减少。我们的生活就像德国邦联，是由很多个州组成的，它的边界永远在扩张，以至于德国人也无法告诉你德国的边界是怎样划定的。这个国家虽然有所谓的内部改善，而这些内部改善，顺便说一句，也都是外部的和表面的，而它本身只是一个笨重的生长过大的机构，就和这片陆地上的上百万个家庭一样，其中充满了凌乱的家具，被自己设下的圈套绊倒，因沉迷于奢华挥霍、缺乏计算和崇高的目标而毁灭。对于德国和那些家庭来说，唯一的治疗方法就是一个严格的生活，比生活简单的斯巴达克人更加严酷。生活过得太快了。人们认为对这个国家来说最重要的是拥有贸易，出口冰块，通过电报谈话和一小时旅行30英里，无论他们是否真的做这些事情，他们的观点都是确定无疑的；然而对于我们是应该像狒狒一样生活还是像人一样生活却有一点儿不确定。如果我们不生产枕木，制造铁轨，把日日夜夜都奉献给这项工作，而是对我们的生活加以修补和改

暮色山水

善，那么谁会去建设铁路呢？如果铁路没有建成的话，那么我们怎样才能按时到达天堂呢？但是如果我们待在家里，关心自己的事情的话，那么又有谁会想要铁路呢？不是我们在铁路身上，而是铁路在我们身上……

时间只是一条我在其中钓鱼的小溪。我从中取水喝，然而在我喝水的同时，我看到了沙子的溪底，发现它是多么浅啊。它细细的支流流走了，但永恒却留下了。我要从更深的地方取水，在天空中钓鱼，它的溪底里躺满了卵石般的星星。我一个数也不会数，字母表里的第一个字母我都不知道。我一直感到遗憾的是我不像我出生那天那样聪明。智慧就像一把大刀，它辨别出道路，一直割进事物的奥秘中去。我不希望我的手比必要的程度更加忙碌。我的头就是我的手和脚，我感到我所有最好的部分都集中在那里面了。我的直觉告诉我，我的头是一个用来挖掘的器官，就像有些动物用它们的鼻子和前爪来挖掘一样，而我将使用我的头脑在这些小山中挖洞前进。我想那最富饶的矿脉就在这左右的什么地方，所以我凭借那占卜杖和薄薄升起的蒸气来判断，我要在这里开始采矿……

结论(节选)

我离开森林的理由和我到那里去的理由一样充分。可能在我看来我还有几种生活要去体验，不能再在那一种上花费更多的时间。值得注意的是我们很容易不知不觉地遵循某条路线，为自己踩出一条踏平了的轨迹。我在那里住了一个星期，就踩出了一条从我的门口到湖边的小路。虽然从我把它踩出来到现在已经有五六年了，它却还是很容易分辨。我想，恐怕是有其他的人也走过这条路，才保持了它的现状。地球的表面是柔软的，人们的脚可以在上面留下印记；而思想旅行的道路也是这样。那么，世界上的道路将被多少人踩踏过，多么尘土飞扬啊；传统和服从的辙迹又是多么深重啊！我并不想从此移居到木屋里，而是想站在世界之船的甲板上、桅杆前，因为在那里我能最清楚地看到群山之间的月光。现在我不想到下面去。

至少，通过我的实验我学到了这一点：如果一个人充满信心地向着他梦想的方向前进，努力争取他想象的生活，他将会取得在平常的时候无法预料的成功。他将会把一些事情抛到身后，越过一条无形的边界；在他身边和内心里将会建立起新的、普遍的、更加自由的法律；或者旧的法律将会在一个更自由的范围上得到新的解释；而他将会生活在一种更高级的生命的特许之下。

与他对自己的生活简化的程度成正比，宇宙间的法律也会显得不那么复杂，孤单将不是孤单，贫穷不是贫穷，弱小也不再是弱小。如果你建筑了空中楼阁，你的工作不一定是白费了；那正是它们应该属于的地方。现在在它们下面加上地基……

我们为什么要那样不顾一切地急着成功，又有着那样不顾一切的进取心呢？如果一个人没有和他的同伴保持步调的一致，那很可能是因为他听到了不同的鼓点。让他按照自己听到的音乐去迈步吧，无论那音乐是怎样缓慢或遥远。他不必像一棵苹果树或橡树那样迅速地成熟。他要把自己的春季转变成夏季吗？如果我们所要求的情况还不够条件，我们能用来代替的任何现实又算得了什么呢？我们不会在一个毫无价值的真实上毁灭。我们要艰难地在自己身上树立起一个带有蓝色玻璃的天空，在它建好之后我们还会傻傻地盯着远方那真正的天空，就好像从未建立一样吗？

无论你的生活是多么低贱，你都需迎接它，体验它；不要避开它，不要咒骂它。生活并不像你本身那样坏。当你最富有的时候，你的生活看起来最贫穷。吹毛求疵的人甚至在天堂里都能找出毛病。热爱你的生活，虽然它很贫穷。即使在一个贫困的家庭里，你也有可能有快乐的、令人兴奋的、光荣的时刻。夕阳从济贫院的窗户上反射出的光彩和从富人的房子上反射出的同样光芒四射；济贫院门前的白雪在春天也一样早早融化。我认为一个宁静的灵魂在那里可以像在一个宫殿里一样生活满足，拥有快乐的思想。在我看来城里的穷人经常过着最独立的生活。也许他们只是伟大得足以不带任何疑虑地接受生活。大多数人认为他们在上面，整个城镇支持着他们的生活，而普遍的实际情况是，他们没有用适当的手段维持自己的生活，这令他们很不光彩。培养你的贫穷，就好像它是花园里的香草，就像鼠尾草。别费太多神去得到新的东西，无论是衣服还是朋友。改变旧的东西，再回到它们身边。东西不改变，我们改变。卖掉你的衣服，保留你的思想。上帝会看到你不想要社会。如果我像一只蜘蛛一样整天都被拘禁在阁楼的一角，只要我有我的思想，世界对我来说就仍旧那么大。哲人说过："一个人可以带走三个师的师长，使军队陷入混乱；然而即使是最卑鄙粗俗的人也无法从一个人那里带走他的思想。"不要太急切地寻求发展，使自己屈从于许多可以利用的影响力；这都只是浪费而已。谦卑和黑暗一样都能揭示天堂的光辉。贫穷和低贱的阴影聚集在我们周围。"然

后，呼！创造在我们眼前放宽。”经常会有人提醒我们，即使把克罗瑟斯的财富赋予我们，我们的目标仍然一样，我们的手段也基本上不变。此外，如果你因为贫穷而被限制在你的范围内，例如说，如果你买不起书和报纸，你也只是被限制在最重要最必不可少的经验之中；这样的环境激发你去处理能生产最多的糖浆和淀粉的材料。最贴近骨头的生活才是最甜蜜的。你被贫穷保护着，因而不会成为在琐事上虚度光阴的人。没人会因为较高层次的慷慨而在较低的层次上失去什么。多余的财富只能买到多余的东西。要买到灵魂必需的东西，钱并不是必要的……

我们身体中的生命就像河水。这一年它就可能涨到人所未见的高度，并且淹没那些已经干透的高地，这一年甚至可能就是那重大的一年，将会淹没我们所有的麝鼠。我们居住的并不总是干燥的土地。我看到远在内陆就有些河岸，远在科学还没有记录它们的泛滥之前，就曾受过江河的冲击。所有人都听说过那个在新英格兰四处传扬的故事，一只强壮美丽的虫子从一段老苹果树的干木层中爬出来，这段木头在一个农夫的厨房里放了60年，最早在康奈克提卡特，后来又到了马萨诸塞——还要早很多年以前，在这棵活着的树里留下了一个虫卵。这是根据木头上虫卵以外的年轮算出来的，这只虫子就从这个卵里爬了出来，它是偶然被一个缸里传来的热量所孵化，于是人们连续几个星期都听到它在向外啃咬。听到这个故事，谁能不感到自己对于复活和生命不朽的信念被加强了呢？那个美丽的长着翅膀的生命，最初的卵被遗留在那绿色有生命的树木边材中，这棵树渐渐被变成了那虫卵被风干的坟墓，它多少年来被埋在死板干燥的刻满年轮的木层之中——多年以后的现在，当这个家

雪景

庭围坐在喜筵的桌边时，他们偶然间惊讶地听到那向外啃咬的声音——它可能出人意料地从社会中最微不足道的只付了订金的家具里钻出来，最后来享受它那完美的夏日生活。

我并不是说约翰或乔纳森这些普通人都会认识到所有这些，但是这就是那个明天的特质，仅靠时间的流逝永远也无法使它破晓。熄灭我们眼神的光对我们来说就是黑暗。只有那一天破晓时，我们才会因它而苏醒。有更多的白昼需要破晓。太阳只是一颗晨星罢了。

文学和生活

读者反应　根据你的看法，独自在一个自然环境中度过两年时光的有利之处和不利之处是什么？

主题焦点　梭罗可能对今天快节奏的社会有什么看法？你生活中的什么具体事情可能会特别让他担忧？

阅读理解

1. 梭罗在想象中做了什么事情？

2. (a)梭罗为什么住在森林里？(b)他最后为什么离开了森林？

3. 他从他的“试验”中学到了什么？

4. 梭罗对那些生活在贫困中的人提出了什么忠告？

思考

解释

1. 梭罗的评论“受到一个农场的束缚和受到国家监狱的束缚并没有什么不同”是什么意思？(分析)

2. 用你自己的话来描述梭罗对于个人主义和遵守常规的态度。(解释)

3. 根据梭罗的观点，为什么穷人要比富人好？(证据支持)

应用

4. 你认为梭罗有可能在今天的社会里进行他的“试验”吗？解释原因。(假设)

扩展

5. 今天的旅行社和假期活动组织者为想回归自然的人们设计假期。为什么这样的旅行很有吸引力？(职业连线)

论公民的不服从(节选)

亨利·大卫·梭罗

我衷心地接受这句箴言:"最好的政府是管理得最少的政府"。而且我希望能看到这句话被快速自动地实践。当它被付诸实践之后,最后就等于这个我也同样相信的判断:"最好的政府是根本就不管理的政府"。而当人们做好了这样的准备时,这就会成为他们将要拥有的那种政府。政府最多也就只是一种权宜之计,但多数政府有时往往并不能有所助益。对于一支人数众多、队伍庞大、应该获胜的常备军队的反对最后也可能发展成为对长期政府的反对。常备军队只是长期政府的一个武器而已。政府本身也只是人民选来执行自己意愿的方式,但在人民通过它有所作为之前,它也一样很容易被歪曲或滥用。见证了现在的这场墨西哥战争,就是少数几个人利用长期政府作为自己的工具的结果;因为在最初的时候,人民就不会同意采取这个行动。

这个美国政府——它不过是一种传统,尽管其历史还不久,但却竭力使自己原封不动地届届相传,可是每届却都丧失掉一些自身的诚实和正直。它并不具有一个活着的人的生命力和力量,因为一个人就能使它屈从于自己的意志。它就是一种对着人民自己的木枪,而如果他们真心地想把它作为一支真枪来彼此对抗的话,它就必然会碎裂。但它并不因此就损失任何必要性,因为人们必须要有这种或其他种类的复杂机器,并且听到它的喧嚣轰鸣,才能满足他们关于政府的想法。于是,政府的存在表明,为了人民的利益,可以成功地利用、欺骗人民,甚至可以使人民利用、欺骗自己。这非常好,我们所有的人都必须同意,然而这个政府自己却从未增长任何进取心,却加快了它出轨的速度。它没有使这个国家保持自由;它没有平息西部;它没有教育;所有的成就都是美国人民固有的品质取得的,而且如果不是政府有时候妨碍他们的话,他们本来还可以取得更多的成就。因为政府是一种权宜之计,通过它人们会很乐意不打扰彼此,而且,正如我们所说过的,当它最能有所助益的时候,它最不干扰那些被管理的人。贸易和商业如果不是由印第劫匪组成的话,它们就永远也不会成功越过立法者不断为它们设置的障碍；而且，如果谁要是完全根据这些立法者的行为结果来判断他们，而没有部分地考虑他们的意图的话，他们就应该和那些在路上摆路障的匪徒归为一类，并一同受到惩罚。

但是，以一个公民的身份客观来说，我不像那些自称是无政府主义的人，我要求的不是立即取消政府，而是拥有一个更好的政府。让每个人都说出什么样的政府能够赢得他的尊敬，那将成为获得那种政府的第一步……

文学和生活

读者反应 什么样的政府能够赢得你的尊敬？为什么？

主题焦点 梭罗对于政府的观点与先验主义者对于人类精神和自然界的看法是相互一致的还是彼此冲突的？做出解释。

小组讨论 讨论梭罗对于政府作用的看法。然后列出五件他会认为政府应该做的事情和五件他会认为政府不应该做的事。

阅读理解

1. 梭罗衷心接受的是哪句箴言？

2. 梭罗认为人民可以怎样对于改进政府作出贡献？

思考

解释

1. 梭罗暗示谁应该对墨西哥战争负责任？（推断）

2. 根据梭罗的观点，为什么一小部分人可以滥用政府而免受惩罚？（分析）

3. 根据梭罗的观点，什么时候美国人将会获得在可能范围内的最好的政府？（得出结论）

评价

4. 关于一个人应该反对他所不同意的政府政策，梭罗所做的论述是否具有说服力？（评价）

应用

5. 梭罗说："如果他们（人们）真心地想把它（政府）作为一支真枪来彼此对

抗的话，它就必然会碎裂。”根据你的历史知识对这一论断做出判断。(社会研究连线)

文学聚焦

风格　一个作家把思想用文字表述出来的方式就叫做风格。梭罗的风格的特点就在于他不断地加强自己的观点的力度。有些评论家认为梭罗夸大了他的论点。然而，梭罗认为关于人类潜力的真理是怎样也不可能夸大的。他有意地重复他的主要观点来加强他所传达的信息。

1. (a)在《瓦尔登湖》中简单的段落怎样说明了梭罗把所有的句子建筑在一起以达到高潮的写作方式？(b)找出另一个用这种方式来组织的段落。

2. 梭罗经常用讨论具体的事件或例子作为一个段落的开始，然后再把这讨论应用到一个更大范围的真理中。找出一个这样的段落。

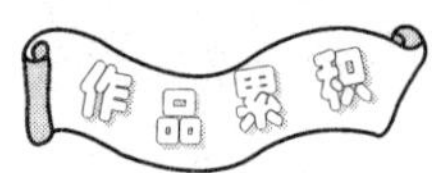

点子库

写作

1. 写给编辑的信　梭罗的哲学观点在今天能怎样应用？给一份报纸的编辑写一封信，宣传人们应该简化自己的生活的观点。

2. 报告　为了抗议墨西哥战争，梭罗在监狱里度过了一夜。写一篇报告解释这场战争的起因和结果，以及美国民众的反应。(社会研究连线)

3. 比较和对比　写一篇文章比较爱默生和梭罗的信念，利用他们作品中的段落和细节作为支持的证据。

项目

1. 今天的瓦尔登湖　调查研究今天的瓦尔登湖的状况。如果可能的话，收集关于该地区的照片。把你调查的结果报告给班里的同学。然后讨论从梭罗的年代到现在，瓦尔登湖发生了什么变化。

2. 自然日志　到一个在你附近并且能观察自然的地区去游览几次——无论是一个公园，一片森林，还是一片海滩。把你的观察结果记录在一篇自然日志中，并给你的同学看。(科学连线)

微型写作课

说服性文章

梭罗在他感情强烈的观点的写作中表现得很有说服力。选择一个对于你来说很重要的事件，然后写一篇文章说服别人接受你的观点，并采取行动。使用一个因果关系的组织结构来对你的读者表明采取行动的结果——或者不采取行动的后果。

写作技巧重点：因果关系的组织结构

为了说明一件事之所以发生或将要发生的原因或方式，使用一个因果关系的组织结构来连接你的观点。按照以下两种方法：

• 陈述一个原因——也就是某件事已经发生或将要发生的证据——然后陈述从这个原因中产生或将要产生的结果。

• 另一种方式：陈述一系列相互关联的结果，然后再通过你的证据论证产生的原因。

构思

想一想你要表达的主要观点和你将需要作为支持的证据。为了帮助你收集原因和结果的证据，使用下表：

题目：______________________________

原因	结果

写稿

在一段短序中清楚地陈述你的观点。对你想写成单独段落的观点进行展开，把你的观点按逻辑顺序组织好。参考你的原因和结果列表来展开讨论。

修改

重新阅读你的草稿，在必要的地方添加细节使你的辩论更加有力，把所有的因果关系都表现清楚。

Guide for Interpreting

Henry David Thoreau (1817—1862)

From the time he was a child, Henry David Thoreau was known by his Concord, Massachusetts, neighbors as an eccentric. He rarely followed rules. He was independent, strong willed, and not very dedicated to his studies, but his mother's love of nature and her own drive convinced him to pursue an education. Thoreau went to Concord Academy, a college preparatory school, and five years later he enrolled at Harvard, where he pursued his studies in his own unique style. Although Harvard University's code called for students to wear black, Thoreau wore green.

Questioning Authority Thoreau always questioned the rules that were presented to him. When his objection to corporal punishment forced him to quit his first teaching job, Thoreau and his older brother John opened their own school in Concord. The school was quite successful, but they had to close it when John became ill.

In 1842, Thoreau moved into the house of another famous Concord resident, Ralph Waldo Emerson. He lived there for two years, performing odd jobs to pay for his room and board. While there, Thoreau was fascinated by Emerson's Transcendentalist beliefs, and soon Thoreau became Emerson's close friend and devoted disciple. Deciding not to go back to teaching and refusing to pursue another career, Thoreau dedicated himself to testing the Transcendentalist philosophy through experience. By simplifying his needs, Thoreau was able to devote the rest of his life to exploring and writing about the spiritual relationship between humanity and nature and supporting his political and social beliefs.

On Walden Pond For two years (1845–1847) Thoreau lived alone in a cabin he built himself at Walden Pond outside of Concord. Thoreau's experiences during this period provided him with the material for his masterwork, Walden (1854). Condensing his experiences at Walden Pond into one year, Thoreau used the four seasons as a structural framework for the book. A unique blend of natural observation, social criticism, and philosophical insight, Walden is now generally regarded as the supreme work of Transcendentalist literature. Carefully and deliberately crafted, Thoreau's work reflects the economy for which he strove throughout his life and about which he wrote in Walden.

When Henry, David Thoreau died of tuberculosis at the age of forty-four, his work had received little recognition. However, his reputation has steadily grown since his death. His work has inspired writers, environ mentalists, and social and political leaders. It has made generations of readers aware of the possibilities of the human spirit and the limitations of society.

Background for Understanding

HISTORY: THOREAU AND THE MEXICAN WAR

The Mexican War was a conflict between Mexico and the United States that took place from 1846 to 1848. The war was caused by a dispute over the boundary between Texas and Mexico, as well as Mexico's refusal to discuss selling California and New Mexico to the United States. Believing that President Polk had intentionally provoked the conflict before having congressional approval, Thoreau and many other Americans strongly objected to the war. To demonstrate his disapproval, Thoreau refused to pay his taxes and was forced to spend a night in jail for his convictions. After that experience, Thoreau wrote "Civil Disobedience", urging people to resist governmental policies with which they disagree.

Literature and your Life

CONNECT YOUR EXPERIENCE

In today's world, we rely on countless modern conveniences — cellular

phones, computers, televisions. Not long ago, all of these things existed only in the imagination. Although most of us don't ever think about it, some people wonder whether technological advances have really made life better — or just more complicated.

Journal Writing Explain what you think it would be like to live in the woods without modern conveniences.

THEMATIC FOCUS: THE HUMAN SPIRIT AND THE NATURAL WORLD

The time in which Thoreau lived was also an age in which modernization was bringing about rapid change. As the experiences described in Walden reveal, Thoreau believed that people needed to simplify their lives and rekindle their connection with nature.

Literary Focus

STYLE

Style refers to the manner in which a writer puts his or her thoughts into words. In Walden, Thoreau's style is closely related to his purpose, which is to encourage us to examine the way we live and think. To achieve his purpose, Thoreau constructs paragraphs so that the sentences build to a climax.

Like Emerson, who admired Thoreau's style, most contemporary readers and critics are struck by the strength and vigor of Thoreau's writing. Within his most effective paragraphs, the sentences build to create an effect that can be compared to a hammer driving a nail into wood.

Walden

Henry David Thoreau

from Where I Lived, and What I Lived For

At a certain season of our life we are accustomed to consider every spot as the possible site of a house. I have thus surveyed the country on every side within a dozen miles of where I live. In imagination I have bought all the farms in succession, for all were to be bought, and I knew their price. I walked over each farmer's premises, tasted his wild apples, discoursed on husbandry with him, took his farm at his price, at any price, mortgaging it to him in my mind; even put a higher price on it—took everything but a deed of it—took his word for his deed, for I dearly love to talk—cultivated it, and him too to some extent, I trust, and withdrew when I had enjoyed it long enough, leaving him to carry it on. This experience entitled me to be regarded as a sort of real-estate broker by my friends. Wherever I sat, there I might live, and the landscape radiated from me accordingly. What is a house but a sedes, a seat?-better if a country seat. I discovered many a site for a house not likely to be soon improved, which some might have thought too far from the village, but to my eyes the village was too far from it. Well, there might I live, I said; and there I did live, for an hour, a summer and a winter life; saw how I could let the years run off, buffet the winter through, and see the spring come in, The future inhabitants of this region, wherever they may place their houses, may be sure that they have been anticipated. An afternoon sufficed to lay out the land into orchard woodlot and pasture, and to decide what fine oaks or pines should be left to stand before the door, and whence each blasted tree could be seen to the best advantage; and then I let it lie, fallow perchance, for a man is rich in proportion to the number of things which he can afford to let alone.

My imagination carried me so far that I even had the refusal of several farms—the refusal was all I wanted—but I never got my fingers burned by actual possession. The nearest that I came to actual possession was when I bought

the Hollowell Place, and had begun to sort my seeds, and collected materials with which to make a wheelbarrow to carry it on or off with; but before the owner gave me a deed of it, his wife — every man has such a wife — changed her mind and wished to keep it, and he offered me ten dollars to release him. Now, to speak the truth, I had but ten cents in the world, and it surpassed my arithmetic to tell, if I was that man who had ten cents, or who had a farm, or ten dollars, or all together. However, I let him keep the ten dollars and the farm too, for I had carried it far enough; or rather, to be generous, I sold him the farm for just what I gave for it, and, as he was not a rich man, made him a present of ten dollars, and still had my ten cents, and seeds, and materials for a wheelbarrow left. I found thus that I had been a rich man without any damage to my poverty. But I retained the landscape, and I have since annually carried off what it yielded without a wheel barrow. With respect to landscapes:

"I am monarch of all I survey, My right there is none to dispute."

I have frequently seen a poet withdraw, having enjoyed the most valuable part of a farm, while the crusty farmer supposed that he had got a few wild apples only. Why, the owner does not know it for many years when a poet has put his farm in rhyme, the most admirable kind of invisible fence, has fairly impounded it, milked it, skimmed it, and got all the cream, and left the farmer only the skimmed milk.

The real attractions of the Hollowell farm, to me, were: its complete retirement, being about two miles from the village, half a mile from the nearest neighbor, and separated from the high way by a broad field; its bounding on the river, which the owner said protected it by its fogs from frosts in the spring, though that was nothing to me; the gray color and ruinous state of the house and barn, and the dilapidated fences, which put such an interval between me and the last occupant; the hollow and lichen-covered apple trees, gnawed by rabbits, showing what kind of neighbors I should have; but above all, the recollection I had of it from my earliest voyages up the river, when the house was concealed behind a dense grove of red maples, through which I heard the house-dog bark. I was in haste to buy it, before the proprietor finished getting out some rocks, cutting down the hollow apple trees, and grubbing up some young birches which had sprung up in the pasture, or, in short, had made any more of his improvements. To enjoy these advantages I was ready to carry it on; like Atlas, to take the world on my shoulders — I never heard what compensation he received for that — and do all those things which had no other motive or excuse but that I might pay for it and be unmolested in my possession of it; for I knew all the while that it would yield the most abundant crop of the kind I wanted if I could only afford to let it alone. But it turned out as I have said.

All that I could say, then, with respect to farming on a large scale (I have always cultivated a garden) was that I had had my seeds ready. Many think that seeds improve with age. I have no doubt that time discriminates between the good and the bad; and when at last I shall plant, I shall be less likely to be disappointed. But I would say to my fellows, once for all, As long as possible live free and uncommitted. It makes but little difference whether you are committed to a farm or the county jail.

Old Cato, whose "De Re Rustica" is my "Cultivator", says, and the only translation I have seen makes sheer nonsense of the passage, "When you think of getting a farm, turn it thus in your mind, not to buy greedily; nor spare your pains to look at it, and do not think it enough to go round it once. The oftener you go there the more it will please you, if it is good." I think I shall not buy greedily, but go round and round it as long as I live, and be buried in it first, that it may please me the more at last...

I do not propose to write an ode to dejection, but to brag as lustily as chanticleer in the morning, standing on his roost, if only to wake my neighbors up.

When first I took up my abode in the woods, that is, began to spend my nights as well as days there, which, by accident, was on Independence Day, or the fourth of July, 1845, my house was not finished for winter, but was merely a defense against the rain, without plastering or chimney, the walls being of rough weatherstained boards, with wide chinks, which made it cool at night. The upright white hewn studs and freshly planed door and window casings gave it a clean and airy look, especially in the morning, when its timbers were saturated with dew, so that I fancied that by noon some sweet gum would exude from them. To my imagination it retained throughout the day more or less of this auroral character, reminding me of a certain house on a mountain which I had visited the year before. This was an airy and unplastered cabin, fit to entertain a traveling god, and where a goddess might trail her garments. The winds which passed over my dwelling were such as sweep over the ridges of mountains, bearing the broken strains, or celestial parts only, of terrestrial music. The morning wind forever blows, the poem of creation is uninterrupted; but few are the ears that hear it.

I went to the woods because I wished to live deliberately, to front only the essential facts of life, and see if I could not learn what it had to teach, and not, when I came to die, discover that I had not lived. I did not wish to live what was not life, living is so dear; nor did I wish to practice resignation, unless it was quite necessary. I wanted to live deep and suck out all the marrow of life, to live so sturdily and Spartanlike as to put to rout all that was not life, to cut a broad swath and shave close, to drive life into a comer, and reduce it to its lowest terms, and, if it proved to be mean, why then to get the whole and genuine meanness of it, and publish its meanness to the world; or if it were sublime, to know it by experience, and be able to give a true account of it in my next excursion. For most men, it appears to me, are in a strange uncertainty about it, whether it is of the devil or of God, and have somewhat hastily concluded that it is the chief end of man here to "glorify God and enjoy him forever".

Still we live meanly, like ants; though the fable tells us that we were long ago changed into men; like pygmies we fight with cranes: it is error upon error, and clout upon clout, and our best virtue has for its occasion a superfluous and evitable wretchedness. Our life is frittered away by detail. An honest man has hardly need to count more than his ten fingers, or in extreme cases he may add his ten toes, and lump the rest. Simplicity, simplicity, simplicity! I say, let your affairs be as two or three, and not a hundred or a thousand; instead of a million count half a dozen, and keep your accounts on your thumbnail. In the midst of this chopping sea of civilized life, such are the clouds and storms and quicksands and thousand-and-one items to be allowed for, that a man has to live, if he would not founder and go to the bottom and not make his port at all, by dead reckoning, and he must be a great calculator indeed who succeeds. Simplify, simplify. Instead of three meals a day, 'if it be necessary eat but one; instead of a hundred dishes, five; and reduce other things in proportion. Our life is like a German Confederacy, made up of petty states, with its boundary forever fluctuating, so that even a German cannot tell you how it is bounded at any moment. The nation itself, with all its so-called internal improvements, which, by the way, are all external and superficial, is just such an unwieldy and overgrown establishment, cluttered with furniture and tripped up by its own traps, ruined by luxury and heedless expense, by want of calculation and a worthy aim, as the million households in the land; and the only cure for it as for them is in a rigid economy, a stern and more than Spartan simplicity of life and elevation of purpose. It lives too fast. Men think that it is essential that the Nation have commerce, and export ice, and talk through a telegraph, and ride thirty miles an hour, without a doubt, whether they do or not; but whether we should live like baboons or like men, is a little uncertain. If we do not get out sleepers, and forge rails, and devote days and nights to the work, but go to tinkering upon our lives to improve them, who will build railroads? And if railroads are not built, how shall we get to heaven in season? But if we stay at home and mind our business, who will want railroads? We do not ride on the railroad; it rides upon us....

Time is but the stream I go a-fishing in. I drink at it; but while I drink I see the sandy bottom and detect how shallow it is. Its thin current slides away, but eternity remains. I would drink deeper; fish in the sky, whose bottom is pebbly with stars. I cannot count one. I know not the first letter of the alphabet. I have always been regretting that I was not as wise as the day I was born. The intellect is a cleaver; it discerns and rifts its way into the secret of things. I do not wish to be any more busy with my hands than is necessary. My head is hands and feet. I feel all my best faculties concentrated in it. My instinct tells me that my head is an organ for burrowing, as some creatures use their snout and forepaws, and with it I would mine and burrow my way through these hills. I think that the richest vein is somewhere hereabouts; so by the divining rod and thin rising vapors I judge; and here I will begin to mine....

From The Conclusion

I left the woods for as good a reason as I went there.Perhaps it seemed to me that I had several more lives to live, and could not spare any more time for that one.It is remarkable how easily and insensibly we fall into a particular route, and make a beaten track for ourselves.I had not lived there a week before my feet wore a path from my door to the pondside; and though it is five or six years since I trod it, it is still quite distinct.It is true, I fear that others may have fallen into it, and so helped to keep it open. The surface of the earth is soft and impressible by the feet of men; and so with the paths which the mind travels. How worn and dusty, then, must be the highways of the world. how deep the ruts of tradition and conformity! I did not wish to take a cabin passage, but rather to go before the mast and on the deck of the world, for there I could best see the moonlight amid the mountains. I do not wish to go below now.

I learned this, at least, by my experiment: that if one advances confidently in the direction of his dreams, and endeavors to live the life which he has imagined, he will meet with a success unexpected in common hours.He will put some things behind, will pass an invisible boundary; new, universal, and more liberal laws will begin to establish themselves around and within him; or the old laws be expanded, and interpreted in his favor in a more liberal sense, and he will live with the license of a higher order of beings. In proportion as he simplifies his life, the laws of the universe will appear less complex, and solitude will not be solitude, nor poverty poverty, nor weakness weakness. If you have built castles in the air, your work need not be lost; that is where they should be. Now put the foundations under them....

Why should we be in such desperate haste to succeed, and in such desperate enterprises? If a man does not keep pace with his companions, perhaps it is because he hears a different drummer. Let him step to the music which he hears, however measured or far away. It is not important that he should mature as soon as an apple tree or an oak. Shall he turn his spring into summer? If the condition of things which we were made for is not yet, what were any reality which we can substitute? We will not be shipwrecked on a vain reality. Shall we with pains erect a heaven of blue glass over ourselves, though when it is done we shall be sure to gaze still at the true ethereal heaven far above, as if the former were not?...

However mean your life is, meet it and live it; do not shun it and call it hard names. It is not so bad as you are. It looks poorest when you are richest. The faultfinder will find faults even in paradise. Love your life, poor as it is. You may perhaps have some pleasant, thrilling, glorious hours, even in a poorhouse. The setting sun is reflected from the windows of the almshouse as brightly as from the rich man's abode; the snow melts before its door as early in the spring. I do not see but a quiet mind may live as contentedly there, and have as cheering thoughts, as in a palace. The town's poor seem to me often to live the most independent lives of any. Maybe they are simply great enough to receive without misgiving. Most think that they are above being supported by the town; but it oftener happens that they are not above supporting themselves by dishonest means, which should be more disreputable. Cultivate poverty like a garden herb, like sage. Do not trouble yourself much to get new things, whether clothes or friends. Turn the old; return to them. Things do not change; we change. Sell your clothes and

keep your thoughts. God will see that you do not want society. If I were confined to a corner of a garret all my days, like a spider, the world would be just as large to me while I had my thoughts about me. The philosopher said: "From an army of three divisions one can take away its general, and put it in disorder; from the man the most abject and vulgar one cannot take away his thought." Do not seek so anxiously to be developed, to subject yourself to many influences to be played on; it is all dissipation. Humility like darkness reveals the heavenly lights. The shadows of poverty and meanness gather around us, "and lo! creation widens to our view." We are often reminded that if there were bestowed onus the wealth of Croesus, our aims must still be the same, and our means essentially the same. Moreover, if you are restricted in your range by poverty, if you cannot buy books and newspapers, for in stance, you are but confined to the most significant and vital experiences; you are compelled to deal with the material which yields the most sugar and the most starch. It is life near the bone where it is sweetest. You are defended from being a trifler. No man loses ever on a lower level by magnanimity on a higher. Superfluous wealth can buy superfluities only. Money is not required to buy one necessary of the soul ....

The life in us is like the water in the river. It may rise this year higher than man has ever known it, and flood the parched uplands; even this may be the eventful year, which will drown out all our muskrats. It was not always dry land where we dwell. I see far inland the banks which the stream anciently washed, before science began to record its freshets. Everyone has heard the story which has gone the rounds of New England, of a strong and beautiful bug which came out of the dry leaf of an old table of apple-tree wood, which had stood in a farmer's kitchen for sixty years, first in Connecticut, and afterward in Massachusetts—from an egg deposited in the living tree many years earlier still, as appeared by counting the annual layers beyond it;which was heard gnawing out for several weeks, hatched perchance by the heat of an urn. Who does not feel his faith in a resurrection and immortality strengthened by hearing of this? Who knows what beautiful and winged life, whose egg has been buried for ages under many concentric layers of woodenness in the dead dry life of society, deposited at first in the alburnum of the green and living tree, which has been gradually converted into the semblance of its well-seasoned tomb-heard perchance gnawing out now for years by the astonished family of man, as they sat round the festive board—may unexpectedly come forth from amidst society's most trivial and handselled furniture, to enjoy its perfect summer life at last!

I do not say that John or Jonathan will realize all this; but such is the character of that morrow which mere lapse of time can never make to dawn. The light which puts out our eyes is darkness to us. Only that day dawns to which we are awake. There is more day to dawn. The sun is but a morning star.

Civil Disobedience

Henry David Thoreau

I heartily accept the motto, "That government is best which governs least"; and I should like to see it acted up to more rapidly and systematically. Carried out, it finally amounts to this, which also I believe: "That government is best which governs not at all"; and when men are prepared for it, that will be the kind of government which they will have. Government is at best but an expedient; but most governments are usually, and all governments are sometimes, inexpedient. The objections which have been brought against a standing army, and they are many and weighty, and deserve to prevail, may also at last be brought against a standing government. The standing army is only an arm of the standing government. The government itself, which is only the mode which the people have chosen to execute their will, is equally liable to be abused and perverted before the people can act through it. Witness the present Mexican war, the work of comparatively a few individuals using the standing government as their tool; for in the outset, the people would not have consented to this measure.

This American government — what is it but a tradition,

though a recent one,endeavoring to transmit itself unimpaired to posterity, but each instant losing some of its integrity? It has not the vitality and force of a single living man; for a single man can bend it to his will. It is a sort of wooden gun to the people themselves; and, if ever they should use it in earnest as a real one against each other, it will surely split. but it is not the less necessary for this; for the people must have some complicated machinery or other, and hear its din, to satisfy that idea of government which they have.Governments show thus how successfully men can be imposed on, even impose on themselves, for their own advantage. It is excellent, we must all allow; yet this government never of itself furthered any enterprise,but by the alacrity with which it got out of its way. It does not keep the country free.It does not settle the West.It does not educate. The character inherent in the American people has done all that has been accomplished; and it would have done somewhat more, if the government had not sometimes got in its way. For government is an expedient by which men would fain succeed in letting one another alone; and, as has been said, when it is most expedient, the governed are most let alone by it. Trade and commerce, if they were not made of India rubber, would never manage to bounce over the obstacles which legislators are continually putting in their way; and, if one were to judge these men wholly by the effects of their actions, and not partly by their intentions,they would deserve to be classed and punished with those mischievous persons who put obstructions on the railroads.

But,to speak practically and as a citizen, unlike those who call themselves no government men, I ask for, not at once no government,but at once a better government.Let every man make known what kind of government would command his respect, and that will be one step toward obtaining it...

Literature of the Expanding Frontier

第4部分

Unit Four

分裂、和解与扩展

Division, Reconciliation and Expansion

时代故事

1850—1914

1850年至1914年之间的那个年代见证了美国的一次变革。在那些年中，美国从一个权力分散的、大部分是农业地区的国家，变成了我们今天所知的现代化的工业国家。这次变革是随着内战开始的。内战时期是一个充满激烈斗争的时代。美国人拿起武器与另一部分美国人作战，来决定哪一方能够获胜：是北方还是南方？是自由还是奴隶制？是联邦还是各州的权力？北方战胜了，联邦继续存在，奴隶制被废除了，然而这些都使这个国家付出了几近毁灭的代价。

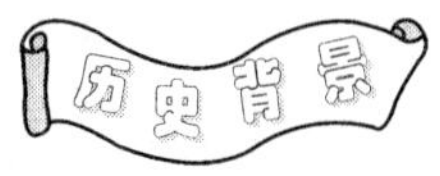

战争序曲 关于奴隶制的不同意见并不是什么新生事物，然而这一争论在1850年由于《逃亡奴隶法案》的通过而被再次激起。这个法案要求所有的公民——既包括自由州的也包括奴隶州的——帮助追捕逃跑的奴隶。南方人认为这是一条合理的法律，而北方人则认为这是暴行。

奴隶制向西部的扩展也是一个激烈争论的话题。1854年，当《堪萨斯——内布拉斯加法案》使一大片本来是自由制的西部土地向奴隶制敞开大门时，争论变成了一场战斗。一位来自纽约的参议员坚持道："我们要参加对堪萨斯那片处女地的争夺。"那场"争夺"将堪萨斯变成了一片血腥的战场。

MERCURY

EXTRA:

Passed unanimously at 1.15 o'clock, P. M., December 20th, 1860.

AN ORDINANCE

To dissolve the Union between the State of South Carolina and other States united with her under the compact entitled "The Constitution of the United States of America."

THE

UNION

IS

DISSOLVED!

关于南卡罗来纳州脱离联邦的新闻报道

这场关于奴隶制的争论占据了政治的重心，吸引了全国的注意，同样，它也影响了当时的文学——在一个经典的事件中，文学加剧了争论。哈丽特·比彻·斯托的长篇小说《汤姆叔叔的小屋》发表于1852年，这部小说生动地描述了奴隶制的残酷。这部书成为反对奴隶制的一件有力的武器，在一年之内就卖出了30余万册。它的影响力是如此之大，以至于在随后的3年之内出现了30余部南方立场的长篇小说，试图对抗它的影响。

1859年，国家的分裂进一步深化了。在约翰·布朗的领导下，一群反奴隶制的极端主义者袭击了一所联邦兵工厂。他们本来的意图是能诱发一次奴隶的武装叛乱。然而，他们并没能实现预期的目标，约翰·布朗因为叛国罪被处死，但这次事件激化了矛盾，并使之即将到达失去控制的程度。

联邦的解体 1860年亚伯拉罕·林肯当选总统，北方与南方之间的矛盾达到了顶点。林肯是新成立的共和党的代表，这个党致力于遏制奴隶制的扩张。南卡罗来纳州曾经威胁说如果林肯当选的话，它就要脱离联邦，在11月，它的威胁变成了现实。其他6个州紧随南卡罗来纳之后也脱离了联邦。1861年2月，分裂州成立了美国南部邦联。

1861年4月11日，南部邦联的炮兵在查尔斯顿港向联邦军队控制的萨姆特要塞开炮，战斗打响了。双方都有很多人认为这场战争将以本方的胜利很快结束。没人能够预料到将会发生什么——安提爱塔姆大屠杀，2.3万人在一天之内丧生；威克斯堡被围困时的物资匮乏，人们靠吃狗和老鼠才幸存下来；还有联邦将军威廉姆·T.·谢尔曼的军队向大海进军时，对佐治亚的大规模破坏。事实上，那场毁灭性的战争将要持续漫长的四年。

到了1865年春天，南部邦联将军罗伯特·E.·李向联邦将军尤利西斯·S.·格兰特投降时，已经有超过62万名士兵失去了生命，还有大约同样多的士兵受伤。整个南方成为一片废墟，城市被夷为平地，农场和种植园被破坏无遗。

扩展的美国 如果说内战时期的特点是矛盾，那么接下来的那个时期的特点就应该是令人震惊的大范围的变化。在那以后的50年中，地理上的扩张和工业化改变了我们的环境、经济、社会及我们自身。

1862年的《宅地法》许诺任何人只要耕种一片160英亩的土地达到五年时间，这片土地就归其所有。这条法案使西进运动的发展达到了最快的速度。50万名农民，其中包括几万名得到解放的美国黑人，在那片大平原上获得了属于自己的土地。数以千计的采矿人受到掘金致富的诱惑，来到了西部。还有其他人搬到西部来，成为牧场经营者。1868年，第一条横贯美洲大陆的铁路完工推进了西进运动。随着国内铁路线的发展，铁路取代了有篷货车——美国拓荒者的象征——成为主要的交通方式。

逐渐消失的边疆地带 到1890年为止，美国人几个世纪以来所熟悉的边疆地带已经不复存在了。不断汇集的定居者，铁路的出现，采矿业和牧场的发展——所有这些因素共同改变了西部。大群的水牛不见了，荒野不见了，取而代之的是大片相连的耕地和牧场，数英里长的带倒钩的铁丝篱笆将其隔开。

印第安民族也不见了。其中有很多部落原本依靠水牛为生。到了1890年，实际上所有在西部的美国土著人都被迫离开了自己的土地。几十年激烈流血的抵抗最终被证明毫无作用。据说，1877年，内兹波赛部落的首领约瑟夫被美国军队最终抓获时说：“我已经厌倦战斗了。”与其他被征服的部落一样，约瑟夫酋长和他的人民被送去住在印第安居留地，也就是现在的俄克拉何马州。然而，即使是这些在1834年由国会划出的印第安居留地，也不能躲过白人的侵蚀。1889年，印第安居留地中没有分配的土地对白人定居者开放了。

边疆地区可能是消失了，但是它遗留下来的文化却继续存在于西部丰富的民间传统中。像派克斯·比尔这样被夸大的民间英雄们仍然在故事和传说中被人们津津乐道。边疆地区也继续保存在草地管理者、铁路工人、养牛人和矿工们的歌声中。

年轻的南军士兵

变化的美国社会 随着19世纪80年代电力

战后的南方某镇

的引入，第二次工业革命正式开始了。在很多手工制造业中，电力取代了蒸汽动力。我们现在所熟悉的现代生活的标志开始出现：电灯，电话，汽车，电影，留声机。消费产品的大批量生产引起了一种重要的新传媒的兴起和发展：那就是广告。摩天大楼、百货商店和大众交通成为城市生活的组成部分——同样还有噪声、交通堵塞、空气污染、犯罪和贫民窟。

这个国家的工业和城市发展也受到了移民的推动。在1865年至1915年之间，2500万人来到美国寻求自由和经济发展机会（作为对比，在内战结束时整个国家的人口是3150万）。大多数新移民在城市里定居。在同一时期，数百万美国人离开农场和小城镇，搬到大城市里寻找工作。这种汇集使城市人口急剧膨胀，为工业发展提供了用之不竭的廉价劳动力。

在19世纪晚期的工业繁荣中产生了新的贫富两极分化。工人的薪水如此之低，以至于一个工人，甚至两个，经常都不能养活一个家庭。童工成为贫穷的工人阶层中的普遍现象。移民家庭经常住在阴暗狭窄、通风不畅、没有卫生间的公寓里，在这样的条件下，疾病极其猖獗。

而同时，相对来说的一小部分人——大工业企业的拥有者们——发了大财，过着皇室一样的生活。他们的奢华使得马克·吐温将这个时期称为“镀金年代”，暗喻其金玉其外、败絮其中。

实际上，就在国家表层的繁盛之下正滋生着不满。妇女、黑人和工人鼓动着要求改变他们的社会、经济和政治地位。妇女仍然没有选举权；黑人虽然得到了解放，但大多数人在1914年的情况并没有比1850年时有多少改善；而劳工改革则迫在眉睫。渐渐出现的工会组织与管理阶层之间爆发了激烈的斗争。

战时的声音 在战争期间，人们创作了成千上万篇日记、信件、日志和演讲，详尽感人地记录了美国人——从地位最低的士兵到李将军本人——所经历的一切。玛丽•彻斯纳特是一位南部邦联高级军官的妻子，她40万字的日记就是内战时期卓越文学成果的一个明显范例。

这个世纪中期，最伟大的语言大师之一就是林肯总统。他的演讲和信件就是清晰和雄辩的模范。他的《葛底斯堡演说》长度只有10个句子，却成为对美国民主含义的经典表达。

林肯带领着这个国家度过了有史以来最严重的危机。然而，最终他却没有机会重建联邦。就在李将军投降后几天，林肯遇刺，并于1865年4月15日逝世。这个饱受战争创伤、疲惫不堪的国家，又不得不面对这令人生畏的重任：在没有林肯的领导的情况下进行和解和重建。

边疆的声音 在美国向西扩张的同时，美国文学也同样在向西扩张。在这个时期，中西部及更遥远的西海岸史无前例地涌现出一批代表性的作家。有些作家，例如布赖特•哈特和威拉•卡瑟，出生在东部或南部，但后来移居西部。哈特在青年时期从纽约移居到加利福尼亚，而卡瑟童年时就从弗吉尼亚搬到了内布拉斯加。在美国文学中最伟大的作家之一——马克•吐温——在密苏里州的哈尼巴尔长大，但他四处旅行，在内战时期定居在内华达的一个矿区城镇里。吐温在他的第一篇短篇小说《卡拉维拉斯县著名的跳蛙》中吸收了西部丰富的语言和夸张的情感。

边疆生活的严酷现实加上艺术家们对内战的反应，共同引起了一个美国新文学运动的兴起，这个运动就叫做现实主义。文学中的现实主义开始于内战以后。虽然这场战争的结果给了这个国家一种来之不易的统一感，但是人们在战争中付出的巨大代价粉碎了国家的理想主义。年轻作家们不再采用战前流行的浪漫主义，而是开始着重描述普通人的“真实生活”，并且试图用诚实、客观、几乎是纯事实的方法来表现人物和事件。例如，威拉•卡瑟就是一名现实主义作家，她因为无所畏惧地刻画了大草原上的生活的孤独和文化隔绝感而著称于世。在《一场瓦格纳音乐会》中，她将这种隔绝感与一座东部城市

中丰富的文化生活进行了对比。

现实主义的一个重要的文学分支就是自然主义。自然主义作家也描写真实情景中的真实人，但是他们相信是大于个人的力量——包括自然、天命、遗传——塑造了个人的命运。例如，杰克·伦敦很多小说的背景都设置在阿拉斯加，那里的环境残酷恶劣。人类在面对压倒一切的自然力量时表现的耐力，是贯穿其小说的主题，《生火》这篇作品也是如此。

如果说这些作家描述的现实看起来总是很严酷，那是因为艰苦的生活影响了他们的艺术视角。他们的视角扎根于战争和边疆，且逐渐移向于发展中的城市。

表达不满的文学 工业化中产生的社会问题落入了当时很多优秀作家敏锐的视野中，并在他们的笔下反映了出来。例如，凯特·肖邦的写作就探讨了妇女对平等和独立的渴望。在自然主义作家看来，与工业化这股力量相比，个人是软弱无力的。斯蒂芬·克瑞恩作为自然主义运动的一名领袖，在他的第一部长篇小说《玛吉：街上的女孩》中就采用了这个观点，这部小说是对纽约城贫民窟中的生活的现实描绘。而保罗·劳伦斯·顿巴的《我们戴着面具》则揭示了美国黑人感受到的疏远，他们在白人的社会中微笑着掩饰自己的绝望。

到了1914年，美国已经成长起来；从某种意义上说，美国的文学也已经成长起来。内战、开拓边疆和工业化共同使美国丧失了纯真，使美国的个性从理想主义转向了实用主义。美国作家对浪漫主义的拒绝和对现实主义的接纳就反映了这种变化。

The Story of the Times
1850—1914

The years between 1850 and 1914 witnessed a transformation of the United States. During those years, America changed from a decentralized, mostly agricultural nation to the modern industrial nation that we know today. This trans formation began with the Civil War. The Civil War era was a time of intense conflict. Americans took up arms against other Americans to determine which should prevail: North or South? freedom or slavery? the federal Union or states' rights? The North won, the Union held, and slavery was abolished, but at a devastating cost to the nation.

Historical Background

Prelude to War Disagreements over slavery were nothing new, but the controversy was rekindled in 1850 by passage of the Fugitive Slave Act. It required all citizens—of free states as well as slave states—to help catch runaway slaves. Southerners saw the law as just; northerners, as an outrage.

The expansion of slavery into the West was hotly contested. When, in 1854, the Kansas-Nebraska Act opened up a vast area of previously free western land to slavery, the argument became a fight. "We will engage in competition for the virginsoil of Kansas", a senator from New York insisted. The "competition" turned Kansas into a bloody battleground.

Just as it dominated politics and preoccupied the nation, the controversy over slavery influenced the literature of the day — and in one classic case, literature fueled the controversy. Harriet Beecher Stowe's novel Uncle Tom's Cabin, published in 1852, vividly depicted the cruelty of slavery. The book became a powerful antislavery weapon, selling more than 300,000 copies within a year. Its impact was such that within three years no fewer than thirty southern novels came out attempting to counter its influence.

The deep national division intensified in 1859 when a group of antislavery extremists raided a federal arsenal. Led by John Brown, the group had intended to provoke an armed slave revolt. The attempt failed, and Brown was executed for treason, but this only fed the controversy which now threatened to escalate out of control.

The Union Is Dissolved The conflict between North and South came to a head when Abraham Lincoln was elected in 1860. Lincoln represented the newly formed Republican party, which had dedicated itself to halting the spread of slavery. South Carolina had threatened to secede if Lincoln was elected, and in December it did so. Six states followed South Carolina out of the Union. In February 1861, the secessionist states established the Confederate States of America.

Fighting began on April 11, 1861, when Confederate artillery fired on Union troops holding Fort Sumter, in Charleston Harbor. Many on both sides anticipated a short war ending in victory. No one could know what lay ahead—the carnage of Antietam, where 23,000 men fell in a single day ; the deprivation of the seige of Vicksburg, where people survived by eating dogs and rats: the wholesale destruction of Georgia, when Union general William T. Sherman's troops marched to the sea. In fact, the devastating war would last four long years.

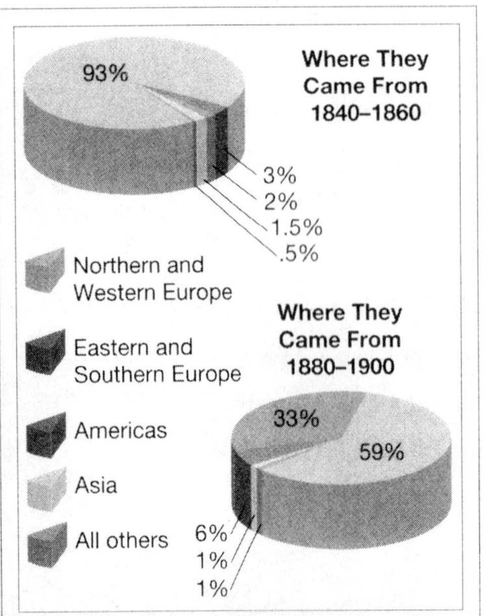

By the time Confederate general Robert E. Lee surrendered to Union general Ulysses S. Grant in the spring of 1865, more than 620,000 soldiers had lost their lives. Nearly that number had been wounded. The South lay in ruins, its cities razed, its farms and plantations destroyed.

An Expanding America If conflict characterized the Civil War years, change — on an astonishing scale — characterized the period that followed. Over the next fifty years, physical expansion and industrialization transformed our landscape, economy, society, and identity.

The Homestead Act of 1862 promised 160 acres of land to anyone who would farm it for five years. This shifted the westward movement into high gear. Half a million farmers, including tens of thousands of emancipated African Americans, staked claims on the Great Plains. Miners went west by the thousands, lured by the prospect of striking it rich in gold. Still others moved west to become cattle ranchers. Westward expansion was boosted by completion of the first transcontinental railroad in 1868. As the national railroads grew, the covered wagon — symbol of the American pioneer — was replaced by the railroad as the main means of transportation.

The Disappearing Frontier By 1890, the frontier as Americans had known it for centuries had ceased to exist. The steady influx of settlers, the burgeoning railroads, the growth of mining and cattle ranching — all had combined to transform the West. Gone were the great herds of buffalo. Gone was the expanse of open range. In its place was an enormous patchwork of plowed field and grazing lands, separated by miles of barbed wire fencing.

Gone, too, were the Indian nations, many of which had depended on the buffalo for survival. By 1890, virtually all the Native Americans in the West had been forced from their land. Decades of fierce and bloody resistance had ultimately proved futile. "I am tired of fighting," Chief Joseph of the Nez Perce reportedly said after being hunted down by the United States Army in 1877. Like others before them, Chief Joseph and his people were sent to live in Indian Territory, in what is now Oklahoma. However, even Indian Territory, which Congress had set aside in 1834, was not safe from white encroachment. In 1889, unas-

signed land in Indian Territory was opened up to settlers.

The frontier may have disappeared, but its legacy lived on in a rich western folk tradition. Larger–than–life folk heros like Pecos Bill were celebrated in tall tales and legends. The frontiersurvived, too, in the songs of the sod busters and railroad workers, cowpokes, and miners.

A Changing American Society With the introduction of electricity in the 1880's, the second Industrial Revolution began in earnest Electricity replaced steam power in many manufacturing industries. The now familiar trappings of modern life began to make their appearance: the electric light, telephone, automobile, motion picture, phonograph. The mass production of consumer goods sparked the rise of an important new medium: advertising. Skyscrapers, department stores, and mass transportation became part of city life—as did noise, traffic Jams air pollution, crime, and slums.

The country's industrial and urban growth were both fueled by immigration. Between 1865 and 1915, 25 million people came to the United States seeking freedom and economic opportunity (By comparison, the population of the entire nation at the end of the Civil War was 31.5 million). Most, though not all, of the newcomers settled in cities. In the same period, millions of Americans left farms and small towns and moved to the cities seeking work. This influx swelled urban populations and provided an inexhaustible supply of cheap labor for industry.

The industrial boom of the late nineteenth century created new extremes of wealth and poverty. The wages of industrial workers were so low that a single

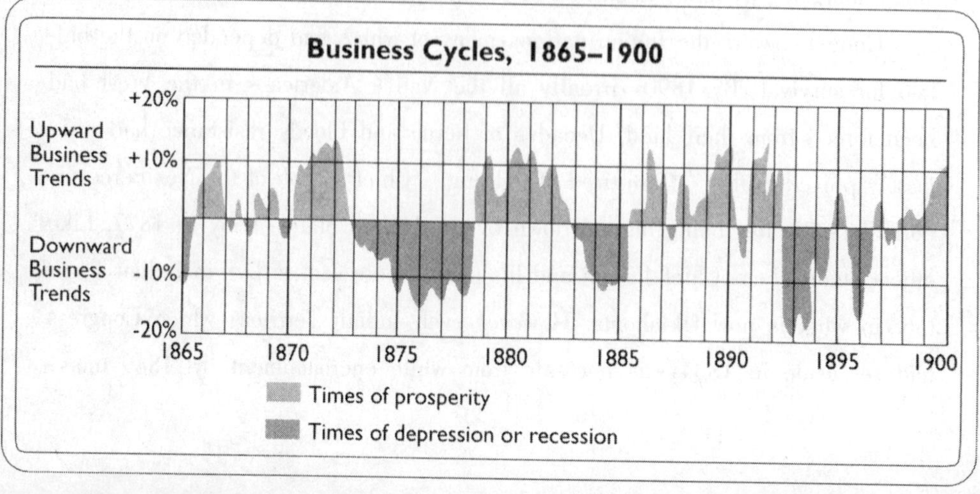

worker, or even two, often could not support a family. Child labor became the norm among the poor working class. Immigrant families often lived in small, dark, unventilated apartments with no toilet. In these conditions, disease was rampant.

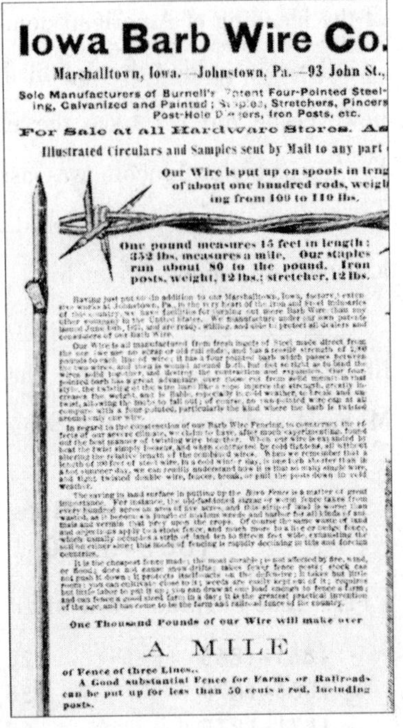

Meanwhile, a relative handful of men—the owners of big industrial corporations—made fortunes and lived like royalty. Their ostentatious displays of wealth led Mark Twain to dub this period "the Gilded Age", implying a thin veneer of glitter over something of poor quality.

Indeed, just beneath the nation's prosperity, discontentment grew. Women, African Americans, and workers agitated for changes in their social, economic, and political status. Women still did not have the vote; most African Americans, despite emancipation, were hardly better off in 1914 than they had been in 1850; labor reform was desperately needed. Bitter struggles erupted between emerging workers' unions and management.

Literature of the Period

Wartime Voices Thousands of diaries, letters, journals, and speeches were produced during the war, providing a richly detailed and moving record of what Americans — from the lowliest private to General Lee himself experienced. The 400,000-word diary of Mary Chesnut, the wife of a high-ranking Confederate officer, is a notable example of the extraordinary literary output of the Civil War years.

One of the greatest masters of the language at mid-century was President Lincoln. His speeches and letters are models of clarity and eloquence. His Gettysburg Address, a mere ten sentences in length, has become a classic expression

of the meaning of American democracy.

Lincoln guided the nation through the worst crisis in its history. At the end, however, he did not have the chance to reconstruct the Union. Just days after Lee's surrender, Lincoln was assassinated. He died on April 15, 1865. The nation, war-torn and weary, would have to face the daunting tasks of reconciliation and reconstruction without him.

Frontier Voices As America expanded west- ward, so, too, did America's literature. In this period, for the first time, a number of writers represented the Midwest and the Far West. Some, like Bret Harte and Willa Cather, were born in the East or South but later moved West. As a young man, Harte moved from New York to California. Cather moved from Virginia to Nebraska as a child. One of the greatest writers in all of American literature—Mark Twain—grew up in Hannibal, Missouri. but traveled widely, settling in a Nevada mining town during the Civil War. Twain drew on the colorful language and outsized sensibility of the West for his first short story, "The Notorious Jumping Frog of Calaveras County".

United States Patents Issued 1861–1900

Five-Year Periods	Number of Patents
1861–1865	20,725
1866–1870	58,734
1871–1875	60,976
1876–1880	64,462
1881–1885	97,156
1886–1890	110,358
1891–1895	108,420
1896–1900	112,188

The harsh reality of frontier life coupled with artists' reactions to the Civil War gave rise to a new movement in American literature called Realism. Realism in literature began after the Civil War. Though the war's outcome had given the nation a hard-won sense of unity, the war's enormous cost in human life had shattered the nation 's idealism. Young writers turned away from the Romanticism that was popular before the war, Instead, writers began to focus on portraying "real life" as ordinary people lived it and attempted to show characters and events in an honest, objective, almost factual way. Willa Cather, for example, was a Realist noted for her unflinching portrayal of the loneliness and cultural isolation of life on the prairie. In "A Wagner Matinee", she contrasts this isolation with the cultural richness of an eastern city.

An important literary offshoot of Realism was Naturalism. Naturalist writers also depicted real people in real situations, but they believed that forces larger than the individual—nature, fate, heredity—shaped individual destiny. Jack London, for example, set much of his fiction in Alaska, where the environment was cruel and unforgiving. The theme of human endurance in the face of overwhelming natural forces pervades his fiction, including "To Build a Fire".

If the reality these writers depicted seemed always to be a harsh one, it was because hardship influenced their artistic vision. It was a vision rooted in war, in the frontier, and, increasingly, in America's growing cities.

Literature of Discontent The social ills that grew out of industrialization came under the sharp eye and pen of many talented writers of the day. Kate Chopin's writing, for example, explored women's desire for equality and independence. The Naturalists saw industrialization as a force against which individuals were powerless. Stephen Crane, a leader of the Naturalist movement, took this view in his first novel, Maggie:A Girl of the Streets, a realistic depiction of life in New York City's slums.Poets, too, captured a growing sense of dissatisfaction. Paul Laurence Dunbar's "We Wear the Mask" revealed the alienation of African Americans who smile in white society to mask despair.

By 1914, America had grown up; in a sense, American literature had, too. The Civil War, the closing of the frontier, and industrialization had brought about a loss of innocence, a shift from idealism to pragmatism in the American character. In their rejection of Romanticism and embrace of Realism, American writers reflected this change.

第一课

战争插曲

斯蒂芬·克瑞恩 (1871—1900)

斯蒂芬·克瑞恩出生在美国内战结束之后，然而他最值得纪念的却是他对那场战争的引人入胜的描述。在他悲剧性的短暂的一生中，克瑞恩确立了自然主义运动领导人和当时最伟大的作家之一的地位。

斯蒂芬·克瑞恩

在他事业的早期，克瑞恩是纽约城的一名报纸写手，他在那里的经历为他的第一部长篇小说提供了灵感，这就是《玛吉：街上的女孩》(1893)。这部小说对于城市贫民窟生活的冷酷的现实主义描写是那样的坦率和惊人，以至于克瑞恩找不到出版商愿意出版这本书，只好自己出资把它出版。

他的第二部小说出版于1895年，即《勇气的红色徽章：美国内战中的一段插曲》(以下简称《战争插曲》)。这部小说是对一名年轻士兵在敌人炮火下的思想和情绪反应的心理探索，它获得了极大的成功，为这位24岁的作家赢得了国际上的喝彩。虽然那时克瑞恩还从未经历过军事战斗，但他在写出逼真的战斗场景之前，访问了内战老兵，研究了照片、战斗计划和传记性的记录。

后来克瑞恩在1897年的希腊–土耳其战争和1898年的美西战争中作为一家报纸的战地通信记者，亲历了战争。他在战争中的经历为他的一部诗集《战争善良》(1899)提供了素材，然而这些诗却让他付出了健康的代价。他在28岁时就死于肺结核。

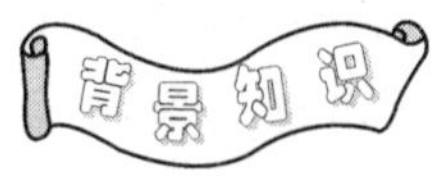

历史：美国内战的血腥遗赠

这篇短故事和这首歌的灵感来自于美国内战，美国历史上最血腥的战争。这次战争夺去了60万名士兵的生命——比美国参加的其他所有战争中的伤亡总数还要多。还有另外几十万名士兵因为战争中受伤和简陋的医疗条件而变成了残疾人。

在你阅读《战争插曲》的时候，请记住那时对于受伤肢体的惯例治疗方法就是截肢。一个受伤的士兵知道他面临危险：外科医生会锯下自己受伤的胳膊或腿。

在战争开始的时候，双方都没有做好照顾伤员的准备。他们没有救护车把伤员从战场上运下来，没有医疗组织对他们进行治疗，没有药品，也没有护士。谷仓、货栈和学校被变成了临时医院，就像这篇小说中描述的一样，情况非常恶劣。甚至轻伤也可能导致死亡，最常见的是由于疾病的感染，死于感染的士兵人数是战争中直接伤亡人数的两倍。

联系你的经历 处于“可控”状态和做出负责任的决定会帮助你建立一种对生活的控制感。然而，在很多情况下，你却经常没有控制的权利——无论那情况是好的还是坏的。设想在内战中作战的战士们的感觉，他们能否控制自己的命运？

日志写作 是否曾经有一个偶然的事件对你的生活产生了影响？把这次经历以及它所产生的影响写下来。

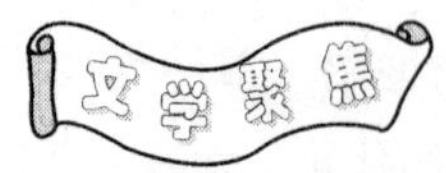

现实主义和自然主义 《战争插曲》是一个严酷的故事，讲述了一个偶然事件怎样永远改变了一名内战军官的生活。这篇短篇小说具有两个新的文学运动的特征，这两个文学运动是作为对浪漫主义的反应而兴起的，浪漫主义是19世纪的文学运动，强调情感、想象和对自然的欣赏。其中第一个运动是现实主义，它追求尽可能忠实并且准确地反映现实生活。现实主义者聚焦于面对日常生活的冷酷现实的普通人。

自然主义产生于现实主义运动，同样也聚焦于忠实地反映普通人的生活。然而，自然主义者认为一个人的命运是由环境、遗传和偶然因素决定的。因此，他们经常描述一类人，这些人的生活是由他们无法理解也无法控制的力量塑造的，然而他们坚强而不失尊严地忍受一切，因此肯定了他们生命的意义。

战争插曲(节选)

斯蒂芬·克瑞恩

中尉把他的橡胶毯铺在地上，然后把供给连队的咖啡倒在上面。下士和其他建起防护矮墙的肮脏干渴的人的代表都来到这里领取每个班的那一份。

中尉皱着眉，对待这分配的任务态度非常严肃。当他用剑在那一堆咖啡中划出不同的线时，他的嘴唇皱拢在一起，一直到大小惊人平均的棕色正方形的咖啡堆出现在毯子上。他几乎感到一阵算术求解后的巨大喜悦，下士们蜂拥而上，每个人都收获了一个小正方形，这时中尉突然尖叫起来，很快地盯着他身边的一个人看，仿佛他怀疑这是一次个人袭击事件。当其他人看到中尉袖子上的血时，他们也叫了起来。

他像一个被蜇了的人一样退缩，并且危险地摇晃着，然后站直了身子。人们可以清楚地听到他粗重的呼吸声。他悲伤神秘的目光越过那道矮墙，看着一片树林的绿色的表面，现在那里有很多小股的白烟。在这段时间里，那些人像雕像一般沉默地盯视着他的周围，为这次灾难感到震惊恐惧，因为它发生在人们毫无预见的时候——在他们有空闲时间去仔细观察它的时候。

就在中尉盯着那森林的同时，他们也摇晃着头，接下来所有的人仍然沉默着，都仔细打量着那远处的森林，仿佛他们的思维都固定在一颗子弹的神秘旅程上。

当然，这军官已经被情况迫使着把剑拿在了左手里，他不是拿着剑柄，而是笨拙地握着剑锋的中部。他把眼神从那充满敌意的森林转回来，看着他举在那里的剑，好像不知道要拿它做什么，把它放在哪里。简单地说，这武器突然间对于他来说变成了一个陌生的东西。他仿佛在麻醉的状态中看着它，就好像别人给了他一杆三叉戟、一根节杖或是一柄铲剑。

最后他试着把它插回到鞘里。要把一把用左手握住剑锋中部的剑，插到一个挂在左边臀部的剑鞘里，简直是一个值得在马戏团里表演的技巧了。这位受伤的军官绝望地与这柄剑和摇晃的剑鞘作着斗争，同时像一个摔跤手那样呼吸着。

但是就在这时，那些人，那些旁观的人，从他们石头般的状态中苏醒过来，充满同情地围了上来。值班军士拿过剑，轻柔地把它放到剑鞘里。做这事的时候，他紧张地向后仰着身子，甚至不让自己的手指碰到中尉的身体。一个创伤会赋予受伤的人一种奇怪的高贵。没受伤的人都会因为他的这种新的可怕的庄严而向后惊退。……他的同伴们若有所思地睁大眼睛看着他。而且，他们还模模糊糊地害怕一个手指放在他身上的重量就可能使他向前栽倒在地上，促成那悲剧的发生，立刻把他投入那模糊灰暗的未知世界。所以值班军士

受伤的士兵

受伤的海军中尉

在把剑插到剑鞘里的时候才紧张地向后仰着身子。

其他人也提供了帮助。有一个人胆怯地贡献出他的肩膀，问中尉是否愿意靠在上面，可是后者悲伤地摆摆手拒绝了他。他的神情如同一个人知道自己成为一种可怕疾病的牺牲品，也了解自己的无助。他再一次越过矮墙盯着森林，然后，转过身，慢慢地向后走去。他轻柔地用左手握着右手腕，仿佛那受伤的胳膊是用易碎的玻璃做成的。

那些人沉默地看着森林，又看看离开的中尉；然后又看看森林，看看中尉。

在这位受伤的军官穿过战场边线时，他看到了很多作为战争参与者所不知道的事情。他看到一个将军骑在黑色的战马上，瞪视着站在绿色树林前一排排穿着蓝色军服的步兵，就是那片树林的遮掩造成了他的麻烦。一名副官疯狂地疾驰而来，突然勒马停下，敬了一个礼，然后交给将军一份文件。奇怪的是，这就像一幅历史油画。

在将军和他的随从身后是一小队人，由一个喇叭手、两三个勤务兵和军旗手组成，他们都骑在狂躁的马上，拼命努力站在原地，保持他们表示敬意的距离，而同时炮弹就在他们身旁轰隆作响，使他们的战马狂暴地颤抖着跳起来。

一个炮兵连，喧闹闪亮的一群人，向右边席卷而过。马蹄重击地面的轰响，骑士们叫喊着责备和赞扬、威胁和鼓励，最后，还有车轮的咆哮声和闪亮的枪支的斜面，这些都使中尉专注地停了下来。炮兵连横扫过去的曲线使人心灵激动，它的停顿就像波浪猛撞在石头上一样生动，而当它消失在前方时，这车轮、杠杆和发动机的集合成为一个美丽的整体，仿佛一枚火箭。它的声音就是到达人类情感深处的战争的合唱。

中尉仍然举着自己的胳膊，仿佛它是玻璃做的一样。他站在那里看着炮兵连，直到所有的细节都消失了，只剩下骑士们的身影，一上一下，在一团黑影上方挥舞着鞭子。

后来，他把眼睛转向了战场，在那里枪声有时像篝火一样噼啪作响，有时毫无规律令人恼怒，也有时像雷声一样回响。他看到翻滚上升的烟，还看到人们奔跑欢呼，或站在那里向着莫测的远方不断射击。

他碰到了几个掉队的人，他们告诉他怎样找到战地医院。他们描述了医院的确切位置。实际上，这些人虽然不再在战斗中拥有一席之地，却比其他人更了解它。他们讲述着每个兵团和每个师的表现，还有每一位将军的看法。中尉向后扶着自己受伤的胳膊，用惊奇的目光看着他们。

在路边有一群人正在煮咖啡，他们"嗡嗡"的谈话声就像寄宿学校中的女孩子们一样。几个军官出来见他，询问了一些他根本就不知道的事情。有一个看见了他的胳膊，于是开始责骂他："哎呀，伙计，这可不是办法，你应该把那玩意儿固定住。"他纠正了中尉对伤势的处理。他把袖子剪下来，露出伤臂，胳膊上的每条神经都在他的碰触下微微颤动。他把自己的手帕绑在伤口上，同时一直不停地责骂。他的语气使人认为他已经习惯于每天都受伤了。中尉垂下头，在这个人面前感到自己不知道该怎样正确地受伤。

医院低矮的白色帐篷聚集在一座古旧的学校建筑的周围。这里正有着一阵异常的骚乱。在最显眼的位置，两辆救护车的轮子深陷在泥里。两个司机前前后后地抱怨，打着手势严厉地责骂着，而从那两辆塞满了伤员的救护车里，不时传来一声悲吟。一群打着绷带的人在来来往往，还有很多人坐在树下，照料着自己的头或是胳膊或是腿。在那学校大楼的楼梯上有人在愤怒地争论。有一个人靠着一棵树坐着，正在安详地吸着一个玉米穗轴做的烟斗，他的脸灰得像一张新的军毯。中尉想冲上前去，告诉他他快要死了。

一个忙碌的外科医生从中尉附近经过，"早上好。"他脸上带着友好的微笑说。然后他看到了中尉的胳膊，立刻就变了脸。"哎，让我们来看一看。"他似乎突然间对中尉非常轻蔑，那伤口很明显使后者处在了一个非常低的社会地位。那医生不耐烦地叫道："到底是哪个蠢货把它绑成这样的？"中尉回答说："哦，一个人。"

当那伤口露出来时，医生轻蔑地用手指拨弄了一下。"哼，"他说，"你跟我来，我会照顾你的。"他声音里的蔑视就仿佛他是在说："你要进监狱了。"

中尉一直很逆来顺受，但是现在他的脸涨红了，他直视着医生的眼睛，说："我猜不用把这胳膊切断吧。""胡说，伙计！胡说！胡说！"那医生叫道，"过

残酷的战争场面

来，来吧。我不会把它切断的。来吧。别幼稚了。”

“放开我。”中尉一边说一边愤怒地向后挣，他的目光固定在那所旧学校的门上，在他看来那门就像通往死亡的大门一样凶恶。

这就是中尉怎样失去了他的胳膊的故事。当他到家的时候，他的姐妹、他的母亲、他的妻子看到那平平的袖管都抽泣了很长时间。“哦，好了，”他说，站在这些泪水中间表情羞愧，“我想这不那么要紧。”

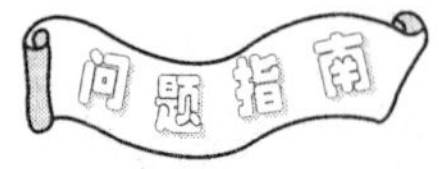

文学和生活

读者反应 你认为《战争插曲》中的哪些方面特别具有悲剧性或令人不安？解释理由。

阅读理解

1. 为《战争插曲》中中尉的伙伴“若有所思地睁大眼睛看着他”但却不愿碰触他的举动给出两个理由。

2. 在作品中，医生最终采取了什么办法医治中尉受伤的胳膊？

思考

解释

1. 作品中的中尉受伤的方式怎样使他成为一个令人同情的人物？（分析）

2. 在作品中，中尉以一种超然事外的眼光在路上行走，就像一个人看着

别人的梦魇。造成他这种麻木状态的原因是什么？（推断）

应用

3. 根据自然主义者的观点，人类在具有决定性的力量面前是弱小而没有影响力的生命。从《战争插曲》中找到例证来支持这种观点。（支持）

文学聚焦

现实主义和自然主义

《战争插曲》包含了现实主义和自然主义的因素。现实主义是强调忠实准确地描述普通生活的文学运动。而自然主义一般描述被自己无法控制的力量所操纵的人。

1. 在《战争插曲》中，中尉被射伤的同时正在分配咖啡，这对于表现文章的现实主义特点有什么作用？

2. 这个情节从哪方面可以作为这篇文章是典型的自然主义文章的支持例证？

3. 给出两个例子，表现中尉安静勇敢地忍受痛苦的这种典型的自然主义作品特征。

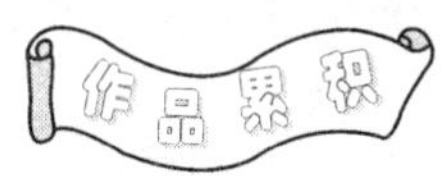

点子库

写作

1. 信　作为中尉，给你的妻子写一封信，告诉她你如何失去了胳膊。

2. 社论　在美国内战中，由于缺乏基本卫生条件而引起的感染致死的士兵比战斗创伤杀死的还要多。写一篇报纸社论，揭露疾病和恶劣的卫生条件是战争中最大的杀手。

3.定义性文章　这个故事中的哪些事件反映出人类在自己无法控制的事情面前非常无助的理论？在一篇文章中，利用《战争插曲》来定义自然主义。

项目

1. 士兵的剪贴簿　制作一本剪贴簿，收录一位想象中的内战士兵的经历记录。收入历史书和内战书籍中照片的复印件，并为每幅照片写出简短的说

明。(社会研究连线;艺术连线)

2. 关于内战中女英雄的口头报告研究多罗西亚·迪克西、伊丽莎白·布莱克威尔、克拉拉·巴顿或其他内战女英雄的事迹。把你的研究结果作成一次口头报告。

微型写作课

医院情况的战地报告

想象中尉的上级是一位上校，他想知道为什么他的很多士兵都死于轻伤。作为中尉写一份给上校的报告,报告你在军队医院住院期间接受的治疗和你观察到的问题。

写作技巧重点:精确的细节

为了让你的报告或任何写作生动完整,你都应该包含精确的细节来支持你的看法和观点。例如,简单地陈述,说受伤的士兵受到了忽视,是无法为上校提供足够的信息帮助他解决问题的。加入精确的细节可以提供一幅更完整的医院情况的全景。

范例

伤员经常在肮脏的床上或地板上一躺就是几小时甚至几天,却没有人喂他们吃饭、给他们洗澡或对他们进行医治。

构思

列出要报告的要点。记下你要用来支持每个要点的确切细节。如果你觉得还需要更多的信息,那么可以参考一本内战参考书。

写稿

在陈述你报告的目的的一个简短的开始段落后,用单独的段落来陈述你的每一个要点和支持的细节。然后,在结论中总结你报告中所有的要点。记得要使用正式的语言。

修改

重读你的报告,检查你是否按照逻辑顺序给出了要点,并且有足够的细节来支持。考虑你还能做什么来改善你的组织结构,还能有哪些信息能使你的写作得到加强或清晰化。

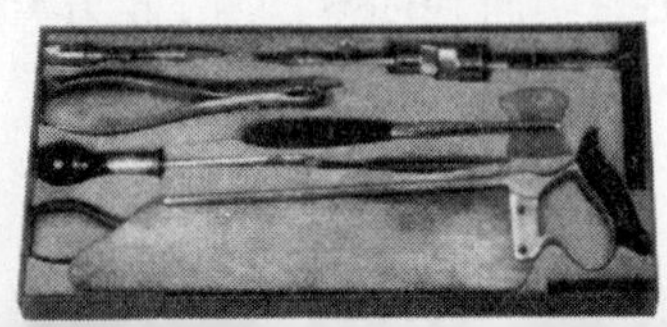

Guide for Interpreting

Stephen Crane (1871—1900)

Stephen Crane hadn't even been born when the last battle of the American Civil War was fought, yet he is best remembered for his compelling depiction of the conflict. During his tragically brief life, Crane established himself as both a leader of the Naturalist movement and one of the greatest writers of his time.

Early in his career, Crane worked as a newspaper writer in New York City. His experiences there inspired his first novel, Maggie:A Girl of the Streets (1893). Its grimly realistic portrayal of life in the city's slums was so frank and shocking that Crane was unable to find a publisher, so he printed the book at his own expense.

His second novel, published in 1895, was The Red Badge of Courage:An Episode of the American Civil War. A psychological exploration of a young soldier's mental and emotional reactions under enemy fire, the wildly successful novel earned international acclaim for the twenty-four-year-old. Though Crane had never experienced military combat, he interviewed Civil War veterans and studied photographs, battle plans, and biographical accounts before writing the realistic battle scenes.

Crane later viewed war firsthand when he served as a newspaper correspondent during the Greco-Turkish War in 1897 and the Spanish-American War in 1898. His war experiences provided material for a collection of poetry, War Is Kind (1899), but they took their toll on his health. He died of tuberculosis at the age of twenty-eight.

Background for Understanding

HISTORY: THE BLOODY LEGACY OF THE AMERICAN CIVIL WAR

Both this short story and this song were inspired by the American Civil War, the bloodiest war in American history. The conflict claimed the lives of 600, 000 soldiers — more American casualties than the total of all other wars in which the United States has fought. Hundreds of thousands more were left maimed by battle wounds and crude medical care.

As you read "An Episode of War," keep in mind that amputation was routine treatment for injured limbs. A wounded soldier knew that he risked losing his injured arm or leg to a surgeon's saw, like those in this Civil War medical kit.

When the war began, neither side was prepared to care for the wounded. There were no ambulances to transport them from the battlefield, no medical corps to treat them, no medicines, no nursing staff. Barns, warehouses, and schools were converted into makeshift hospitals, like the one described in this story. The conditions were terrible. Even a minor injury was liable to result in death, most often from disease; twice as many Civil War soldiers died of infections than of combat wounds.

Literature and your Life

CONNECT YOUR EXPERIENCE

Being "in control" of a situation and making responsible decisions help to make you feel in command of your life. Often, however, you don't have control over the situations — good and bad — that life presents. Do you imagine that the soldiers who fought in the Civil War felt as if they were in control of their destinies?

<u>Journal Writing</u> Has a chance event ever had an effect on your life? Write about the experience and its impact.

Literary Focus

REALISM AND NATURALISM

"An Episode of War" is a harsh tale of how a chance event forever changes the life of a Civil War officer. The story is characteristic of two new literary movements that sprang up in reaction to Romanticism — an earlier nineteenth-century literary movement that stressed emotion, imagination, and an appreciation of nature. The first movement, Realism, sought to portray real life as faithfully and accurately as possible. Realists focused on ordinary people faced with the harsh realities of everyday life.

From the Realism movement grew Naturalism, which also focused on truthfully portraying the lives of ordinary people. Naturalists, however, believed that a person's fate is determined by environment, heredity, and chance. As a result, they offen depicted characters whose lives were shaped by forces they could neither understand nor control, but endured with strength and dignity, thereby affirming the significance of their existence.

An Episode of War

Stephen Crane

The lieutenant's rubber blanket lay on the ground, and upon it he had poured the company's supply of coffee. Corporals and other representatives of the grimy and hot-throated men who lined the breastwork had come for each squad's portion.

The lieutenant was frowning and serious at this task of division. His lips pursed as he drew with his sword various crevices in the heap, until brown squares of coffee, astoundingly equal in size, appeared on the blanket. He was on the verge of a great triumph in mathematics, and the corporals were thronging forward, each to reap a little square, when suddenly the lieutenant cried out and looked quickly at a man near him as if he suspected it was a case of personal assault. The others cried out also when they saw blood upon the lieutenant's sleeve.

He had winced like a man stung, swayed dangerously, and then straightened. The sound of his hoarse breathing was plainly audible. He looked sadly, mystically, over the breast-work at the green face of a wood, where now were many little puffs of white smoke. During this moment the men about him gazed statuelike and silent, astonished and awed by this catastrophe which happened when catastrophes were not expected—when they had leisure to observe it.

As the lieutenant stared at the wood, they too swung their heads, so that for another instant all hands, still silent, contemplated the distant forest as if their minds were fixed upon the mystery of a bullet's journey.

The officer had, of course, been compelled to take his sword into his left hand. He did not hold it by the hilt. He gripped it at the middle of the blade, awkwardly. Turning his eyes from the hostile wood, he looked at the sword as he held it there, and seemed puzzled as to what to do with it, where to put it. In short, this weapon had of a sudden become a strange thing to him. He looked at it in a kind of stupefaction, as if he had been endowed with a trident, a sceptre, or a spade.

Finally he tried to sheathe it. To sheathe a sword held by the left hand, at the middle of the blade, in a scabbard hung at the left hip, is a feat worthy of a sawdust ring. This wounded officer engaged in a desperate struggle with the sword and the wobbling scabbard, and during the time of it breathed like a wrestler.

But at this instant the men, the spectators, awoke from their stone-like poses and crowded forward sympathetically. The orderly-sergeant took the sword and tenderly placed it in the scabbard. At the time, he leaned nervously backward, and did not allow even his finger to brush the body of the lieutenant. A wound gives strange dignity to him who bears it. Well men shy from his new and terrible majesty. Moreover, they fear vaguely that the weight of a finger upon him might send him headlong precipitate the tragedy, hurl him at once into the dim, grey unknown. And so the orderly-sergeant, while sheathing the sword, leaned nervously backward.

There were others who proffered assistance. One timidly presented his shoulder and asked the lieutenant if he cared to lean upon it, but the latter waved him away mournfully. He wore the look of one who knows he is the victim of a terrible disease and understands his helplessness. He again stared over the breast-work at the forest, and then, turning, went slowly rearward. He held his right wrist tenderly in his left hand as if the wounded arm was made of very brittle glass.

And the men in silence stared at the wood, then at the departing lieutenant; then at the wood, then at the lieutenant.

As the wounded officer passed from the line of baffle, he was enabled to see many things which as a participant in the fight were unknown to him. He saw a general on a black horse gazing over the lines of blue infantry at the green woods which veiled his problems. An aide galloped furiously, dragged his horse suddenly to a halt, saluted, and presented a paper. It was, for a wonder, precisely like a historical painting.

To the rear of the general and his staff a group, composed of a bugler, two or three ordefiles, and the bearer of the corps standard, all upon maniacal horses, were working like slaves to hold their ground, preserve their respectful interval, while the shells boomed in the air about them, and caused their chargers to make furious quivering leaps.

A battery, a tumultuous and shining mass, was swirling toward the right. The wild thud of hoofs, the cries of the riders shouting blame and praise, menace and encouragement, and, last, the roar of the wheels, the slant of the glistening guns, brought the lieutenant to an intent pause. The battery swept in curves that stirred the heart; it made halts as

dramatic as the crash of a wave on the rocks, and when it fled onward this aggregation of wheels, levers, motors had a beautiful unity, as if it were a missile. The sound of it was a war-chorus that reached into the depths of man's emotion.

The lieutenant, still holding his arm as if it were of glass, stood watching this battery until all detail of it was lost, save the figures of the riders, which rose and fell and waved lashes over the black mass.

Later, he turned his eyes toward the battle, where the shooting sometimes crackled like bush-fires, sometimes sputtered with exasperating irregularity, and sometimes reverberated like the thunder. He saw the smoke rolling upward and saw crowds of men who ran and cheered, or stood and blazed away at the inscrutable distance.

He came upon some stragglers, and they told him how to fred the field hospital. They described its exact location. In fact, these men, no longer having part in the battle, knew more of it than others. They told the performance of every corps, every division, the opinion of every general. The lieutenant, carrying his wounded arm rearward, looked upon them with wonder.

At the roadside a brigade was making coffee and buzzing with talk like a girls' boarding-school. Several officers came out to him and inquired concerning things of which he knew nothing. One, seeing his arm, began to scold. "Why, man, that's no way to do. You want to fix that thing." He appropriated the lieutenant andthe lieutenant's wound. He cut the sleeve and laid bare the arm, every nerve of which softly fluttered under his touch. He bound his handkerchief over the wound, scolding away in the meantime. His tone allowed one to think that he was in the habit of being wounded every day. The lieutenant hung his head, feeling, in this presence, that he did not know how to be correctly wounded.

The low white tents of the hospital were grouped around an old schoolhouse. There was here a singular commotion. In the foreground two ambulances interlocked wheels in the deep mud. The drivers were tossing the blame of it back and forth, gesticulating and berating, while from the ambulances, both crammed with wounded, there came an occasional groan. An interminable crowd of bandaged men were coming and going. Great numbers sat under the trees nursing heads or arms or legs. There was a dispute of some kind raging on the steps of the schoolhouse. Sitting with his back against a tree a man with a face as grey as a new army blanket was serenely smoking a corncob pipe. The lieutenant wished to rush forward and inform him that he was dying.

A busy surgeon was passing near the lieutenant. "Good-morning," he said, with a friendly smile. Then he caught sight of the lieutenant's arm, and his face at once changed. "Well, let's have a look at it." He seemed possessed suddenly of a great contempt for the lieutenant. This wound evidently placed the latter on a very low social plane. The doctor cried out impatiently, "What mutton-head had tied it up that way anyhow?" The lieutenant answered, "Oh, a man."

When the wound was disclosed the doctor fingered it disdainfully. "Humph," he said. "You come along with me and I'll tend to you." His voice contained the same scorn as if he were saying: "You will have to go to jail."

The lieutenant had been very meek, but now his face flushed, and he looked into the doctor's eyes. "I guess I won't have it amputated," he said.

"Nonsense, man! Nonsense! Nonsense!" cried the doctor. "Come along, now. I won't amputate it. Come along. Don't be a baby."

"Let go of me," said the lieutenant, holding back wrathfully, his glance fixedupon the door of the old schoolhouse, as sinister to him as the portals of death.

And this is the story of how the lieutenant lost his arm. When he reached home, his sisters, his mother, his wife, sobbed for a long time at the sight of the fiat sleeve. "Oh, well," he said, standing shamefaced amid these tears, "I don't suppose it matters so much as all that."

第二课

葛底斯堡演说

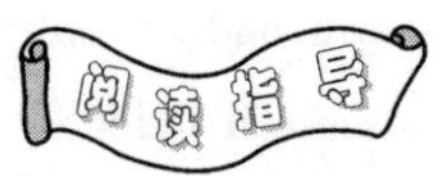

亚伯拉罕·林肯 (1809—1865)

作为美国历史上最悲惨时期的总统，亚伯拉罕·林肯为了把这个被战争分裂的国家重新联合在一起而努力奋斗。他面对无法避免的国家危机时所表现出来的勇气、力量和献身精神使他成为最受人崇拜和尊敬的美国总统之一。

亚伯拉罕·林肯

林肯出身低贱，但他很早就表现出对政治的兴趣。他曾经在伊利诺斯州的立法院和美国国会工作，这些工作使他赢得了奴隶解放运动支持者的声誉。1858年，他与斯蒂芬·道格拉斯竞选美国参议院席位。虽然林肯没有在这次选举中获胜，但他与道格拉斯白热化的辩论使他获得了全国范围内的承认，并帮助他在1860年成为了总统。

在他当选不久之后，美国内战爆发了。在战争的过程中，林肯表现出了巨大的力量和勇气，也展示了他演讲的天赋。1863年11月，他被邀请在将葛底斯堡战场确立为国家公墓的启用典礼上讲“几句合适的话”。整个世界很长时间以来都记得他在那里说过的话。

罗伯特•E.•李 (1807—1870)

罗伯特•E.•李

在内战中指挥南部邦联的军队并不是罗伯特•E.•李所希望的工作。随着关于奴隶制的争论不断升级，李的精神经受着巨大的折磨。他信任联邦，他反对奴隶制，也反对从联邦脱离出来，而且他被认为是美国军队中最优秀的军事将领之一。然而，当林肯总统提出让他指挥联邦军队的时候，他却拒绝率领一支军队与他自己故乡的州作战，他从军队中辞职，并且发誓只为保卫弗吉尼亚而战。

与其他南部邦联的领导人不同，李对于南部的力量不抱任何幻想。他最初就任北弗吉尼亚的军队指挥官，后来又成为全部邦联军队的总指挥官，他预料到了那场战争将要引起的大范围的流血和破坏。他是一位卓越不凡的军事将领，他面对对方压倒性的力量时所取得的成就和表现出来的正直的人格鼓舞了士兵和平民的强烈忠诚感。

在辞去美国军队职务的前夕，李在《给儿子的信》中探究了自己被分裂的忠诚。

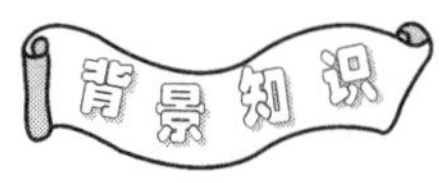

历史：林肯为在葛底斯堡的演讲做准备

1863年7月发生在宾夕法尼亚州的葛底斯堡的战斗是联邦的一次重大胜利，标志着战争中的一个转折点。5.1万多名士兵在那场战斗中受伤。1863年11月19日，在这个战场上建立的一个军人公墓正式启用。典礼的组织者因为不能肯定总统是否能够到场，所以只把他作为了一名次要的演讲者，只请他讲“几句合适的话”。在准备这篇简短的演讲稿时，林肯想带领1.5万名参加公墓启用典礼的美国人经历一次情感的最后典礼，他也需要为一场还远远没有胜利的血腥的斗争赢得继续的支持。

关于林肯写演讲稿的故事有很多：他一周以前写好了稿；他前一夜写的；

他在火车上写的；他写在一片废纸上。可以肯定的是，他在演讲的同时还在进行修改，加入了“在上帝的庇佑下”这个词组来形容这个国家。作为一名有经验的演讲家，林肯很可能预料到了这种来自于神的对于美国和它自由的目标的赞许会对听众产生什么样的正面影响。

联系你的经历 在那个很多人感到自己与故乡的州的联系比和国家之间的联系更加紧密的时代，像罗伯特•E.•李这样分裂的忠诚是很普遍的。而现在虽然选择不同了，但是分裂的忠诚却仍然普遍存在。对于重要事情与朋友有相反的看法，在学校和工作中不同的义务——这些都能成为你为忠诚而挣扎斗争的根源。

日志写作 描述一个情况——在你的生活中、一部电影或一本书中或是最近的公共事件——在那种情况中分裂的忠诚需要做出不同的选择。探讨那些选择是怎样做出的。

专题聚焦：一个分裂的国家 合理的话语经常可以克服分裂。在“第二次就职演说”中，林肯总统设法治愈一个分裂的国家。一个对于共同信仰和目标的感人的描述能发挥什么作用，使人们把分歧抛到一边？

措辞 你将会注意到李在给他儿子写信时的措辞——或者说词语的选择——比林肯总统写公众演讲稿时所用的措辞要不正式。词语的选择——无论是正式的还是非正式的，具体的或抽象的——都使一位作家的声音具有独一无二的特质。例如，李的句子“我看见4个州已经宣布了脱离联邦……”就比林肯的论述“叛乱者们却在设法……通过谈判来解散联邦，分裂国家”要更加个人化和不正式。注意到每位作家的措辞怎样反映出了他的读者（听众）和目的。

葛底斯堡演说

亚伯拉罕•林肯

1863年11月19日

87年前，我们的父辈使一个新的国家诞生在这片大陆上，这个国家孕育于自由之中，并致力于人生而平等的信念。

现在我们正在进行一场伟大的内战，这场战争检验我们的国家或任何一个像我们这样孕育并执著追求这种主张的国家是否能够长久存在。我们聚集在这场战争中的一个伟大的战场上，有些人在这里为了这个国家的生存而牺牲了自己的生命，我们此时将这个战场上的一块土地奉献给他们，作为他们的最终安息之所。我们这样做是完全合适和正确的。

亚伯拉罕•林肯葛底斯堡演讲

然而，从更广阔的意义上来说，我们无法奉献这片土地——我们无法使之神圣——我们也无法使之光荣。是那些勇敢的人，无论活着的还是死了的，是那些曾在这里战斗的人，使它变得神圣伟大，这远非我们微薄的力量所能予以增减的。这个世界不会注意也不会长时间记得我们在这里说的话，但是它永远也不会忘记勇士们在这里的业绩。对于我们这些活着的人来说，真正要做的是献身于勇士们未竟的事业。他们曾在这里战斗，并英勇地将这项事业推向前进。我们要做的是献身于留在我们面前的伟大的使命——他们已光荣牺牲，而我们会更加献身于他们为之付出一切的事业——我们在这里坚定地承诺烈士的鲜血绝不能白流——这个国家，在上帝的庇佑下，将会获得一次自由的新生——这个民有、民治、民享的政府一定会与世长存。

第二次就职演说

亚伯拉罕·林肯

1865年3月4日

因为这是我第二次出现在这里宣誓就任总统,所以没有必要像第一次就任时那样发表一次很长的演说。那么对于我们将要进行的行动的比较详细的叙述看起来是合适的。现在,我的前四年任期已满。在这四年里,由于这场伟大的竞赛仍然吸引着人们的注意并且占据着这个国家的精力,所以在它的每个时间点和阶段都不断地引出了公开宣言,因此没有什么新的情况可以报告了。我们军备的进步,因为其他各方面都依靠于这一方面,所以公众了解的和我自己了解的也一样多了;而我相信,这情况对所有人来说都是相当令人满意和鼓舞的。我们对未来抱有很高的希望,但不能冒险做出任何相关的预测。

在四年前相应的这个时候,所有的思绪都焦急地指向一场正在迫近的内战。所有人都害怕它——所有人都设法避免它。那次在这里做出的就职演说完全致力于不通过战争来拯救这个国家,而同时城市中的叛乱者们却在设法不通过战争来破坏它——他们设法通过谈判来解散联邦,分裂国家。两方面都反对战争;但是他们中的一方宁愿制造战争也不愿让这国家继续存在;另一方却宁愿接受战争也不愿让这国家灭亡。于是战争来了。

我们全部人口的八分之一是黑人奴隶,但他们不是普遍地分布在整个联邦,而是集中在南部地区。这些奴隶构成了一种奇怪然而强大的利益。所有的人都知道正是这种利益以某种方式引起了战争。叛乱者甚至不惜通过战争来分裂国家的目的就是为了加强、持续并且扩展这种利益;而政府要求的只不过是有权利限制这种利益在地域上的扩大。双方都没有预料到这场战争,也没有预料到它已经达到的严重程度和时间长度。双方都没有预料到这场战争的起因随着战争的结束、甚至在战争结束之前就消除了。每一方都寻求一种比较容易的胜利,期望结局不至于涉及根本,令人震惊。双方都读同一本《圣经》,向同一个上帝祈祷;而每一方都祈求上帝帮助他们与对方斗争。这可能看起来很奇怪:居然有人敢于请求一位公正的上帝来帮助他压榨别人的血汗积累自己的财富;不过让我们先别断定自己就不会受到审判。双方的祈祷都不可能得到回应;实际上双方的祈祷也都没有完全得到回应。全能的上帝有他自己的目的。“因为罪过，让悲伤降临到世界上！因为罪过必须到来；但是要让悲伤降临到那带来罪过的人身上！”如果我们认为美国的奴隶制属于在上帝的天意中必须到来的罪过，但已经延续了上帝所指定的时间，他现在就希望消除它。因此他把这场可怕的战争给了南方和北方，作为带来罪过的那些人的悲伤的话，“活着的上帝”的信徒们认为他具有神圣的特性，我们是不是要看清楚对于那些特性的任何偏离呢？我们天真地希望——我们热切地祈祷——这强大的战争的苦难根源可以很快地消亡。然而，如果上帝希望它继续下去，一直到奴隶250年没有报偿的劳作积累起来的财富全部毁灭；一直到从鞭子上流下的每一滴血都从剑上留下的血中得到了报复，就像3万年前所说的那样，现在我们仍然要说：“主的审判是完全准确公正的。”

林肯纪念堂

我们对任何人都没有怨恨；我们对所有人都怀有博爱；我们对正确的事情态度坚定，因为上帝使我们能辨认正确的事情，并让我们继续斗争，结束我们正在进行的事业；包扎好国家的伤口；照料参加了这场战争的人，他们的遗孀和他们的孤儿——采取所有的行动去获得并且珍视一个公正持久的和平，我们自己的，以及与其他国家之间的和平。

给儿子的信

罗伯特·E.·李

1861年1月23日

我收到了你寄给我的爱弗莱特①的《华盛顿的生活》，仔细读过了。要是他能看到他那伟大工作遭到的毁坏，他将会感到多么悲伤啊！然而，除非所有的

① 爱弗莱特：指爱德华·爱弗莱特（1789-1865），一位美国学者和演说家，林肯在葛底斯堡发表那次著名的演讲之前，爱德华·爱弗莱特先作了一次很长的发言。

希望都不复存在，否则我不会允许自己相信他那高尚行为的成就将要被破坏，而他那宝贵的忠告和美德的范例这么快就要被他的国人遗忘。根据那些文件，我判断现在我们正处在一种介于无政府和内战之间的状态。但愿上帝能使我们躲开这两种罪恶！我恐怕人类将有很多年都不能像基督徒那样承受没有制约和武力的状态。我看见4个州已经宣布了脱离联邦，很显然还有4个会追随他们的先例。然后，如果边境的州都卷入这次革命的漩涡之中的话，那么这个国家的一半就会摆开阵势来与另一半作战。我必须试着耐心等待结果，因为我既没法加快也没法拖延它的到来。

在我看来，正如你所说的，南方受到了北方的行动的侵害。我感觉到了这种侵犯，也愿意采取任何适当的措施来弥补。我是为原则奋斗，而不是为了个人或私己的利益。作为一名美国公民，我为我的国家的繁荣和制度，感到无比骄傲，如果有任何一个州的权利受到侵害，我都愿意去护卫它。但是我能预料到这个国家要遭到的是联邦解体的灾难。这将会是我们抱怨的所有罪恶的累积的结果，而我愿意牺牲除了荣誉之外的任何东西使联邦保持完整。因此，我希望能先尝试所有宪法规定的方法，最后再付诸武力。脱离联邦就是革命。我们"宪法"的筹划者们耗尽了劳动、智慧和忍耐来完成它，在它周围设下了那么多保卫和安全措施，并不是为了让联邦的每个成员随意破坏它的。根据宪法引言中所表述的，它是为了"永恒的联邦"而制定的，是为了建立一个政府，而不是一个契约，这政府只有通过革命或者全体大会成员的一致同意才能解体。谈论脱离是没有用的。无政府状态将要产生，没有一个政府，无论是华盛顿、汉密尔顿、杰弗逊、麦迪逊，还是其他美国革命时期的爱国者的政府……然而，一个只有靠剑和刺刀才能维持的联邦，一个冲突和内战要代替亲兄弟般的爱和善良的联邦，对我而言没有任何魅力。我会悼念我的国家和人类的幸福及进步。如果联邦解体了，政府也分裂了，我就要回到我的家乡的州，和我的人民一起分担苦难，并且，除非是为了自卫，我不会用我的剑对着任何人。

文学和生活

读者反应　你认为林肯的演讲中最值得纪念的是哪些语句？

主题焦点　(a)林肯是怎样利用语言来安慰和治愈听众的心灵的？(b)李对于一个“只有靠剑才能维持”的联邦的厌恶能为他将弗吉尼亚的利益置于联邦利益之上的决定做出合理的辩护吗？

日志写作　内战以后，罗伯特·E.·李申请完全赦免他带领邦联军队对抗联邦军队的行为。如果你是一名国会议员，你会投票同意赦免他吗？为什么？写一篇简短的日志来讨论你的回答。

阅读理解

1. 简要地叙述林肯做出这两次演讲的时候的情况。
2. 林肯在这些演讲中表达了对于奴隶制的怎样的观点？
3. 在信中，李在考虑什么选择？
4. 对于李脱离联邦是怎样解释的？

思考

解释

1. (a)除了为启用公墓所作的献词以外，林肯的《葛底斯堡演说》的主要目的是什么？(b)他《第二次就职演说》的主要目的是什么？(推断)

2. 林肯以描述他对于这个国家的最后重生的展望作为这两次演讲的结尾，考虑到他的目的，为什么这是组织这两次演讲的有效方法？(联系)

3. 林肯是怎样试图在他的演讲中使南方和北方之间达成和解或向双方都伸出调停之手的？(分析)

4. 用你自己的话来解释罗伯特·E.·李反对脱离联邦的论证。(讲述)

5. 李怎样将他收到他儿子的礼物和他的论证联系了起来？(联系)

6. 李和林肯都具有什么共同的品质？(联系)

应用

7. 林肯的演说与现代总统的讲话有什么不同之处？(讲述)

文学聚焦

措辞

措辞指的是作家对词语的选择。林肯总统使用了正式的词句使自己的演讲优雅而又具有重要性。李将军不那么正式的语言则在他的信中制造出了更加亲切和私人化的感觉。每位作家都使用了适合他的主题、读者(听众)、情况和文学形式的语言。

1. 从《第二次就职演说》中找出两个正式措辞的例子。

2. 从李的《给儿子的信》中找出两个非正式、个人化措辞的例子。

3. 为什么两位作家的措辞都很适宜?

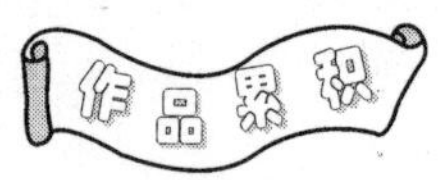

点子库

写作

1. 回信　假设你是李的儿子,写一封非正式的信,对你父亲信中的看法做出回应。(社会研究连线)

2. 日志写作　这是葛底斯堡演说的前夜,作为林肯,描述你想通过这还未写完的演讲稿传达的信息。你希望人们记住它的哪些方面呢?

3. 报纸专栏　作为一名记者写一篇关于《葛底斯堡演说》的专栏文章,对这次演讲做出评价。你是同意林肯的观点,认为这次演讲是个失败,还是同意与他共同发言的爱德华·爱福瑞特的观点,对这次演讲充满崇敬之情?用例证来支持你的观点。(职业连线)

项目

1. 纪念拼贴画　从图书馆里或因特网上找到关于葛底斯堡战役的照片或图画的复印件。用文字把它们结合在一起制成一幅拼贴画。(艺术连线)

2. 网页制作　做出制作一个因特网页的计划,提供与美国内战相关的信息和图片。制作一个流程图来说明你的网页将要包含的链接。(传媒连线;科技连线)

微型写作课

调查信

选择美国内战使你一直感兴趣的一个方面，写一封调查信或请求信，来收集相关信息。把你的信发给着重于研究这一阶段美国历史的机构、图书馆、或历史社团之一。使用适合于商业信函的语言和格式，使你的信收到效果。

写作技巧重点：适合于目的的语言

适合的语言可以确保你的读者理解你的要求并且感到你很感谢他们的帮助。使用礼貌正式的语言。写清机构的名称，选择精炼的词句，按照正式标准组织你的句子。

构思

找出一个可以提供你所需资料的机构或个人。为了达到这个目的，你可以研究网上资源或图书馆资源，例如：美国政府手册和华盛顿信息指南。回答下列问题：我需要什么信息？谁是最适合询问的人？我怎样简化我的问题才能得到最有用的回答？

写稿

在信的开头写清你自己的住址，日期和你收信人的姓名和住址，还有问候。在信的主体部分，清楚简洁地陈述你的要求。然后感谢收信人，签名，并在手写的签名下打印出你的姓名。

修改

大声朗读你的信，确定你使用了适合你的读者和目的的表示敬意的语言，并且清楚地表明了你需要的信息。此外，确认收信人的姓名、地址和机构名称都拼写正确。

Guide for Interpreting

Abraham Lincoln (1809—1865)

Serving as president during one of the most tragic periods in American history, Abraham Lincoln fought to reunite a nation torn apart by war. His courage, strength, and dedication in the face of an over whelming national crisis have made him one of the most admired and respected American presidents. A man of humble origins, Lincoln developed an early interest in politics. He served in the Illinois state legislature and the United States Congress, where he earned a reputation as a champion of emancipation. In 1858, he ran for the United States Senate against Stephen Douglas. Lincoln lost the election, but his heated debates with Douglas brought him national recognition and helped him win the presidency in 1860.

Shortly after his election, the Civil War erupted. Throughout the war, Lincoln showed great strength and courage. He also demonstrated his gift for oratory. He was invited to make "a few appropriate remarks" in November 1863 for a dedication of the Gettysburg battlefield as a national cemetery. The world has long remembered what he said there.

Robert E. Lee (1807—1870)

The job of commanding the Confederate army during the Civil Was wasn't one that Robert E.Lee wanted. As the dispute over slavery grew, Lee was torn. He believed in the Union, he opposed both slavery and secession, and he was regarded as one of the finest military leaders in the United States Army. When President Lincoln offered him command of the Union forces, however, Lee refused to lead an army against his native state and resigned from the army, vowing to fight only in defense of Virginia.

Unlike many Confederate leaders, Lee had no illusions about the South's power. Serving initially as commander of the army of northern Virginia and later of all the Confederate armies, he expected the widespread bloodshed and destruction caused by the war. He was an extraordinary military leader whose accomplishments and personal integrity in the face of overwhelming odds inspired great loyalty in both soldiers and civilians.

On the eve of resigning his U.S. Army commission, Lee explored his divided loyalties in "Letter to His Son."

Background for Understanding

HISTORY: LINCOLN PREPARES TO SPEAK AT GETTYSBURG

The battle of Gettysburg, Pennsylvania, fought in July 1863, was an important Union victory and marked a turning point in the war. More than 51,000 soldiers were injured in the battle. On November 19, 1863, a military cemetery on the battlefield was dedicated. Unsure of President Lincoln's availability, the dedication organizers slated him as a secondary speaker, asking him to make only "a few appropriate remarks" In drafting that brief address, Lincoln wanted to lead the 15,000 American citizens at the cemetery dedication through an emotional final rite of passage. He also needed to gain continuing support for a bloody conflict that was far from won.

Stories abound regarding Lincoln's drafting of the speech: He wrote it the week before; he wrote it the night before; he wrote it on the train; he wrote it on a piece of scrap paper. Certainly, he was still revising even as he spoke, adding the phrase "under God" to describe the nation. An experienced speaker, Lincoln probably anticipated the positive effect this suggestion of divine approval of the United States and its goals of freedom would have on the audience.

Literature and your Life

CONNECT YOUR EXPERIENCE

Divided loyalties like Robert E. Lee's were common in a time when many

felt more closely tied to their home state than to the nation. Divided loyalties are still common, though the choices are different. Friends with opposing priorities, commitments at school and work—all can become forces in a tug of war for your loyalty.

Journal Writing Describe a situation — in your life, a film or book, or recent public events — where divided loyalties required a difficult choice. Explore how the decision was made.

THEMATIC FOCUS: A NATION DIVIDED

The right words can often overcome division.In the "Second Inaugural Address", President Lincoln sought to heal a torn nation. How can a moving description of common beliefs and goals encourage enemies to set aside their differences?

Literary Focus

DICTION

You'll notice that Lee's diction—or word choice—in writing to his son was more informal than that of President Lincoln in drafting a public speech. Word choice—formal or informal, concrete or abstract — gives a writer's voice its unique quality. For example, Lee's phrase, "I see that four states have declared themselves out of the Union..." is more personal and informal than Lincoln's statement"insurgent agents were..., seeking to dissol[v]e the Union, and divide effects, by negotiation." Notice how each writer's diction reflects his audience and purpose.

The Gettysburg Address

Abraham Lincoln

November 19, 1863

Four score and seven years ago our fathers brought forth on this continent a new nation, conceived in Liberty, and dedicated to the proposition that all men are created equal.

Now we are engaged in a great civil war, testing whether that nation, or any nation so conceived and so dedicated, can long endure. We are met on a great battle-field of that war. We have come to dedicate a portion of that field, as a final resting place for those who here gave their lives that that nation might live. It is altogether fitting and proper that we should do this.

But, in a larger sense, we cannot dedicate—we cannot consecrate—we cannot hallow—this ground. The brave men, living and dead, who struggled here, have consecrated it, far above our poor power to add or detract. The world will little note, nor long remember what we say here, but it can never forget what they did here. It is for us the living, rather, to be dedicated here to the unfinished work which they who fought here have thus far so nobly advanced. It is rather for us to be here dedicated to the great task remaining before us—that from these honored dead we take increased devotion to that cause for which they gave the last full measure of devotion—that we here highly resolve that these dead shall not have died in vain—that this nation, under God, shall have a new birth of freedom—and that government of the people, by the people, for the people, shall not perish from the earth.

Second Inaugural Address

Abraham Lincoln

March 4, 1865

At this second appearing to take the oath of the presidential office, there is less occasion for an extended address than there was at the first. Then a statement, somewhat in detail, of a course to be pursued, seemed fitting and proper.

Now, at the expiration of four years, during which public declarations have been constantly called forth on every point and phase of the great contest which still absorbs the attention, and engrosses the energies of the nation, little that is new could be presented. The progress of our arms, upon which all else chiefly depends, is as well known to the public as to myself; and it is, I trust, reasonably satisfactory and encouraging to all. With high hope for the future, no prediction in regard to it is ventured.

On the occasion corresponding to this four years ago, all thoughts were anxiously directed to an impending civil war. All dreaded it — all sought to avert it. While the inaugural address was being delivered from this place, devoted altogether to saving the Union without war, insurgent agents were in the city seeking to destroy it without war–seeking to dissolve the Union, and divide effects, by negotiation. Both parties deprecated war; but one of them would make war rather than let the nation survive; and the other would accept war rather than let it perish. And the war came.

One eighth of the whole population were colored slaves, not distributed generally over the Union, but localized in the Southern part of it. These slaves constituted a peculiar and powerful interest. All knew that this interest was, somehow, the cause of the war. To strengthen, perpetuate, and extend this interest was the object for which the insurgents would rend the Union, even by war; while the government claimed no right to do more than to restrict the territorial enlargement of it. Neither party expected for the war, the magnitude, or the duration, which it has already attained. Neither anticipated that the cause of the conflict might cease with, or even before, the conflict itself should cease. Each looked for an easier triumph, and a result less fundamental and astounding. Both read the same Bible, and pray to the same God; and each invokes His aid against the other. It may seem strange that any men should dare to ask a just God's assistance in wringing their bread from the sweat of other men's faces; but let us Judge not that we be not judged. The prayers of both could not be answered; that of neither has been answered fully. The Almighty has his own purposes. "Woe unto the world because of offences! for it must needs be that offences come; but woe to that man by whom the offence cometh! "If we shall suppose that American Slavery is one of those offences which, in the providence of God, must needs come, but which, having continued through His appointed time, He now wills to remove, and that He gives to both North and South, this terrible war, as the woe due to those by whom the offence came, shall we discern therein any departure from those divine attributes which the believers in a Living God always ascribe to Him? Fondly do we hope—fervently do we pray—that this mighty scourge of war may speedily pass away. Yet, if God wills that it continue, until all the wealth piled by the bond-man's two hundred and fifty years of unrequited toil shall be sunk, and until every drop of blood drawn with the lash, shall be paid by another drawn with the sword, as was said three thousand years ago, so still it must be said "the judgments of the Lord, are true and righteous altogether."

With malice toward none; with charity for all; with firmness in the right, as God gives us to see the right, let us strive on to finish the work we are in; to bind up the nation's wounds; to care for him who shall have borne the battle, and for his widow, and his orphan—to do all which may achieve and cherish a just and lasting peace, among ourselves, and with all nations.

Letter to His Son

Robert E. Lee

January 23, 1861

I received Everett's[1] Life of Washington which you sent me, and enjoyed its perusal. How his spirit would be grieved could he see the wreck of his mighty labors! I will not, however, permit myself to believe, until all ground of hope is gone, that the fruit of his noble deeds will be destroyed, and that his precious advice and virtuous example will so soon be forgotten by his countrymen. As far as I can judge by the papers, we are between a state of anarchy and civil war. May

① Everett's: Referring to Edward Everett (1789–1865), an American scholar and orator who made a long speech at Gettysburg before Lincoln delivered his famous address.

God avert both of these evils from us! I fear that mankind will not for years be sufficiently Christianized to bear the absence of restraint and force. I see that four states have declared themselves out of the Union; four more will apparently follow their example. Then, if the border states are brought into the gulf of revolution, one half of the country will be arrayed against the other. I must try and be patient and await the end, for I can do nothing to hasten or retard it.

The South, in my opinion, has been aggrieved by the acts of the North, as you say. I feel the aggression and am willing to take every proper step for redress. It is the principle I contend for, not Individual or private benefit. As an American citizen, I take great pride in my country, her prosperity and institutions, and would defend any state if her rights were invaded. But I can anticipate no greater calamity for the country than a dissolution of the Union. It would be an accumulation of all the evils we complain of, and I am willing to sacrifice everything but honor for its preservation. I hope, therefore, that all constitutional means will be exhausted before there is a resort to force. Secession is nothing but revolution. The framers of our Constitution never exhausted so much labor, wisdom, and forbearance in its formation, and surrounded it with so many guards and securities, if it was intended to be broken by every member of the Confederacy at will. It was intended for "perpetual union", so expressed in the preamble, and for the establishment of a government, not a compact, which can only be dissolved by revolution or the consent of all the people in convention assembled. It is idle to talk of secession. Anarchy would have been established, and not a government, by Washington, Hamilton, Jefferson, Madison, and the other patriots of the Revolution.... Still, a Union that can only be maintained by swords and bayonets, and in which strife and civil war are to take the place of brotherly love and kindness, has no charm for me. I shall mourn for my country and for the welfare and progress of mankind. If the Union is dissolved, and the government disrupted, I shall return to my native state and share the miseries of my people; and, save in defense, will draw my sword on none.

第三课

内战中的声音

内战是美国历史上最痛苦的篇章之一，它影响了几百万士兵和人民的生活。以下的日记、日志和信件就讲述了内战中的故事，它们的讲述者都是生活受到了内战影响的人们。

1860年4月12日，当战争的第一声枪声在萨姆特要塞打响时，没有人受到伤害，但是玛丽•波耶金•彻斯纳特却似乎感觉到了即将来临的大屠杀。玛丽•波耶金的父亲是一名棉花种植园主，同时也是美国的参议员。玛丽成长在南卡罗来纳州查尔斯顿的一个贵族家庭里，17岁时，她嫁给了詹姆斯•彻斯纳特，一名富有的律师和未来的参议员。她的日记表现了内战开始阶段乐观和恐惧交织于一起的感情。

男人们都急着应征入伍，去参加一场大多数人认为是迅速而光荣的战争。正如我们从联邦士兵沃伦•李•高斯的记录中所了解的那样，有些年轻人把参军看做是赢得尊敬和提升的机会。然而训练营和战场上严酷的现实很快就使双方的士兵都明白了赢得光荣要付出生命或肢体残缺的代价。在葛底斯堡战役中他们付出的代价格外高昂——这是邦联将军罗伯特•E.•李的一次令人惊愕的惨败。邦联士兵兰道尔夫•麦克吉姆在自己的日记中记录了他的同伴们的勇敢，这些人中有很多都属于在葛底斯堡战役中伤亡的5.1万人。

南部邦联将军和军事策略家托马斯•乔纳森•“石壁”•杰克逊（1824—

1863）由于在1861年布伦战役中的坚定和果决而在战争早期就赢得了他的绰号。杰克逊在给他妻子的一封信中讲述了这次战斗，并在取得这次巨大胜利的两年之后逝世。他意外地被自己的军队射中，死于并发症。

1862年，由林肯总统发布的《解放黑奴宣言》改变了这场战争的目的。这个宣言宣布1863年1月1日起所有的奴隶都将得到解放，由此这场战争变成了一场结束奴隶制的战争，同时也是重新恢复联邦的战争。亨利·M.特纳牧师是一位出身自由的美国黑人，他住在华盛顿特区，他记录了黑人们对于这个消息的反应。

1865年，当这场战争结束时，废奴主义者索约娜·特鲁斯（1797–1883）却刚刚开始与种族歧视的战斗。特鲁斯是一名牧师，早先她本人就是奴隶，人们认为她也是主张妇女权利、禁酒以及要求改善工作环境和监狱改革的倡导者。

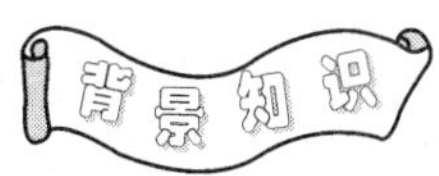

传媒：历史在《内战》中复活

1990年10月上旬的5个晚上，美国人坐在电视机前，被一部名叫《内战》的公共电视纪录片吸引住了。这突如其来的冲击创造了PBS历史上纪录片的最高收视率，它以前所未有的视角表现了战争的故事：用那些亲身经历了战争的人的语言。在制作《内战》的过程中，电影制作人肯·伯恩斯收集了2500个人的语录和1.6万幅原始的照片。

整个美国对这部系列纪录片的着迷程度充分证明了第一手记录吸引和感动我们的力量。在随之发行的图书中，伯恩斯解释了普通人是怎样抓住战争的很多侧面，而历史学家是无法做到这一点的。

“1861年爆发战争的美国很可能是地球上最有文化的国家。在前线的战士们和在家里的居民们留下了令人惊讶的丰富感人的关于他们所见所感的记录……描述，沉思，观点，愤怒的叫声，嘲讽，悲伤，大笑和胜利……在美国人经历的范围内发出了成百上千种声音，正是这些人的生活受到了战争的影响、破坏或永远被战争改变。”

联系你的经历 在今天的世界里，你几乎可以即时地了解所有的重大事件。你可以看到捕捉了事件中的景象和声音的新闻镜头，听到相关的人们在访谈中讲述所发生的事情和他们的感觉。然而，内战的发生远在电视摄像机发明之前，因此，了解那场战争以及被裹入其中的人们的经历的最好方法，就是通过信件、日志、日记和照片。

日志写作 描述你已经知道的内战对人们生活产生的影响。在你读过课文之后，注意你收集到的任何补充的观点。

专题聚焦：分裂、战争与和解 这些信件、日记和日志中提供了哪些大多数历史书没有涉及的观点？

日记、日志和信件 日记和日志是对于事件、思想、感受和评论的个人记录。它们以每天的写作为基础，使人们可以记录自己的经历和即时的反应。因为日记和日志一般是为个人使用而保留下来的，所以一般都用能表现作者的观点和感情的非正式语言写成。与之类似的是，私人信件的写作目的也不是为了发表。然而，因为信是写给另一个人看的，所以它不是完全的私人写作。

玛丽·彻斯纳特的内战（节选）

玛丽·彻斯纳特

在1861年4月上旬，北方和南方之间的紧张局势不断恶化，整个国家都屏住了呼吸。4月12日，内战的第一枪在萨姆特要塞打响了，这是一个在南卡罗来纳州南部查尔斯顿的联邦军营，而那时城里的居民就在他们的屋顶上注视着这一切。玛丽·彻斯纳特在她的日志中描写了当时的情感剧变。

1861年4月7日

今天形势看起来有一点儿确定了。

一个人只能希望风平浪静。林肯或是席沃德曾经那么愚蠢地前进，然后又更加愚蠢地后退了。无论如何，可能还有和平的希望。

事情发生得那么快。

我丈夫被任命为布里奇德将军的一名副官。

3个小时以前我们在安静地收拾东西准备回家。大会休会了。

现在他告诉我可能会在今晚对萨姆特要塞发动进攻。这取决于安德森(当时驻守萨姆特要塞的联邦军队将领——译者注)和外面的舰队。那传令官说这次围栏外面的战争表演是为了给得克萨斯看的。

约翰•曼宁带着他的剑和红色肩带进来了。他因为能在队伍前进时成为布里奇德的手下而高兴得像个孩子。他和威格福一起带着命令去找哈特斯蒂恩上尉了。

彻斯纳特先生还在赶着完成一份要交给大会的报告。

海恩太太打了电话来。她说，她"只有一种感觉，那就是替不在这里的人感到遗憾。"

杰克•普勒斯顿，威利•阿尔斯顿——别人叫他们"轻松生活的人"——和约翰•格林"大胆儿"一起作为志愿士兵去了那个岛。

700人被派了出去。运军火的大车整夜都在街上隆隆地行驶。安德森点着了蓝色的灯——我猜是给外面的舰队发出的信号或暗示。

在今天的晚餐上没有提到查尔斯顿港那边的事情，但有一股强烈的兴奋的暗流。这群人是再杰出不过的了。除了我们通常的四人小组(威瑟斯法官，朗顿•彻威斯，还有特瑞斯科特)，我们的两位州长敏斯和曼宁也和我们一起共进晚餐。

这些人谈得那样兴高采烈。在我一生中只有这次认真倾听。

晚餐结束后，正事开始了。敏斯州长诚挚地从什么地方仔细翻找出了一把剑和一条红色肩

士兵在战壕中看报

带，准备给彻斯纳特上校，上校已前往萨姆特要塞要求对方投降。

现在，耐心——我们必须等待。

安德森那笨蛋为什么要进驻萨姆特要塞里去呢？那之后所有的事情都不对了。现在他们从他那里截获了一封信，他在信里催促他们让他投降。他描述了一幅在他们不许他投降的情况下将要发生的恐怖图景。

在把头伸到那洞里之前他就应该想到这一切。

1861年4月12日

安德森不愿有条件投降。

昨天是我们有过的最快乐、最疯狂的晚餐。男人们都更加大胆地机智诙谐。我们有一种没说出来的预感：这将是我们最后一次快乐的聚会了。迈尔斯先生今天和我们一起吃了饭。亨利•金太太冲了进来：“新闻，我带来了最新的新闻——金家所有的男人都在岛上了”——她似乎为此感到很骄傲。

当她在这里的时候，我们的和平谈判者——或者说特使——进来了。也就是说，彻斯纳特先生回来了——大家对他和安德森上校的谈话非常感兴趣——但是他却不太愿意谈话，而是想吃饭。他好像有些同情安德森，已给戴维斯总统发了电报请求指示。

给安德森什么回答，等等，等等。他带着附加的命令又回到萨姆特要塞去了。

就在他们正要离开码头的时候，A. H. 波耶金极其兴奋地跳到了船上，他认为自己没有受到重用。他那么热爱战斗——却把他留在了后面！

我没有假装睡着，我怎么能睡得着呢？如果安德森不接受条件——四点钟，命令是——向他开火。

我数到了四点——圣米歇尔教堂的钟响了。我开始希望。四点半，响起了一座大炮沉重的爆炸声。

我跳下床。双膝跪下——匍匐着——我以前所未有的虔诚祈祷。

房子里到处都是骚动的声音——走廊里快步的脚步声——仿佛都赶往同一个方向。我穿上我的两层长袍，披上披肩，也赶过去了。那是朝着房顶的方向。

炮弹在爆炸。在黑暗中我听到一个男人说“浪费弹药”。

我知道我的丈夫正在那黑暗的海湾中的某个地方划船。而炮弹笼罩了那个海湾——朝要塞飞去。如果安德森很顽固——他就会下令我们这边的要塞开火。射击肯定已经开始了。大炮有规律的轰响声——就在那里。谁又能说得出每次群射造成了多少死亡和破坏。

女人们在房顶上，全都失控了。女人的祈祷，男人的咒骂，然后一颗炮弹就会照亮这场面。他们说，今晚军队就要试图登陆。

哈利亚特路号的舵手室被炸烂了，于是开回到了海里。

我们在上面那儿望着——每个人都在奇怪。萨姆特要塞一枪未开。

今天敏斯和曼宁，他们现在是上校了——布里奇德将军的副官——和我们一起吃饭。后者希望我维持秩序。但我只对他说了祝福的话，因为他将要日夜冒着炮火，在海湾里传达命令，等等。

昨晚——其实是今早——在房顶上我是那么虚弱疲倦，于是我坐在了一个看起来像一个黑色凳子的东西上。

"站起来，你这傻女人——你的裙子着火了。"一个男人叫道。然后他把我拉了起来。

那是一截烟囱，火星引着了我的衣服。然后苏珊•普莱斯顿和维纳伯先生上来了。但是我身上的火在变成大火苗之前已经熄灭了。

你知道么，在所有这些嘈杂和我们的眼泪和祈祷之后，竟然没有任何人受伤。声音和狂怒，什么也不代表。一种错觉和陷阱……

刚才有人进来，报告说彻斯纳特上校在布里奇德将军房间里的沙发上睡着了。经过这样的两夜之后，他一定累得在什么地方都能睡着了……

1861年4月13日

无论如何，没有人受伤。昨晚我们是多么高兴啊。

我们认为那些可怕的大炮发出那样的轰响是对所有屠杀的恐惧的反应。

甚至没有一个连受到损伤。

萨姆特要塞着火了。他还没有使我们的任何一支枪缄默。副官们——他们还佩戴着剑和红色的肩带作为制服——是这样告诉我们的。

但是那些枪声还是使我们不可能正常地进餐。没有人坐在餐桌旁，但是走廊里到处都是茶盘。

有些人带着焦虑的心情躺在床上，在孤单的痛苦中悲叹。威格福夫人和我在我的房间里用茶来使自己得到安慰。

这些女人有着非常值得信赖的忠诚。

1861年4月15日

我以前从不知道人能经历这样激动兴奋的日子。

他们喊道:"出来——来了一群人。"

实际上是一群暴民,只不过是由彻斯纳特上校和曼宁上校带领的。

人群叫喊着,把这两个人作为带来好消息的使者。他们被大家护送着去了布里奇德将军的总部。萨姆特要塞投降了。

那些房顶上的人对我们喊道:"要塞起火了。"以前这种情况已经发生过一两次了。

当我们镇静下来的时候,彻斯纳特上校——如果他的宁静中有什么比平常稍显不安定的话,他的态度也足够平静——向我们讲述了投降是怎么发生的。

威格福和他们一起在莫里斯岛上,当他看见要塞里的火光,他就跳上了一艘小船,把他的手帕作为一面白旗,向萨姆特要塞划去。威格福从一个炮门进去了。

彻斯纳特上校不久以后也到达了,他被从正规的入口接了进去。安德森上校告诉他要小心地挑选道路,因为那地方布满了地雷。

根据我所能理解的,要塞是向威格福投了降。

然而一切都是一团混乱。我们的旗帜在那里飘扬,消防车也被派去灭火。

每个人都告诉你什么事情的一半,然后就冲到别处去讲其他的事情或去听最新的消息……

一个士兵的回忆

沃伦·李·高斯

攻击萨姆特要塞后的几周里,双方都有成千上万的男人志愿参加战斗。在前期的入伍者中就有马萨诸塞州的沃伦·李·高斯。

经过不眠的一夜,我起身下床时"冰冷的寒气"在我后背上下游移。我刮了胡子,为另一次不顾一切的英勇行为做着准备。那时我20岁,当我要做任何不同寻常的事情时,例如战斗或求爱,我就会刮胡子。

我站在招募新兵办公室的门前，全身紧张地颤动着，心脏像低沉的鼓一样重重地敲打着，在转动门把手进门之前，我把贴在门上的招募新兵的广告读了又读，一直到我了解了它所有的特性。许诺的“旅游和提升”的机会看起来不错，我想，我把战争想得那么严肃可能是个错误。“旅游的机会！”现在，当了四年兵之后，我必须承认那“旅游的机会”并不是神话；但“提升”就有点儿不确定而且来得很缓慢了。

我一点儿也不着急开门。虽然我已经下定决心应征入伍了，但我却有些倾向于稍微延迟一会儿；我的欲望波动不定；我既懦弱又勇敢；我想入伍，然而——在这里我转动了门把手，得到了解脱……

我的第一套军服极不合适：我的裤子长了三四英寸；法兰绒衬衫又粗又不舒服，脖子周围太大，其他地方又太短。步兵帽就是一个难看的袋子，顶和皮帽舌是由纸板做的；宽松上衣是唯一看起来得体的部分；而那外套大衣让我觉得我就像一个长在很大的外壳里的发育不良的玉米穗。除了“弗吉尼亚泥”以外，再没有什么东西使我对军队的盛况的看法降得如此之低了。

从军之后，我得到的结果并不像我曾经预料过的那样。公正地评价我得到的东西，那么我穿着军装的外表就没什么可令人兴奋的。他们教了我左右转，当时，在挺肩、传令和举臂的问题上，我认为训练教官有些不必要的小题大做。那时因为获得火枪很困难，所以人们经常先接受连队或团队的固定动作训练，很久以后才能学习武器手册。我们早一点儿拿到了枪，但是在背了几个小时以后，我们会很情愿地把它们扔在一边。经过一个小时的训练，那火枪似乎更沉重，而且也没有刚开始看起来那么漂亮了。

我去接受训练的第一天，因为厌倦了一遍遍地做同样的事情，所以我对那训练军士说：“让咱们别做这种傻事了，到杂货店去吧。”他唯一的回答是说给一个下士听的：“下士，带这个人出去，训练他。”而那下士就真的那么做了！

我发现人们在军队里不像在平常生活中那样感谢建议，而没有什么聪明才智能抵得上训练教官的“向右看”、“向左转”和“右，斜身，开步走”。一个没有经验的新兵要花上一些时间才能学会他不是来思考或提建议，而是来服从的。有些人永远学不会，而我最终在谦卑和泥浆里学到这一点，那很难。然而我怀疑在我前三个星期的训练中，我的爱国主义是否能有膝盖那么高。训练在一个旁观者看来很容易，但事实不是那样。过了一段时间，我剪短了我的制服，以便我能忍受它；我也有效地克服了训练，熬过了它。然后命令来了：去华盛顿！……

葛底斯堡战役邦联方的叙述

兰道尔夫•麦克吉姆

从1863年7月1日至7月3日，北部联邦军队和南部邦联军队在宾夕法尼亚的一个叫做葛底斯堡的小镇附近交战。在北部联邦军队控制了小镇周围的山丘之后，罗伯特·E.·李指挥的南部邦联军队对联邦兵力最强大的阵地发起了一次冒险的进攻。这次进攻失败了，邦联军队在付出了惨重的生命代价之后被迫撤退。这场战役是李指挥的军队第一次被击败，标志着这场战争中的一个转折点。南部邦联士兵兰道尔夫·麦克吉姆在一篇日记中描述了这场战役的最后一天。

然后爱威尔将军下令发动进攻，去攻击我们右侧的考尔普山的山顶……我们将要猛攻的那些工事几乎与我们的工事成直角。此外，还有一条双层壕沟的防线，一条在另一条的上面，每条壕沟里都布满了军队。除了在正面要面对那双层防线的火力之外，在发动进攻的行进过程中，我们还要暴露在我们左肋树林中的扫射火力下，在我们左后方还有一个炮兵连埋伏在一座小山上，可以近距离对我们开炮……

那个人数很少的英勇的旅，北卡罗来纳第三旅在战线的右侧向前移动，旁边就是玛丽兰德第二旅，然后是三个弗吉尼亚团（第10、第23和第37团），还有北卡罗来纳第一旅在最左边向前挺进。这支队伍的人员已经严重削减了，精力也因为早晨那六个小时可怕的战斗而大大衰竭了，但勇气和精神却没有丝毫减弱。然而，很快左侧和中间的队伍就被阻住并且击退了，很可能是因为侧面树林里的猛烈火力。北卡罗来纳第三旅剩余的一小部分人和比较强大的玛丽兰德第二旅一起（我不记得看见任何其他团队的旗帜了）则在战线的其他部分向前挺进得很远。他们推进到了对方阵地里大约20或30步的地方——他们是人数很少然而非常英勇的一队英雄，敢于尝试血肉之躯无法做到的事情。

战斗很快就结束了。我们在一片茫然中被打退回到那条战线，我们是遭受了惨重的损失才得以从那里推进过来的。不过敌人并没有反攻。通过战线上的军官和士兵们的艰苦努力，终于恢复了秩序，我们在最初出发的那些矮防护墙那里重组了队伍，又一次要暴露在威力比早晨那次还要大的炮火下。剩下能说的就是，像那天后来皮科特的人[①]一样，这个小队被丢下来毫无支援地面对敌人的工事。在那次进攻中间和之后，丹尼尔的旅一直待在矮防护墙里，无论是从那支部队还是其他部队我们都没得到任何支援。当然我们应该认为丹尼尔将军是遵命而行。这次进攻之后，我们在这道矮防护墙里停留了一小时左右，最后放弃了邦联的壕沟，退到了山脚下。

布尔伦战役的叙述

“石壁”·杰克逊

南部邦联的将军托马斯·“石壁”·杰克逊在这封写给他妻子的信中讲述了南方军队在战争中的第一次胜利：1861年7月进行的一场战役，在华盛顿特区外一条名叫布尔伦的小溪附近。

我心爱的宝贝：

昨天我们打了一场大仗，取得了伟大的胜利，它的光荣都归于上帝一人。虽然连续几个小时冒着猛烈的炮火，但我只受了一处伤，我左手最长的手指被打伤了；不过医生说这手指还保得住。它是在手掌和指节中间的地方被打断的，子弹从食指旁的那一边穿了过去。如果它打到了中心的话，我就要失去这个手指了。我的马受了伤，不过没有死。你（送我）的外套在臀部附近裂了个很难看的口子，不过我的仆人非常手巧，他已经把它补得不是很明显了。就像这次光荣的胜利一样，我能活下来也全都归功于我们的上帝，让所有的荣誉、

① 皮科特的人：乔治·皮科特将军是一位南部邦联军官，他率领部队对联邦阵地进行了不成功的进攻。

赞扬和光荣都属于他。这场战役是我参加过的最艰难的一场，但是炮火不是那么激烈。我主要指挥中间的军队，我的一个团也向右边伸展出去了一段距离。我的左右也有其他的指挥官。虽然很大一部分功劳应该属于我们勇敢的军队的其他部分，但上帝使我的旅在打退敌人的主要进攻中发挥了更大的作用。这只是说给你听的——别对别人提起这事。让别人说出赞扬的话，而不是我自己。

对《解放黑奴宣言》的反应

亨利·M. 特纳牧师

1862年9月22日，林肯总统发表了《解放黑奴宣言》，宣布叛乱州的所有奴隶将在1863年1月1日被解放。因为当时那些州并不在北方联邦的控制之下，所以在那一天并没有奴隶被真正解放。然而，《宣言》对那些仍处在奴隶制中的人来说是一个有力的希望的标志，并且激起了自由的美国黑人支持北部联邦的一阵热潮。在这篇记述中，亨利·M. 特纳牧师，一个住在华盛顿特区的出身自由的美国黑人，描述了黑人对于《宣言》的反应。

看见我的教堂里面和周围拥挤着那么多人，我急忙跑到了第一家能印刷《解放黑奴宣言》的报社，叫做《晚星报》，然后挤进了那等待着报纸的稠密的人群中。第一张印着《宣言》的报纸被我们中的三个人抓住了，但是一个机敏的年轻人拿到了它，逃走了。下一张被几个人抓住了，撕成了碎纸条。从报社里出来的第三张也被几个人抓住了，但是我成功地拿到了印着《宣言》的主要部分，拼命地逃走了。我顺着潘索威尼亚大道逃命似的跑着，当人们看到我手里拿着报纸到来的时候，他们发出了一阵震耳欲聋的欣喜的叫声。很多的人围在我身边，把我举到了一个大台子上，我开始朗读《宣言》。可我差不多跑了一英里，上气不接下气，没法读下去。于是我把报纸递给了辛顿先生，他有力清楚地朗读了出来。在他朗读的时候，人们做出了各种表现和手势。男人尖叫，女人昏倒，狗狂吠，白人和黑人握手，歌声响起了。在这个时候，海军院

联邦军总司令格兰特将军

子里的大炮开始开火，随之而来的是已经在白宫后面响了一阵的吼叫声……黑人和白人的大队人马在白宫前来回游行着，人们庆贺着林肯总统发布了《宣言》。总统出现在窗户前，回应地鞠躬，成千上万的人告诉他，如果他走出白宫的话，人们会把他拥抱死的……这真是一个独一无二的历史时刻，人的一生中再也不能看到这样的场面了。

一次经历种族歧视的记录

索约娜•特鲁斯

虽然内战终结了奴隶制，对抗种族歧视的斗争却刚刚开始。在下面这封写于1865年10月1日的信里，索约娜·特鲁斯描述了一次与种族主义的遭遇。

几星期以前我和我的朋友约瑟芬•S.•格里芬在一起，一辆街车上的售票员拒绝为我停车，虽然我紧紧跟在约瑟芬的后面，而且已经抓住了车上的铁杆。他们拖着我开出了很远，她才拦住他们。她把这个售票员的行为报告给了城市轨道的主管，他马上就开除了这个售票员，然后告诉我当我受到售票员或司机的不公正待遇时，就把那辆车的车号记下来。13日，我为了弗里得医院的病人们必须要到那里去一趟，我已经在那里做了很多个月的咨询建议工作了。这次因为我和另一个朋友，密歇根的劳拉•S.•哈维兰德同行，所以我以为坐车时不会遇到什么麻烦。在我登上那辆车的平台上时，那个售票员却推了我一下，说："回去——下去。"我告诉他我不会下去的，然后他就狂怒地说："那我就把你扔下去！"他双手紧紧抓住我的右臂，用了那么猛的力气，马上就要把我推下去了，这时候哈维兰德夫人对他说他不能把我扔下去。他用一种又快又生气的语气说："她是你的吗？"她回答道："她不是我的，但她是人。"我们记下了那辆车的车号，主管一接到我们的报告就马上开除了那个售票员，并且建议以攻击和殴打的罪名将他逮捕，因为在他努力要把我扔下车去的时候，我的肩膀扭伤了。根据这个建议，他被逮捕了，并且由汤普森法官审判了这个案子。我的胳膊那时非常僵痛，而且肿得厉害，不过现在好多了。灭亡陈旧的奴隶制思想是很难的。但它必须消亡……

文学和生活

读者反应　在内战的早期，你会志愿参战吗？为什么？

主题焦点　这些选文在哪些方面使你增加了对内战的理解？

阅读理解

1. 玛丽·彻斯纳特在她的日记中描述了什么事件？

2. 总结这三名士兵的叙述中描述的事件。

3. 特纳牧师的会众对《解放黑奴宣言》有什么反应？

思考

解释

1. 玛丽·彻斯纳特的日记揭示了她对这场战争的什么态度？（解释）

2. 士兵高斯在入伍后的态度和期望发生了哪些变化？（分析）

3. 你将会怎样描述(a)兰道尔夫·麦克吉姆(b)“石壁”·杰克逊的叙述的语气？（分析）

4. 为什么《解放黑奴宣言》对已经自由的美国黑人产生了那样的情感上的影响？（推断）

5. 看到特鲁斯以为她乘车时“不会遇到什么麻烦”，“因为我和劳拉·S.·哈维兰德同行”，你可以合理地对哈维兰德做出什么推断？（推断）

应用

6. 如果玛丽·彻斯纳特是北方的人，那么她的日记会有怎样的不同？（修改）

扩展

7. 特鲁斯要战胜种族歧视的决心预示了哪些后来的领导人和重大事件？（社会研究连线）

文学聚焦

日记、日志与信件

这些日记、日志和信件描述了内战中的事件和人们以及作者的反应。

1. 玛丽•彻斯纳特的很多描述都受到了她对战争的反感的影响。给出至少两个表现出这种反感的例子。

2. “石壁”•杰克逊的信是写给他妻子一个人看的。如果这是一份用于发表的报告，找到三个杰克逊可能会省略掉的细节或观点。

3. 索约娜•特鲁斯的信揭示了她自己的什么个性？

点子库

写作

1. 总结　写一份事实总结，总结《玛丽•彻斯纳特的内战》的节选部分中描述的事件。使用连接词来连接观点并表明事件的时间顺序。

2. 书的封面　设计一本收录了内战日记、日志和信件的书的封面，解释这些记录提供的对于这场战争的独特视角，说服读者购买这本书。

3. 思考性文章　今天，很少有人花时间来通信或写日志了。这为什么是一种损失？写一篇文章，探索进行这类写作的个人收益和历史价值。使用这些选文来说明你的观点。

项目

1. 时间线　到林肯就任总统时，已经有7个州脱离了联邦。研究1860年的总统选举，了解林肯的胜利对于南方意味着什么。做出一条导致了内战的事件发生的时间线。

2. 模型/地图　组成一个小组对葛底斯堡战役进行研究。制作这个战场的一个模型或一张地图。用解释性的标题标明重要事件发生的地点。

微型写作课

第一手的人物传记

你本人认识什么人，他/她的成就或经历是值得记录的吗？在一篇第一手的人物传记中描述她/他生活中的事件，反映你对这个人的观点。这篇简洁但有揭示性的略传应该包括对于这个人的描述，传记性的信息，和你对他/她成就和人格的印象。利用描述动作的动词使你的人物栩栩如生，以吸引读者。

写作技巧重点：生动的动词

有力准确的动词就叫做生动的动词，这类动词能增加写作的生动性。它

们表现具体的动作，因而帮助读者看到作者描述的事件。例如，高斯的《一个士兵的回忆》中的这个段落如果只是简单地陈述高斯“感到紧张”，那么就不可能这样有效果。然而，生动的动词却惟妙惟肖地表现了他准备应征入伍时的体会。

士兵高斯叙述中的范例：全身紧张地颤动着，心脏像低沉的鼓一样重重地敲打着……

构思

列出你要描写的对象的成就或经历，还有他/她的个人品质——性格、外貌、举止，诸如此类。如果可能的话，与你的对象进行面谈，以收集具体的可用于传记的信息。然后决定哪些细节能最好地表现你对你描写对象的观点。

写稿

重点描写最有力的事实、细节和轶闻。考虑引用你描写对象的话或对话，以表现他/她的个性。使用生动的动词来使你的写作保持生动。

修改

将你的文稿与你打腹稿时列出的清单做对比，在你的描写过程中是否表现了你对他/她的看法？你应该添加哪些细节？哪些是不必要的？你能把哪些沉闷的动词换成生动的动词？

Guide for Interpreting

Civil War Voices

The Civil War was One of the most painful chapters of American history, touching the lives of millions of soldiers and civilians. The following diaries, journals, and letters tell the story of the war through the eyes of just a few of those whose lives were affected by it.

No one was hurt when the opening shots of the war were fired on Fort Sumter on April 12, 1860, but Mary Boykin Chesnut (1823–1886) seems to have sensed the carnage to come. The daughter of a cotton plantation owner and United States senator, Mary Boykin was raised in an aristocratic family in Charleston, South Carolina. At the age of seventeen, she married James Chesnut, Jr., a wealthy lawyer and future senator. Her journal entries convey the mingled optimism and dread that marked the opening days of the Civil War.

Men hurried to enlist in what most believed would be a swift and glorious war. Some young men, as we learn from the account of Union soldier Warren Lee Goss, saw the military as an opportunity for respect and advancement. The harsh realities of the training camp and battlefield soon taught soldiers on both sides that lives and limbs were the price of glory. The cost was especially high at the Battle of Gettysburg — a stunning defeat for Confederate general Robert E. Lee. In his diary, Confederate soldier Randolph McKim recounts the bravery of companions, many of whom were among the 51,000 killed or wounded at Gettysburg.

Confederate general and military strategist Thomas Jonathan "Stonewall" Jackson (1824–1863) earned his nickname early in the war for his steadiness and determination during the Battle of Bull Run in 1861. Jackson, who recounted the battle in a letter to his wife died two years after his great victory; he was acci-

dentally shot by his own troops and died of complications.

The Emancipation Proclamation, issued by President Lincoln on September 22, 1862, changed the purpose of the war. By declaring that all slaves would be freed on January 1, 1863, the Proclamation made the conflict into a war to end slavery, as well as a war to restore the Union. Reverend Henry M. Turner, a free-born African American who lived in Washington, D.C., recounts his community's reaction to the news.

When the war ended in 1865, abolitionist Sojourner Truth (1797–1883) had only begun to battle discrimination. A preacher and former slave, Troth is also recognized as an advocate of women's rights, temperance, and workplace and prison reform.

Background for Understanding

MEDIA: THE PAST COMES TO LIFE IN THE CIVIL WAR

For five nights in early October 1990, Americans sat riveted by a public-television documentary called The Civil War. This unexpected hit, which garnered the highest rating of any series in PBS history, presented the story of the war as it had never been told: in the words of those who had lived it. In the course of creating The Civil War, film- maker Ken Burns worked with 2,500 first-person quotations and 16,000 original photographs.

America's fascination with the series is a testament to the power of firsthand accounts to engage and move us. In the companion book, Burns explains how ordinary people captured the many facets of the war as no historian ever could.

"The America that went to war in 1861 was perhaps the most literate nation on earth. Soldiers at the front and civilians at home left an astonishingly ric-hand moving record of what they saw and felt..., descriptions, reflections, opinions, cries of outrage, cynicism, sorrow, laughter and triumph...hundreds of voices from across the spectrum of American experience, men and women whose lives were touched or destroyed or permanently changed by the war."

Literature and your Life

CONNECT YOUR EXPERIENCE

In today's world, you can learn about key events almost instantly. You can see news footage that captures the sights and sounds of an event, and hear interviews in which the people involved describe what happened and share their feelings. The Civil War took place long before television cameras were invented, however, so the best way to learn about the war and share the experiences of those involved is through letters, journals, diaries, and photographs.

Journal Writing Describe what you already know about the impact of the Civil War on people's lives. When you've finished reading, note any additional insights you've gathered.

THEMATIC FOCUS: DIVISION, WAR, AND RECONCILIATION

What insights about the Civil War do these letters, diaries, and journals provide that aren't captured in most history books?

Literary Focus

DIARIES, JOURNALS, AND LETTERS

Diaries and journals are personal records of events, thoughts, feelings, and observations. Written on a day-to-day basis, they allow people to record immediate responses to experiences. Because diaries and journals are generally kept for personal use, they are usually written in an informal style that captures the writer's ideas and emotions. Similarly, a personal letter is written without the intention of publication. Yet because it is written to another person, it is not entirely private writing.

Mary Chesnut's Civil War

Mary Chesnut

In the early days of April 1861, the nation held its collective breath as the tension between North and South mounted steadily. On April 12, the opening shots of the Civil War were fired on Fort Sumter, a Union military post in Charleston, South Carolina, as the city's citizens watched from their rooftops. Mary Chesnut captured the emotional upheaval of the time in her journal.

April 7, 1861.

Today things seem to have settled down a little.

One can but hope still. Lincoln or Seward have made such silly advances and then far sillier drawings back. There may be a chance for peace, after all.

Things are happening so fast.

My husband has been made an aide-de- camp of General Beauregard.

Three hours ago we were quietly packing to go home. The convention has adjourned.

Now he tells me the attack upon Fort Sumter may begin tonight. Depends upon Anderson and the fleet outside. The Herald says that this show of war outside of the bar is intended for Texas.

John Manning came in with his sword and red sash. Pleased as a boy to be on Beauregard's staff while the row goes on. He has gone with Wigfall to Captain Hartstene with instructions.

Mr. Chesnut is finishing a report he had to make to the convention.

Mrs. Hayne called. She had, she said, "but one feeling, pity for those who are not here."

Jack Preston, Willie Alston—"the take-life-easys", as they are called—with John Green, "the big brave," have gone down to the island—volunteered as privates.

Seven hundred men were sent over. Ammunition wagons rumbling along the streets all night. Anderson burning blue lights — signs and signals for the fleet outside, I suppose.

Today at dinner there was no allusion to things as they stand in Charleston Harbor. There was an undercurrent of intense excitement. There could not have been a more brilliant circle. In addition to our usual quartet (Judge Withers, Langdon Cheves, and Trescot) our two governors dined with us, Means and Manning.

These men all talked so delightfully. For once in my life I listened.

That over, business began. In earnest, Governor Means rummaged a sword and red sash from somewhere and brought it for Colonel Chesnut, who has gone to demand the surrender of Fort Sumter.

And now, patience—we must wait.

Why did that green goose Anderson go into Fort Sumter? Then everything began to go wrong.

Now they have intercepted a letter from him, urging them to let him surrender. He paints the horrors likely to ensue if they will not.

He ought to have thought of all that before he put his head in the hole.

April 12, 1861.

Anderson will not capitulate.

Yesterday was the merriest, maddest dinner we have had yet. Men were more audaciously wise and witty. We had an unspoken foreboding it was to be our last pleasant meeting. Mr. Miles dined with us today. Mrs. Henry King rushed in: "The news, I come for the latest news — all of the men of the King family are on the island" — of which fact she seemed proud.

While she was here, our peace negotiator—or envoy—came in. That is, Mr. Chesnut returned—his interview with

Colonel Anderson had been deeply interesting—but was not inclined to be communicative, wanted his dinner. Felt for Anderson. Had telegraphed to President Davis for instructions.

What answer to give Anderson, etc., etc. He has gone back to Fort Sumter with additional instructions.

When they were about to leave the wharf, A.H.Boykin sprang into the boat, in great excitement; thought himself illu-sed. A likelihood of fighting—and he to be left behind!

I do not pretend to go to sleep. How can I? If Anderson does not accept terms—at four—the orders are—he shall be fired upon.

I count four—St. Michael chimes. I begin to hope. At half-past four, the heavy booming of a cannon.

I sprang out of bed. And on my knees—prostrate—I prayed as I never prayed before.

There was a sound of stir all over the house—pattering of feet in the corridor—all seemed burying one way. I put on my double gown and a shawl and went, too. It was to the housetop.

The shells were bursting. In the dark I heard a man say "waste of ammunition."

I knew my husband was rowing about in a boat somewhere in that dark bay. And that the shells were roofing it over—bursting toward the fort. If Anderson was obstinate—he was to order the forts on our side to open fire. Certainly fire had begun. The regular roar of the cannon—there it was. And who could tell what each volley accomplished of death and destruction.

The women were wild, there on the house top. Prayers from the women and imprecations from the men, and then a shell would light up the scene. Tonight, they say, the forces are to attempt to land.

The Harriet Lane had her wheelhouse smashed and put back to sea.

We watched up there—everybody wondered. Fort Sumter did not fire a shot.

Today Miles and Manning, colonels now—aides to Beauregard—dined with us. The latter hoped I would keep the peace. I give him only good words, for he was to be under fire all day and night, in the bay carrying orders, etc.

Last night—or this morning truly—up on the housetop I was so weak and weary I sat down on something that looked like a black stool.

"Get up, you foolish woman—your dress is on fire," cried a man. And he put me out.

It was a chimney, and the sparks caught my clothes. Susan Preston and Mr. Venable then came up. But my fire had been extinguished before it broke out into a regular blaze.

Do you know, after all that noise and our tears and prayers, nobody has been hurt. Sound and fury, signifying nothing. A delusion and a snare....

Somebody came in just now and reported Colonel Chesnut asleep on the sofa in General Beauregard's room. After two such nights he must be so tired as to be able to sleep anywhere....

April 13, 1861.

Nobody hurt, after all. How gay we were last night.

Reaction after the dread of all the slaughter we thought those dreadful cannons were making such a noise in doing.

Not even a battery the worse for wear.

Fort Sumter has been on fire. He has not yet silenced any of our guns. So the aides—still with swords and red sashes by way of uniform—tell us.

But the sound of those guns makes regular meals impossible. None of us go to table. But tea trays pervade the corridors, going everywhere.

Some of the anxious hearts lie on their beds and moan in solitary misery. Mrs. Wigfall and I solace ourselves with tea in my room.

These women have all a satisfying faith.

April 15, 1861.

I did not know that one could live such days of excitement.

They called, "Come out—there is a crowd coming."

A mob indeed, but it was headed by Colonels Chesnut and Manning.

The crowd was shouting and showing these two as messengers of good news.

They were escorted to Beauregard's headquarters. Fort Sumter had surrendered.

Those up on the housetop shouted to us, "The fort is on fire". That had been the story once or twice before.

When we had calmed down. Colonel Chesnut, who had taken it all quietly enough—if anything, more unruffled than usual in his serenity—told us how the surrender came about.

Wigfall was with them on Morris Island when he saw the fire in the fort, jumped in a little boat and, with his handkerchief as a white flag, rowed over to Fort Sumter. Wigfall went in through a porthole.

When Colonel Chesnut arrived shortly after and was received by the regular entrance. Colonel Anderson told him he had need to pick his way warily, for it was all mined.

As far as I can make out, the fort surrendered to Wigfall.

But it is all confusion. Our flag is flying there. Fire engines have been sent to put out the fire.

Everybody tells you half of something and then rushes off to tell something else or to hear the last news....

Recollections of a Private

Warren Lee Goss

In the weeks that followed the attack on Fort Sumter, thousands of men on both sides volunteered to fight. Among the early enlistees was Warren Lee Goss of Massachusetts.

"Cold chills" ran up and down my back as I got out of bed after the sleepless night, and shaved preparatory to other desperate deeds of valor. I was twenty years of age, and when any thing unusual was to be done, like fighting or courting, I shaved.

With a nervous tremor convulsing my system, and my heart thumping like muffled drumbeats, I stood before the door of the recruiting office, and before turning the knob to enter read and reread the advertisement for recruits posted thereon, until I knew all its peculiarities. The promised chances for "travel and promotion" seemed good, and I thought I might have made a mistake in considering war so serious after all. "Chances for travel!" I must confess now, after four years of soldiering, that the "chances for travel" were no myth; but "promotion" was a little uncertain and slow.

I was in no hurry to open the door. Though determined to enlist, I was half inclined to put it off awhile; I had a fluctuation of desires; I was fainthearted and brave; I wanted to enlist, and yet—Here I turned the knob, and was relieved....

My first uniform was a bad fit: My trousers were too long by three or four inches; the flannel shirt was coarse and unpleasant, too large at the neck and too short elsewhere. The forage cap was an ungainly bag with pasteboard top and leather visor; the blouse was the only part which seemed decent; while the overcoat made me feel like a little nubbin of corn in a large preponderance of husk. Nothing except "Virginia mud" ever took down my ideas of military pomp quite so low.

After enlisting I did not seem of so much consequence as I had expected. There was not so much excitement on account of my military appearance as I deemed justly my due. I was taught my facings, and at the time I thought the drillmaster needlessly fussy about shouldering, ordering, and presenting arms. At this time men were often drilled in company and regimental evolutions long before they learned the manual of arms, because of the difficulty of obtaining muskets. These we obtained at an early day, but we would willingly have resigned

them after carrying them a few hours. The musket, after an hour's drill, seemed heavier and less ornamental than it had looked to be.

The first day I went out to drill, getting tired of doing the same things over and over, I said to the drill sergeant: "Let's stop this fooling and go overto the grocery." His only reply was addressed to a corporal: "Corporal, take this man out and drill him"; and the corporal did! I found that suggestions were not so well appreciated in the army as in private life, and that no wisdom was equal to a drillmaster's "Right face," "Left wheel," and "Right, oblique, march." It takes a raw recruit some time to learn that he is not to think or suggest, but obey. Some never do learn. I acquired it at last, in humility and mud, but it was tough. Yet I doubt if my patriotism, during my first three weeks' drill was quite knee high. Drilling looks easy to a spectator, but it isn't. After a time I had cut down my uniform so that I could see out of it, and had conquered the drill sufficiently to see through it. Then the word came: on to Washington! ...

A Confederate Account of the Battle of Gettysburg

Randolph McKim

From July 1 to July 3, 1863, Union and Confederate troops fought near the small town of Gettysburg, Pennsylvania. After Union troops gained control of the hills surrounding the town, the Confederate troops commanded by Robert E. Lee launched a risky attack on the strongest Union position. When the attack failed, the Confederate troops were forced to retreat at a great cost of lives. The battle, the first in which troops commanded by Lee were defeated, marked a turning point in the war. In a diary entry, Confederate soldier Randolph McKim described the final day of the battle.

Then came General Ewell's order to assume the offensive and assail the crest of Culp's Hill, on our right....The works to be stormed ran almost at right angles to those we occupied. Moreover, there was a double line of entrenchments, one above the other, and each filled with troops. In moving to the attack we were

exposed to enfilading fire from the woods on our left flank, besides the double line of fire which we had to face in front, and a battery of artillery posted on a hill to our left rear opened upon us at short range ....

On swept the gallant little brigade, the Third North Carolina on the right of the line, next the Second Maryland, then the three Virginia regiments (10th, 23d, and 37th), with the First North Carolina on the extreme left. Its ranks had been sadly thinned, and its energies greatly depleted by those six fearful hours of battle that morning; but its nerve and spirit were undiminished. Soon, however, the left and center were checked and then repulsed, probably by the severe flank fire from the woods; and the small remnant of the Third North Carolina, with the stronger Second Maryland (I do not recall the banners of any other regiment), were far in advance of the rest of the line. On they pressed to within about twenty or thirty paces of the works—a small but gallant band of heroes daring to attempt what could not be done by flesh and blood.

The end soon came. We were beaten back to the line from which we had advanced with terrible loss, and in much confusion, but the enemy did not make a countercharge. By the strenuous efforts of the officers of the line and of the staff, order was restored, and we reformed in the breastworks from which we had emerged, there to be again exposed to an artillery fire exceeding in violence that of the early morning. It remains only to say that, like Pickett's men later in the day, this single brigade was hurled unsupported against the enemy's works. Daniel's brigade remained in the breastworks during and after the charge, and neither from that command nor from any other had we any support. Of course it is

to be presumed that General Daniel acted in obedience to orders. We remained in this breastwork after the charge about an hour before we finally abandoned the Federal entrenchments and retired to the foot of the hill.

An Account of the Battle of Bull Run

Stonewall Jackson

In this letter to his wife, Confederate General Thomas "Stonewall" Jackson recounts the first southern victory of the war: a battle fought in July 1861, outside Washington, D.C., near a small stream named Bull Run.

My precious pet,

Yesterday we fought a great battle and gained a great victory, for which all the glory is due to God alone. Although under a heavy fire for several continuous hours, I received only one wound, the breaking of the longest finger of my left hand; but the doctor says the finger can be saved. It was broken about midway between the hand and knuckle, the ball passing on the side next [to] the fore-finger. Had it struck the center, I should have lost the finger. My horse was wounded, but not killed. Your coat got an ugly wound near the hip, but my servant, who is very handy, has so far repaired it that it doesn't show very much. My preservation was entirely due, as was the glorious victory, to our God, to whom be all the honor, praise and glory. The battle was the hardest that I have ever been in, but not near so hot in its fire. I commanded the center more particularly, though one of my regiments extended to the right for some distance. There were other commanders on my right and left. Whilst great credit is due to other

parts of our gallant army, God made my brigade more instrumental than any other in repulsing the main attack. This is for your information only—say nothing about it. Let others speak praise, not myself.

Reaction to the Emancipation Proclamation

Reverend Henry M. Turner

On September 22, 1862, President Lincoln issued the Emancipation Proclamation, declaring that all slaves in states still in rebellion would be free as of January 1, 1863. Because those states were not under Union control at the time, no slaves were actually set free that day. The Proclamation, however, was a powerful symbol of hope for those still in slavery and inspired a wave of Union support from free African Americans. In this account, Reverend Henry M. Turner, a free-born African American living in Washington, D.C., describes his people's reaction to the news of the Proclamation.

Seeing such a multitude of people in and around my church, I hurriedly sent up to the office of the first paper in which the proclamation of freedom could be printed, known as the Evening Star, and squeezed myself through the dense crowd that was waiting for the paper. The first sheet run off with the proclamation in it was grabbed for by three of us, but some active young man got possession of it and fled. The next sheet was grabbed for by several, and was torn into tatters. The third sheet from the press was grabbed for by several, but I succeeded in procuring so much of it as contained the proclamation, and off I went for life and death. Down Pennsylvania Avenue I ran as for my life, and when the people saw me coming with the paper in my hand they raised a shouting cheer that was almost deafening. As many as could get around me lifted me to a great platform, and I started to read the proclamation. I had run the best end of a mile, I was out of breath, and could not read. Mr. Hinton, to whom I handed the paper, read it with great force and clearness. While he was reading every kind of demonstration and gesticulation was going on. Men squealed, women fainted, dogs barked, white

and colored people shook hands, songs were sung, and by this time cannons began to fire at the navy yard, and follow in the wake of the roar that had for some time been going on behind the White House.... Great processions of colored and white men marched to and fro and passed in front of the White House and congratulated President Lincoln on his proclamation. The President came to the window and made responsive bows, and thousands told him, if he would come out of that palace, they would hug him to death....It was indeed a time of times, and nothing like it will ever be seen again in this life.

An Account Of an Experience With Discrimination

Sojourner Truth

Although the Civil War brought an end to slavery, the struggle against racial discrimination was just beginning. In the following letter, written on October 1, 1865, Sojourner Truth describes an encounter with racism.

A few weeks ago I was in company with my friend Josephine S. Griffing, when the conductor of a streetcar refused to stop his car for me, although [I was] closely following Josephine and holding on to the iron rail. They dragged me a number of yards before she succeeded in stopping them. She reported the conductor to the president of the City Railway, who dismissed him at once, and told me to take the number of the car whenever I was mistreated by a conductor or driver. On the 13th I had occasion to go for necessities for the patients in the Freedmen's Hospital where I have been doing and advising for a number of months. I thought now I would get a ride without trouble as I was in company with another friend, Laura S. Haviland of Michigan. As I ascended the platform of the car, the conductor pushed me, saying "Go back—get off here." I told him I was not going off, then "I'll put you off" said he furiously, clenching my right arm with both hands, using such violence that he seemed about to succeed, when Mrs. Haviland told him he was not going to put me off. "Does she belong to you?" said he in a hurried angry tone. She replied, "She does not belong to me, but she belongs to human beings. We reported to the president, who advised his arrest for assault and battery as my shoulder was sprained by his effort to put me off. Accordingly I had him arrested and the case tried before Justice Thompson. My shoulder was very lame and swollen, but is better. It is hard for the old slave-holding spirit to die. But die it must....